D1164744

The Faber Book of
ART ANECDOTES

The Faber Book of

ART ANECDOTES

EDITED BY
EDWARD LUCIE-SMITH

faber and faber

First published in 1992
by Faber and Faber Limited
3 Queen Square London WC1N 3AU

Photoset by Wilmaset Ltd, Wirral
Printed in England by Clays Ltd, St Ives plc

All rights reserved

This anthology © Edward Lucie-Smith, 1992

Edward Lucie-Smith is hereby identified as editor of
this work in accordance with Section 77 of the Copyright,
Designs and Patents Act 1988

A CIP record of this book is available from
the British Library

ISBN 0–571–14382–2

2 4 6 8 10 9 7 5 3 1

for Michael Leonard
artist-friend
who may occasionally recognize
himself in these pages

CONTENTS

INTRODUCTION

What is an 'anecdote'? Originally, the *OED* tells us, the word meant something 'unpublished' – thus by implication secret or private. It comes from the Greek, and was, so the *Dictionary* informs us, 'applied by Procopius to his *Unpublished Memoirs* of the Emperor Justinian, which consisted chiefly of tales of the private life of the court, whence the application to short stories'. Eventually the application of the word broadened. It came to mean: 'The narrative of a detached incident, or of a single event, told as being in itself interesting or striking'. That is obviously the sense in which it is being used in the title of this book.

There is in fact something paradoxical about publishing a book of anecdotes at this particular moment. The appetite for brief, striking, picturesque stories has never been greater. They make up the larger part of the content of our newspapers, especially the tabloids, where the brevity of the actual narrative is reinforced by the use of pictorial illustration. Television, too, has found a way of adapting the anecdote to its own purposes. You might say that the 'sound-bites' used with such effect by television news programmes represent the ultimate, electronic development of the age-old taste for anecdote.

On the other hand academic history tends to reject the brief, picturesque incident in favour of something duller but seemingly more coherent and, as historians say, 'more rounded'. The anecdote thus seems out of favour, and the adjective anecdotal has become a term of abuse. The tendency is to concentrate on the evidence offered by the work of art itself, and upon written evidence which is certainly not narrative – the contract between an artist and his patron, for instance, or the successive reappearances of a particular painting in a set of family inventories. Where the art of the past is concerned, therefore, anecdotal evidence is increasingly mistrusted and unwelcome.

The situation is apparently different only for certain artists of the immediate present. In a society where a few successful artists become major celebrities, there is an unquenchable appetite for gossip about their doings; for news, however improbable, about their foibles, misdeeds, peculiarities and eccentricities. A considerable industry has grown up around the personality of Picasso; there is another, more recent but almost as large, around that of Andy Warhol. In cases such as these, the line between historiography and gossip remains thin.

The difficulty here, however, is a curious one. What is generally missing is the succinctness, the combination of brevity and completeness, which gives a good anecdote its hold upon our imaginations. There is another difficulty as well. Modern research techniques frequently call into question the veracity of the more striking stories which have clustered round a particular personality; or they offer alternative versions, so that the impact of some crucial incident is subtly blurred. Thus the biographer, even when offering proof that the anecdote is in fact in all essentials true, is moved to put it in a context which deprives it of what seemed to be its real significance.

What I am suggesting is that there exists, within the good and memorable anecdote, a certain tension between truth and untruth. Anecdotes achieve impact in various ways, but one of the most important of these is the element of surprise. Where the reader is concerned, this surprise can take different forms. Some of these brief stories – a very few – act like a lightning flash. A whole character – in the case of an artist, a whole creative personality – is suddenly and briefly illuminated, but illuminated with a distinctness which can be achieved in no other way. By contrast there are stories which simply seem grotesque or bizarre, when put in the context of what we otherwise know about a particular artist's life and work. It seems strange, for instance, that Guido Reni, one of the great masters of the Baroque altarpiece, should have been an obsessional gambler, and constantly in financial trouble because of it.

Increasingly, in reading and researching for this book, I became convinced that historical anecdotes of any kind, and anecdotes about art and artists in particular, could no longer be presented naïvely, as if they were all of absolutely equal value and enjoyed equal authority. It also occurred to me that many stories which seemed untrustworthy as contributions to biography, were still of great value because of what they had to say about the attitudes adopted, at a given moment, towards art and artists. What the main part of this book has to offer is not just a sequence of stories – perhaps striking, perhaps illuminating, perhaps even believable – about artists from the Renaissance to the present day, but a kind of capsule history of the way in which attitudes to the visual arts have constantly developed and altered. The anecdotes and brief fragments I have chosen illustrate not only what may have happened, what individual artists and their patrons may have said and done, but how the educated public of the time understood visual art and its functions, social and aesthetic.

That is, the book gives glimpses of what art was, and, more importantly, it often demonstrates what the public of a given moment wanted it to be. It also does something else: it illustrates the dialogue between artists and styles of art and literary intellectuals.

This distinction cannot, of course, be drawn with absolute rigidity. Many of the chief source-books for anecdotes about artists are the work of men who were themselves practising artists. One need look no further than Giorgio Vasari (1511–74), whose *Lives of the Most Excellent Italian Architects, Painters and Sculptors* is the most celebrated collection of its kind ever published and who was himself a practising artist of considerable distinction, court-painter and court-architect to Cosimo de' Medici, first Grand Duke of Tuscany. Yet it is also fair to point out two things. The first and more evident is that Vasari's fame as a biographer eventually eclipsed his reputation as an artist. The second is that he belonged to a part of the Italian artistic tradition which was itself intellectualized, and that his book can be read as a polemic in favour of a theory of art which was soon to be very seriously challenged by a new generation.

The division between the two traditions or streams of development in Italian art can most easily be understood, not by looking at the generation to which Vasari himself belonged – that of fully developed, academizing Mannerism – but at that which immediately followed, the generation of Annibale Carracci and Michelangelo Merisi da Caravaggio. Carracci and Caravaggio had more things in common than they are usually given credit for, notably a commitment to realism, or more precisely to naturalism which exposed the self-conscious artificiality of their predecessors. Yet, as contemporaries recognized, these two great artists developed along opposing lines, and had a totally different impact on the future of Italian art, and thus of Western European art in general. Caravaggio almost immediately attracted a swarm of imitators, first in Rome, then in Naples, and finally almost throughout Europe. He exercised a major influence over certain Dutch and French artists. Indeed, there is a case for saying that the most gifted and significant of his followers were non-Italians. Some major Caravaggists, such as the Lorrainer Georges de La Tour, seem never to have visited Italy nor to have been in direct contact with Caravaggio himself.

The story of Caravaggism contains a paradox. Many of those who encountered his work at first hand in Rome, and were seduced by it, soon renounced their allegiance. The important French painter Simon Vouet, for example, was a Caravaggist in Italy, but soon loosened his connection with the style when he returned home.

Annibale Carracci did not offer style so much as a method. Committed to naturalism in his youth, influenced by Giorgione and the Venetians just as Caravaggio was, he evolved steadily towards a grand, idealizing classicism. This, in turn, was founded upon a revision of High Renaissance studio practice inherited from the generation of Raphael. This practice developed into a coherent theory of art which could be passed on to others, through spoken and written precept as well as through imitation in the studio.

For more than two hundred years the main tradition of European painting stemmed from the so-called Bolognese Academy, which Annibale founded in conjunction with his brother Agostino and his cousin Lodovico. It took deep root in France as well as in Italy. In France, it seemed to weaken under the impact of the Rococo, but was revived by Neo-classicism, recodified by David and then by Ingres, and passed on to the painters of the nineteenth century through the Ecole des Beaux-Arts in Paris. One of the last inheritors to make original and creative use of it was Degas.

If we look at the 'anecdotal heritage' left behind by Annibale Carracci on the one hand and Caravaggio on the other, we immediately discover that the stories which have come down to us are not only different in tone, but often very different in point of view. Bernini, talking to Chantelou during his visit to Paris, clearly perceives a line of succession which descends from Michelangelo to Annibale, and then to himself and his own contemporaries. Stories about Annibale, whether related by Bernini or by one of Vasari's chief successors as a writer of artists' lives, G. P. Bellori, are often constructed so as to enshrine some apophthegm about the nature of art – that is, they are stories-with-a-moral, and also stories told by artistic insiders about another insider.

In Caravaggio's case, precisely the contrary seems to be true. The stories about him emphasize the bizarre aspects of his character, his personal faroucheness, and at the same time the unsystematic nature of his art. In a wider context, they invite the reader to wonder about the inexplicable nature of art itself.

During the twentieth century, it is this second set of attitudes which has triumphed – which is why there is currently far more popular interest in Caravaggio than there is in his once-triumphant rival. What we enjoy today are anecdotes which stress the otherness of artistic talent, and its magical or shamanistic aspects. This is the fundamental point of many of the stories told about such artists as Picasso, Jackson Pollock and Joseph Beuys. At the same time, new techniques in biography, and new criteria for what is true or untrue, mean that these stories are often undermined or contradicted even as they are being told.

In order to understand the phenomena I have just described, we have to set them in a much broader context. In his preface to the second, 1568, edition of the *Lives* (which had first appeared eighteen years earlier), Vasari gives the reader some idea of how he expected his work to be read. He speaks first of the Ancient Near East and of Ancient Egypt (for both these he relies on the Bible, and for the second on Diodorus and Pliny as well). He then turns to what he thinks of as the true exemplars for the artists of his own day – the Greeks and the Romans. One of the important distinctions he makes is between what is 'antique', and therefore praiseworthy, and what is simply 'old':

But that my readers may the better comprehend what it is that I call 'old', and what 'antique', I add that the antique are works executed before the time of Constantine, in Corinth, Athens, Rome, and other far-famed cities, down to the times of Nero, Vespasian, Trajan, Adrian, and Antonine; 'old' are such as were executed from the days of St. Silvester, downwards by a certain residue of the Greeks, whose profession was rather that of dyeing than painting. For the greater part of the excellent earlier artists being extirpated in those times of war, there remained, as I have said, nothing to these Greeks ('old', but not 'antique') save only the first rude outlines on a ground of colour, as is made sufficiently manifest by a crowd of mosaics executed throughout Italy by these Greeks, and which may be seen in any old church of whatsoever city you please, through all the land.[1]

In writing his *Lives*, Vasari not only exalted the qualities of ancient art, as defined above, but consciously modelled himself upon ancient

1. Introduction to the *Lives*, trans. Mrs J. Foster, London, 1850.

authors. In terms of form, his most important model was probably Plutarch. He writes of his artist-heroes in more or less the same fashion that Plutarch wrote about the warrior heroes of antiquity. Just as in Plutarch, he inserts brief stories or anecdotes in order to illustrate their qualities, and bring them alive for the reader's imagination.

A more immediate and practically useful source, however, was Pliny. The descriptions of celebrated Greek painters and their works given in the Book XXXV of Pliny's immense *Natural History* – and, to a lesser extent, the descriptions and characterizations of the great Greek sculptors given in Book XXXVI – provided Vasari with a suggestive model. A problem with Pliny's descriptions of the work of such artists as Zeuxis and Apelles, so widely famous in the ancient world, was that there was no way of verifying them: all their works were lost. Vasari and his contemporaries had to rely on written accounts alone, and all they had to help them were a few discoveries already made in the ruins of Rome – for instance, the paintings and stucco decorations in Nero's Golden House, which provided so powerful a stimulus to Raphael and members of his school.

Renaissance painters did of course try to reconstruct the lost masterpieces of antiquity that ancient writers described. A favourite was the so-called *Calumny of Apelles*, an allegorical representation of Slander described by the Hellenistic Greek writer Lucian. Botticelli made a painting inspired by this, and Mantegna made an elaborate drawing.

Inevitably, because the originals were missing, Pliny's descriptions of the artists, rather than the works, tended to occupy a primary position. The influence of these descriptions was threefold. First, artists learned from them what to attempt and what their relationship with the patron, especially the princely patron, ought to be. Second, the patron learned that the ancients had thought of major artists as being much more than artisans, in the medieval model. Finally, writers about art, caught up in the revival of Classical culture, began to shape their descriptions of art and artists to bring them into conformity with the literary models supplied by Pliny and other writers.

There is another influence to be found in Vasari's work especially in the earlier artists he discusses – those who had lived long before his own time and for whose lives he was forced to rely largely on folk memory and hearsay. This was a combination of the medieval 'merry tale' and the moral fables of the same epoch. The derivation becomes clear if we look at the work of a number of slightly earlier Italian Renaissance authors – men who belong to the fifteenth not the sixteenth century. They include Poggio Bracciolini (1380–1459), Ludovico Carbone (1435–82) and Angelo Poliziano (1454–94). All of these men were humanists, and all produced collections of witty and sometimes licentious anecdotes, of a kind which came to be called *facetiae*.

These collections, like Vasari's *Lives*, owe much to Classical models, in this case Latin rather than Greek. Sources include the *Attic Nights* of Aulus Gellius, the *Saturnalia* of Macrobius and Cicero's *De Oratore*, which cites a large number of anecdotes as part of a general analysis of wit and humour. Yet Classical sources are not the only pedigree which can be cited for these collections. They also stem from the humorous stories used by medieval preachers trying to hold the attention of their congregations, and from the jests told by medieval *jougleurs* or professional entertainers.

The derivation from the first of these sources can be seen in the collection of tales which cluster round the personality of Piovano [Priest] Arlotto. Arlotto Mainardi, or 'Priest Arlotto', was a real personage, who lived from 1396 to 1484. Shortly after his death an anonymous author put together a collection of brief stories about him, which stress his qualities, his peasant shrewdness and earthy wisdom. Many were of the kind which might have adorned a successful sermon. A typical example runs as follows:

'What prayer do you recommend that I say in the morning, so that it will avail me?' a man asked Priest Arlotto.

He replied: 'When you rise, make the sign of the holy cross and say devotedly a Hail Father and a Hail Mary, and then say these words: "My lord Jesus Christ, protect me from the fury and the hands of peasants, from the conscience of priests, from doctors' prescriptions, from the so-ons and so-forths of lawyers, from a man who hears two Masses every morning, and from those who always say 'On my word of honour . . .'"'[1]

Another collection of stories of the same period centres round the exploits not of a priest but of the jester Pietro Gonella, a Florentine who lived towards the middle of the fourteenth century and was

---

1. Quoted in Charles Speroni, *Wit and Wisdom of the Italian Renaissance*, 1964.

employed at the court of Obizzo d'Este, Marquis of Ferrara. Gonella's pleasantries are less moralizing, but just as earthy as those of Priest Arlotto.

None of the stories about Priest Arlotto or Gonella concern artists. Art does, however, make its appearance in the collection called *Il bel libretto*, the 'beautiful little book', which the best modern scholarship attributes to Angelo Poliziano, though it was first published, with an additional section written by himself, by the sixteenth-century historian Ludovico Domenichi (1515–64). The first edition appeared in 1548, two years before the first edition of Vasari. Among the artists who figure in Poliziano's collection of stories are Mino da Fiesole, Donatello and Botticelli. Domenichi added further stories of his own about an artist of a later generation, Raphael.

The difference between Poliziano's and Vasari's treatment of their artist subjects is simply this – in Poliziano's text, Donatello appears in order to make a particular point; the joke or witticism explodes, and the story has served its purpose and is over. In Vasari's text, such stories serve as parts of a larger whole, and their chief function is to illuminate the inner recesses of artistic temperament and character. Vasari attempts something more complex than anything written about the visual arts by the humanists of an earlier generation. In dismantling his work, to present his anecdotal material stripped of its context, one does him an injustice.

When writing about Donatello, Vasari was, in historical terms, within touching distance of his subject. Donatello died in 1466: Vasari was born in 1511. They were therefore just under fifty years apart. It is conceivable that Vasari was able to speak to people who had themselves known the great sculptor: it is certain that he was able to question some whose fathers had known him.

With earlier subjects, the case is obviously different. Vasari gives a surprising amount of space to an artist called Buonamico Buffalmacco (1262/72–1340). In terms of present-day art history Buffalmacco is not a great name. He is now tentatively identified with the so-called Master of St Cecilia (named from an altarpiece now in the Uffizi), whom Berenson curtly describes as a 'close follower of the youthful Giotto; attractive in small figures, but less so in larger ones'. Vasari is less interested in Buffalmacco's achievements than in his personality. He portrays him as a slightly clownish figure, and a characteristic story concerns a painting of St Christopher, commissioned by a peasant.

Because of the nature of the contract, the figure is forced into a space much too small for it, thus fulfilling the letter of the agreement but outraging the disappointed client. This tale (p. 16) has much of the rustic savour of the stories linked to Priest Arlotto and the jester Gonella.

The central tradition of anecdotes about painters and painting is undoubtedly an Italian one, and it reflects the superior status of the artist within Italian society. As a compiler of artists' lives, Vasari found many successors and imitators during the seventeenth and eighteenth centuries: Bellori, Baldinucci, Malvasia, Baglione, Ridolfi. When the idea of writing artists' biographies transferred itself to northern Europe, in the hands of such writers as Joachim von Sandrart and Carel van Mander, the Italian influence was still manifest.

There was not, however, the close and constant contact between artists and literary intellectuals which seems to have been the norm in Italy. Dürer's close relationship with Willibald Pirckheimer and Holbein's more temperate friendship with Erasmus were not the start of a tradition. As the Reformation established itself more firmly in northern Europe, intellectual circles and artistic ones actually seemed to draw apart.

In addition, the profession of artist was more slowly and uncertainly separated from the medieval artisanal tradition in regions north of the Alps. One of the frustrations of scholarship in dealing with the art of the Low Countries, for example, is the curiously uneven and capricious distribution of biographical information. For example, Carel van Mander's *Schilderboek* (1604) is a treasury of information about Northern Mannerists, giving a full biography of the important painter and virtuoso engraver Hendrik Goltzius, a close personal friend of the author. About major figures such as Rembrandt and Hals, however, it remains silent, simply because it was published too early.

No comparable writer took van Mander's place, with the result that the biographical tradition for the golden age of Dutch painting is a defective one. Most of the biographical information we have about seventeenth-century Dutch painters comes to us, not directly through Dutch sources, but via French authors of the eighteenth century, at a period when Dutch cabinet painting had become fashionable with wealthy French collectors. Enthusiasm for the work of artists like Adriaen Brouwer fuelled a lively curiosity about their lives.

In Brouwer's case there already seems to have been a strong oral tradition, nourished by the sheer eccentricity of the artist's character and strengthened by his contact with Rubens, who admired and collected his work (this is attested by inventories as well as hearsay). Because he played a double role, as a diplomat and statesman as well as an artist, Rubens was fully visible to his educated contemporaries. He is therefore one of the few northern artists of the time concerning whom there are trustworthy accounts.

Brouwer, by contrast, emerges as a type, rather than an individual. He represents the artist in his role as a naïve clown, a spendthrift and feckless Bohemian. In his case, a legend can be seen in the process of accretion about a small nucleus of fact, as the pearl forms round a piece of grit in an oyster. The anecdotes told about Brouwer carry an echo of earlier traditions. For example, the story about the artist improvising elaborately painted garments for himself is a variant of a tale told about Mabuse. Brouwer, however, is not the conclusion of this line of descent. There are strong similarities between what is said about him and the tales which attached themselves to the personality of the late eighteenth-century English painter George Morland.

It seems to me that complex cultural and psychological forces are at work here. Brouwer is in one sense simply another reincarnation of the medieval 'wise fool' or jester, to whom the artist had long been assimilated in popular tradition. In a second sense, the picture offered of Brouwer's personality is an example of society's instinctive adroitness in dealing with creative recalcitrance and reluctance to be assimilated to the bourgeois norm. In yet a third sense, paradoxically opposed to this second one, Brouwer is offered as a role model, an example of the way in which the true creative artist certifies his own talent and makes himself recognizable. The elaborate story of Brouwer painting a picture to prove his identity, after having been imprisoned as a spy in the citadel at Antwerp, serves as a kind of parable illustrating this (p. 166).

Though Rembrandt is a much more important artist than Brouwer, the biographical tradition concerning him is far less elaborate and complete. He seems to have lived without any kind of intellectual intimacy, or at least with none which has been recorded. That is not the same thing as saying that his paintings failed to communicate with his contemporaries. Like Caravaggio, he was an artist whose influence spread throughout Europe. It was felt not only by his numerous pupils in Holland, but by leading artists elsewhere, often several generations removed. Those he influenced included G. B. Castiglione in Genoa, G. B. Tiepolo in Venice, and Fragonard in France.

The few anecdotes about Rembrandt, however, are mere scraps of information, not all of it very convincing. Their central theme is one which tends to shock posterity: his supposed avarice.

As a complex, fully developed personality Rembrandt remained mute until the nineteenth century. It was only then that he came to be regarded as a Shakespeare among artists. The chief instrument in this transformation was his large corpus of self-portraits, which the Romantics interpreted in the light of their own preoccupations. In this context it is necessary to remember that the biographical facts about an artist, especially if he is a major figure, are constantly interpreted and reinterpreted in the light of current reactions to his work. It is these reactions which supply the necessary context which makes them meaningful to the audience.

The reinterpretation of Rembrandt's personality did, however, have roots in a remoter past than Romanticism. It was connected with the cult of genius, which the Romantics did not invent, though they certainly carried it to new heights. It is sometimes said that this cult is primarily a literary phenomenon, which only afterwards spilled over into the interpretation of art and music. In fact, almost the contrary is the case. Our modern conception of genius first formed around the personality of Michelangelo, the subject of Vasari's longest, most intimate life and also of another contemporary biography written by Ascanio Condivi.

As these two accounts make clear, in Michelangelo's own lifetime his younger contemporaries already hailed him as an individual who broke the common mould, and who, in doing so, changed the whole nature of art. They found his personality as important as his artistic achievements, and they tried to define what was unique about it.

Some precedents for the attitudes they adopted were already to be found in Pliny. In the *Natural History*, Pliny remarks that the Greek artist Parrhasius described himself as 'the Prince of Painters': 'Above all saying that he was sprung from the lineage of Apollo and that his picture of Heracles at Lindos presented the hero as he had often appeared to him in his dreams' (*Natural History*, XXXVI 71–2). Pliny even seemed on one occasion to make the now established modern distinction between talent and genius, saying of another painter, Timanthes, that 'his execution, though consummate, is always surpassed by his *ingenium*' (XXXV 74). This term, which I have left in the original Latin, is not exactly the same as our English word 'genius', but in this context it seems to come close.

Nevertheless in the sixteenth century Michelangelo's reputation was essentially a new cultural phenomenon. For the first time the creative person, though visibly moral and subject to all human ills and frailties, came close to being regarded as a demi-god.

The psychoanalyst Lange-Eichbaum, author of one of the most thorough and interesting studies of genius, notes that a religious response still survives in the post-Renaissance approach to the subject: 'Among modern civilized beings a reverence for genius has often become a substitute for the lost dogmatic religions of the past. Genius has come to be regarded as, so to say, a justification of the goal towards which humanity is marching.' This is near to the tone adopted by Michelangelo's contemporary biographers, though they also stressed the human side of the artist's personality. Every fact about him became interesting, thanks to the presence of genius.

In this sense, Michelangelo is the first artist whose life can be regarded as providing a kind of religious text. This element has again become visible – even more visible, in fact – during the twentieth century. A recent case is the German sculptor Joseph Beuys. Beuys openly acknowledged the shamanistic aspect of his own activity, and it is this which is stressed by his enthusiastic disciples.

Since the religious or at least the transcendental element does indeed play a part in some of the texts chosen for inclusion in this anthology, it is worth quoting again from Lange-Eichbaum. He sees the reverence for genius as something which is culturally conditioned and far from universal. In his view, it is a typically bourgeois phenomenon: 'In paying homage to the productive writer and the sculptor, the bourgeois is, as it were, paying homage to himself, is elevating his own nobility, intellectual nobility, to the level of the ideal.'

What the anecdotes about artists and the (more fully elaborated) artists' biographies written in the Western tradition teach us is that the very concept of the artist as a special form of human being is not universal. It was invented, in a rather tentative way, by Hellenistic Greek and Roman writers. It disappeared with the collapse of the

Roman Empire, and for a long period the artist was indistinguishable from the artisan. It was conclusively reinvented by the Renaissance humanists and has continued to flourish until the present day.

It is interesting to reflect why this should be so. The only non-Western culture, for example, which seems to have been interested in the systematic collection of stories about art and artists was classical Chinese civilization. There seem to be almost no stories about the great artists of India, Africa or Oceania, who for the most part remain anonymous.

Chinese painting, from the T'ang Dynasty onwards, was always closely connected with Chinese literary culture. Stories about Chinese art concern themselves almost exclusively with the lives and work of scholar-painters. The themes they embrace cover some which are also familiar in the annals of Western art – personal eccentricity, virtuoso skill in the manipulations of the artist's materials – and others which are more peculiarly Chinese, such as the artist's apparent amateurism and unwillingness to work for money (the mark of the gentleman–scholar as opposed to the mere tradesman), and the desire to achieve harmony with nature. A few characteristic Chinese anecdotes form the final section of this book.

Because Chinese civilization remained separated from our own, it is possible to take a much more detached view of this kind of material. The process of decoding is therefore much easier. My contention is that the main body of anecdotal material about art and artists, stretching roughly from the period of Giotto to the present day, and confined to what can in the broadest sense be called European art, needs to be decoded in similar fashion.

This is not to denigrate its human interest. I think many of the anecdotes included here cast a searching light on human nature, and especially upon the creative temperament. Many celebrated artists suddenly seem to speak to us directly, as the thick veil of art-historical interpretation is drawn aside. Yet it makes no sense to pretend that this represents wholly unprejudiced information. The anecdote is always filtered through the preconceptions of the person who has chosen to record it, even when that person is in fact the artist himself. Even so, I have tended to avoid purely autobiographical fragments, on the ground that these generally go beyond the scope of the anecdote as it is most usefully defined. It is for this reason, for example, that I have included only one extract from Cellini's *Autobiography*, chosen less for what Cellini tells us about himself than for what the whole excerpt has to say in general about the Renaissance artist and his princely patron. The contest between Cellini and François I's mistress, Mme d'Etampes, for the king's approval and attention is revealing, not least – in a metaphorical sense – about Cellini's powerful but unstable position within the king's immediate circle. We are left with the impression, unintended by the writer, that he and the lady were rivals almost in a sexual sense.

The stories, sayings and brief episodes collected here (with the exception of Part XXIII) trace the emergence of the artist in Western civilization as a figure distinguishable from the mere artisan. They show how his newly achieved status was defined through relationships with other people, the princely patron above all, then – much later – the intellectual class and the general bourgeois public.

Because collecting facts about art and the writing of artists' lives were activities pioneered by Renaissance humanism, there has been a general tendency to assume that artists and literary intellectuals have always been on close terms with one another. In fact, this seems to be a misconception. It is further the case that when intellectuals *have* interested themselves in art, they have frequently seemed to look in the wrong direction.

There have been moments in the history of Western painting and sculpture when artists and intellectuals seemed to draw close together, and to some extent to make common cause. The first of these was the mature period of Mannerism, typified by Vasari himself, and to some extent also by Cellini. An art based on the *concetto* (which can be translated as either 'conceit' or 'concept') was also, necessarily, an art which provoked verbal explication, and which perhaps relied upon this explication to make its fullest effect.

It is, nevertheless, worth remembering that there are major Mannerist artists who have almost entirely slipped through the anecdotal net. If Michelangelo's personality is well recorded, that of Giambologna, the greatest Mannerist sculptor of the following generation, is not – and this despite the fact that he spent his career at the Florentine court. Vasari added a brief biography of Giambologna, then just under forty years old, to the second edition of his *Lives*, but had nothing especially vivid to say about him. The one striking story is told by Baldinucci, and, significantly, concerns an encounter between Giambologna and

Michelangelo. Giambologna seems, in old age, to have told it against himself. What happened was that Giambologna, a Fleming by birth, went to see the aged Michelangelo soon after his arrival in Rome, taking with him a laboriously finished wax *modello* he had just completed. Michelangelo did not approve – he took the wax, crushed it, then swiftly turned the material into a far more vigorous new composition, commenting: 'Now go off and learn to model properly, before you try to give a finish to anything.'

This belongs to a well-established category of art anecdote – the kind which offers the layman a quick glimpse into the kitchen. It is a fragment of *ad hoc* practical advice; and if it offers a glimpse of character it is of Michelangelo's character, not Giambologna's.

There are two reasons why Giambologna did not generate a penumbra of stories. First, he had an equable character and was highly professional in his working methods. He had a large, well-organized studio, undertook great quantities of commissions, and delivered them on time. He seems to have had a complete absence of what is now called artistic temperament. More important than this, however, were his actual aesthetic preoccupations, which have to be deduced from his work. Charles Avery puts it well in his authoritative book about the sculptor:[1]

Unlike the intense and neurotic genius Michelangelo, Giambologna was not deeply involved with the spiritual content of his work, nor even (to the dismay of his more literal-minded contemporaries) with the narrative aspect of his subjects. He concentrated instead (and this was completely novel) on perfecting certain distinct types of composition, for example the single figure, and the group with two or three figures, in a conceptual – almost 'abstract' – way. The ingenuity of his solution to a complex problem of design and the technical accomplishment of carving it in marble or chasing it in bronze were paramount in Giambologna's aesthetic. Fortunately this coincided with the expectations of his patrons, the Medici dukes and other distinguished heads of state, including successive Roman Emperors and Popes.

What was missing in Giambologna's case was a language in which what he was doing could be explained. His temperament offered the anecdotalist no purchase; nor did his art – which ensured that the

1. Charles Avery, *Giambologna: The Complete Sculpture*, Phaidon/Christies, Oxford, 1985.

makers and circulators of stories about artists very largely passed him by.

Baroque art represented, to some extent, a rejection of the intellectual preoccupations of middle and late Mannerism in favour of the emotions. This rejection hinged on a change in religious climate, at least in that part of Europe which still adhered to the doctrines of the Catholic church.

The rejection of intellectual preoccupations was still more emphatic – at least on the surface – in the art of seventeenth-century Holland. The work of Vermeer, for example, is intellectual, but intellectual through its exquisitely refined sense of abstract design, which is then clothed in mundane dress. As a personality, however, Vermeer has left no record. A similar oblivion has swallowed the personality of another painter – by courtesy French though in fact from the then still-independent duchy of Lorraine – Georges de La Tour.

Concerning La Tour's personality some fragments of information remain, but they hardly amount to anything which can be described as an anecdote. We know, for instance, that a painting of his – a *St Sebastian Tended by Holy Women* (now apparently lost) – belonged to Louis XIII, and hung in the king's bedroom. We also know, from a petition sent by some of the inhabitants of Lunéville to the Duke of Lorraine, that La Tour had pretensions to the status of gentleman rather than tradesman, and 'made himself odious to the people by the number of dogs he kept, both greyhounds and spaniels'. Yet these hardly add up to what is usually defined as an anecdote.

When we contemplate the careers of these two artists, both now regarded as major figures, we are forced to admit that art could exist, at this period, in a universe of its own, quite separate from any world which has left a trace in literature.

The situation only started to change in the eighteenth century, and it did not change rapidly or immediately. The one leading artist of the Rococo who has left a substantial trace in the writings of his contemporaries is Antoine Watteau. His admirers and commercial heirs seem to have wished to put him on the same footing as the Dutch cabinet painters who were then so fashionable. Largely what they portray is a more civilized Brouwer. It is remarkable how little we know about the personality of Boucher, despite his lofty official position as Premier Peintre du Roi. We know equally little about

Fragonard. The personality of the great Venetian decorative painter G. B. Tiepolo also remains an enigma — we know far more about his rival at the court of Madrid, the pioneer Neo-classicist, Anton Rafael Mengs.

The contrast is not accidental. What changed attitudes to art and artists were two linked events — the birth of Neo-classicism and the beginnings of modern art criticism. Like the Renaissance before it, Neo-classicism embarked on a revolution in art by making an appeal to the remote past. However, the leading Neo-classical theorists, such as Winckelmann, were better informed historically than their fifteenth-century predecessors, and had more material at their disposal. They did not have to rely nearly so much on ancient texts. They could make their appeal to the evidence offered by a multitude of ancient statues and even paintings. In the case of the latter, knowledge of what Greek and Roman painting really looked like had been revolutionized by the discoveries made in the buried cities of Pompeii and Herculaneum, which included both copies after Greek masters and original Roman compositions.

What Neo-classicism lacked, certainly to begin with, were major artists. Anton Rafael Mengs was no match for Raphael himself. One of the reasons why David made such a tremendous impact on the art of his time was that he was the first Neo-classical painter whose commitment to the new movement and whose stature as an artist were alike unquestionable. His emergence, however, did not alter the fact that Neo-classicism was the first European art movement to be invented by theoreticians, who afterwards looked for artists to carry out the programme they had announced. It can thus also be described as the first avant-garde art movement, in the sense in which we now use the term. Surrealism, so different in every other respect, followed a similar pattern of development, in that it was invented by literary men who found artists to carry out their prescriptions.

The *Encyclopédiste* Denis Diderot, though not the first art critic in the modern sense, can be thought of as the first important one. David did not arrive on the scene early enough for Diderot, whose significant alliance was with a much weaker painter, Jean-Baptiste Greuze. His moralizing genre paintings, addressed to a bourgeois public (which they reached not only through exposure at the Salon, but through reproduction in engravings), were used by Diderot as an oblique way of chastising the vices of the court.

Diderot did not import morality into Greuze's paintings. Greuze was quite capable of doing that for himself, creating compositions which owed much to contemporary stage practice – dramas frozen at the decisive moment, with both the function and the moral stature of every participant carefully indicated. What Diderot did do, however, was to turn the discussion of art into an activity in which moral judgements played a primary part. Despite occasional attempts to change its direction, it has retained this moralizing character right up to the present day.

All of this revived and strengthened the anecdotal impulse in a number of different ways. First, the alliance between art and literature was now formally acknowledged. It had, of course, existed previously: both Renaissance and Baroque artists used themes taken from the classics. Baroque painters made extensive use of Ariosto's *Orlando Furioso* and Tasso's *Gerusalemme Liberata*, and there is a strong link between some of Poussin's classicizing paintings and the contemporary French drama of Corneille and Racine. Up till now, however, the artist had not seemed to rival the writer. Greuze not only used literary themes, but made paintings which were meant to be read, rather than looked at.

Even so, his work did not wholly satisfy the expectations which commentators like Diderot had now begun to arouse. When Greuze applied for membership of the Académie Royale, submitting a scene from Roman history, *The Death of Septimius Severus*, which was distinctly reminiscent of Poussin, the Académie refused to receive him, as he had hoped, as a *peintre d'histoire*, but insisted that he be admitted only as a painter of genre scenes. Greuze was cut to the quick. To be classified thus was to be excluded from a world of intellectual discourse where art was placed on the same footing as purely cerebral occupations. What his intellectually inclined contemporaries were looking for was defined by the immediate enthusiasm which greeted David's *Oath of the Horatii*.

In the circumstances I have outlined, the inclusion of the artist's life, as well as his productions, within this essentially literary framework, seemed only logical. David's subsequent activities as a committed revolutionary and member of the Convention seemed to confirm the justice of this judgement. The paintings he produced were only one facet of a far more complex biographical whole.

It was also significant that the eighteenth century saw a great increase in sophistication in the craft of biography itself. Boswell's *Life of Johnson* is a much more complex, as well as a much longer work, than any individual life written by Vasari — even his life of Michelangelo — and this represents the direction taken by biography in general, though artists had in fact to wait until the next century before they regularly became the subjects of studies of this degree of elaboration. Ambitious biographers realized that a plentiful supply of anecdotal material had an important role to play in making the subject live for the reader.

This situation has now been partly obscured for us by the development of the modern illustrated book, dependent on the invention first of photography and then of new printing techniques which enable photographs to be reproduced in book form. This has played some part in switching the emphasis back to close visual analysis of the works of art themselves. The main focus, certainly in the case of pre-modern artists where authentic biographical material is often scarce, is now on the analysis of stylistic development, with biographical material perhaps relegated to an appendix. Even so, the changeover has not been complete. Elaborate biographies of artists continue to appear, side by side with fully illustrated volumes cataloguing their work.

The second thing which strengthened the impulse to collect and preserve information about the lives of artists — especially revealing or amusing anecdotes where these could be found — was the fact that by the eighteenth century they had definitely entered the ranks of the professional classes. The professional characteristically claimed not only increased status during his life, but the recollection of this status even after death.

As can be seen from many of the stories collected here, those who gathered information about artists' lives, from the mid-sixteenth century onwards, were always particularly interested in defending the artist's status, and for a long time this defence remained difficult. Over and over again the great artist is portrayed as the intimate of kings. Dürer consorts with the Emperor Maximilian, Titian with Charles V, Holbein with Henry VIII, Velásquez with Philip IV of Spain. But such intimacy was of a precarious kind, perpetually challenged by the nobility who surrounded the monarch. Indeed, this is one of the things which such anecdotes most consistently tell us.

By the eighteenth century the challenge had receded. Of the knighthoods conferred on artists by English monarchs, that given to Joshua Reynolds was not the earliest. Charles I had knighted Rubens and Van Dyck; knighthoods were also conferred upon Lely and Kneller. These honours recognized the artists' connection with the court. Reynolds, on the other hand, was recognized as the leader and President of a newly formed professional body, the Royal Academy, whose specific purpose was to confirm the professional status of the artist in the eyes of the public. Increased status, in turn, seemed to legitimize curiosity about art as an activity and about those who were involved with it.

Because of the nature of nineteenth-century biographical conventions, the hundred years between 1800 and 1900 offer perhaps the richest and most varied supply of anecdotes about art. The technique of the biographer, at this period, though far more developed than it had been previously, was less demanding than it has since become. The author introduced his witnesses one after the other, and let them ramble on almost at will. Where the subject was of recent vintage, as he was in C. R. Leslie's justly famous life of Constable, the result was a rich harvest of undoctored, but also unquestioned, eye-witness accounts. Significantly, the correct title of the book is *Memoirs of the Life of John Constable, R.A.* In this, as in other classic nineteenth-century biographies, there is in fact little distinction to be made between biography and reminiscences. In modern biographies, by contrast, the significant anecdote is often difficult to separate from the matrix of comment and analysis in which it is embedded.

Certain modern artists, however, have so much fascinated their contemporaries that they have become the subjects, often during their own lifetimes, of volumes of reminiscences which carry forward a purer form of the anecdotal tradition. Picasso is an outstanding case: there are books by his mistresses (Fernande Olivier and Françoise Gilot), his secretary (Jaime Sabartès) and his literary friends (Jean Cocteau, Hélène Parmelin), and by one of the most important of his dealers (Daniel-Henry Kahnweiler). Not all of these books are entirely devoted to Picasso, but he plays a substantial role in all of them. This mass of twentieth-century material threatens to overwhelm the selector, and enforces thought about how the position of the contemporary artist differs from that of artists in the past.

One aspect has already been touched upon, in connection with Beuys. The nineteenth-century artist, with rare exceptions, aimed to achieve an established position in the social hierarchy. This was true even of painters who now seem to us revolutionary, for example Manet. One of the most puzzling aspects of Manet's character – indeed, it seems to have mystified even Manet himself – was the fact that his gift for provocation appeared to be exercised in spite of himself: he was always surprised by the uproar his work aroused.

In the twentieth century, artists have often wanted to break away from the social framework. Their claim, implicit and sometimes explicit, has been that artistic talent is *sui generis*. The successful artist is now often regarded as a radical being, capable of transforming any situation into which he is put. In addition, the artist remains a person of his own time; in other words, he or she is a creation of and responds to, modern means of communication.

The first artist to be projected to the public in this way was inevitably Picasso, and this took place only late in his long career. The most significant step in the process was probably Henri-Georges Clouzot's film, *Le Mystère Picasso*, made in 1955. In this, the artist was seen apparently at the very moment of creation – the drawing or painting developed on the screen before the spectator's eyes. At the same time, the 'Picasso' of the title became a role – one enacted by the artist himself.

The most significant aspects of the modern artist, as opposed to his predecessors, seem to be threefold. One is a special kind of spontaneity, in which art manifests itself directly from the subconscious mind. We find this in Picasso; we find it yet more strongly developed in Pollock, where personal brutishness seems to offer a telling contrast to the evident sensitivity of the product. Another is passivity. Duchamp and Warhol are examples of artists who seemed to manipulate events around them by calculated non-intervention. The artist's personal magic is such that he becomes a catalyst. He transforms his surroundings, and changes the nature of objects, simply by being present. The third is activity of a ritual or shamanistic kind. The ritual itself is the point, not any physical object which may be an end product. The most extreme instance of this is of course Beuys.

Rather than trying to cover the whole spectrum of twentieth-century art, I have therefore limited my selection to anecdotes about the five artists I have just named.

One issue necessarily raised by a collection of this kind is whether or not the anecdotes it contains are true. I have included some which are self-evidently fiction, others which seem implausible on the face of it, and many others which are unverifiable. I have already suggested, at the start of this introductory essay, that good anecdotes often contain a certain tension between truth and untruth, reality and fiction. This is best expressed in the proverbial Italian phrase *si non è vero, è ben trovato*.

Even when they are apparently plausible, or even verifiable, anecdotes only tell us what some witness saw, or thought he saw; heard, or thought he heard. The shape the story takes can be affected by any number of things. Two of the most important are a desire to make a neat and telling story out of the persistent untidiness of real life (in other words, the instinct for dramatization, sometimes combined with the wish to point a moral), and the witness's own preconceptions. These embrace not only his feelings or prejudices about the individual who is at the centre of the story, but his feelings about art and artists in general.

Exploring what one may call the 'anecdotal heritage' of Western art, the researcher soon begins to recognize certain old friends – anecdotes, usually of the least plausible kind, which are told in almost identical form about different artists. One such concerns the dying artist who rejects the crucifix that the priest holds out to him on the grounds that it is too ugly to contemplate. This is told of Alonso Cano and also of Watteau. Another concerns the artist who, in order to create a truly realistic Crucifixion, pinions a living victim and stabs him to death in order to watch his death agony. Late sources attach this grotesque story to the personalities of both Giotto and Michelangelo.

What underpins these tales, and makes them interesting, is the way in which they seem to reflect popular opinions about the nature of art and of the artistic temperament. The first story, about the rejected crucifix, states that the artist is apt to put artistic integrity and the sense of aesthetic quality above even the most sacred things, and that he will continue to do so even in extreme and desperate situations. The second says something about the popular view of realism – or, more exactly, of verisimilitude – and its place in art. It also offers a comment on the relationship between artistic necessity and conventional morality.

While few stories repeat themselves absolutely exactly, there is a definite pattern to be found in many others. A frequent theme, as has already been noted, is the artist's intimacy with his princely patron. Others which recur are the power of naturalistic imitation – the work of art which deceives the eye because of the way it replicates reality – and the violent reaction of the creative spirit when it feels that its efforts have been insufficiently rewarded. There are numerous stories about artists destroying their own work in a fit of pique. These anecdotes tell us, first, what the audience expected art itself to be; and second, what the artist's position was within the social framework.

The theme of social relationships is also stressed in the numerous stories about portrait painting. Often it is the sitter himself or herself who tells the story and thus provides an intimate glimpse of the creative process – a glimpse which can be obtained in no other way. An apple could not report on what it was like to be painted by Cézanne, nor a Suffolk landscape on what it was like to be depicted by Constable.

Many of the stories told about art and artists before about 1850, or even 1900, now provide graphic evidence of how much attitudes towards art have changed in Western society. The coherence of this earlier material does, nevertheless, suggest that we ought to look for a similar coherence in the tales which circulate about the art of our own time.

It also suggests that we ought to look for things which have been carried over from the pre-modern epoch. The developing reverence for the idea of genius, and the idea that artistic activity has something intrinsically magical about it are cases in point. Artists, the Western tradition tells us, deal in transformation – of materials, social situations, physical perceptions and surroundings. Like primitive magicians they are both powerful and abject. Often they seem to be both at the same time.

Essentially, therefore, the anecdotes gathered together in this book, however convincing in themselves, however authentic their origins, must be looked upon as a collective attempt to explain the inexplicable, which is the essence of art itself.

I

THE ANCIENT WORLD

୧୬

This small group of extracts from Pliny's Natural History, *given in Philemon Holland's stately Elizabethan translation in order to mark their distance from other extracts included in the book, demonstrates the way in which Vasari and those who followed him in writing artists' lives took over and remoulded concepts about art and those who made it which they found in ancient authors.*

Themes to note are the emphasis on the perfect imitation of life (Zeuxis' grapes, and Parrhasius' trompe l'oeil representation of a piece of cloth), and on virtuoso skills (the contest between Protogenes and Apelles, where the text also implies that the 'handwriting' of a great artist is unmistakable). In apparent contrast, there is a story about the role of chance: Protogenes trying to paint the foam which came from the dog's mouth.

More important still for the future is the stress Pliny puts on the artist's special relationship with the prince. Apelles rebukes the world-conqueror Alexander the Great for his ignorance about art, and Alexander accepts the rebuke. In the story which immediately follows, and forms part of the same extract, Alexander actually makes Apelles a present of a favourite courtesan, with whom the painter has fallen in love. This story provided a favourite subject for Renaissance and Baroque artists. It was titillatingly erotic and voyeuristic, but also served to glorify the painter's profession.

The story of the relationship between Protogenes and Demetrius Poliorcetes ('the besieger'), King of Macedon (336–283 BC) refers to the latter's unsuccessful siege of Rhodes in 305 BC. Pliny fancifully links Demetrius' failure to capture the city and island to his unwillingness to endanger a masterpiece, and by so doing exalts the importance of art.

Zeuxis (fl. late 5th century BC) and Success

He grew in processe of time to such wealth by the means only of his excellent hand, that for to make shew how rich he was, when he went to the solemnity of the games at Olympia, he caused his owne name to be imbrodered in golden letters, within the lozenge worke of his clokes, whereof he had change,* and which he brought thither to be seen. In the end, he resolved with himselfe to work no longer for mony, but to give away al his pictures, saying, That he valued them above any price.

* Whereof he had many changes.

[Pliny, *Natural History*, xxxv]

Parrhasius (fl. late 5th century BC) and Zeuxis

Parrhasius by report was so bold as to challenge Zeuxis openly and to enter the lists with him for the victory; in which contention and triall, Zeuxis for proofe of his cunning, brought upon the scaffold a table [painting on panel], wherein were clusters of grapes so lively painted, that the very birds of the aire flew flocking thither for to bee pecking at the grapes. Parrhasius againe for his part to shew his workmanship, came with another picture, wherin he had painted a linnen sheet, so like to a sheet indeed, that Zeuxis in a glorious bravery and pride of his heart, because the birds had approved of his handy-worke, came to Parrhasius with these words by way of a scorn and frumpe, Come on sir, away with your sheet once, that we may see your goodly picture. But taking himselfe with the manner, and perceiving his own error, he was mightily abashed, and like an honest minded man yeelded the victory to his adversary, saying withall, Zeuxis hath beguiled poore birds, but Parrhasius hath deceived Zeuxis, a professed artisane.

This Zeuxis, as it is reported, painted afterwards another table, wherein he had made a boy carrying certaine bunches of grapes in a flasket, and seeing again that the birds flew to the grapes, he shook the head, and comming to his picture, with the like ingenious mind as before, brake out into these words, and said, Ah, I see well enough where I have failed, I have painted the grapes better than the boy, for if I had don him as naturally, the birds would have bin afraid and never approched the grapes.

[Pliny, *Natural History*, xxxv]

Protogenes and Apelles (both fl. 4th century BC)

And to this purpose impertinent it is not, to report a pretty occurrent
that fell between Protogenes and him [Apelles]: for being very desirous
to be acquainted with Protogenes, a man whom hee had never seen,
and of his works, whereof there went so great a name, he imbarqued
and sailed to Rhodes, where Protogenes dwelt: and no sooner was hee
landed, but he enquired where his shop was, and forthwith went
directly thither. Protogenes himselfe was not at home, only there was
an old woman in the house who had the keeping of a mighty large table
set in a frame, and fitted ready for a picture: and when he enquired for
Protogenes, she made answer, that he was not within; and seeing him
thereupon ready to depart, demanded what his name was, and who
she should tell her master asked for him. Apelles then, seeing the
foresaid table standing before him, tooke a pensil [brush] in hand and
drew in colour a passing fine and smal line through the said table,
saying to the woman, Tell thy master, that he who made this line
enquired for him; and so he went his wayes. Now when Protogenes
was returned home, the old woman made relation unto him of this that
hapned in his absence; and as it is reported, the artificer had no sooner
seene and beheld the draught of this small line, but he knew who had
been there, and said withall, Surely Apelles is come to town; for
unpossible it is, that any but hee should make in colour so fine
workemanship.

With that hee takes me the pensill, and with another colour drew
within the same line a smaller than it: willing the woman when hee
went forth of dores, that if the party came againe, she should shew him
what he had done, and say withall, that there was the man whom he
inquired after. And so it fell out indeed, for Apelles made an errand
againe to the shop, and seeing the second line, was dismaied at first and
blushed withal to see himselfe thus overcome; but taking his pensil, cut
the foresaid colours throughout the length, with a third colour distinct
from the rest, and left no room at all for a fourth to be drawn within it.
Which when Protogenes saw, hee confessed that he had met with his
match and his master both; and made all the hast he could to the haven
to seek for Apelles to bid him welcome and give him friendly
entertainment.

[Pliny, *Natural History*, xxxv]

Apelles and Alexander the Great (356–323 BC)

Over and besides, very courteous he was and faire spoken, in which regard King Alexander the Great accepted the better of him, and much frequented his shop in his owne person: for, as I have said before, he gave streight commandment, That no painter should bee so hardie as to make his picture but only Apelles. Now when the King being in his shop, would seeme to talke much and reason about his art, and many times let fal some words to little purpose, bewraying his ignorance; Apelles after his mild manner, would desire his grace to hold his peace, and said, sir, no more words, for feare the prentise boies there that are grinding of colours, do laugh you to scorn: So reverently thought the king of him, that being otherwise a cholericke prince, yet hee would take any word at his hands in that familiar sort spoken in the best part, and be never offended.

And verily, what good reckoning Alexander made of him, he shewed by one notable argument; for having among his courtesans one named Campaspe, whom he fancied especially above the rest, in regard as well of that affection of his as her incomparable beauty, he gave commandement to Apelles for to draw her picture all naked: but perceiving Apelles at the same time to be wounded with the like dart of love as wel as himself, he bestowed her on him most frankly. By which example, hee shewed moreover, that how great a Commander, and high minded a prince he was otherwise, yet in this mastering and commanding of his affections, his magnanimity was more seen: and in this act of his he wan as much honor and glory, as by any victory over his enemies; for now he had conquered himselfe, and not onely made Apelles partner with him of his love, but also gave his affection clean away from her unto him, nothing mooved with the respect of her whom before he so dearly loved, that being the concubin of a king, she should now become the bedfellow of a painter. Some are of opinion, That by the patterne of this Campaspe, Apelles made the picture of *Venus Anadyomene*.

[Pliny, *Natural History*, xxxv]

Apelles and Ptolemy I of Egypt

As for Apelles, he had such a dexterity in drawing pourtraits so lively, and so neer resembling those for whom they were made, that hardly one could be known from the other; insomuch, as Appio the Grammarian hath left in writing (a thing incredible to be spoken) that a certain Physiognomist or teller of Fortune, by looking onely upon the face of men and women, such as the Greekes call Metoposcopos, judged truly by the portraits that Apelles had drawne, how many yeres they either had lived or were to live, for whom those pictures were made. But as gracious as he was otherwise with Alexander and his train, yet he could never win the love and favor of prince Ptolomaeus, who at that time followed the court of K[ing] Alexander, and was afterwards king of Egypt. It fortuned, that after the decease of Alexander, and during the reigne of K[ing] Ptolomae aforesaid, this Apelles was by a tempest at sea cast upon the coast of Aegypt, and forced to land at Alexandria; where, other painters that were no well willers of his, practised with a jugler or jeaster of the kings, and suborned him in the kings name to train* Apelles to take his supper with the king. To the court came Apelles accordingly, and shewed himself in the presence. Ptolomae having espied him, with a stern and angry countenance demanded of him what he made there, and who had sent for him? and with that shewed unto him all his servitors who ordinarily had the inviting of ghests to the kings table, commanding him to say which of all them had bidden him: whereat Apelles, not knowing the name of the party who had brought him thither, and beeing thus put to his shifts, caught up a dead cole of fire from the hearth thereby, and began therewith to delineate and draw upon the wall the proportion of that cousiner beforesaid. He had no sooner pourfiled a little about the visage, but the king presently tooke knowledge thereby of the party that had played this pranke by him and wrought him this displeasure.

* Persuade.

[Pliny, *Natural History*, xxxv]

Protogenes and the Siege of Rhodes by Demetrius Poliorcetes

About the same time, there flourished (as I have said before) Protogenes; born he was at Caunos a city in Cilicia, and subject to the Rhodians: he was so exceeding poore at the beginning, and withall, so studious, intentive, and curious in his worke without all end, that fewer pictures by that means came out of his hands, and himselfe never rise to any great wealth . . . But of all the painted tables that ever he wrought, that of Ialysus* is accounted the principall, which is now dedicated at Rome within the temple of Peace: whiles he was in painting this Ialysus, it is said, that he lived only upon steeped Lupines, which might serve him in stead of meat and drinke both, to satisfie his hunger and quench his thirst: and this hee did, for feare least too much sweetnesse of other viands should cause him to feed over liberally, and so dul his spirit and senses. And to the end that this picture should be lesse subject to other injuries, and last the longer, he charged it with foure grounds of colours, which he laid one upon another: that ever as the upper coat went, that underneath might succeed in the place and shew fresh againe.

In this table, the pourtraiture of a dog is admirable and miraculous; for not only art, but fortune also met together in the painting thereof; for when he had done the dog in all parts to the contentment of his owne minde (and that ywis was a very hard and rare matter with him) and could not satisfie and please himselfe in expressing the froth which fell from his mouth as he panted and blowed almost windlesse with running; displeased he was with the very art it selfe: and albeit he thought that he had bin long enough already about the said froth, and spent therein but too much art and curiositie, yet somewhat (he wist not what) was to be diminished or altered therein: the more workmanship and skill that went thereto, the farther off it was from the truth indeed and the nature of froth (the onely marke that he shot at): for when he had done all that he could, it seemed still but painted froth, and not that which came out of the dogs mouth; whereas it should have been the very same and no other, which had been there before. Hereat he was troubled and vexed in his mind, as one who would not have any thing seene in a picture of his, that might be said like, but the very same indeed. Many a time he had changed his pensill and colours; as often, he had wiped out that which was done, and al to see if he could hit upon it, but it would not be, for yet it was not to his fansie.

At the last, falling clean out with his own workmanship, because the art might be perceived in it, in a pelting chase he flings me the spungeful of colours that he had wiped out, full against that unhappy place of the table which had put him to all this trouble: but see what came of it! the spunge left the colours behind, in better order than hee could have laied them, and in truth, as well as his heart could wish. Thus was the froth made to his full mind, and naturally indeed by meere chance, which all the wit and cunning in his head could not reach unto. (After whose example, Nealces another painter did the like, and sped as wel, in making the froth falling naturally from a horses mouth; namely, by throwing his spunge against the table before him, at what time as he painted a horse-rider cheering and cherking up his horse, yet reining him hard as he champed upon his bit.) Thus (I say) Fortune taught Protogenes to finish his dog.

This picture of Ialysus and his dog, was of such name and so highly esteemed, that K[ing] Demetrius when hee might have forced the city of Rhodes, on that side onely where Protogenes dwelt, forbare to set it on fire, because he would not burne it among other painted tables: and thus for to spare a picture, he lost the opportunitie of winning a towne. During this strait siege and hot assault of Rhodes, it chanced that Protogenes himselfe was at worke in a little garden that he had by the townes side, even as a man would say within the compasse of Demetrius his camp. And for all the fury of warre and the daily skirmishes within his sight and hearing, yet he went on still with his workes that he had in hand, and never discontinued one hour. But being sent for by the king, and demanded, How he durst so confidently abide without the walls of the city in that dangerous time? he answered, That he knew full well that Demetrius warred against the Rhodians, and had no quarrell to good Arts and Sciences. The king then (glad in his heart that it lay now in his hand to save those things, which he had spared before, and whereof he had so good respect) bestowed a very strong guard about Protogenes for his better safety and security: and as great an enemy as he was to the Rhodians, yet he used otherwhiles to visit Protogenes of his owne accord in proper person, because he would not eftsoones call him out of his shop from worke: and setting aside the maine point and occasion of lying before Rhodes, which was the winning thereof, the thing that he so much desired; even amid the assaults, skirmishes, and battels, hee would finde time to come to Protogenes, and took great pleasure to see his worke.

* A worthy knight, sonne of Ochimus.

[Pliny, *Natural History*, xxxv]

II

THE EARLY RENAISSANCE

ॐ

In the opinion of Vasari and his contemporaries, the first truly modern artist – the first to shake off what they regarded as the bondage of the Middle Ages – was Giotto. However, Giotto died more than two hundred years before the first publication of Vasari's Lives, *and it is unlikely that Vasari had access to much, or indeed any, written information about him. What he did have were stories which had been passed down by word of mouth. These, for the most part, had an 'exemplary' character. They were designed to explain just why it was that Giotto had achieved such unique importance.*

Probably the best remembered story about Giotto, since, as Vasari himself tells us, it acquired proverbial status, was the tale of the drawing Giotto made for the emissary of Pope Benedict IX – a perfect freehand circle. As the context gives us to understand, this was at the same time a declaration of superiority over all competitors and a kind of signature – something to be compared with the lines made successively by Apelles and Protogenes, in the story related by Pliny.

Other themes which first appear in Pliny recur: familiar relations with the great; supreme powers of naturalistic imitation. A story concerning Giotto from a very late source, totally out of character with the description Vasari gives of this great artist, stresses Machiavellian wickedness and cruelty. It is included because it demonstrates the way in which a striking anecdote, deeply implausible but representing something which people want to think or believe about art (i.e. that it contains a demonic element), will try to achieve credibility by attaching itself to a great name. The demonic element also appears in another form in the tale Vasari tells about an artist of the later fourteenth century, Spinello Aretino.

The connection between the stories told about Giotto's contemporary Buonamico Buffalmacco and the humorous stories of the purely medieval tradition has already been discussed in the Introduction. The anecdote about Giotto decorating a shield for a peasant is in the same vein.

Giotto (1276–1337) and Cimabue (c. 1240–?1302)

This great man was born at the village of Vespignano, in the district of Florence, fourteen miles distant from that city, in the year 1276, from a father named Bondone, a tiller of the soil and a simple fellow. He, having had this son, to whom he gave the name Giotto, reared him conformably to his condition; and when he had come to the age of ten, he showed in all his actions, although childish still, a vivacity and readiness of intelligence much out of the ordinary, which rendered him dear not only to his father but to all those also who knew him, both in the village and beyond. Now Bondone gave some sheep into his charge, and he, going about the holding, now in one part and now in another, to graze them, and impelled by a natural inclination to the art of design, was for ever drawing, on stones, on the ground, or on sand, something from nature, or in truth anything that came into his fancy. Wherefore Cimabue, going one day on some business of his own from Florence to Vespignano, found Giotto, while his sheep were browsing, portraying a sheep from nature on a flat and polished slab, with a stone slightly pointed, without having learnt any method of doing this from others, but only from nature; whence Cimabue, standing fast all in a marvel, asked him if he wished to go to live with him. The child answered that, his father consenting, he would go willingly. Cimabue then asking this from Bondone, the latter lovingly granted it to him, and was content that he should take the boy with him to Florence; whither having come, in a short time, assisted by nature and taught by Cimabue, the child not only equalled the manner of his master, but became so good an imitator of nature that he banished completely that rude Greek manner and revived the modern and good art of painting, introducing the portraying well from nature of living people, which had not been used for more than two hundred years.

[Vasari, *Lives of the most Eminent Painters, Sculptors and Architects*, revised edition 1568]

Giotto's Circle

Pope Benedict IX of Treviso sent one of his courtiers into Tuscany to see what sort of man was Giotto, and of what kind his works, having designed to have some pictures made in S. Pietro. This courtier, coming in order to see Giotto and to hear what other masters there were in Florence excellent in painting and in mosaic, talked to many masters in Siena. Then, having received drawings from them, he came to Florence, and having gone into the shop of Giotto, who was working, declared to him the mind of the Pope and in what way it was proposed to make use of his labour, and at last asked him for some little drawing, to the end that he might send it to His Holiness. Giotto, who was most courteous, took a paper, and on that, with a brush dipped in red, holding his arm fast against his side in order to make a compass, with a turn of the hand he made a circle, so true in proportion and circumference that to behold it was a marvel. This done, he smiled and said to the courtier: 'Here is your drawing.' He, thinking he was being derided, said: 'Am I to have no other drawing but this?' ''Tis enough and to spare,' answered Giotto. 'Send it, together with the others, and you will see if it will be recognized.' The envoy, seeing that he could get nothing else, left him, very ill-satisfied and doubting that he had been fooled. All the same, sending to the Pope the other drawings and the names of those who had made them, he also sent that of Giotto, relating the method that he had followed in making his circle without moving his arm and without compasses. Wherefore the Pope and many courtiers that were versed in the arts recognized by this how much Giotto surpassed in excellence all the other painters of his time. This matter having afterwards spread abroad, there was born from it the proverb that is still wont to be said to men of gross wits: 'Tu sei più tondo che l' O di Giotto!' ('Thou art rounder than Giotto's circle'). This proverb can be called beautiful not only from the occasion that gave it birth, but also for its significance, which consists in the double meaning; tondo being used, in Tuscany, both for the perfect shape of a circle and for slowness and grossness of understanding.

[Vasari, *Lives*, 1568]

Giotto Paints a Buckler

The story: 'Everyone must have heard already who was Giotto, and how great a painter he was above every other. A clownish fellow, having heard his fame and having need, perchance for doing watch and ward, to have a buckler of his painted, went off incontinent to the shop of Giotto, with one who carried his buckler behind him, and, arriving where he found Giotto, said, "God save thee, master, I would have thee paint my arms on this buckler." Giotto, considering the man and the way of him, said no other word save this, "When dost thou want it?" And he told him; and Giotto said, "Leave it to me", and off he went. And Giotto, being left alone, ponders to himself, "What meaneth this? Can this fellow have been sent to me in jest? Howsoever it may be, never was there brought to me a buckler to paint, and he who brings it is a simple manikin and bids me make him his arms as if he were of the blood-royal of France; i' faith, I must make him a new fashion of arms." And so, pondering within himself, he put the said buckler before him, and, having designed what seemed good to him, bade one of his disciples finish the painting, and so he did; which painting was a helmet, a gorget, a pair of arm-pieces, a pair of iron gauntlets, a cuirass and a back-piece, a pair of thigh-pieces, a pair of leg-pieces, a sword, a dagger, and a lance. The great man, who knew not what he was in for, on arriving, comes forward and says, "Master, is it painted, that buckler?" Said Giotto, "Of a truth, it is; go, someone, and bring it down." The buckler coming, that would-be gentleman begins to look at it and says to Giotto, "What filthy mess is this that thou hast painted for me?" Said Giotto, "And it will seem to thee a right filthy business in the paying." Said he, "I will not pay four farthings for it." Said Giotto, "And what didst thou tell me that I was to paint?" And he answered, "My arms." Said Giotto, "And are they not here? Is there one wanting?" Said the fellow, "Well, well!" Said Giotto, "Nay, 'tis not well, God help thee! And a great booby must thou be, for if one asked thee, 'Who art thou?' scarce wouldst thou be able to tell; and here thou comest and sayest, 'Paint me my arms!' An thou hadst been one of the Bardi, that were enough. What arms dost thou bear? Whence art thou? Who were thy ancestors? Out upon thee! Art not ashamed of thyself? Begin first to come into the world before thou pratest of arms as if thou wert Dusnam of Bavaria. I have made thee a whole suit of armour on thy buckler; if there be one piece wanting, name it, and I will have it painted." Said he, "Thou dost use vile words to me, and hast spoilt me a buckler;" and taking himself off, he went to the justice and had Giotto summoned. Giotto appeared and had him summoned, claiming two florins for the painting, and the other claimed them from him. The officers, having heard the pleadings, which Giotto made much the better, judged that the other should take his buckler so painted, and should give six lire to Giotto, since he was in the right. Wherefore he was constrained to take his buckler and go, and was dismissed; and so, not knowing his measure, he had his measure taken.'

[Franco Sacchetti, quoted in Vasari, *Lives*, 1568]

Giotto and the King of Naples

But to return to Naples; Giotto made many works in the Castel dell' Uovo, and in particular the chapel, which much pleased that King, by whom he was greatly beloved that many times, while working, Giotto found himself entertained by the King[1] in person, who took pleasure in seeing him at work and in hearing his discourse. And Giotto, who had ever some jest on his tongue and some witty repartee in readiness, would entertain him with his hand, in painting, and with pleasant discourse, in his jesting. Wherefore, the King saying to him one day that he wished to make him the first man in Naples, Giotto answered, 'And for that end am I lodged at the Porta Reale, in order to be the first in Naples.' Another time, the King saying to him, 'Giotto, an I were you, now that it is hot, I would give over painting for a little;' he answered, 'And I, i' faith, an I were you.'

[Vasari, *Lives*, 1568]

Giotto Tricks his Master

It is said that Giotto, while working in his boyhood under Cimabue, once painted a fly on the nose of a figure that Cimabue himself had made, so true to nature that his master, returning to continue his work, set himself more than once to drive it away with his hand, thinking that it was real, before he perceived his mistake.

[Vasari, *Lives*, 1568]

Giotto's Crucifixion

Giotto intending to make a painting of the Crucifixion, induced a poor man to suffer himself to be bound to a cross, under the promise of being set at liberty in an hour, and handsomely rewarded for his pains. Instead of this, as soon as Giotto had made his victim secure, he seized

1. Robert of Anjou, King of Naples (1309–42).

a dagger, and, shocking to tell, stabbed him to the heart! He then set about painting the dying agonies of the victim to his foul treachery. When he had finished his picture, he carried it to the Pope; who was so well pleased with it, that he resolved to place it above the altar of his own chapel. Giotto observed, that as His Holiness liked the copy so well, he might perhaps like to see the original. The Pope, shocked at the impiety of the idea, uttered an exclamation of surprise. 'I mean,' added Giotto, 'I will show you the person whom I employed as my model in this picture; but it must be on condition that your Holiness will absolve me from all punishment for the use which I have made of him.' The pope promised Giotto the absolution for which he stipulated, and accompanied the artist to his workshop. On entering, Giotto drew aside a curtain which hung before the dead man, still stretched on the cross and covered with blood.

The barbarous exhibition struck the Pontiff with horror; he told Giotto he could never give him absolution for so cruel a deed, and that he must expect to suffer the most exemplary punishment. Giotto, with seeming resignation, said that he had only one favour to ask, that His Holiness would give him leave to finish the piece before he died. The request had too important an object to be denied; the Pope readily granted it; and in the meantime a guard was set over Giotto, to prevent his escape. On the painting being replaced in the artist's hands, the first thing he did was to take a brush, and dipping it into a thick varnish, he daubed the picture all over with it, and then announced that he had finished his task. His Holiness was greatly incensed at this abuse of the indulgence he had given, and threatened Giotto that he should be put to the most cruel death, unless he painted another picture equal to the one which he had destroyed. 'Of what avail is your threat,' replied Giotto, 'to a man whom you have doomed to death at any rate?' 'But,' replied His Holiness, 'I can revoke that doom.' 'Yes,' continued Giotto, 'but you cannot prevail on me to trust to your verbal promise a second time.' 'You shall have a pardon under my signet before you begin.' 'On that condition,' said Giotto, 'I shall make the trial.' The conditional pardon was accordingly made out and given to Giotto, who taking a wet sponge, in a few minutes wiped off the coating with which he had bedaubed the picture; and instead of a copy, restored the original in all its beauty to His Holiness.

[*The Percy Anecdotes*, 1821–3]

Buonamico Buffalmacco (1262/72–1340) and the Peasant's Contract

A peasant desiring that Buonamico should make him a S. Christopher, they came to an agreement in Florence and arranged a contract in this fashion, that the price should be eight florins and that the figure should be twelve braccia high. Buonamico, then, having gone to the church where he was to make the S. Christopher, found that by reason of its not being more than nine braccia either in height or in length, he could not, either without or within, accommodate the figure in a manner that it might stand well; wherefore he made up his mind, since it would not go in upright, to make it within the church lying down. But since, even so, the whole length would not go in, he was forced to bend it from the knees downwards on to the wall at the head of the church. The work finished, the peasant would by no means pay for it; nay, he made an outcry and said he had been cozened. The matter, therefore, going before the Justices, it was judged, according to the contract, that Buonamico was in the right.

[Vasari, *Lives*, 1568]

Buffalmacco and the Ape

It is said that in the year 1302 he was summoned to Assisi, and that in the Church of S. Francesco, in the Chapel of S. Caterina, he painted all the stories of her life in fresco, which have been very well preserved; and there are therein some figures that are worthy to be praised. This chapel finished, on his passing through Arezzo, Bishop Guido, by reason of having heard that Buonamico was a gay fellow and an able painter, desired him to stop in that city and paint for him, in the Vescovado, the chapel where baptisms are now held. Buonamico, having put his hand to the work, had already done a good part of it when there befell him the strangest experience in the world, which was, according to what Franco Sacchetti relates, as follows. The Bishop had an ape, the drollest and the most mischievous that there had ever been. This animal, standing once on the scaffolding to watch Buonamico at work, had given attention to everything, and had never taken his eyes off him when he was mixing the colours, handling the flasks, beating the eggs for making the distempers, and in short when he was doing anything else whatsoever. Now, Buonamico having left off working one Saturday evening, on the Sunday morning this ape, notwithstanding that he had, fastened to his feet, a great block of wood which the Bishop made him carry in order that thus he might not be able to leap wherever he liked, climbed on to the scaffolding whereon Buonamico was used to stand to work, in spite of the very great weight of the block of wood; and there, seizing the flasks with his hands, pouring them one into another and making six mixtures, and beating up whatever eggs there were, he began to daub over with the brushes all the figures there, and, persevering in this performance, did not cease until he had repainted everything with his own hand; and this done, he again made a mixture of all the colours that were left him, although they were but few, and, getting down from the scaffolding, went off. Monday morning having come, Buonamico returned to his work, where, seeing the figures spoilt, the flasks all mixed up, and everything upside down, he stood all in marvel and confusion. Then, having pondered much in his own mind, he concluded finally that some Aretine had done this, through envy or through some other reason; wherefore, having gone to the Bishop, he told him how the matter stood and what he suspected, whereat the Bishop became very much disturbed, but, consoling Buonamico, desired him to put his hand again to the work and to repaint all that was spoilt. And because the Bishop had put faith in his words, which had something of the probable, he gave him six of his men-at-arms, who should stand in hiding with halberds while he was not at work, and, if anyone came, should cut him to pieces without mercy. The figures, then, having been painted over again, one day that the soldiers were in hiding, lo and behold! they hear a certain rumbling through the church, and a little while after the ape climbing on to the scaffolding; and in the twinkling of an eye, the mixtures made, they see the new master set himself to work over the saints of Buonamico. Calling him, therefore, and showing him the culprit, and standing with him to watch the beast at his work, they were all like to burst with laughter; and Buonamico in particular, for all that he was vexed thereby, could not keep from laughing till the tears came. Finally, dismissing the soldiers who had mounted guard with their halberds, he went off to the Bishop and said to him: 'My lord, you wish the painting to be done in one fashion, and your ape wishes it done in another.' Then, relating the affair, he added: 'There was no need for you to send for painters from elsewhere, if you had the true master at home. But he, perhaps, knew not so well how to make the mixtures; now that he knows, let him do it by himself, since I am no more good here. And his talent being revealed, I am content that there should be nothing given to me for my work save leave to return to Florence.' The Bishop, hearing the affair, although it vexed him, could not keep from laughing, and above all as he thought how an animal had played a trick on him who was the greatest trickster in the world. However, after they had talked and laughed their fill over this strange incident, the Bishop persuaded Buonamico to resume the work for the third time, and he finished it. And the ape, as punishment and penance for the crime committed, was shut up in a great wooden cage and kept where Buonamico was working, until this work was entirely finished; and no one could imagine the contortions which that creature kept making in this cage with his face, his body, and his hands, seeing others working and himself unable to take part.

[Vasari, *Lives*, 1568]

Spinello Aretino (?1346–1410) in Old Age

And although he [Spinello] was very old when he returned to Arezzo, and, having ample means, could have done without working, yet, as one who was ever used to working, he knew not how to take repose, and undertook to make for the Company of S. Agnolo in that city certain stories of S. Michael, which he sketched in red on the intonaco[1] of the wall, in that rough fashion wherein the old craftsmen used generally to do it; and in one corner, for a pattern, he wrought and coloured completely a single story, which gave satisfaction enough. Then, having agreed on the price with those who had charge thereof, he finished the whole wall of the high-altar, wherein he represented Lucifer fixing his seat in the North; and he made there the Fall of the Angels, who are being transformed into devils and raining down to earth; while in the air is seen a S. Michael, who is doing combat with the ancient serpent of seven heads and ten horns; and below, in the centre, there is a Lucifer already transformed into a most hideous beast. And Spinello took so much pleasure in making him horrible and deformed, that it is said (so great, sometimes, is the power of imagination) that the said figure painted by him appeared to him in a dream, asking Spinello where he had seen him so hideous, and why

---

1. The final layer of plaster on which a fresco is painted.

he had offered him such an affront with his brushes; and that he, awaking from his sleep, being unable to cry out by reason of his fear, shook with a mighty trembling, insomuch that his wife, awaking, came to his rescue. But he was none the less thereby in peril – his heart being much strained – of dying on the spot by reason of such an accident; and although he lived a little afterwards, he was half mad, with staring eyes, and he slipped into the grave, leaving great sorrow to his friends, and to the world two sons, of whom one was Forzore, the goldsmith, who worked admirably at Florence in niello, and the other was Parri, who, imitating his father, laboured continually at painting, and surpassed him by a long way in design.

[Vasari, *Lives*, 1568]

III

THE QUATTROCENTO AND
CINQUECENTO IN ITALY

෨

The idea that artists were a separate breed, quite different from mere artisans, first appeared in Florence, the most intellectually active city in Italy. It is therefore no accident that all but one of the stories included in this section feature Florentine artists. The exception, which concerns Giorgione, is about an argument between the Venetian painter and the Florentine sculptor Verrocchio, who was no doubt the means of its transmission back to Florence.

One subtext of the stories is fierce professional pride. It is now that we first begin to find stories about artists destroying their own work when they feel they have been underpaid, or, alternatively, when they feel they are being unduly harried by the patron. Donatello (Donato in some of the extracts) and Verrocchio are both said to have destroyed the heads of their two great equestrian statues, the Gattamelata *and the* Colleoni. *According to Vasari, Donatello destroyed another bronze head, when he thought he had been offered too little for it. Leonardo, paid what was agreed, was nevertheless fussy about the form in which he took the money. His remark: 'I am no penny painter' is an assertion that he is not a journeyman, working for daily wages.*

Leonardo, too, is the subject of an anecdote about the magical, transformative power of art, when he threatened to take the importunate Prior of S. Maria delle Grazie in Milan as his model for the head of Judas in The Last Supper.

Other subtexts are rather different. One which emerges with surprising frequency is the artist's fear of want in his old age. There is even a story of this kind about Donatello, who is undoubtedly the dominant personality in Florentine artistic circles at this period – one of the few who made an impression on authors other than Vasari. He was remembered not only for the trenchancy of his sayings, but for a new professionalism of attitude, and an outspoken pride in his own talent. In the Florentine art world, simultaneously close-knit and intensely competitive, he was a far more central figure than Leonardo, who did not remain in Florence, and who in any case seems to have been regarded as a dilettante.

Donatello (1386–1466) and Filippo Brunelleschi (1377–1446)

He [Donatello] made a Crucifix of wood with extraordinary care; and when he had finished this, thinking that he had made a very rare work, he showed it to Filippo di Ser Brunellesco, who was very much his friend, wishing to have his opinion. Filippo, whom the words of Donato had led to expect something much better, smiled slightly on seeing it. Donato, perceiving this, besought him by all the friendship between them to tell him his opinion; whereupon Filippo, who was most obliging, replied that it appeared to him that Donato had placed a ploughman on the Cross, and not a body like that of Jesus Christ, which was most delicate and in all its parts the most perfect human form that was ever born. Donato, hearing himself censured, and that more sharply than he expected, whereas he was hoping to be praised, replied, 'If it were as easy to make this figure as to judge it, my Christ would appear to thee to be Christ and not a ploughman; take wood, therefore, and try to make one thyself.' Filippo, without another word, returned home and set to work to make a Crucifix, without letting any one know; and seeking to surpass Donato in order not to confound his own judgment, after many months he brought it to the height of perfection. This done, he invited Donato one morning to dine with him, and Donato accepted the invitation. Whereupon, as they were going together to the house of Filippo, they came to the Mercato Vecchio, where Filippo bought some things and gave them to Donato, saying, 'Do thou go with these things to the house and wait for me there, I am coming in a moment.' Donato, therefore, entering the house and going into the hall, saw the Crucifix of Filippo, placed in a good light; and stopping short to study it, he found it so perfectly finished, that, being overcome and full of amazement, like one distraught, he spread out his hands, which were holding up his apron; whereupon the eggs, the cheese, and all the other things fell to the ground, and everything was broken to pieces. But he was still marvelling and standing like one possessed, when Filippo came up and said with a laugh, 'What is thy intention, Donato, and what are we to have for dinner, now that thou hast upset everything?' 'For my part,' answered Donato, 'I have had my share for this morning: if thou must have thine, take it. But enough; it is thy work to make Christ and mine to make ploughmen.'

[Vasari, *Lives*, 1568]

Donatello's Statue of Il Zuccone

For the main front of the Campanile of S. Maria del Fiore he wrought four figures in marble, five braccia in height, of which the two in the middle are portrayed from life, one being Francesco Soderini as a youth, and the other Giovanni di Barduccio Cherichini, now called Il Zuccone.* The latter was held to be a very rare work and the most beautiful that Donato ever made, and when he wished to take an oath that would command belief he was wont to say, 'By the faith that I place in my Zuccone'; and the while that he was working on it, he would keep gazing at it and saying, 'Speak, speak, plague take thee, speak!'

* i.e. Bald-head.

[Vasari, *Lives*, 1568]

Donatello Destroys his own Work

It is said that a Genoese merchant caused Donato to make a life-size head of bronze, which was very beautiful and also very light, because it had to be carried to a great distance; and that the commission for this work came to him through the recommendation of Cosimo. Now, when the head was finished and the merchant came to pay for it, it appeared to him that Donato was asking too much; wherefore the matter was referred to Cosimo, who had the head carried to the upper court of the palace and placed between the battlements that overlook the street, to the end that it might be seen better. When Cosimo sought to settle the difference, he found the offer of the merchant very far from the demand of Donato, and he turned round and said that it was too little. Whereupon the merchant, thinking it too much, said that Donato had wrought it in a month or little more, and that this meant a gain of more than half a florin a day. Donato, thinking this too much of an insult, turned round in anger and said to the merchant that in the hundredth part of an hour he would have been able to spoil the value of a year's labour; and giving the head a push, he sent it flying straightway into the street below, where it broke into a thousand pieces; saying to him that this showed that he was more used to bargaining for beans than for statues. Wherefore the merchant, regretting his meanness, offered to give him double the sum if he would make another; but neither his promises nor the entreaties of Cosimo could induce Donato to make it again.

[Vasari, *Lives*, 1568]

Donatello's Fair Price

In Florence the Consuls of the Wool Guild were planning to have a statue made; so they called in Donatello, a famous and excellent sculptor and painter. But as he asked fifty ducats for the execution of the statue, the Consuls, who had not expected him to ask so much, became angry at him and turned the order over to a rival of his – Giovanni, who was a mediocre sculptor.

In due time, after Giovanni had sculptured the statue as well as he could, he asked for eighty ducats. Completely amazed by this, the Consuls complained to him, protesting that Donatello, who was such an excellent man, had asked no more than fifty ducats to do it. Finally, since they were unable to settle the matter satisfactorily, they referred it to Donatello himself, who immediately decreed that the Consuls should pay Giovanni seventy ducats.

When the Consuls became indignant and reminded him that he himself would have been satisfied with fifty ducats, Donatello graciously said, 'It is true; and I had reasons to be satisfied with that amount, because with my experience I would have made the statue in less than one month; but this poor man, who could hardly be my apprentice, spent over six months on it!'

[L. Guiccardini, *L'hore di ricreatione*, 1568, trans. C. Speroni]

Donatello Praises a Lesser Sculptor

In the days of the excellent sculptor Donatello, there was in Florence another sculptor, Lorenzo of Bartoluccio; but he was a pale star next to that brilliant sun. This Lorenzo had sold a piece of property called Lepricino, from which he had been receiving little profit. Donatello was asked which was the best thing that the said Lorenzo had ever done; and the man who asked, of course, had in mind Lorenzo's sculptures.

Donatello replied, 'Selling Lepricino.'
[Niccolo Angeli dal Bucine, from a MS compiled c. 1486–92, trans. C. Speroni]

Donatello under Pressure

Donatello was making a bronze statue of Captain Gattamelata;[1] and since he was constantly goaded to hurry with it, he took a hammer and crushed the head of the statue. When the Signori of Venice[2] heard about this, they asked him to come in and, among other threats, they told him that they would bash his head in just as he had done to the statue.

[Angelo Poliziano, first published in Domenichi's *Facetie e motti*, 1548, trans. C. Speroni] Vasari tells an identical story in the *Lives*, but applies it to Verrocchio's equestrian statue of Colleoni, in Venice itself.

Donatello Quarrels with an Apprentice

'He smiled at me, and I smiled at him.' This saying originated with the sculptor Donatello. When a young apprentice of Donatello's with whom he had had a quarrel left him, Donatello went to see Cosimo[3] to secure letters of introduction to the Marquis of Ferrara, where the youth had fled; and he stated to Cosimo that he wanted to go after him and kill him. Cosimo, who knew his temperament, wrote him the letters he wanted; but he secretly informed the Marquis of Donatello's nature. The Marquis granted Donatello permission to kill his apprentice on sight. However, when the youth ran into Donatello, he began smiling at him from a distance; and Donatello, who suddenly felt reconciled, smiled back at him and ran toward him. When the Marquis asked him if he had killed him, Donatello replied to him: 'No, I should say not! For he smiled at me, and I smiled at him.'

[Angelo Poliziano, from a lost MS entitled *Il bel libretto*, compiled c. 1477–99 and incorporated into L. Domenichi, *Facetie e Motti*, first published 1548, trans. C. Speroni]

1. Erasmo di Narni. The statue stands near the Santo in Padua.
2. Padua was in Venetian territory.
3. Cosimo de' Medici.

Donatello's Old Age

He was most liberal, gracious, and courteous, and more careful for his friends than for himself; nor did he give thought to money, but kept his in a basket suspended by a cord from the ceiling, wherefore all his workmen and friends could take what they needed without saying a word to him. He passed his old age most joyously, and, having become decrepit, he had to be succoured by Cosimo and by others of his friends, being no longer able to work. It is said that Cosimo, being at the point of death, recommended him to the care of his son Piero, who, as a most diligent executor of his father's wishes, gave him a farm at Cafaggiuolo, which produced enough to enable him to live in comfort. At this Donato made great rejoicing, thinking that he was thus more than secure from the danger of dying of hunger; but he had not held it a year before he returned to Piero and gave it back to him by public contract, declaring that he refused to lose his peace of mind by having to think of household cares and listen to the importunity of the peasant, who kept pestering him every third day – now because the wind had unroofed his dovecote, now because his cattle had been seized by the Commune for taxes, and now because a storm had robbed him of his wine and his fruit. He was so weary and disgusted with all this, that he would rather die of hunger than have to think of so many things. Piero laughed at the simplicity of Donato; and in order to deliver him from this torment, he accepted the farm (for on this Donato insisted), and assigned him an allowance of the same value or more from his own bank, to be paid in cash, which was handed over to him every week in the due proportion owing to him; whereby he was greatly contented. Thus, as a servant and friend of the house of Medici, he lived happily and free from care for the rest of his life.

[Vasari, *Lives*, 1568]

Paolo Uccello (1397–1475): Strange Tastes at S. Miniato

In a cloister of S. Miniato without Florence, also, he wrought the lives of the Holy Fathers, chiefly in terra-verde, and partly in colour; wherein he paid little regard to effecting harmony by painting with one colour, as should be done in painting stories, for he made the fields blue, the cities red, and the buildings varied according to his pleasure; and in this he was at fault, for something which is meant to represent

[27]

stone cannot and should not be tinted with another colour. It is said that while Paolo was labouring at this work, the Abbot who was then head of that place gave him scarcely anything to eat but cheese. Wherefore Paolo, having grown weary of this, determined, like the shy fellow that he was, to go no more to work there; whereupon the Abbot sent to look for him, and Paolo, when he heard friars asking for him, would never be at home, and if peradventure he met any couples of that Order in the streets of Florence, he would start running and flying from them with all his might. Now two of them, more curious than the rest and younger than Paolo, caught him up one day and asked him for what reason he did not return to finish the work that he had begun, and why he fled at the sight of a friar; and Paolo answered: 'You have murdered me in a manner that I not only fly from you, but cannot show myself near any carpenter's shop or pass by one, and all because of the thoughtlessness of your Abbot, who, what with pies and with soups always made of cheese, has crammed so much cheese into me that I am in terror lest, being nothing but cheese, they may use me for making glue. And if it were to go on any longer, I would probably be no more Paolo, but cheese.' The friars, leaving him with peals of laughter, told everything to the Abbot, who made him return to his work, and ordered him some other fare than cheese.

[Vasari, *Lives*, 1568]

Paolo Uccello's Wound in the Side

It is said that having been commissioned to paint, over the door of S. Tommaso in the Mercato Vecchio, that Saint feeling for the wound in the side of Christ, Paolo put into that work all the effort that he could, saying that he wished to show therein the full extent of his worth and knowledge; and so he caused a screen of planks to be made, to the end that no one might be able to see his work until it was finished. Wherefore Donato, meeting him one day all alone, said to him: 'And what sort of work may this be of thine, that thou keepest it screened so closely?' And Paolo said in answer: 'Thou shalt see it. Let that suffice thee.' Donato would not constrain him to say more, thinking to see some miracle, as usual, when the time came. Afterwards, chancing one morning to be in the Mercato Vecchio buying fruit, Donato saw Paolo uncovering his work, whereupon he saluted him courteously, and was asked by Paolo himself, who was curious and anxious to hear his judgment on it, what he thought of that picture. Donato, having studied the work long and well, exclaimed: 'Ah, Paolo, thou oughtest to be covering it up, and here thou art uncovering it!' Whereupon Paolo was much aggrieved, feeling that he was receiving much more by way of blame than he expected to receive by way of praise for this last labour of his; and not having courage, lowered as he was, to go out any more, he shut himself up in his house, devoting himself to perspective, which kept him ever poor and depressed up to his death. And so, growing very old, and having but little contentment in his old age, he died in the eighty-third year of his life, in 1432, and was buried in S. Maria Novella.

He left a daughter, who had knowledge of drawing, and a wife, who was wont to say that Paolo would stay in his study all night, seeking to solve the problems of perspective, and that when she called him to come to bed, he would say: 'Oh, what a sweet thing is this perspective!' And in truth, if it was sweet to him, it was not otherwise than dear and useful, thanks to him, to those who exercised themselves therein after his time.

[Vasari, *Lives*, 1568]

Filippo Lippi (c. 1406–69) Gains Freedom through his Art

Now, chancing to be in the March of Ancona, he was disporting himself one day with some of his friends in a little boat on the sea, when they were all captured together by the Moorish galleys that were scouring those parts, and taken to Barbary, where each of them was put in chains and held as a slave; and thus he remained in great misery for eighteen months. But one day, seeing that he was thrown much into contact with his master, there came to him the opportunity and the whim to make a portrait of him; whereupon, taking a piece of dead coal from the fire, with this he portrayed him at full length on a white wall in his Moorish costume. When this was reported by the other slaves to the master (for it appeared a miracle to them all, since drawing and painting were not known in these parts), it brought about his liberation from the chains in which he had been held for so long.

[Vasari, *Lives*, 1568]

Filippo Lippi: Slavery and Release again

It is said that he was so amorous, that, if he saw any women who pleased him, and if they were to be won, he would give all his possessions to win them; and if he could in no way do this, he would paint their portraits and cool the flame of his love by reasoning with himself. So much a slave was he to this appetite, that when he was in this humour he gave little or no attention to the works that he had undertaken; wherefore on one occasion Cosimo de' Medici, having commissioned him to paint a picture, shut him up in his own house, in order that he might not go out and waste his time; but after staying there for two whole days, being driven forth by his amorous – nay, beastly – passion, one night he cut some ropes out of his bed-sheets with a pair of scissors and let himself down from a window, and then abandoned himself for many days to his pleasures. Thereupon, since he could not be found, Cosimo sent out to look for him, and finally brought him back to his labour; and thenceforward Cosimo gave him liberty to go out when he pleased, repenting greatly that he had previously shut him up, when he thought of his madness and of the danger that he might run.

[Vasari, *Lives*, 1568]

The Generosity of Alessio Baldovinetti (?1423–99)

Alesso lived eighty years, and when he began to draw near to old age, as one who wished to be able to attend with a quiet mind to the studies of his profession, he retired into the Hospital of S. Paolo, as many men are wont to do. And perhaps to the end that he might be received more willingly and better treated (or it may have been by chance), he had a great chest carried into his room in the said hospital, giving out that it contained a good sum of money. Wherefore the Director and the other officials of the hospital, believing this to be true, and knowing that he had bequeathed to the hospital all that might be found after his death, showed him all the attention in the world. But on the death of Alesso, there was nothing found in it save drawings, portraits on paper, and a little book that explained the preparation of the stones and stucco for mosaic and the method of using them. Nor was it any marvel, so men said, that no money was found there, because he was so open-handed that he had nothing that did not belong as much to his friends as to himself.

[Vasari, *Lives*, 1568]

Andrea del Verrocchio (1435–88) and his Statue of Colleoni

The Venetians, meanwhile, wishing to honour the great valour of Bartolommeo da Bergamo[1], thanks to whom they had gained many victories, in order to encourage others, and having heard the fame of Andrea, summoned him to Venice, where he was commissioned to make an equestrian statue of that captain in bronze, to be placed on the Piazza di SS. Giovanni e Polo. Andrea, then, having made the model of the horse, had already begun to get it ready for casting in bronze, when, thanks to the favour of certain gentlemen, it was determined that Vellano da Padova should make the figure and Andrea the horse. Having heard this, Andrea broke the legs and head of his model and returned in great disdain to Florence, without saying a word. The Signoria, receiving news of this, gave him to understand that he should never be bold enough to return to Venice, for they would cut his head off; to which he wrote in answer that he would take good care not to, because, once they had cut a man's head off, it was not in their power to put it on again, and certainly not one like his own, whereas he could have replaced the head that he had knocked off his horse with one even more beautiful. After this answer, which did not displease those Signori, his payment was doubled and he was persuaded to return to Venice, where he restored his first model and cast it in bronze; but even then he did not finish it entirely, for he caught a chill by overheating himself during the casting, and died in that city within a few days; leaving unfinished not only that work (although there was only a little polishing to be done), which was set up in the place for which it was destined, but also another which he was making in Pistoia, that is, the tomb of Cardinal Forteguerra, with the three Theological Virtues, and a God the Father above; which work was afterwards finished by Lorenzetto, a sculptor of Florence.

[Vasari, *Lives*, 1568]

---

1. Bartolommeo Colleoni (1400–75), famous condottiere

[31]

Nanni Grosso (second half of fifteenth century), a Pupil of Verrocchio: The Badly Wrought Crucifix

It is also told of him that once, having returned from S. Maria Nuova completely cured of some sickness, I know not what, he was visited by his friends, who asked him how it went with him. 'Ill,' he answered. 'But thou art cured,' they replied. 'That is why it goes ill with me,' said he, 'for I would dearly love a little fever, so that I might lie there in the hospital, well attended and at my ease.' As he lay dying, again in the hospital, there was placed before him a wooden Crucifix, very rude and clumsily wrought; whereupon he prayed them to take it out of his sight and to bring him one by the hand of Donato, declaring that if they did not take it away he would die in misery, so greatly did he detest badly wrought works in his own art.

[Vasari, *Lives*, 1568] This story later became attached to more famous names – those of Alonso Cano and Antoine Watteau (see Introduction).

Luca Signorelli (1441–1524) Commemorates his Son

It is said that a son of his, most beautiful in countenance and in person, whom he loved dearly, was killed at Cortona; and that Luca, heart-broken as he was, had him stripped naked, and with the greatest firmness of soul, without lamenting or shedding a tear, portrayed him, to the end that, whenever he might wish, he might be able by means of the work of his own hands to see that which nature had given him and adverse fortune had snatched away.

[Vasari, *Lives*, 1568]

The Honesty of Pietro Perugino (c. 1450–1523)

The said Prior [of the convent of the Ingesuati, Florence], so I once heard tell, was very excellent at making ultramarine blues, and, therefore, having an abundance of them, he desired that Pietro should use them freely in all the above-mentioned works [paintings commissioned from Perugino]; but he was nevertheless so mean and suspicious that he would never trust Pietro, and always insisted on being present when he was using blue in the work. Wherefore Pietro, who had an honest and upright nature, and had no desire for another man's goods save in return for his own labour, took the Prior's distrust very

[32]

ill, and resolved to put him to shame; and so, having taken a basin of water, and having laid on the ground for draperies or for anything else that he wished to paint in blue and white, from time to time he caused the Prior, who turned grudgingly to his little bag, to put some ultramarine into the little vase that contained the tempera-water, and then, setting to work, at every second stroke of the brush Pietro would dip his brush in the basin, so that there remained more in the water than he had used on the picture. The Prior, who saw his little bag becoming empty without much to show for it in the work, kept saying time after time: 'Oh, what a quantity of ultramarine this plaster consumes!' 'Does it not?' Pietro would answer. After the departure of the Prior, Pietro took the ultramarine from the bottom of the basin, and gave it back to him when he thought the time had come, saying: 'Father, this is yours; learn to trust honest men, who never cheat those who trust them, although, if they wished, they could cheat such distrustful persons as yourself.'

    [Vasari, *Lives*, 1568] This is one of a number of stories which record friction between Renaissance artists and ecclesiastical patrons.

The Worldliness of Pietro Perugino

Pietro was a man of very little religion, and he could never be made to believe in the immortality of the soul – nay, with words in keeping with his head of granite, he rejected most obstinately every good suggestion. He placed all his hopes in the goods of fortune, and he would have sold his soul for money. He earned great riches; and he both bought and built houses in Florence, and acquired much settled property both at Perugia and at Castello della Pieve. He took a most beautiful young woman to wife, and had children by her; and he delighted so greatly in seeing her wearing beautiful head-dresses, both abroad and at home, that it is said that he would often tire her head with his own hand.

    [Vasari, *Lives*, 1568]

Leonardo da Vinci (1452–1519) Paints a Buckler

It is said that Ser Piero da Vinci,[1] being at his villa, was besought as a favour, by a peasant of his, who had made a buckler with his own

1. Leonardo's father (the artist was illegitimate).

hands out of a fig-tree that he had cut down on the farm, to have it painted for him in Florence, which he did very willingly, since the countryman was very skilful at catching birds and fishing, and Ser Piero made much use of him in these pursuits. Thereupon, having had it taken to Florence, without saying a word to Leonardo as to whose it was, he asked him to paint something upon it. Leonardo, having one day taken this buckler in his hands, and seeing it twisted, badly made, and clumsy, straightened it by the fire, and, having given it to a turner, from the rude and clumsy thing that it was, caused it to be made smooth and even. And afterwards, having given it a coat of gesso, and having prepared it in his own way, he began to think what he could paint upon it, that might be able to terrify all who should come upon it, producing the same effect as once did the head of Medusa. For this purpose, then, Leonardo carried to a room of his own into which no one entered save himself alone, lizards great and small, crickets, serpents, butterflies, grasshoppers, bats, and other strange kinds of suchlike animals, out of the number of which, variously put together, he formed a great ugly creature, most horrible and terrifying, which emitted a poisonous breath and turned the air to flame; and he made it coming out of a dark and jagged rock, belching forth venom from its open throat, fire from its eyes, and smoke from its nostrils, in so strange a fashion that it appeared altogether a monstrous and horrible thing; and so long did he labour over making it, that the stench of the dead animals in that room was past bearing, but Leonardo did not notice it, so great was the love that he bore towards art. The work being finished, although it was no longer asked for either by the countryman or by his father, Leonardo told the latter that he might send for the buckler at his convenience, since, for his part, it was finished. Ser Piero having therefore gone one morning to the room for the buckler, and having knocked at the door, Leonardo opened to him, telling him to wait a little; and, having gone back into the room, he adjusted the buckler in a good light on the easel, and put to the window, in order to make a soft light, and then he bade him come in to see it. Ser Piero, at the first glance, taken by surprise, gave a sudden start, not thinking that that was the buckler, nor merely painted the form that he saw upon it, and, falling back a step, Leonardo checked him, saying, 'This work serves the end for which it was made; take it, then, and carry it away, since this is the effect that it was meant to produce.' This thing appeared to Ser Piero nothing short of a miracle, and he praised very greatly the ingenious idea of Leonardo; and then, having privately bought from a pedlar another buckler, painted with a heart transfixed by an arrow, he presented it to the countryman, who remained obliged to him for it as long as he lived. Afterwards, Ser Piero sold the buckler of Leonardo secretly to some merchants in Florence, for a hundred ducats; and in a short time it came into the hands of the Duke of Milan, having been sold to him by the said merchants for three hundred ducats.[1]

[Vasari, *Lives*, 1568]

Leonardo da Vinci Shadows his Subjects

He was so delighted when he saw certain bizarre heads of men, with the beard or hair growing naturally, that he would follow one that pleased him a whole day, and so treasured him up in idea, that afterwards, on arriving home, he drew him as if he had had him in his presence.

[Vasari, *Lives*, 1568]

Leonardo da Vinci's 'Last Supper' in
S. Maria delle Grazie, Milan

It is said that the Prior of that place kept pressing Leonardo, in a most importunate manner, to finish the work; for it seemed strange to him to see Leonardo sometimes stand half a day at a time, lost in contemplation, and he would have liked him to go on like the labourers hoeing in his garden, without ever stopping his brush. And not content with this, he complained of it to the Duke,[2] and that so warmly, that he was constrained to send for Leonardo and delicately urged him to work, contriving nevertheless to show him that he was doing all this because of the importunity of the Prior. Leonardo, knowing that the intellect of that Prince was acute and discerning, was pleased to discourse at large with the Duke on the subject, a thing which he had never done with the Prior: and he reasoned much with him about art, and made him understand that men of lofty genius sometimes accomplish the most when they work the least, seeking out

1. This is a much elaborated variant of a similar story about Giotto (see p. 12).
2. Lodovico il Moro.

inventions with the mind, and forming those perfect ideas which the hands afterwards express and reproduce from the images already conceived in the brain. And he added that two heads were still wanting for him to paint; that of Christ, which he did not wish to seek on earth; and he could not think that it was possible to conceive in the imagination that beauty and heavenly grace which should be the mark of God incarnate. Next, there was wanting that of Judas, which was also troubling him, not thinking himself capable of imagining features that should represent the countenance of him who, after so many benefits received, had a mind so cruel as to resolve to betray his Lord, the Creator of the world. However, he would seek out a model for the latter; but if in the end he could not find a better he should not want that of the importunate and tactless Prior. This thing moved the Duke wondrously to laughter, and he said that Leonardo had a thousand reasons on his side. And so the poor Prior, in confusion, confined himself to urging on the work in the garden, and left Leonardo in peace, who finished only the head of Judas, which seems the very embodiment of treachery and inhumanity; but that of Christ, as has been said, remained unfinished.

[Vasari, *Lives*, 1568] This is a variant of a story also told about Michelangelo and the *Last Judgement* in the Sistine Chapel.

Leonardo da Vinci's Multifarious Talents

Leonardo had very great spirit, and in his every action was most generous. It is said that, going to the bank for the allowance that he used to draw every month from Piero Soderini,[1] the cashier wanted to give him certain paper-packets of pence; but he would not take them, saying in answer, 'I am no penny-painter.' Having been blamed for cheating Piero Soderini, there began to be murmurings against him; wherefore Leonardo so wrought upon his friends, that he got the money together and took it to Piero to repay him; but he would not accept it.

He went to Rome with Duke Giuliano de' Medici, at the election of Pope Leo,[2] who spent much of the time on philosophical studies, and particularly on alchemy; where, forming a paste of a certain kind of

1. Gonfaloniers of the Florentine Republic – the Medici were in exile.
2. Leo x, a member of the Medici family.

wax, as he walked he shaped animals very thin and full of wind, and, by blowing into them, made them fly through the air, but when the wind ceased they fell to the ground. On the back of a most bizarre lizard, found by the vine-dresser of the Belvedere, he fixed, with a mixture of quicksilver, wings composed of scales stripped from other lizards, which, as it walked, quivered with the motion; and having given it eyes, horns, and beard, taming it, and keeping it in a box, he made all his friends, to whom he showed it, fly for fear. He used often to have the guts of a wether completely freed of their fat and cleaned, and thus made so fine that they could have been held in the palm of the hand; and having placed a pair of blacksmith's bellows in another room, he fixed to them one end of these, and, blowing into them, filled the room, which was very large, so that whoever was in it was obliged to retreat into a corner; showing how, transparent and full of wind, from taking up little space at the beginning they had come to occupy much, and likening them to virtue. He made an infinite number of such follies, and gave his attention to mirrors; and he tried the strangest methods in seeking out oils for painting, and varnishing for preserving works when painted.

[Vasari, *Lives*, 1568]

Leonardo's Heavenly Gift

On a Holy Saturday, as is customary, a priest was making the rounds of his parish, blessing homes with holy water. He came into the room of a painter, and as he sprinkled holy water over one of his paintings, the painter turned to him angrily and asked him why he was wetting his paintings. Then the priest said that it was the custom, and that it was his duty to carry it out. He added that he was doing the right thing, for he who does good can expect the same or better in return; it is God's promise that for every good thing one does on earth, one will receive a hundredfold from above.

The painter waited for the priest to leave his house, and then he went to the window and threw a large bucketful of water on top of him, saying: 'Here is the hundredfold that is coming to you from above, as you said you would get for the good you were doing me with your holy water, which ruined half of my paintings.'

[C. Speroni, *Wit and Wisdom of the Italian Renaissance*, 1964] This story was recorded by Leonardo in his notebooks.

Bernardino Pinturicchio (1454–1513)
Brings Good Luck to the Friars

Afterwards, having reached the age of fifty-nine, he was commissioned to paint the Nativity of Our Lady on a panel in S. Francesco at Siena. To this he set his hand, and the friars assigned to him a room to live in, which they gave to him, as he wished, empty and stripped of everything, save only a huge old chest, which appeared to them too awkward to remove. But Pinturicchio, like the strange and whimsical man that he was, made such an outcry at this, and repeated it so often, that finally in despair the friars set themselves to carry it away. Now their good fortune was such, that in removing it there was broken a plank which contained 500 Roman ducats of gold; at which Pinturicchio was so displeased, and felt so aggrieved at the good luck of those poor friars, that it can hardly be imagined – nay, he took it so much to heart, being unable to get it out of his thoughts, that it was the death of him.

[Vasari, *Lives*, 1568]

Sandro Botticelli (c. 1445–1510)
Plays a Trick on his Pupil

Sandro was a man of very pleasant humour, often playing tricks on his disciples and his friends; wherefore it is related that once, when a pupil of his who was called Biagio had made a round picture exactly like the one mentioned above [a Madonna with angels], in order to sell it, Sandro sold it for six florins of gold to a citizen; then, finding Biagio, he said to him, 'At last I have sold this thy picture; so this evening it must be hung on high, where it will be seen better, and in the morning thou must go to the house of the citizen who has bought it, and bring him here, that he may see it in a good light in its proper place; and then he will pay thee the money.' 'O, my master,' said Biagio, 'how well you have done.' Then, going into the shop, he hung the picture at a good height, and went off. Meanwhile Sandro and Jacopo, who was another of his disciples, made eight caps of paper, like those worn by citizens, and fixed them with white wax on the heads of the eight angels that surrounded the Madonna in the said picture. Now, in the morning, up comes Biagio with his citizen, who had bought the picture and was in the secret. They entered the shop, and Biagio, looking up, saw his

Madonna seated, not among his angels, but among the Signoria of Florence, with all those caps. Thereupon he was just about to begin to make an outcry and to excuse himself to the man who had bought it, when, seeing that the other, instead of complaining, was actually praising the picture, he kept silent himself. Finally, going with the citizen to his house, Biagio received his payment of six florins, the price for which his master had sold the picture; and then, returning to the shop just as Sandro and Jacopo had removed the paper caps, he saw his angels as true angels, and not as citizens in their caps. All in a maze, and not knowing what to say, he turned at last to Sandro and said: 'Master, I know not whether I am dreaming, or whether this is true. When I came here before, these angels had red caps on their heads, and now they have not; what does it mean?' 'Thou art out of thy wits, Biagio,' said Sandro; 'this money has turned thy head. If it were so, thinkest thou that the citizen would have bought the picture?' 'It is true,' replied Biagio, 'that he said nothing to me about it, but for all that it seemed to me strange.' Finally, all the other lads gathered round him and wrought on him to believe that it had been a fit of giddiness.

[Vasari, *Lives*, 1568]

Botticelli's Sense of Humour

To one who said, 'I wish I had one hundred tongues,' Sandro Botticelli said the following: 'You are asking for so many tongues, and you already have one-half more than you need; why don't you ask for some brains, poor fellow, of which you have none?'

[Angelo Poliziano, from the lost MS *Il bel libretto*, compiled c. 1477–99, incorporated into L. Domenichi, *Facetie e motti*, 1548]

Piero di Cosimo (1462–?1521): Nature and Imagination

Even better did he show this after the death of Cosimo,[1] when he kept himself constantly shut up, and would not let himself be seen at work, leading the life of a man who was less man than beast. He would never have his rooms swept, he would only eat when hunger came to him, and he would not let his garden be worked or his fruit-trees pruned; nay, he allowed his vines to grow, and the shoots to trail over the ground, nor were his fig-trees ever trimmed, or any other trees, for

1. Cosimo Rosselli (1439–1507), Piero de Cosimo's master.

it pleased him to see everything wild, like his own nature; and he declared that Nature's own things should be left to her to look after, without lifting a hand to them. He set himself often to observe such animals, plants, or other things as Nature at times creates out of caprice, or by chance; in which he found a pleasure and satisfaction that drove him quite out of his mind with delight; and he spoke of them so often in his discourse, that at times, although he found pleasure in them, it became wearisome to others. He would sometimes stop to gaze at a wall against which sick people had been for a long time discharging their spittle, and from this he would picture to himself battles of horsemen, and the most fantastic cities and widest landscapes that were ever seen; and he did the same with the clouds in the sky.

[Vasari, *Lives*, 1568]

Idiosyncracies of Piero di Cosimo

And in truth, in all that there is to be seen by his hand, one recognizes a spirit very different and far distant from that of other painters, and a certain subtlety in the investigation of some of the deepest and most subtle secrets of Nature, without grudging time or labour, but only for his own delight and for his pleasure in the art. And it could not well be otherwise; since, having grown enamoured of her, he cared nothing for his own comfort, and reduced himself to eating nothing but boiled eggs, which, in order to save firing, he cooked when he was boiling his glue, and not six or eight at a time, but in fifties; and, keeping them in a basket, he would eat them one by one. In this life he found such peculiar pleasure that any other, in comparison with his own, seemed to him slavery. He could not bear the crying of children, the coughing of men, the sound of bells, and the chanting of friars; and when the rain was pouring in torrents from the sky, it pleased him to see it streaming straight down from the roofs and splashing on the ground. He had the greatest terror of lightning; and, when he heard very loud thunder, he wrapped himself in his mantle, and, having closed the windows and the door of the room, he crouched in a corner until the storm should pass. He was very varied and original in his discourse, and sometimes said such beautiful things, that he made his hearers burst with laughter. But when he was old, and near the age of eighty, he had become so strange and eccentric that nothing could be done with him. He would not have assistants standing round him, so that his misanthropy had robbed him of all possible aid. He was sometimes seized by a desire to work, but was not able, by reason of the palsy, and fell into such a rage that he tried to force his hands to labour; but, as he muttered to himself, the mahl-stick fell from his grasp, and even his brushes, so that it was pitiable to behold. Flies enraged him, and even shadows annoyed him. And so, having become ill through old age, he was visited by one or two friends, who besought him to make his peace with God; but he would not believe that he was dying, and put them off from one day to another; not that he was hard of heart, or an unbeliever, for he was a most zealous Christian, although his life was that of a beast. He discoursed at times on the torments of those ills that destroy men's bodies, and of the suffering endured by those who come to die with their strength wasting away little by little, which he called a great affliction. He spoke evil of physicians, apothecaries, and those who nurse the sick, saying that they cause them to die of hunger; besides the tortures of syrups, medicines, clysters, and other martyr-doms, such as not being allowed to sleep when you are drowsy, making your will, seeing your relatives round you, and staying in a dark room. He praised death by the hand of justice, saying that it was a fine thing to go to your death in that way; to see the broad sky about you, and all that throng; to be comforted with sweetmeats and with kind words; to have the priest and the people praying for you; and to go into Paradise with the Angels; so that whoever departed from this life at one blow, was very fortunate. And as he discoursed, he would twist everything to the strangest meanings that were ever heard. Wherefore, living in such strange fashion, he reduced himself to such a state with his extravagant fancies, that one morning he was found dead at the foot of a staircase, in the year 1521; and he was given burial in S. Piero Maggiore.

[Vasari, *Lives*, 1568]

Mariotto Albertinelli (1474–1515) on Life versus Art

Mariotto was a most restless person, devoted to the pleasures of love, and a good liver in the matter of eating; wherefore, conceiving a hatred for the subtleties and brain-rackings of painting, and being often wounded by the tongues of other painters (according to the undying custom among them, handed down from one to another), he resolved

[41]

to turn to a more humble, less fatiguing, and more cheerful art. And so, having opened a very fine inn, without the Porta S. Gallo, and a tavern and inn on the Ponte Vecchio, at the Dragon, he followed that calling for many months, saying that he had chosen an art without foreshortenings, muscles, and perspectives, and, what was much more important, free from censure, and that the art which he had given up was quite the contrary of his new one, since the former imitated flesh and blood, and the latter made both blood and flesh; and now, having good wine, he heard himself praised all day long, whereas before he used to hear nothing but censure.

[Vasari, *Lives*, 1568]

Giorgione (1477/8–1510) on Painting versus Sculpture

It is related that Giorgione, at the time when Andrea Verrocchio was making his bronze horse [the statue of Bartolommeo Colleoni in Venice], fell into an argument with certain sculptors, who maintained, since sculpture showed various attitudes and aspects in one single figure to one walking round it, that for this reason it surpassed painting, which only showed one side of a figure. Giorgione was of the opinion that there could be shown in a painted scene, without any necessity for walking round, at one single glance, all the various aspects that a man can present in many gestures – a thing which sculpture cannot do without a change of position and point of view, so that in her case the points of view are many, and not one. Moreover, he proposed to show in one single painted figure the front, the back, and the profile on either side, a challenge which brought them to their senses; and he did it in the following way. He painted a naked man with his back turned, at whose feet was a most limpid pool of water, wherein he painted the reflection of the man's front. At one side was a burnished cuirass that he had taken off, which showed his left profile, since everything could be seen on the polished surface of the piece of armour; and on the other side was a mirror, which reflected the other profile of the naked figure; which was a thing of most beautiful and bizarre fancy, whereby he sought to prove that painting does in fact, with more excellence, labour, and effect, achieve more at one single view of a living figure than does sculpture. And this work was greatly extolled and admired, as something ingenious and beautiful.

[Vasari, *Lives*, 1568]

IV

THE HIGH RENAISSANCE AND
ITALIAN MANNERISM:
THE FLORENTINE TRADITION

&

A number of the anecdotes in this section are the work of eye-witnesses, recording what they actually heard or saw. The stories are evidence not only of an art-historical evolution – the way in which Italian artists, especially those from Tuscany, began to travel abroad, taking the ideas of the Renaissance with them – but of a social and psychological one as well.

Vasari's accounts of Sodoma and of the obscure Jacone – both artists who were destined to be remembered more for their way of life than for anything they created – show the evolution of an anti-bourgeois way of living long before the concept of 'bohemian' lifestyle was formulated. There is also something of this in the delightful story of the painter Rosso's pet ape. The psychological change is noticeable too. Artists such as Rosso and Pontormo are now presented as deeply neurotic. This development was foreshadowed in Vasari's anecdotes about Piero di Cosimo, but it becomes more consistently noticeable in stories concerning the leading artists of the early sixteenth century.

The Death of Pietro Torrigiano (1472–1528)

He went at last to Seville, where he set himself up and did a superb terracotta crucifix, today in the monastery of San Jeronimo outside the city, and a fine St Jerome with his lion. He also made an image of the Madonna, with her precious child in her arms. This was so beautiful that a great nobleman who was at that time living in Seville commissioned Torrigiano to make another like it, and offered to pay as much as he asked. He did the job, thinking, such had been the Duke's promises, that he would be rich for life. However, the nobleman, having received the sculpture and having praised it highly, next day sent two men loaded with money, but this was in maravedises (there were a lot of these coins in Analusia then, and even today there are quite a few).[1] Torrigiano, seeing a lot of money, but not recognizing the coins, called in a fellow Italian who was familiar with the currencies of Spain and Italy to tell him what the money was worth in Italian terms and discovered that it amounted to barely thirty ducats. At this point, since he interpreted the payment as a gesture of contempt, he took an axe and went in a rage to the Duke's house, where he chopped the image to pieces. The sculpture was lifesize, as can be seen from a hand which escaped destruction. It was raised to the Madonna's breast in order to offer this to the child. Painters keep casts of it among their models: it is a fine thing, and is known as the Hand of the Breast. The heads of the Virgin and of the Child are also still preserved by painters.

The Duke, thinking himself insulted by this extreme behaviour, called in the Holy Inquisition and falsely accused Torrigiano of heresy. The deed itself, and the fact that Torrigiano had come from England[2] (though heresy was not so rampant there at that time), together with the other excesses of Torrigiano's nature, were thought to offer circumstantial evidence. However, I will not give the Duke's name here because I do not believe that he exhibited the kind of behaviour that befits a great lord. I also omit it because he was a Spaniard and the deed was all the worse because it was committed against a foreigner, an eminent and proud man made angry by the contempt shown for his

1. A maravedi was an almost worthless small coin.
2. Torrigiano made the effigy of Henry VII in Westminster Abbey.

work. It was against this that Torrigiano's impetuosity was directed, without regard for the work itself.

His case was tried and, with so much against him and with such a powerful adversary, the Holy Tribunal sentenced Torrigiano, who had already suffered a long imprisonment, to an ignominious death. When he heard this, since he was already in the grip of deep melancholy, he stopped eating and, either by design or through lack of appetite, died wretchedly in the Inquisition's prison in Seville, around 1522, aged about fifty.[1] Alas, such is the power of malign fate!

[A. Palomino, El parnaso espanol pintoresco laureado, 1724] A version of this story also appears in Vasari.

The Modesty of Giuliano Bugiardini (1475–1574)

Giuliano once relating to Bronzino[2] how he had seen a very beautiful woman, after he had praised her to the skies, Bronzino said, 'Do you know her?' 'No,' answered Giuliano, 'but she is a miracle of beauty. Just imagine that she is a picture by my hand, and there you have her.'

[Vasari, Lives, 1568] Bugiardini was considered to be a second-rate artist, and Vasari meant this story to be taken as an example of artistic hubris.

Sodoma [Giovanni Antonio da Verzelli] (1477–1549) and his Companions

Besides this, he was a gay and licentious man, keeping others entertained and amused with his manner of living which was far from creditable. In which life, since he always had about him boys and beardless youths, whom he loved more than was decent, he acquired the by-name of Sodoma; and in this name, far from taking umbrage or offence, he used to glory, writing about it songs and verses in terza rima, and singing them to the lute with no little facility. He delighted, in addition, to have about the house many kinds of extraordinary animals; badgers, squirrels, apes, marmosets, dwarf asses, horses, barbs [Barbary horses] for running races, little horses from Elba, jays,

1. The date of death and Torrigiano's age are both incorrect.
2. Agnolo Bronzino (1493–1568), Florentine Mannerist painter, famous for his portraits of the family of Cosimo de' Medici, Grand Duke of Tuscany.

dwarf fowls, Indian turtle-doves, and other suchlike animals, as many as he could lay his hands on. But, besides all these beasts, he had a raven, which had learned from him to speak so well, that in some things it imitated exactly the voice of Giovanni Antonio, and particularly in answering to anyone who knocked at the door, doing this so excellently that it seemed like Giovanni Antonio himself, as all the people of Siena know very well. In like manner, the other animals were so tame that they always flocked round anybody in the house, playing the strangest pranks and the maddest tricks in the world, insomuch that the man's house looked like a real Noah's Ark.

[Vasari, *Lives*, 1568]

The Anger of Franciabigio (1482/3–1525)

Not long after this, on the occasion of a festival, the friars wished that the scenes of Andrea,[1] and likewise that of Francia, should be uncovered; and the night after Francia had finished his with the exception of the base, they were so rash and presumptuous as to uncover them, not thinking, in their ignorance of art, that Francia would want to retouch or otherwise change his figures. In the morning, both the painting of Francia and those of Andrea were open to view, and the news was brought to Francia that Andrea's works and his own had been uncovered; at which he felt such resentment, that he was like to die of it. Seized with anger against the friars on account of their presumption and the little respect that they had shown to him, he set off at his best speed and came up to the work; and then, climbing on to the staging, which had not yet been taken to pieces, although the painting had been uncovered, and seizing a mason's hammer that was there, he beat some of the women's heads to fragments, and destroyed that of the Madonna, and also tore almost completely away from the wall, plaster and all, a nude figure that is breaking a rod. Hearing the noise, the friars ran up, and, with the help of some laymen, seized his hands, to prevent him from destroying it completely. But, although in time they offered to give him double payment, he, on account of the hatred that he had conceived for them, would never restore it. By

---

1. Andrea del Sarto. Both artists had been working in the cloister of Santa Annunziata in Florence, Franciabiagio on the *Marriage of the Virgin*, Andrea del Sarto on the *Birth of the Virgin* and the *Magi*.

reason of the reverence felt by other painters both for him and for the work, they have refused to finish it; and so it remains, even in our own day, as a memorial of that event.

[Vasari, *Lives*, 1568]

Raphael (1483–1520) Answers a Prudish Admirer

Raphael from Urbino, a remarkable and most excellent painter, was painting the loggia in Agostino Chigi's garden in Rome. He had painted many Goddesses and graces there, and also a very large Polyphemus and a thirteen-year-old Mercury. One morning there came to the loggia a lady who considered herself cultured and intelligent; she admired and praised the paintings highly, and then said: 'Undoubtedly all these figures are most excellent; but for the sake of modesty I wish you would paint a lovely rose or a vine-leaf on Mercury's shame.'

Raphael said smiling: 'Pardon me, madam, it was very inconsiderate of me.' And then he added: 'But why didn't you ask me to do the same for Polyphemus, whom you praised so much a while ago, and who has a much larger shame?'

[L. Domenichi, *Facetie e motti*, 1548, trans. C. Speroni]

Raphael's Pope Julius II

Pope Julius had the rooms in which he lived painted by Raphael, a very excellent painter. In one of the rooms he had himself painted kneeling during Mass, and on the opposite wall, as he was returning from Belvedere carried by his footmen. In the latter portrait the colours were much more intense than in the former, and some people blamed Raphael and said that he had made a mistake not to use the same colours in both portraits. Marco Antonio Colonna intervened and told the faultfinders that they were wrong and that Raphael had indeed observed decorum; for, whereas the Pope was sober during Mass, upon returning from Belvedere, his face was flushed and ruddy because he had indulged in drinking.[1]

[L. Domenichi, *Facetie, motti et burle di diversi signori et persone private*, 1564, revised and enlarged from his *Facetie e motti* of 1548,

---

1. A celebrated condottiere (1535–84). The witticism dates from after the death of the pope and of Raphael.

trans. C. Speroni] When Raphael was working in Rome, he belonged to
the faction that clustered round the architect Bramante (1444–1514),
which was opposed to the group surrounding Michelangelo. The anecdotal tradition concerning him is therefore much less rich than that relating
to Michelangelo. Moreover, Raphael died young, and he was of Umbrian
not Tuscan origin and thus, despite an important period in Florence, was
never fully accepted by Florentine artists. Vasari is surprisingly uncom-
municative about Raphael's personality.

Raphael Defends Himself

In a similar manner also, the painter Raphael replied to two cardinals
with whom he was on friendly terms, who, to tease him, were
criticizing in his presence a picture he had painted in which St. Peter
and St. Paul were represented, saying that the two figures were too red
in the face. Then Raphael quickly said, 'My Lords, there is no reason
for amazement: I was fully aware of what I was doing, for we have
good grounds to believe that St. Peter and St. Paul must be as red in
heaven as you see them here, out of shame that their Church is being
ruled by such men as you.'

[Baldassare Castiglione, *The Courtier*, 1528]

Andrea del Sarto (1486–1530): 'Genius in Double Harness'

Now Federigo II, Duke of Mantua, in passing through Florence on his
way to make obeisance to Clement VII, saw over a door in the house of
the Medici that portrait of Pope Leo between Cardinal Giulio de'
Medici and Cardinal de' Rossi, which the most excellent Raffaello da
Urbino had formerly painted; and being extraordinarily pleased with
it, he resolved, being a man who delighted in pictures of such beauty,
to make it his own. And so, when he was in Rome and the moment
seemed to him to have come, he asked for it as a present from Pope
Clement, who courteously granted his request. Thereupon orders were
sent to Florence to Ottaviano de' Medici, under whose care and
government were Ippolito and Alessandro, that he should have it
packed up and taken to Mantua. This matter was very displeasing to
the Magnificent Ottaviano, who would never have consented to
deprive Florence of such a picture, and he marvelled that the Pope
should have given it up so readily. However, he answered that he
would not fail to satisfy the Duke; but that, since the frame was bad, he

was having a new one made, and when it had been gilt he would send the picture with every possible precaution to Mantua. This done, Messer Ottaviano, in order to 'save both the goat and the cabbage,' as the saying goes, sent privately for Andrea and told him how the matter stood, and how there was no way out of it but to make an exact copy of the picture with the greatest care and send it to the Duke, secretly retaining the one by the hand of Raffaello. Andrea, then, having promised to do all in his power and knowledge, caused a panel to be made similar in size and in every respect, and painted it secretly in the house of Messer Ottaviano. And to such purpose did he labour, that when it was finished even Messer Ottaviano, for all his understanding in matters of art, could not tell the one from the other, nor distinguish the real and true picture from the copy; especially as Andrea had counterfeited even the spots of dirt, exactly as they were in the original. And so, after they had hidden the picture of Raffaello, they sent the one by the hand of Andrea, in a similar frame, to Mantua; at which the Duke was completely satisfied, and above all because the painter Giulio Romano, a disciple of Raffaello, had praised it, failing to detect the trick. This Giulio would always have been of the same opinion, and would have believed it to be by the hand of Raffaello, but for the arrival in Mantua of Giorgio Vasari, who, having been as it were the adoptive child of Messer Ottaviano, and having seen Andrea at work on that picture, revealed the truth. For Giulio making much of Vasari, and showing him, after many antiquities and paintings, that picture of Raffaello's, as the best work that was there, Giorgio said to him, 'A beautiful work it is, but in no way by the hand of Raffaello.' 'What?' answered Giulio. 'Should I not know it, when I recognize the very strokes that I made with my own brush?' 'You have forgotten them,' said Giorgio, 'for this picture is by the hand of Andrea del Sarto; and to prove it, there is a sign (to which he pointed) that was made in Florence, because when the two were together they could not be distinguished.' Hearing this, Giulio had the picture turned round, and saw the mark; at which he shrugged his shoulders and said these words, 'I value it no less than if it were by the hand of Raffaello – nay, even more, for it is something out of the course of nature that a man of excellence should imitate the manner of another so well, and should make a copy so like. It is enough that it should be known that Andrea's genius was as valiant in double harness as in single.' Thus, then, by the wise judgment of Messer Ottaviano, satisfaction was given to the

Duke without depriving Florence of so choice a work, which, having been presented to him afterwards by Duke Alessandro, he kept in his possession for many years; and finally he gave it to Duke Cosimo, who has it in his guardaroba together with many other famous pictures.

[Vasari, *Lives*, 1568]

Jacopo Sansovino (1486–1570) and his Apprentice

All these works caused Sansovino to held by the men of art and by all Florence to be a most excellent and gracious master; on which account Giovanni Bartolini, having caused a house to be built in his garden of Gualfonda, desired that Sansovino should make for him a young Bacchus in marble, of the size of life. Whereupon the model for this was made by Sansovino, and it pleased Giovanni so much, that he had him supplied with the marble, and Jacopo began it with such eagerness, that his hands and brain flew as he worked. This work, I say, he studied in such a manner, in order to make it perfect, that he set himself to portray from the life, although it was winter, an assistant of his called Pippo de Fabbro, making him stand naked a good part of the day. Which Pippo would have become a capable craftsman, for he was striving with every effort to imitate his master; but, whether it was the standing naked with the head uncovered at that season, or that he studied too much and suffered hardships, before the Bacchus was finished he went mad, copying the attitudes of that figure. And this he showed one day that it was raining in torrents, when, Sansovino calling out 'Pippo!' and he not answering, the master afterwards saw him mounted on the summit of a chimney on the roof, wholly naked and striking the attitude of his Bacchus. At other times, taking a sheet or other large piece of cloth, and wetting it, he would wrap it round his naked body, as if he were a model of clay or rags, and arrange the folds; and then, climbing up to some extraordinary place, and setting himself now in one attitude and now in another, as a Prophet, an Apostle, a soldier, or something else, he would have himself portrayed, standing thus for a period of two hours without speaking, not otherwise than as if he had been a motionless statue. Many other amusing follies of that kind poor Pippo played, but above all he was never able to forget the Bacchus that Sansovino had made, save only when he died, a few years afterwards.

[Vasari, *Lives*, 1568]

Baccio Bandinelli (1493–1568) and his 'Hercules and Cacus'

Desiring to know what was being said of his work,[1] he sent to the Piazza a pedagogue whom he kept in his house, telling him that he should not fail to report to him the truth of what he might hear said. The pedagogue, hearing nothing but censure, returned sadly to the house, and, when questioned by Baccio, answered that all with one voice were abusing the giants, and that they pleased no one. 'And you,' asked Baccio, 'what do you say of them?' 'I speak well of them,' he replied, 'and say, may it please you, that they please me.' 'I will not have them please you,' said Baccio, 'and you, also, must speak ill of them, for, as you may remember, I never speak well of anyone; and so we are quits.'

[Vasari, *Lives*, 1568]

Jacopo da Pontormo (1494–1557): Reflections

Pontormo had very beautiful manners, and he was so afraid of death, that he would not even hear it spoken of, and avoided having to meet dead bodies. He never went to festivals or to any other places where people gathered together, so as not to be caught in the press; and he was solitary beyond all belief. At times, going out to work, he set himself to think so profoundly on what he was to do, that he went away without having done any other thing all day but stand thinking.

[Vasari, *Lives*, 1568]

Rosso Fiorentino (1494–1540) Frightens away a Patron

The Director of the Hospital of S. Maria Nuova commissioned him to paint a panel: but when he saw it sketched, having little knowledge of that art, the Saints appeared to him like devils; for it was Rosso's custom in his oil-sketches to give a sort of savage and desperate air to the faces, after which, in finishing them, he would sweeten the

---

1. The *Hercules and Cacus* (1534), in the Piazza della Signoria in Florence. This work was a direct challenge to Michelangelo's *David*.

expressions and bring them to a proper form. At this the patron fled from his house and would not have the picture, saying that the painter had cheated him.

[Vasari, *Lives*, 1568]

Rosso's Ape

While Rosso was engaged on this work [*Jacob Giving Drink to the Women at the Well*], he was living in the Borgo de' Tintori, the rooms of which look out on the gardens of the Friars of S. Croce; and he took much pleasure in a great ape, which had the intelligence rather of a man than a beast. For this reason he held it very dear, and loved it like his own self; and since it had a marvellous understanding, he made use of it for many kinds of service. It happened that this beast took a fancy to one of his assistants, by name Battistino, who was a young man of great beauty; and from the signs that his Battistino made to him he understood all that he wished to say. Now against the wall of the rooms at the back, which looked out upon the garden of the friars, was a pergola belonging to the Guardian, loaded with great Sancolombane grapes; and the young men used to let the ape down with a rope to the pergola, which was some distance from their window, and pull the beast up again with his hands full of grapes. The Guardian, finding his pergola stripped, but not knowing the culprit, suspected that it must be mice, and lay in hiding; and seeing Rosso's ape descending, he flew into a rage, seized a long pole, and rushed at him with hands uplifted in order to beat him. The ape, seeing that whether he went up or stayed where he was, the Guardian could reach him, began to spring about and destroy the pergola, and then, making as though to throw himself on the friar's back, seized with both his hands the outermost crossbeams which enclosed the pergola. Meanwhile the friar made play with his pole, and the ape, in his terror, shook the pergola to such purpose, and with such force, that he tore the stakes and rods out of their places, so that both pergola and ape fell headlong on the back of the friar, who shrieked for mercy. The rope was pulled up by Battistino and the others, who brought the ape back into the room safe and sound. Thereupon the Guardian, drawing off and planting himself on a terrace that he had there, said things not to be found in the Mass; and full of anger and resentment he went to the Council of Eight, a tribunal much feared in Florence. There he laid his complaint; and Rosso having been summoned, the ape was condemned in jest to carry a weight fastened to his tail, to prevent him from jumping on pergole, as he did before. And so Rosso made a wooden cylinder swinging on a chain, and kept it on the ape, in such a way that he could go about the house but no longer jump about over other people's property. The ape, seeing himself condemned to such a punishment, seemed to guess that the friar was responsible. Every day, therefore, he exercised himself in hopping step by step with his legs, holding the weight with his hands; and thus, resting often, he succeeded in his design. For, being one day loose about the house, he hopped step by step from roof to roof, during the hour when the Guardian was away chanting Vespers, and came to the roof over his chamber. There, letting go the weight, he kept up for half an hour such a lovely dance, that not a single tile of any kind remained unbroken. Then he went back home; and within three days, when rain came, were heard the Guardian's lamentations.

[Vasari, *Lives*, 1568]

Rosso's Death

By reason of these works and many others, of which nothing is known, he became so dear to the King,[1] that a little before his death he found himself in possession of more than a thousand crowns of income, without counting the allowances for his work, which were enormous; insomuch that, living no longer as a painter, but rather as a prince, he kept a number of servants and horses to ride, and had his house filled with tapestries, silver, and other valuable articles of furniture. But Fortune, who never, or very seldom, maintains for long in high estate one who puts his trust too much in her, brought him headlong down in the strangest manner ever known. For while Francesco di Pellegrino[2], a Florentine, who delighted in painting and was very much his friend, was associating with him in the closest intimacy, Rosso was robbed of some hundreds of ducats; whereupon the latter, suspecting that no one but the same Francesco could have done this, had him arrested by the hands of justice, rigorously examined, and grievously tortured. But he, knowing himself innocent, and declaring nothing but the truth, was finally released; and, moved by just anger, he was forced

1. François I of France – Rosso was employed at Fontainebleau.
2. Francesco di Pellegrino (d. 1552) worked with Rosso at Fontainebleau.

to show his resentment against Rosso for the shameful charge that he had falsely laid upon him. Having therefore issued a writ for libel against him, he pressed him so closely, that Rosso, not being able to clear himself or make any defence, felt himself to be in a sorry plight, perceiving that he had not only accused his friend falsely, but had also stained his own honour; and to eat his words, or to adopt any other shameful method, would likewise proclaim him a false and worthless man. Resolving, therefore, to kill himself by his own hand rather than be punished by others, he took the following course. One day that the King happened to be at Fontainebleau, he sent a peasant to Paris for a certain most poisonous essence, pretending that he wished to use it for making colours or varnishes, but intending to poison himself, as he did. The peasant, then, returned with it; and such was the malignity of the poison, that, merely through holding his thumb over the mouth of the phial, carefully stopped as it was with wax, he came very near losing that member, which was consumed and almost eaten away by the deadly potency of the poison. And shortly afterwards it slew Rosso, although he was in perfect health, he having drunk it to the end that it might take his life, as it did in a few hours.

[Vasari, *Lives*, 1568]

Toto del Nunziata (1498–1556): The Lighter Side of Art

Nunziata, although he was a puppet-painter,[1] was in some things a person of distinction, and above all in preparing fireworks and the girandole[2] that were made every year for the festival of S. John; and, since he was an amusing and facetious person, everyone took great pleasure in conversing with him. A citizen once saying to him that he was displeased with certain painters who could paint nothing but lewd things, and that he therefore wished him to paint a picture of a Madonna that might be seemly, well advanced in years and not likely to provoke lascivious thoughts, Nunziata painted him one with a beard. Another meaning to ask from him a Christ on the Cross for a ground-floor room where he lived in summer, and not being able to say anything but 'I want a Christ on the Cross for summer,' Nunziata, who saw him to be a simpleton, painted him one in breeches.

[Vasari, *Lives*, 1568]

1. A painter of small-scale figures; thus, by implication, of trivial themes.
2. A branched candlestick or candlebracket.

Jacone [Jacopo di Giovanni di Francesco] (d. 1553): Art without Housework

Then hearing once much praise spoken of the façades executed by Polidoro[1] and Maturino[2] at Rome, without anyone knowing about it he went off to that city, where he stayed some months and made some copies, gaining such proficience in matters of art, that he afterwards proved himself in many works a passing good painter. Wherefore the Chevalier Buondelmonte commissioned him to paint in chiaroscuro a house[3] that he had built opposite to S. Trinita, at the beginning of the Borgo S. Apostolo; wherein Jacone painted stories from the life of Alexander the Great, very beautiful in certain parts, and executed with so much grace and design, that many believe that the designs for the whole work were made for him by Andrea del Sarto. To tell the truth, from the proof of his powers that Jacone gave in that work, it was thought that he was likely to produce some great fruits. But, since he always had his mind set more on giving himself a good time and every possible amusement, living in a round of suppers and feastings with his friends, than on studying and working, he was for ever forgetting rather than learning. And that which was a thing to laugh at or to pity, I know not which, was that he belonged to a company, or rather, gang, of friends who, under the pretence of living like philosophers, lived like swine and brute-beasts; they never washed their hands, or face, or head, or beard; they did not sweep their houses, and never made their beds save only once every two months; they laid their tables with the cartoons for their pictures, and they drank only from the flask or the jug; and this miserable existence of theirs, living, as the saying goes, from hand to mouth, was held by them to be the finest life in the world. But, since the outer man is wont to be a guide to the inner, and to reveal what our minds are, I believe, as has been said before, that they were as filthy and brutish in mind as their outward appearance suggested.

[Vasari, *Lives*, 1568]

1. Polidoro da Caravaggio (1490/1500–43).
2. Maturino (1498–1528).
3. In the sixteenth century there was a fashion for painted façade decorations, generally in chiaroscuro (monochrome), and mostly with secular subjects from ancient history or literature. Many painters, including the two named by Vasari, were celebrated for their skill in designing and painting them. Now almost the only evidence that survives consists of preparatory and record drawings, and engravings.

Jacone Put in his Place by Vasari

The sum of the matter is that Jacone spent the best part of his life in jesting, in going off into cogitations, and in speaking evil of all and sundry. For in those days the art of design in Florence had fallen into the hands of a company of persons who paid more attention to playing jokes and to enjoyment than to working, and whose occupation was to assemble in shops and other places, and there to spend their time in criticizing maliciously, in their own jargon, the works of others who were persons of excellence and lived decently and like men of honour. The heads of this company were Jacone, the goldsmith Piloto, and the wood-carver Tasso; but the worst of them all was Jacone, for the reason that, among his other fine qualities, his every word was always a foul slander against somebody. Wherefore it was no marvel that from such a company there should have sprung in time, as will be related, many evil happenings, or that Piloto, on account of his slanderous tongue, was killed by a young man. And since their habits and proceedings were displeasing to honest men, they were generally to be found – I do not say all of them, but some at least – like wool-carders and other fellows of that kidney, playing at chuck-stones at the foot of a wall, or making merry in a tavern.

One day that Giorgio Vasari was returning from Monte Oliveto, a place without Florence, after a visit to the reverend and most cultured Don Miniato Pitti, who was then Abbot of that monastery, he found Jacone, with a great part of his crew, at the Canto de' Medici; and Jacone thought to attempt, as I heard afterwards, with some of his idle talk, speaking half in jest and half in earnest, to hit on some phrase insulting to Giorgio. And so, when Vasari rode into their midst on his horse, Jacone said to him: 'Well, Giorgio, how goes it with you?' 'Finely, my Jacone,' answered Giorgio. 'Once I was poor like all of you, and now I find myself with three thousand crowns or more. You thought me a fool, and the priests and friars think me an able master. I used to be your servant, and here is a servant of my own, who serves me and looks after my horse. I used to dress in the clothes that beggarly painters wear, and here am I dressed in velvet. Once I went on foot, and now I go on horseback. So you see, my Jacone, it goes exceeding well with me. May God be with you.'

When poor Jacone had heard all this recital in one breath, he lost all his presence of mind and stood confused, without saying another word, as if reflecting how miserable he was, and how often the engineer is hoist with his own petard. Finally, having become much reduced by an infirmity, and being poor, neglected, and paralysed in the legs, so that he could do nothing to better himself, Jacone died in misery in a little hovel that he had on a mean street, or rather, alley, called Codarimessa, in the year 1553.

[Vasari, *Lives*, 1568]

Benvenuto Cellini (1500–73) at Fontainebleau

Meanwhile I was making haste to finish the fine silver Jupiter, as also the gilded base for it. This latter I had placed on a wooden plinth, which was hardly seen, fixing in the plinth four castors of hard wood, half hidden in their sockets, like the nut of a crossbow. They were so delicately contrived that a little child could turn the statue round, or move it to and fro, without the least fatigue. Having arranged everything as I wished I set off with it for Fontainebleau, where the King[1] then was. Now about this time Bologna had brought back from Rome the statues I have spoken of, and had them cast in bronze with the greatest care. I knew nothing about it; first, because he had had the business done very secretly, and also because Fontainebleau is forty miles from Paris. When I asked the King where he wished me to place the Jupiter, Madame d'Etampes[2], who was present, said to him that there was no more suitable place for it than his fine gallery. This was what we should call a loggia in Tuscany – nay, more correctly, a corridor, for loggias should be open at one side. The place was more than a hundred paces long, and about twelve wide, and richly adorned with paintings by the hand of the admirable Rosso, our Florentine. Among the pictures were arranged a great many pieces of sculpture, some in the round, others in low relief. Now it was in this gallery also that Bologna[3] had placed all his antique masterpieces, excellently cast in bronze; and he had arranged them beautifully, each one mounted on its pedestal; and, as I have already said, they were copied from the finest antiques in Rome. So when I brought my Jupiter into

1. François I.
2. The King's mistress.
3. Francesco Primaticcio (1504–74), so called because he came from Bologna. He and Cellini were deadly rivals at the French court, and their rivalry was exacerbated because they came from different Italian cities.

this same gallery, and saw the grand display, all arranged with such art, I said to myself, 'This is being under a very hot fire. Now God be my aid!' So I set up my statue, placing it to the very best advantage possible; and then I waited till the great King came in. In his right hand my Jupiter grasped his thunderbolt, as if about to hurl it; in his left he held the world. Among the flames of the bolt I had skilfully inserted a white waxen torch. Now Madame d'Etampes kept the King away till night came on, seeking to harm me, either by preventing him from coming at all, or at least till darkness should hinder my work being seen to advantage. But God protects those who have faith in Him; and so just the contrary happened. For as soon as I saw night falling, I lit the torch in the hand of the Jupiter, and as it was somewhat raised above the head of the statue, the light fell from above and made it seem much more beautiful than it had appeared by daylight.

Well, the King appeared at last, with Madame d'Etampes, the Dauphin, his son (now the King), the Dauphiness, his brother-in-law, the King of Navarre, and Madame Marguerite, his daughter, besides several lords of the Court, who had been schooled by Madame d'Etampes to speak against me. When I saw his Majesty come in, I made my lad Ascanio push the statue gently forward; and as my contrivance was arranged with some skill, this movement gave to the striking figure an additional appearance of life. The antiques were now left standing somewhat behind; and mine was the first to catch the eyes of the spectators. The King exclaimed on the instant, 'This is by far the finest thing which has ever been seen; and much as I delight in works of art and understand them, I could never have imagined the hundredth part of the wonder of this one.' Even the lords, whose part it was to speak against me, seemed as if they could not praise my work enough. But Madame d'Etampes said boldly, 'Surely you have no eyes! Do you not see the fine bronze antiques over there? In them is displayed the real power of the sculptor's art; not in this modern rubbish.' Then the King came forward – the others following him – and glanced at the casts; but as the light was below them, they did not show up well, and he cried, 'Whoever wished to harm this man has done him a great benefit; for this statue of his is now proved to surpass these wonderful figures with which it is compared. So Benvenuto cannot be made too much of; for not only do his works hold their own with the antiques, but they surpass them.' Thereupon Madame d'Etampes said, if they were to see the work by day, it would not seem a thousandth part as fine as now it did by night; besides, they had to consider that I had put a veil over the figure to cover up its faults. Now this was a very thin veil, which I had gracefully hung over the Jupiter, to enhance its majesty. At her words I removed it, lifting it from below, and disclosing the fine genital members. Then, giving vent to my anger, I tore it to pieces. She thought I had uncovered these parts to shame her; but the wise King, seeing her anger, and perceiving, too, that I was overcome by passion, and was about to speak my mind, said, uttering the words deliberately in his own tongue, 'Benvenuto, not a word. Keep silence, and you shall have a thousandfold more money than you can wish for.' When I might not speak, I writhed in my rage, which made her mutter even more angrily; and the King went off much sooner than he would have done, saying aloud, to put heart into me, that he had brought out of Italy the greatest man that ever was born – one full of talents.

[Benvenuto Cellini, *The Life, written by himself*, 1730]

Federico Zuccaro (1540–1609) and Philip II of Spain

Señor, says Zucaro, as he was displaying a painting of the Nativity for the great altar at the Escorial, *you now behold all that art can execute; beyond this, which I have done, the powers of painting cannot go:* The King was silent for a time, and so unmoved, that neither approbation nor contempt could be determined from the expression of his countenance; at last, preserving still the same indifference, he asked if those were eggs, which one of the shepherds, in the act of running, carried in his basket; the painter answered him they were: *'Tis well he did not break them*, said the King, and turned away; the picture was dismissed.

[R. Cumberland, *Anecdotes of Eminent Painters in Spain*, 1787] This is one of the few anecdotes in which a royal patron is allowed the last word in discussion with an artist. The story reflects the hostility of the new naturalistic style, which came in with the work of Caravaggio and Annibale Carracci, to the exhausted academic Mannerism represented by Zuccaro. A later anecdote (p. 110) illustrates Zuccaro's own hostility to the work of Caravaggio.

V
MICHELANGELO

છે.

Michelangelo is the first artist of the Western tradition about whom we possess a mass of detailed information – information, furthermore, related by eye-witnesses. His two first biographers, Giorgio Vasari and Ascanio Condivi, were personal friends of the great artist and wrote while he was still alive. The first version of Vasari's life of Michelangelo appeared in 1550; Condivi's biography was published in 1554. Michelangelo did not die until 1564.

Here, for the first time, the biographers of an artist begin to display curiosity about physical appearance and personal quirks.

The tradition which Vasari and Condivi handed down to posterity is mixed. On the one hand, they portrayed Michelangelo as a man of godlike and lofty spirit; on the other, they revealed a personality full of practical commonsense and earthy wisdom. Michelangelo's comments, both about works of art and about some of the artists who were his immediate predecessors and his contemporaries, were handed down, not only as part of a written tradition, but by word of mouth, as we can see from some of the stories which the seventeenth-century sculptor Gianlorenzo Bernini told to Chantelou, when he came to Paris at the invitation of Louis XIV. What one sees here is the beginning of a coherent studio tradition, which existed and continued to be elaborated until the mid-nineteenth century – a body of received wisdom to which most artists subscribed.

Michelangelo was thus a contradictory figure – a kind of demigod, different in kind from everyone else – and, by the end of his life, the recognized head of his profession. His attitudes and opinions affected the whole artistic climate surrounding him.

The Youth of Michelangelo (1473–1564)

The boy drawing now this thing, now the other, without any fixed place, or course of study, it happened one day that he was taken by Granacci[1] to the garden of the Medici, at San Marco. This garden, Lorenzo the Magnificent, father of Pope Leo, a man of singular worth in all excellent virtues, had adorned with various antique statues and figures. Michelagnolo, seeing these works and being taken with their beauty, did not afterwards go any more to the workshop of Domenico,[2] nor elsewhere, but remained here all the day, as in the better school, ever profiting himself in some thing of that means of study. One day he observed, among other things, the head of a faun, already aged in his look, with a long beard and laughing countenance, although the mouth was hardly to be made out, through the antiquity of the thing, or one would have known what it was; and this pleasing Michelagnolo beyond measure, he set himself to copy it in marble. Now Lorenzo, the Magnificent, was then having executed in that place the marbles, or rather the wrought stonework, to ornament that most noble library which he and his fathers had collected from all parts of the world; and this building, having been abandoned through the death of Lorenzo and other vicissitudes, was many years afterwards resumed by Pope Clement, but nevertheless left unfinished, so that the books are still stored away in chests: these marbles, I say, being in the course of execution, Michelagnolo begged a piece of the masters who were working them, and being provided with tools by them, he set himself to copy the faun with such attention and study, that in a few days he brought it to perfection, adding out of his imagination all that was wanting in the antique; namely, the open mouth in the likeness of a man who is laughing, so that the cavity of it was shown, with all the teeth. The Magnificent, coming in the meanwhile to see how the work was going forward, found the boy, who was about to polish his head, and accosting him a little, having first observed the excellency of the work and remarked his age, was much astonished; and although he praised the work, nevertheless jesting with him, as with a child, he said: 'What, you have made this old faun, and left him all his teeth! Do you not know that some are always wanting to old fellows of his age?'

1. Francesco Granacci (1477–1543).
2. Domenico Ghirlandaio (1449–94).

[63]

It seemed to Michelagnolo, in his eagerness to correct his mistake, a thousand years before the Magnificent went away. Having been left alone, he cut out one of the upper teeth of his old faun, making a hole in the jaw, as if it had come out by the root, and awaited the Magnificent another day, with great expectancy. He, coming and perceiving the good nature and simplicity of the boy, laughed at it greatly; but afterwards having remarked to himself the perfection of the work, and the age of the lad, he, like the father of all the virtues that he was, resolved to help and favour so great a talent, and take him into his house; and having asked him whose son he was: 'Go, tell your father,' he said, 'that I would speak with him.'

[A. Condivi, *The Life of Michelangelo Buonarroti*, 1553]

Michelangelo's 'Cupid'

Having returned to his own country, Michelagnolo set himself to execute in marble a god of Love, between six and seven years of age, lying at length, in the guise of a sleeping boy. Lorenzo di Pier Francesco de' Medici, for whom in the meantime Michelagnolo had made a little Saint John, seeing this figure, and judging it to be an admirable work, said to him: 'If you were to treat it so that it seemed to have been buried in the earth, I would send it to Rome, and it would pass for an antique, and you would sell it at a far better price.' Michelagnolo, hearing that, immediately treated it in such a manner that it appeared to have been made many ages ago; he being a man to whom no mode of skill was unknown. The figure having been sent to Rome in this condition, the Cardinal of San Giorgio bought it as an antique, for two hundred ducats; nevertheless the person who received that sum of money wrote word to Florence, that thirty ducats were due to Michelagnolo, since that was the amount he had received for the Cupid; deceiving, at the same time, both Pier Francesco and Michelagnolo. But in the meantime, it having come to the ears of the cardinal that the Cupid had been made in Florence, he, disdaining to be cheated, sent one of his gentlemen thither, who, pretending to look for a sculptor to execute certain works in Rome, was directed, after going to some others, to the house of Michelagnolo, and finding the young man, in order the more guardedly to discover what he wished to know, requested him to show him something. But Michelagnolo, not having anything to show, took a pen, (for at that time the crayon was not in use,) and with such deftness drew him a hand, that he was astonished at it. The gentleman then asked him if he had ever executed any work in sculpture; and when Michelagnolo replied yes, and amongst other things a Cupid of such a size, and in such an attitude, the gentleman learned what he wished to know. And having related to Michelagnolo how the matter had gone, he promised him, if he would go with him to Rome, to cause the rest of the money to be paid to him, and to get him employment with his patron, whom he knew would gladly accept his service.

[A. Condivi, *Life of Michelangelo*, 1553]

Michelangelo's Pieta[1] in St Peter's

Such were Michelagnolo's love and zeal together in this work, that he left his name – a thing that he never did again in any other work – written across a girdle that encircles the bosom of Our Lady. And the reason was that one day Michelagnolo, entering the place where it was set up, found there a great number of strangers from Lombardy, who were praising it highly, and one of them asked one of the others who had done it, and he answered, 'Our Gobbo from Milan.' Michelagnolo stood silent, but thought it something strange that his labours should be attributed to another; and one night he shut himself in there, and, having brought a little light and his chisels, carved his name upon it.

[Vasari, *Lives*, 1568]

Michelangelo's 'David'

It happened at this time that Piero Soderini, having seen it in place, was well pleased with it, but said to Michelagnolo, at a moment when he was retouching it in certain parts, that it seemed to him that the nose of the figure was too thick. Michelagnolo noticed that the Gonfalonier was beneath the Giant, and that his point of view prevented him from seeing it properly; but in order to satisfy him he climbed upon the staging, which was against the shoulders, and quickly took up a chisel in his left hand, with a little of the marble-dust that lay upon the planks of the staging, and then, beginning to strike lightly with the chisel, let fall the dust little by little, nor changed the nose a whit from what it

1. 1497–1506.

was before. Then, looking down at the Gonfalonier, who stood watching him, he said, 'Look at it now.' 'I like it better,' said the Gonfalonier, 'you have given it life.' And so Michelagnolo came down, laughing to himself at having satisfied that lord, for he had compassion on those who, in order to appear full of knowledge, talk about things of which they know nothing.

[Vasari, *Lives*, 1568]

Michelangelo's Statue of Pope Julius II in Bologna

His Holiness commanded him that he should make a statue of bronze in the likeness of Pope Julius, five braccia in height. In this work he showed most beautiful art in the attitude, which had an effect of much majesty and grandeur, and displayed richness and magnificence in the draperies, and in the countenance, spirit, force, resolution, and stern dignity; and it was placed in a niche over the door of S. Petronio. It is said that while Michelagnolo was working at it, he received a visit from Francia,[1] a most excellent goldsmith and painter, who wished to see it, having heard so much praise and fame of him and of his works, and not having seen any of them, so that agents had been set to work to enable him to see it, and he had obtained permission. Whereupon, seeing the artistry of Michelagnolo, he was amazed: and then, being asked by Michelagnolo what he thought of that figure, Francia answered that it was a most beautiful casting and a fine material. Wherefore Michelagnolo, considering that he had praised the bronze rather than the workmanship, said to him, 'I owe the same obligation to Pope Julius, who has given it to me, that you owe to the apothecaries who give you your colours for painting;' and in his anger, in the presence of all the gentlemen there, he declared that Francia was a fool. In the same connection, when a son of Francia's came before him and was announced as a very beautiful youth, Michelagnolo said to him, 'Your father's living figures are finer than those that he paints.' Among the same gentlemen was one, whose name I know not, who asked Michelagnolo which he thought was the larger, the statue of the Pope or a pair of oxen; and he answered, 'That depends on the oxen. If they are these Bolognese oxen, then without a doubt our Florentine oxen are not so big.'[2]

1. Francesco Francia (c. 1450–1517), the leading Bolognese painter of the period.
2. 'Stupid as an ox' was an Italian proverb.

Michelagnolo had the statue finished in clay before the Pope departed from Bologna for Rome, and his Holiness, having gone to see it, but not knowing what was to be placed in the left hand, and seeing the right hand raised in a proud gesture, asked whether it was pronouncing a benediction or a curse. Michelagnolo answered that it was admonishing the people of Bologna to mind their behaviour, and asked his Holiness to decide whether he should place a book in the left hand; and he said, 'Put a sword there, for I know nothing of letters.'

[Vasari, *Lives*, 1568] The statue referred to was Michelangelo's only sculpture in bronze, begun 1506 and raised to its niche in the façade of the church of S. Petronio on 21 February 1508. The Bolognese resented it as the symbol of the papal conquest of their city, and it was destroyed less than four years later.

Michelangelo and the Sistine Ceiling

Whilst he was painting, Pope Julius would often go to see the work, ascending by a ladder; and Michelagnolo used to hold out his hand to him to assist him in mounting the scaffold. And like the man that he was, naturally eager and impatient of waiting, as soon as the half was done, namely, from the door to the middle of the vault, he ordered Michelagnolo to uncover it; although it was still unfinished, and wanted the last touches. The opinion and the expectation that was held of Michelagnolo drew all Rome to see the work; and thither the pope also went, before the dust that was raised by the removal of the scaffold, had settled.

After this had been done, Raffaello,[1] having seen the new and marvellous manner, as one who had an admirable gift of imitation, sought, by means of Bramante,[2] to paint the rest. At this, Michelagnolo was much perturbed, and having obtained audience of the pope, grievously complained of the injury that Bramante did him, and in his presence, deplored it before the pope, disclosing all the persecutions which he had received at his hands; and then revealed many of his faults, and especially, when he pulled down old Saint Peter's, how he threw to the ground those marvellous columns that were in that church, neither caring nor taking heed to prevent their being shattered

1. Raphael (1483–1520) was always regarded as the ally and henchman of the architect Bramante.
2. Bramante (1444–1514) was of Umbrian origin, like Raphael, and headed a faction hostile to Michelangelo at the court of Julius II.

in pieces, though he might have gently lowered them and preserved them entire; and he showed how easy a thing it was to pile brick upon brick, but to make a column of that kind a most difficult one; together with many other things, which it is not needful to relate: so that the pope, having heard these complaints, ordered that Michelagnolo should proceed; and showed more favours than he had ever shown him. Michelagnolo finished the whole of the work in twenty months without any assistance soever; not even of some one to grind the colours for him. It is true I have heard him say, that it was not finished as he would have wished; having been prevented by the hurry of the pope, who asked him one day when he would finish the chapel, and Michelagnolo replying to him, 'As soon as I shall be able,' added in wrath: 'You wish that I should cause you to be thrown down from that scaffold.' And Michelagnolo hearing this, said to himself: 'You shall not have me thrown down.' And having gone his way, he caused the scaffold to be removed, and uncovered the work on the feast of All Saints; and it was seen with great satisfaction by the pope, who was in chapel that day, and with admiration by all Rome, who flocked together to see it. There were still wanting the retouches of ultramarine 'a secco' and gold in some places, that it might appear the more rich. Julius, his first enthusiasm having abated, wished Michelagnolo to add these; but he, considering the trouble that he would have had in re-erecting the scaffold, replied that what was wanting, was not a matter of importance. 'It is, indeed, necessary to retouch it with gold,' replied the pope; to whom Michelagnolo answered familiarly, as he was wont to do with his holiness: 'I know not wherefore these men should wear gold.' And the pope: 'The work will look poor.' To which he replied, 'They who are painted here were poor, even they.' Thus was the retort made in jest, and thus the paintings remain. Michelagnolo received for his work, including all his expenses, three thousand ducats, out of which he spent in colours, as I have heard him say, about twenty, or twenty-five.

When the work was finished, Michelagnolo, in having for so long a time, whilst he was painting, held his eyes raised towards the vault, was afterwards able to see little when looking down; so that if he had to read a letter, or look at some other small object, it was necessary for him to hold it with his arm raised above his head. Nevertheless he afterwards, little by little, accustomed himself to read.

[A. Condivi, *Life of Michelangelo*, 1553]

Michelangelo and Pope Paul III

In the meanwhile, Clement[1] died and Paul III[2] having been created pope, sent for Michelagnolo, and requested him to enter his service. Michelagnolo, who foresaw that he would be hindered in the work of the tomb,[3] replied that he was not able to do that, since he was bound by contract to the Duke of Urbino, until he had finished the work which he had in hand. The pope was much troubled at this, and said: 'It is already thirty years that I have had this desire; and now that I am pope, am I not able to satisfy it? Where is this contract? for I will tear it up.'

    [A. Condivi, *Life of Michelangelo*, 1553]

Michelangelo's 'Last Judgement'

Michelagnolo had already carried to completion more than three-fourths of the work, when Pope Paul[4] went to see it. And Messer Biagio da Cesena, the master of ceremonies, a person of great propriety, who was in the chapel with the Pope, being asked what he thought of it, said that it was a very disgraceful thing to have made in so honourable a place all those nude figures showing their nakedness so shamelessly, and that it was a work not for the chapel of a Pope, but for a bagnio or tavern. Michelagnolo was displeased at this, and, wishing to revenge himself, as soon as Biagio had departed he portrayed him from life, without having him before his eyes at all, in the figure of Minos with a great serpent twisted round the legs, among a heap of Devils in Hell; nor was Messer Biagio's pleading with the Pope and with Michelagnolo to have it removed of any avail, for it was left there in memory of the occasion, and it is still to be seen at the present day.

    [Vasari, *Lives*, 1568] A similar story is told about Leonardo's *Last Supper* in Milan (see p. 35).

---

1. Clement VII (1523–34).
2. (1534–49).
3. The tomb of Julius II.
4. Pope Paul III.

Michelangelo and the Florence Pietà

Vasari, sent by Julius III[1] to Michelagnolo's house for a design at the first hour of the night, found him working at the Pietà in marble that he broke. Michelagnolo, recognizing him by the knock at the door, left his work and took a lamp with his hand by the handle; Vasari explained what he wanted, whereupon Michelagnolo sent Urbino upstairs for the design, and then they entered into another conversation. Meanwhile Vasari turned his eyes to examine a leg of the Christ at which he was working, seeking to change it; and, in order to prevent Vasari from seeing it, he let the lamp fall from his hand, and they were left in darkness. He called to Urbino to bring a light, and meanwhile came forth from the enclosure where the work was, and said: 'I am so old that death often pulls me by the cloak, that I may go with him, and one day this body of mine will fall like the lamp, and the light of my life will be spent.'

[Vasari, *Lives*, 1568]

Michelangelo and a Gift of Candles

Often during the night, not being able to sleep, he would rise to labour with the chisel; having made a cap of thick paper, and over the centre of his head he kept a lighted candle, which in this way threw light over where he was working without encumbering his hands. Vasari, who had seen the cap several times, reflecting that he did not use wax, but candles of pure goat's tallow, which are excellent, sent him four bundles of these, which weighed forty libbre. And his servant with all courtesy carried them to him at the second hour of the evening, and presented them to him; but Michelagnolo refused them, declaring that he did not want them; and then the servant said: 'They have broken my arms on the way between the bridge and here, and I shall not carry them back to the house. Now here in front of your door there is a solid heap of mud; they will stand in it beautifully, and I will set them all alight.' Michelagnolo said to him: 'Put them down here, for I will not have you playing pranks at my door.'

1. Pope from 1550–55, which dates this incident to the first half of the 1550s. Michelangelo smashed the sculpture sometime late in 1555.

He told me that often in his youth he slept in his clothes, being weary with labour and not caring to take them off only to have to put them on again later.

[Vasari, *Lives*, 1568]

Michelangelo's Character

Michelagnolo has likewise read with great study and attention the sacred scriptures both of the Old and New Testament, as well as those who have laboured to expound them, such as the writings of Savonarola,[1] whom he always has held in great veneration; the memory of his living voice still remaining in his mind. He has, moreover, loved the beauty of the body, as became one who was in the highest degree acquainted with it; and in such sort has he loved it, that to certain carnally minded men, who are not able to understand the love of beauty, unless it be lascivious and shameful, it has given occasion to think and speak ill of him: as if Alcibiades, who was a most lovely youth, had not been chastely loved by Socrates; from whose side, when he lay down with him, he was wont to say that he rose as from the side of his father. I have many times heard Michelagnolo reason and discourse upon love; and have afterwards heard from those that were present, that he spoke not otherwise of love, than according to that which is to be read in the writings of Plato. As for me, I know not what Plato may say about this matter; but I know well, that having thus long and intimately conversed with Michelagnolo, I never heard fall from his lips other than honest words, and such as were able to quench in youth every uncouth and licentious desire that might arise in it. And that unclean thoughts were never bred in him, may be perceived also by this: that he has not only loved the beauty of the human body, but every beautiful thing, without exception; a beautiful horse, a beautiful dog, a beautiful countryside, a beautiful plant, a beautiful mountain, a beautiful wood, and every place and thing, beautiful and rare, in its kind; admiring them with a marvellous passion. And in this way, he would seek out what is beautiful in nature, as the bees gather the honey from the flowers, in order to make use of it afterwards in their works; and thus have all those ever done, who in painting have achieved any renown. That master of antiquity,

1. Girolamo Savonarola (1452–98), religious reformer who was burned at the stake.

in order to make a Venus, was not content to see one virgin only; on the contrary he was minded to contemplate many; and taking from each the most beautiful and perfect part, made use of it in his Venus. And in truth, he who thinks that without this method, (by which one is able to acquire the true theory of the beautiful), he will arrive at some degree of excellence in this art, greatly deceives himself.

Michelagnolo has ever been very frugal in his mode of life, partaking of food rather out of necessity, than for pleasure; especially when he has been at work: at which time, more often than not, he has been content with a piece of bread, which he would eat while he was still working. Though, from a certain period of his life, he has lived more carefully, since his age, already more than mature, has required it. Many times have I heard him say: 'Ascanio, for the rich man that I have been, I have ever lived as a poor one.' And as he has partaken of little food, so of little sleep, which, as he himself says, has rarely done him good; since when he sleeps long, he almost invariably suffers from pain in the head: indeed, too much sleep disorders his stomach. When he was more robust, he often slept in his clothes, and with his buskins on his legs; and these he has always used both on account of cramp, from which he has continually suffered, and for other reasons: and sometimes, he has gone so long before taking them off, that afterwards the skin has come away, like that of a snake, along with the buskins. He was never greedy of money, nor did he set himself to pile up gold; being content with as much as sufficed him to live honestly: for which reason, although very many lords and rich persons have made request to him, with large promises of reward, for some work by his hand, he has rarely executed anything; and that which he has, rather out of friendship and good-will, than for any expectation of gain.

[A. Condivi, *Life of Michelangelo*, 1553]

Michelangelo's Appearance and Habits

Michelagnolo is of good complexion; of body rather nervous and bony, than fleshy and fat; healthy above all, both by nature and by his bodily exercise and continence, as well in coition as in food, although as a child he was feeble and sickly, and as a man he has had two illnesses. He suffered much on that account for several years after, in passing water: and this hurt would have turned into stone, had he not been cured by the work and diligence of Messer Realdo aforesaid. He has always had a good colour in his face; and his stature is as follows: he is of a middle height, large in the shoulders, and the rest of his body proportionate to them, but rather spare than otherwise. The form of that part of the head, which is seen in full face, is of a rounded figure, in such a manner that above the ears it makes a sixth part more than a half round: and thus the temples project somewhat more than the ears, and the ears more than the cheeks, and these more than the rest; so that the head in proportion to the face must be called large. The forehead in this view is square, the nose a little flattened, though not by nature; for when he was a child, one Torrigiano de' Torrigiani, a bestial man and proud, almost crushed with a blow the cartilage of his nose; so that he was carried home for dead. This Torrigiano, therefore, having been banished from Florence, on that account, came to an evil end: and so Michelagnolo's nose, thus as it is, is proportionate to the forehead and the rest of the face. The lips are thin, but the lower one somewhat fuller: so that when seen in profile, it projects a little. The chin agrees well with the parts aforesaid. The forehead when seen in profile almost projects beyond the nose; and this would appear little less than broken, were it not for a little lump in the middle. The eyebrows have few hairs; the eyes might be called small, rather than otherwise, and of the colour of horn, but varied and marked with yellow and blue specks. The ears are well proportioned; the hair is black and so is the beard; except that in this seventy-ninth year of his age the hairs are copiously streaked with white: the beard, moreover, is forked from four to five fingers in length, and not very thick, as may partially be seen from his portraits.

[A. Condivi, *Life of Michelangelo*, 1553]

Michelangelo on Marriage

A priest, his friend, said to him: 'It is a pity that you have not taken a wife, so that you might have had many children and left them all your honourable labours.' And Michelagnolo replied: 'I have only too much of a wife in this art of mine, who has always kept me in tribulation, and my children shall be the works that I may leave, which, even if they are naught, will live a while.'

[Vasari, *Lives*, 1568]

Michelangelo's Powers of Memory

Michelagnolo was a man of tenacious and profound memory, so that, on seeing the works of others only once, he remembered them perfectly, and could avail himself of them in such a manner, that scarcely anyone has ever noticed it; nor did he ever do anything that resembled another thing by his hand, because he remembered everything that he had done. In his youth, being once with his painter-friends, they played for a supper for him who should make a figure most completely wanting in design and clumsy, after the likeness of the puppet-figures which those make who know nothing, scrawling upon walls; and in this he availed himself of his memory, for he remembered having seen one of those absurdities on a wall, and drew it exactly as if he had had it before him, and thus surpassed all those painters – a thing difficult for a man so steeped in design, and accustomed to choice works, to come out of with credit.

[Vasari, *Lives*, 1568]

Michelangelo's Attitude to Death; his Comment on Donatello's St Mark

A friend having spoken to him of death, saying that it must grieve him much, because he had lived in continual labour in matters of art, and had never had any repose, he answered that all that was nothing, because, if life is a pleasure to us, death, being likewise by the hand of one and the same master, should not displease us. To a citizen who found him by Orsanmichele in Florence, where he had stopped to gaze at Donato's[1] statue of S. Mark, and who asked him what he thought of that figure, Michelagnolo answered that he had never seen a figure that had more of the air of a good man than that one, and that, if S. Mark was like that, one could give credence to what he had written.

[Vasari, *Lives*, 1568]

Michelangelo and Titian

Michelagnolo and Vasari, going one day to visit Tiziano [Titian] in the Belvedere, saw in a picture that he had executed at that time a nude

1. i.e. Donatello's.

woman representing Danaë,[1] who had in her lap Jove transformed into a rain of gold; and they praised it much, as one does in the painter's presence. After they had left him, discoursing of Tiziano's method, Buonarroti commended it not a little, saying that his colouring and his manner much pleased him, but that it was a pity that in Venice men did not learn to draw well from the beginning, and that those painters did not pursue a better method in their studies. 'For,' he said, 'if this man had been in any way assisted by art and design, as he is by nature, and above all in counterfeiting the life, no one could do more or work better, for he has a fine spirit and a very beautiful and lively manner.'

> [Vasari, *Lives*, 1568] This much repeated story encapsulates the argument which continued to rage in art between *disegno* and *colore*. It spilled over into later French painting, and represents, for example, the basic difference between Ingres and Delacroix.

Michelangelo, Daniele da Volterra and Bernini

M. Colbert spoke of the great resemblance between Bernini's bust of Louis XIV and the original. Even in the presence of the king himself, the resemblance could not have been more great. The Cavaliere [Bernini] replied that comparisons of this type must always be to the disadvantage of sculpture, or even of painting (even though the latter was imbued with all the colours of life), because the real thing had life and movement. He told a story of how Daniele da Volterra,[2] working one day on a *Pallas Athene*, gave the goddess a shield on her arm. The model was a real shield made of steel. Michelangelo came to the studio one day and found Daniele in a great state of shame and depression because he was unable to endow his work with the glitter of the shield he was imitating. He asked Michelangelo to give a few touches to this area of the picture.

Michelangelo, continued the Cavaliere, thought that the imitation was already as close as anything art could accomplish, so he told Daniele to leave the room, saying that he would not paint in front of him. Once the latter had departed, Michelangelo did not do more than

---

1. Titian was in Rome in 1455–6. The picture was commissioned by Ottavio Farnese and is now in the Gallerie Nazionali of Naples.
2. Daniele da Volterra (1509–66), friend and follower of Michelangelo, who supplied designs for some of his paintings.

take the shield from where it was, and turn it face against the wall. After some time, he called Daniele back, and made him look at the work, which now seemed entirely different, as the real thing was no longer there to be compared with it. Astonished, Daniele asked Michelangelo how he had produced the colours he had used. For some time Michelangelo refused to tell him, but finally admitted that he had not touched the brushes, and had done no more than move the shield.

[Paul Fréart de Chantelou, *Journal du voyage du Cav. Bernini en France*, 1885] Bernini stayed in Paris from June to October 1665.

Michelangelo and the Grotesque Mask

Speaking once again about Michelangelo, the Cavaliere [Bernini] said that, at the Porta Pia, which was one of the gates of Rome, designed by Michelangelo, the latter wanted to carve the mask which ornaments it with his own hand. The same Cardinal Salviati, who was Michelangelo's particular friend, had a vineyard near the gate, and told the artist to go there whenever he wanted. The cardinal also instructed the caretaker to let Michelangelo use the house and garden as he pleased, and to give him anything he needed.

A little later, the cardinal went to the vineyard and asked this caretaker what Michelangelo had been doing. The man replied that 'it was a shame but he had gone mad'. The cardinal was astonished, and asked why he said this. The caretaker said that he had perceived Michelangelo's madness when he found him on several occasions standing alone with his servant. He was making the latter open his mouth, and crying 'More! more!' to make him gape wider. The only thing which interested him was to get his servant to pull faces.

[Chantelou, *Journal du voyage du Cav. Bernini en France*, 1885]

Michelangelo and the Torso Belvedere

Bernini added that one day Michelangelo was looking at the *Torso Belvedere*, and had got down on his knees to examine it more closely. Cardinal Salviati found him thus. Surprised, he accosted Michelangelo, who took some time to reply, so absorbed was he in what he was doing. Coming to himself, and seeing the cardinal, he said: 'This is the work of a man who knew more than Nature itself. It would be a great misfortune were it ever to be lost.'

[Chantelou, *Journal du voyage du Cav. Bernini en France*, 1885]

Michelangelo's Comments on other Artists

Being asked by a friend what he thought of one who had counterfeited in marble some of the most celebrated antique figures, and boasted that in his imitations he had surpassed the antiques by a great measure, Michelagnolo replied: 'He who goes behind others can never go in front of them, and he who is not able to work well for himself cannot make good use of the works of others.' A certain painter, I know not who, had executed a work wherein was an ox, which looked better than any other part; and Michelagnolo, being asked why the painter had made the ox more lifelike than the rest, said: 'Any painter can make a good portrait of himself.' Passing by S. Giovanni in Florence, he was asked his opinion of those doors,[1] and he answered: 'They are so beautiful that they would do well at the gates of Paradise.'

[Vasari, *Lives*, 1568]

Michelangelo: Speaking Professionally

Among other things, [Bernini] reminded me that he had told me how Michelangelo used to say, when shown the work of a talented artist: 'There's a rogue – a real mischief-maker'. Shown something mediocre, he said: 'There's a good fellow – he won't make trouble for anybody'.

[Chantelou, *Journal du voyage du Cav. Bernini en France*, 1885]

Michelangelo and 'the Light of the Piazza'

He went to see a work of sculpture which was about to be sent out because it was finished, and the sculptor was taking much trouble to arrange the lights from the windows, to the end that it might show up well; whereupon Michelagnolo said to him: 'Do not trouble yourself; the important thing will be the light of the Piazza'; meaning to infer that when works are in public places, the people must judge whether they

---

1. The doors to the Florence Baptistry (dedicated to St John the Baptist) by Lorenzo Ghiberti (1375–1455), who won the competition to design them in 1402.

are good or bad. There was a great Prince in Rome who had a notion to play the architect, and he had caused certain niches to be built in which to place figures, each three squares high, with a ring at the top; and having tried to place various statues within these niches, which did not turn out well, he asked Michelagnolo what he should place in them, and he answered: 'Hang bunches of eels from those rings.' There was appointed to the government of the fabric of S. Pietro a gentleman who professed to understand Vitruvius,[1] and to be a critic of the work done. Michelagnolo was told, 'You have obtained for the fabric one who has a great intelligence'; and he answered, 'That is true, but he has a bad judgment.' A painter had executed a scene, and had copied many things from various other works, both drawings and pictures, nor was there anything in that work that was not copied. It was shown to Michelagnolo, who, having seen it, was asked by a very dear friend what he thought of it, and he replied: 'He has done well, but I know not what this scene will do on the day of Judgment, when all bodies shall recover their members, for there will be nothing left of it'.

[Vasari, *Lives*, 1568]

Michelangelo's Not-so-famous Companions

For all this, he took pleasure in certain kinds of men after his taste, such as Menighella, a commonplace and clownish painter of Valdarno, who was a most diverting person. He would come at times to Michelagnolo, that he might make for him a design of S. Rocco or S. Anthony, to be painted for peasants; and Michelagnolo, who was with difficulty persuaded to work for Kings, would deign to set aside all his other work and make him simple designs suited to this manner and his wishes, as Menighella himself used to say. Among other things, Menighella persuaded him to make a model of a Crucifix, which was very beautiful; of this he made a mould, from which he formed copies in pasteboard and other materials, and these he went about selling throughout the countryside. Michelagnolo would burst out laughing at him, particularly because he used to meet with fine adventures, as with a countryman who commissioned him to paint a S. Francis, and was displeased because Menighella had made the vestment grey,

1. Marcus Vitruvius Pollio (fl. first century BC), author of the only surviving Roman treatise on architectural theory.

whereas he would have liked it of a finer colour; whereupon Menighella painted over the Saint's shoulders a pluvial of brocade, and so contented him.

He loved, likewise, the stonecutter Topolino, who had a notion of being an able sculptor, but was in truth very feeble. This man spent many years in the mountains of Carrara, sending marble to Michelagnolo; nor would he ever send a boatload without adding to it three or four little figures blocked out with his own hand, at which Michelagnolo would die of laughing. Finally Topolino returned, and, having blocked out a Mercury from a piece of marble, he set himself to finish it; and one day, when there was little left to do, he desired that Michelagnolo should see it, and straitly besought him that he should tell him his opinion. 'You are a madman to try to make figures, Topolino,' said Michelagnolo. 'Do you not see that your Mercury is more than a third of a braccio too short between the knees and the feet, and that you have made him a dwarf and all misshapen?' 'Oh, that is nothing! If there is nothing else wrong, I will put it right; leave it to me.' Michelagnolo laughed once more at his simplicity; and when he was gone, Topolino took a piece of marble, and, having cut the Mercury a quarter of a braccio below the knees, he let it into the new piece of marble and joined it neatly together, making a pair of buskins for the Mercury, the tops of which were above the joins; and so he added the length required. Then he invited Michelagnolo to come, and showed him his work once again; and the master laughed, marvelling that such simpletons, when driven by necessity, form resolutions of which able men are not capable.

While Michelagnolo was having the tomb of Julius II finished, he caused a marble-hewer to execute a terminal figure for placing in the tomb in S. Pietro in Vincola, saying to him, 'Cut away this to-day,' 'Level that,' 'Polish here'; insomuch that, without the other noticing it, he enabled him to make a figure. Wherefore, when it was finished, the man gazed at it marvelling; and Michelagnolo said: 'What do you think of it?' 'I think it fine,' he answered, 'and I am much obliged to you.' 'Why so?' asked Michelagnolo. 'Because by your means I have discovered a talent that I did not know I possessed.'

[Vasari, *Lives*, 1568]

Michelangelo Paints a Crucifix

It has also been said (but I think this is just a story) that Michelangelo Buonarotti nailed some poor man to a board and pierced his heart with a spear, so as to paint a Crucifixion.

[Francesco Susinno, *Le vite dei pittori messinesi*, 1724] A good example of an apocryphal story from a late source. Virtually the same story attached itself to Giotto (see p.14).

VI

RENAISSANCE ARTISTS FROM VENICE, PARMA AND MILAN

ॐ

Vasari's gaze was fixed chiefly on artists from his own, Florentine milieu. The artists of other schools whom he knew most about were those who had either worked in Florence for a time, like Parmigianino, or who had come into close contact with Michelangelo, like Sebastiano del Piombo.

Because a number of Florentine artists lived and worked in Venice, Vasari also had access to information about the world of artists there. However, it was not nearly as complete as his information about Florence, and in any case he tended to feel unsympathetic to the Venetian approach to art, which exalted colour above drawing (the contrast is exemplified in the story about Michelangelo's comments on Titian's Danaë (see p. 74). In any case, the whole tendency in Venice – the social attitudes of Venetian society – discouraged a cult of artistic personality of the kind Vasari's approach seemed to endorse. It is striking that there are so few anecdotes about Titian, despite the painter's close personal friendship with Pietro Aretino, perhaps the most celebrated Italian writer of the time. Aretino promoted Titian's interests, wrote to him when the two men were apart, but wrote very little about him.

The one Venetian artist who broke the mould was Tintoretto. Though Ridolfi's Le maraviglie dell'arte was not published until 1648, over fifty years after Tintoretto's death, it is clear that the latter left a vivid anecdotal tradition behind him.

Titian (1477/89–1575) and Giorgione

Then in the year 1507, while the Emperor Maximilian was making war on the Venetians, Tiziano [Titian], according to his own account, painted an Angel Raphael with Tobias and a dog in the Church of S. Marziliano, with a distant landscape, where, in a little wood, S. John the Baptist is praying on his knees to Heaven, whence comes a radiance that illumines him; and this work it is thought that he executed before he made a beginning with the façade of the Fondaco de' Tedeschi. Concerning which façade, many gentlemen, not knowing that Giorgione was not working there any more and that Tiziano was doing it, who had uncovered one part, meeting with Giorgione, congratulated him in friendly fashion, saying that he was acquitting himself better in the façade towards the Merceria than he had done in that which is over the Grand Canal. At which circumstance Giorgione felt such disdain, that until Tiziano had completely finished the work and it had become well known that the same had done that part, he would scarcely let himself be seen; and from that time onward he would never allow Tiziano to associate with him or be his friend.

[Vasari, *Lives*, 1568]

Titian and the Emperor Charles V

About the end of that year [1548], summoned by the Emperor Charles V, [Titian] went to the imperial court with an honourable retinue of pages and servitors, bringing with him a painting of the *Pieta*, and a life-sized image of *Venus*. He now painted the Emperor's portrait for the third time, showing him in old age, wearing blackened armour with rich gold decoration (as can be seen from the copies made of the picture). It is said that, while he was painting, he let fall one of his brushes, which the Emperor picked up for him. Titian protested, saying: 'Sire, I am not worthy of such a servant.' To which the Emperor replied: 'Titian is worthy to be served by Caesar.'

[C. Ridolfi, *Le maraviglie dell' arte, overo, le vite degli illustri pittori veneti e dello stato*, 1648]

The Rivalry of Pordenone (c. 1485–1539) and Titian

He disputed the superiority with Titian, and their jealousy of each other was so great, that Pordenone fearing to be insulted by his rival, was always upon his guard, and when he painted the cloyster of St Stephen in Venice, he worked with a sword by his side, and a buckler tied about him, as was the fashion of the bravo's in his time.

[R. de Piles, *Abrégé de la vie des peintres*, 1699; English trans., 1750]

Sebastiano del Piombo (1485–1547) Living Well in Rome

Fra Sebastiano had a passing good house which he had built for himself near the Popolo, and there he lived in the greatest contentment, without troubling to paint or work any more. He used often to say that it was a great fatigue to have to restrain in old age those ardours which in youth craftsmen are wont to welcome out of emulation and a desire for profit and honour, and that it was no less wise for a man to live in peace than to spend his days in restless labour in order to leave a name behind him after death, for all his works and labours had also in the end, sooner or later, to die. And even as he said these things, so he carried them into practice as well as he was able, for he always sought to have for his table all the best wines and the rarest luxuries that could be found, holding life in more account than art. Being much the friend of all men of talent, he often had Molza and Messer Gandolfo to supper, making right good cheer. He was also the intimate friend of Messer Francesco Berni,[1] the Florentine, who wrote a poem to him; to which Fra Sebastiano answered with another, passing well, for, being very versatile, he was even able to set his hand to writing humorous Tuscan verse.

Having been reproached by certain persons, who said that it was shameful that he would no longer work now that he had the means to live, Fra Sebastiano replied in this manner: 'Why will I not work now that I have the means to live? Because there are now in the world men of genius who do in two months what I used to do in two years; and I believe that if I live long enough, and not so long, either, I shall find that everything has been painted. And since these stalwarts can do so much, it is well that there should also be one who does nothing, to the

1. Francesco Berni (1497/8–1535), celebrated burlesque poet.

end that they may have the more to do.' With these and similar pleasantries Fra Sebastiano was always diverting himself, being a man who was never anything but humorous and amusing; and, in truth, a better companion never lived.

[Vasari, *Lives*, 1568]

Tintoretto (1518–94) in Titian's Studio

When [Jacopo Tintoretto] was still a child, he used to draw on walls, using charcoal and his father's dye-colours – these were juvenile scribbles, figures without any elegance. Seeing his natural inclination, his parent thought it ought to be encouraged, so they placed him with Titian, in whose house he remained with other young men, learning from the master's example.

Not long after Tintoretto arrived there, Titian went into the pupils' studio, and there saw, scattered beside a bench, some pieces of paper, upon which were drawn certain grotesque figures. He asked who had done them. Jacopo, who was responsible, and fearing that he had done wrong, admitted he was the author. Whereupon Titian, deducing from these beginnings that Tintoretto would become a fine painter, and would bow to no one in art, impatiently ran up the steps and, putting on his cloak, told his apprentice Girolamo (so much does greed for honour find a place in human hearts) to send Jacopo back to his house – so that the latter, without knowing why, found himself deprived of a master.

[C. Ridolfi, *Le maraviglie dell' arte*, 1648]

Tintoretto and the Scuola di San Rocco

And it is not long since, Tintoretto having executed the Passion of Christ in a large picture in oils and on canvas for the Scuola of S. Rocco, the men of that Company resolved to have some honourable and magnificent work painted on the ceiling above it, and therefore to allot that commission to that one among the painters that there were in Venice who should make the best and most beautiful design. Having therefore summoned Joseffo Salviati,[1] Federigo Zucchero,[2] who

---

1. Giuseppe Porta, il Salviati (c. 1520–75).
2. Federico Zuccaro (1540–1609).

was in Venice at that time, Paolo Veronese,[1] and Jacopo Tintoretto, they ordained that each of them should make a design, promising the work to him who should acquit himself best in this. While the others, then, were engaged with all possible diligence in making their designs, Tintoretto, having taken measurements of the size that the work was to be, sketched a great canvas and painted it with his usual rapidity, without anyone knowing about it, and then placed it where it was to stand. Whereupon, the men of the Company having assembled one morning to see the designs and to make their award, they found that Tintoretto had completely finished the work and had placed it in position. At which being angered against him, they said that they had called for designs and had not commissioned him to execute the work; but he answered them that this was his method of making designs, that he did not know how to proceed in any other manner, and that designs and models of works should always be after that fashion, so as to deceive no one, and that, finally, if they would not pay him for the work and for his labour, he would make them a present of it. And after these words, although he had many contradictions, he so contrived that the work is still in the same place. In this canvas, then, there is painted a Heaven with God the Father descending with many Angels to embrace S. Rocco, and in the lowest part are many figures that signify, or rather represent the other principal Scuole of Venice, such as the Carità, S. Giovanni Evangelista, the Misericordia, S. Marco, and S. Teodoro, all executed after his usual manner.

[Vasari, *Lives*, 1568]

Tintoretto and Aretino

Pietro Aretino spoke badly of him because he belonged to the faction headed by Titian, and therefore did not like Tintoretto. Meeting Aretino one day, Tintoretto asked him to come to the studio so he could paint a portrait. Aretino came, and prepared to sit, when Tintoretto, with every appearance of fury, whipped out a pistol which he had in his doublet. Aretino, frightened, and fearing the repayment of a grudge, began to cry out: 'Jacopo, what are you up to?' And Tintoretto said: 'Be quiet. I'm taking your measurements.' Then starting at the head, and moving towards the feet: 'You are two and a

1. Paolo Veronese (1528–88).

half pistols tall.' Then Aretino, reassured: 'You're a madman – always up to something odd!' But he no longer spoke against Tintoretto, and the two men became friends.

[C. Ridolfi, *Le maraviglie dell' arte*, 1648]

Tintoretto's Manner of Working

He was visited by certain prelates and senators when he was working on the *Paradiso* in the Sala del Maggior Consiglio [in the Palazzo Ducale in Venice]. Seeing how freely and rapidly he painted, they asked why Giovanni Bellini,[1] Titian and other painters were so laborious in their work, while he on the contrary painted by fits and starts. He promptly replied: 'These old men did not have, as I do, so many things filling their heads to bursting.' And no one dared to bother him further.

[C. Ridolfi, *Le maraviglie dell' arte*, 1648]

Tintoretto's Efficiency

He got a letter from his brother, with many requests – then, at the very end, the brother asked whether their mother, who had been ill, was dead. He answered curtly, so as to dispose of the nuisance as quickly as possible: 'Dear brother, to everything you have written me, the answer is no.'

[C. Ridolfi, *Le maraviglie dell' arte*, 1648]

Tintoretto Puts a Critic to the Test

Once, at Signor Jacopo Contarno's, where many good painters and other virtuosi gathered, a female portrait of Titian's was being praised, and someone turned to Tintoretto and said: 'That is how you should paint.' He told the old man he would make him eat his words, then went back to his house and took a canvas upon which was painted a female head by Titian. On top of this he painted the portrait of an old woman who was his neighbour, and smoked it a little, and hid the other image entirely with colour and glue. Then he carried it back to the company, where everyone who saw it praised it as a fine example

1. Giovanni Bellini (c. 1430–1516).

of Titian's work. Then Tintoretto, taking off what he had painted with a sponge, said: 'This is by the hand of Titian, but the other head I painted myself. Note, signori, how far authority and opinion prevail, and how few there are who really understand painting.'

[C. Ridolfi, *Le maraviglie dell' arte*, 1648]

Tintoretto's Advice to a Vain Sitter

Attracted by Tintoretto's reputation, a gentleman came to have his portrait painted, but wanted to be shown in an exaggerated pose. He was also very ugly. The old man said: 'You had better go to Bassano[1] – he'll paint you to the life.'

[C. Ridolfi, *Le maraviglie dell' arte*, 1648]

The Tintoretto Scale

A Venetian gentleman once asked him to do a fresco painting in his garden. Since he had to measure the wall for this, he spread out his arms, to find the breadth of the space. Asked how big it was, he replied: 'Three Tintorettos.'

[C. Ridolfi, *Le maraviglie dell' arte*, 1648]

Tintoretto Returns from Lombardy

He returned from a trip to Lombardy, and was asked by Palma Giovane[2] what the painters were like there. He replied: 'I cannot tell you – I couldn't find them in the dark.'[3]

[C. Ridolfi, *Le maraviglie dell' arte*, 1648]

Tintoretto on Drawing

He was accustomed to say that beautiful colours could be found in the shops of the Rialto, but that drawing came from the strongbox of the mind with much study and hard work, and thus was understood and practised by very few.

[C. Ridolfi, *Le maraviglie dell' arte*, 1648]

1. Jacopo da Ponte, Il Bassano (1510/15–92).
2. Jacopo Negreti, Palma il Giovane (1544–1628), Venetian painter.
3. A hit at the north Italian liking for exaggerated chiaroscuro.

Tintoretto on Colour

Asked which were the most beautiful colours, he answered: 'Black and white. The first gives strength to the figures by deepening the shadows, the second gives relief.'

[C. Ridolfi, *Le maraviglie dell' arte*, 1648]

Annibale Carracci on Tintoretto

In a letter to Ludovico Carracci, he wrote: 'I saw Tintoretto, at times the equal of Titian and at times less than Tintoretto.'

[G. P. Bellori, *Vite de' pittori, scultori e architetti moderni*, 1672]

Veronese (1528–88) Describes the Painter's Profession

He had a great idea of his profession; he used to say it was a gift from heaven; that to judge of it well, a man ought to understand abundance of things; that no Painter would ever do any thing perfectly, if he had not nature present before him; that none but master's pictures should be placed in churches, because admiration only excites devotion; and that the sovereign quality of a true Painter is probity and integrity of manners.

R. de Piles, *Abrégé de la vie des peintres*, 1699, trans. 1750]

Correggio (c. 1489–1534) Reacts to Raphael

It is related of this artist, justly styled the Apelles of Europe, that instigated by the desire of beholding the Frescos of Raffael in the Vatican, he visited Rome; and after having long gazed on these celebrated works, conscious of his own transcendent but less regarded talents, he broke forth with the memorable words, *'anch'io son pittore!'* I also am a painter.

[*The Percy Anecdotes*, 1821–3]

The Death of Correggio

Going on a time to Parma to receive fifty crowns, he was paid in a sort of copper-money called Quadrino's. His joy that he had got it to carry home to his wife, made him that he did not mind the weight of his

[89]

money, with which he loaded himself in the heat of the summer, and being to lug it twelve miles on foot, the burthen, the walk, and the weather, threw him into a pleurisy, of which he died at 40 years old, anno 1513.

[R. de Piles, *Abrégé de la vie des peintres*, 1699, trans. 1750]

Parmigianino (1503–40): His Obsession with Alchemy, and his Death

Meanwhile Francesco began to abandon the work of the Steccata,[1] or at least to carry it on so slowly that it was evident that he was not in earnest. And this happened because he had begun to study the problems of alchemy, and had quite deserted his profession of painting, thinking that he would become rich quicker by congealing mercury. Wherefore, wearing out his brains, but not in imagining beautiful inventions and executing them with brushes and colour-mixtures, he wasted his whole time in handling charcoal, wood, glass vessels, and other suchlike trumperies, which made him spend more in one day than he earned by a week's work at the Chapel of the Steccata. Having no other means of livelihood, and being yet compelled to live, he was wasting himself away little by little with those furnaces; and what was worse, the men of the Company of the Steccata, perceiving that he had completely abandoned the work, and having perchance paid him more than his due, as is often done, brought a suit against him. Thereupon, thinking it better to withdraw, he fled by night with some friends to Casal Maggiore. And there, having dispersed a little of the alchemy out of his head, he painted a panel-picture for the Church of S. Stefano, of Our Lady in the sky, with S. John the Baptist and S. Stephen below. Afterwards he executed a picture, the last that he ever painted, of the Roman Lucretia, which was a thing divine and one of the best that were ever seen by his hand; but it has disappeared, however that may have happened, so that no one knows where it is.

By his hand, also, is a picture of some nymphs, which is now in the house of Messer Niccolò Bufolini at Città di Castello, and a child's cradle, which was painted for Signora Angiola de' Rossi of Parma, wife of Signor Alessandro Vitelli, and is likewise at Città di Castello.

In the end, having his mind still set on his alchemy, like every other

---

1. The church of S. Maria della Steccata, Parma.

man who has once grown crazed over it, and changing from a dainty and gentle person into an almost savage man with long and unkempt beard and locks, a creature quite different from his other self, Francesco went from bad to worse, became melancholy and eccentric, and was assailed by a grievous fever and a cruel flux, which in a few days caused him to pass to a better life.

[Vasari, *Lives*, 1568]

A Portrait by Arcimboldo (c. 1530–93)

At the Emperor Maximilian's[1] command he painted a portrait which was laughable in the highest degree. It showed a certain Doctor (of Law) whose face had been ravaged by syphilis, so that all that remained to him were a few hairs on his chin. The portrait is made up of various roasted animals and fishes, and the likeness so exact that anyone who even glanced at it saw it was the image of the good jurist. It is unnecessary to stress the pleasure this gave to their Majesties and the laughter it caused at the Imperial Court.

[Gregorio Comanini, *Il Figino, overo del fine dalla Pittura*, 1591] Arcimboldo's paintings have been interpreted very differently in the twentieth century, as forerunners of Surrealism. The sixteenth century sense of humour was more robust than our own.

1. Maximilian II, Holy Roman Emperor 1564–1576.

VII

THE RENAISSANCE IN
NORTHERN EUROPE

ह०

Interest in artists and their lives grew more slowly in northern Europe
than it did in Italy, and near-contemporary anecdotal material is
correspondingly much sparser. Of the great German artists of the first
half of the sixteenth century, Cranach has left no trace as a living,
breathing personality, despite his close links with the Reformation.
Dürer's personality is preserved for us in his own writings, most
notably the diary he kept of his trip to the Netherlands. Nevertheless
some anecdotes survive which illustrate his connection, not only with
the imperial court, but with the world of theologians and intellectuals.
Holbein is glimpsed through his connection with the greatest and most
celebrated of the northern humanists, Erasmus.

Where Netherlandish artists are concerned, the chief source is Carel
van Mander. The second and definitive edition of van Mander's
Schilderboek did not appear until 1618. There is a striking contrast
between his stories about earlier artists, which are clearly often
legendary, and his vivid portrait of a man who was a personal friend,
the engraver Hendrick Goltzius. Goltzius's compulsion to travel
evidently had a neurotic element – van Mander makes it clear that it
was the artist's way of escaping from himself. This may also have had
something to do with his decision to travel for the most part incognito.
At the same time, van Mander's account also makes it plain that
Goltzius was a major European celebrity, who was forced to protect
himself from the intrusions of the curious. The artist as 'star' is not a
wholly twentieth-century concept.

Albrecht Dürer (1471–1528)

The story is told among other tales that [the Emperor] Maximilian once asked Albrecht to draw something, rather large, on a wall. The master found he was too short to reach it. The Emperor ordered one of his courtiers forward, and requested him to stand on the back of this man. The latter objected to the Emperor, in all courtesy, saying that such an act was an humiliation to nobility, and that he regarded it as rather contemptible to serve as a footstool to a painter. The Emperor replied that Albrecht was already a nobleman for the excellence of his work of art; and he declared further that he could make a nobleman out of a peasant, very easily, but that it was not in his power to make an artist out of a nobleman.

[Carl van Mander, *Het schilderboek*, 1618] Compare Henry VIII's rebuke to a noble lord who quarrelled with Holbein: 'I tell you, Earl, that if it pleased me to make seven dukes of seven peasants, I could do so, but I could not make of seven earls one Hans Holbein, or anyone as eminent as he.'

Albrecht Dürer and his Wife

In Albrecht Dürer I have lost the best friend I ever had on earth; and nothing grieves me more than that he should have died so cruel a death. I can ascribe it to no one but his wife (after the decree of God), for she so gnawed into his heart and to such a degree tormented him that he departed hence sooner than he would have done. He was shrivelled up like a bundle of straw, and dared never seek for amusement, or go into company, for she was always uneasy, though there was no need for her to be so. She watched him day and night, drove him to work hard for this reason alone that he might earn money and leave it to her when he died. For she always thought she was on the borders of ruin, as, for the matter of that she does still, though Albrecht left her property worth as much as six thousand florins. But there! nothing was enough, and in fact she alone is the cause of his death. I often besought her myself about her ungenerous, criminal conduct, and I warned her and told her what the end of it all would be, but I got nothing but ingratitude for my pains. She was the enemy of all who were kindly disposed to her husband and fond of his society; and this indeed was a great trouble to Albrecht and brought him to his grave. I have never seen her since his death, and she will not have any dealings with me, although I have been helpful to her in many matters, but you can put no confidence there. Whoever opposes her, and does not agree with her in everything, of him she is suspicious, and so I like her better away from me than about me. She and her sister are not indeed loose, but, doubtless, honourable and most God-fearing women; still one would prefer a loose woman, who bore herself friendly, to such a gnawing, suspicious, and scolding pious one, with whom no rest can be had day or night.

[W. M. Conway, *Literary Remains of Albrecht Dürer*, 1889] This apparently authentic letter, written by Willibald Pirckheimer (Dürer's closest friend) soon after the artist's death, was responsible for the persistent rumour that Dürer's wife was a shrew.

Dürer, Giovanni Bellini (c. 1430–1516) and Mantegna (1431–1506)

I cannot forbear to tell, in this place, the story of what happened between him and Giovanni Bellini. Bellini had the highest reputation as a painter at Venice and indeed throughout all Italy. When Albrecht was there he easily became intimate with him, and both artists naturally began to show one another specimens of their skill. Albrecht frankly admired and made much of all Bellini's works. Bellini also candidly expressed his admiration of various features of Albrecht's skill and particularly the fineness and delicacy with which he drew hairs. It chanced one day that they were talking about art, and when their conversation was done Bellini said: 'Will you be so kind, Albrecht, as to gratify a friend in a small matter?' 'You shall soon see,' says Albrecht, 'if you will ask of me anything I can do for you.' Then says Bellini: 'I want you to make me a present of one of the brushes with which you draw hairs.' Dürer at once produced several, just like other brushes, and, in fact, of the kind Bellini himself used, and told him to choose those he liked best, or to take them all if he would. But Bellini, thinking he was misunderstood, said: 'No, I don't mean these but the ones with which you draw several hairs with one stroke; they must be rather spread out and more divided, otherwise in a long sweep such regularity of curvature and distance could not be preserved.' 'I use no other than these,' says Albrecht, 'and to prove it, you may watch me.' Then, taking up one of the same brushes, he drew some very long wavy tresses, such as women generally wear, in the most regular order and symmetry. Bellini looked on wondering, and afterwards confessed to many that no human being could have convinced him by report of the truth of that which he had seen with his own eyes.

A similar tribute was given him, with conspicuous candour, by Andrea Mantegna, who became famous at Mantua by reducing painting to some severity of law – a fame which he was the first to merit, by digging up broken and scattered statues, and setting them up as examples of art. It is true all his work is hard and stiff, inasmuch as his hand was not trained to follow the perception and nimbleness of his mind; still it is held that there is nothing better or more perfect in art. While Andrea was lying ill at Mantua he heard that Albrecht was in Italy and had him summoned to his side at once, in order that he might fortify his (Albrecht's) facility and certainty of hand with scientific knowledge and principles. For Andrea often lamented in conversation with his friends that Albrecht's facility in drawing had not been granted to him nor his learning to Albrecht. On receiving the message Albrecht, leaving all other engagements, prepared for the journey without delay. But before he could reach Mantua Andrea was dead, and Dürer used to say that this was the saddest event in all his life; for high as Albrecht stood, his great and lofty mind was ever striving after something yet above him.

Almost with awe have we gazed upon the bearded face of the man, drawn by himself, in the manner we have described, with the brush on the canvas and without any previous sketch. The locks of the beard are almost a cubit long, and so exquisitely and cleverly drawn, at such regular distances and in so exact a manner that the better anyone understands art the more he would admire it and the more certain would he deem it that in fashioning these locks the hand had employed artificial aid.

[Joachim Cammermeister, preface to the Latin translation of Dürer's *Four Books of Human Proportion*, in W. M. Conway, *Literary Remains of Albrecht Dürer*, 1887]

Dürer and the Reformer Melanchthon (1497–1560)

Melanchthon was often, and for many hours together, in Pirkheimer's company, at the time when they were advising together about the churches and schools at Nürnberg; and Dürer, the painter, used also to be invited to dinner with them. Dürer was a man of great shrewdness, and Melanchthon used to say of him that, though he excelled in the art of painting, it was the least of his accomplishments. Disputes often arose between Pirkheimer and Dürer on these occasions about the matters recently discussed, and Pirkheimer used vehemently to oppose Dürer. Dürer was an excessively subtle disputant and refuted his adversary's arguments, just as if he had come fully prepared for the discussion. Thereupon Pirkheimer, who was rather a choleric man and liable to very severe attacks of the gout, fired up and burst forth again and again into such words as these, 'What you say cannot be painted,' 'Nay!' rejoined Dürer, 'but what you advance cannot be put into words or even figured to the mind.' I remember hearing Melanchthon often tell this story, and in relating it he confessed his astonishment at the ingenuity and power manifested by a painter in arguing with a man of Pirkheimer's renown.

[W. M. Conway, *Literary Remains of Albrecht Dürer*, 1889]

Dürer and the Treasures of the New World

I saw the things which have been brought to the King from the new land of gold (Mexico), a sun all of gold a whole fathom broad, and a moon all of silver of the same size, also two rooms full of armour of the people there, and all manner of wondrous weapons of theirs, harness and darts, very strange clothing, beds, and all kinds of wonderful objects of human use, much better worth seeing than prodigies. These things were all so precious that they are valued at 100,000 florins. All the days of my life I have seen nothing that rejoiced my heart so much as these things, for I saw amongst them wonderful works of art, and I marvelled at the subtle *Ingenia* of men in foreign lands. Indeed I can not express all that I thought there.

[W. M. Conway, *Literary Remains of Albrecht Dürer*, 1889] From Dürer's diary of his visit to the Netherlands (Brussels, 26 August–3 September 1520).

Lucas van Leyden (1494–1533) Falls Ill

Lucas made a tour to Zealand and Brabant, to visit the Painters of those provinces; which journey not only cost him a great deal of money, but his life also, for it is said a Flushinger, of his profession, out of jealousy of his merit, poisoned him at an entertainment to which he had invited him. He lived in a languishing condition six years after, during which time he almost always kept his bed. What troubled him most was, that he could not work at ease; however, he had such a love to his art, that, ill as he was, he could not forbear working a-bed; and being told, that his application to it in the condition he was in would hasten his end, he replied, 'Be it so; I will have my bed to be a bed of honour, and cannot die in a better posture than with my pencil in my hand.'

[R. de Piles, *Abrégé de la vie des peintres*, 1699, trans. 1750]

Holbein (c. 1497–1543) Leaves Basel

The Earl of Arundel, returning from Italy through Basil, saw his works, was charmed with them, and advised him to go into England. At first Holbein neglected this advice: but in 1526, his family and the froward temper of his wife increasing, and his business declining, he determined upon that journey.

At first he said he should quit Basil but for a time, and only to raise the value of his works, which were growing too numerous there; yet before he went he intimated that he should leave a specimen of the power of his abilities. He had still at his house a portrait that he had just finished for one of his patrons – on the forehead he painted a fly, and sent the picture to the person for whom it was designed. The gentleman, struck with the beauty of the piece, went eagerly to brush off the fly – and found the deceit. The story soon spread, and as such trifling deceptions often do, made more impression than greater excellences.

[H. Walpole, *Anecdotes of Painting in England*, 1780] Walpole correctly notes: 'This anecdote is told of many painters.'

Holbein and Erasmus (1485–1536)

When Erasmus wrote his Moriæ Encomium,[1] he sent a copy of it to Hans Holbein, who reading it was so pleased with the several descriptions of folly, that he designed all of them in the margin, but having not room to draw the whole figures, he pasted a piece of paper

1. *In Praise of Folly*, 1509. The Latin title is a pun on the surname of the dedicatee, Sir Thomas More, Holbein's first English patron.

to the leaves where he could not do it; and when he had done so, he sent the book to Erasmus for a present. Erasmus seeing he had drawn the picture of a fat Dutch lover hugging his lass and his bottle, for the representation of an amorous fool, wrote under it, Hans Holbein, and so returned the book to the Painter; who, to be revenged of him, drew the picture of Erasmus for a musty groper, that busied himself in scraping up old manuscripts and antiquities, and wrote under it Adagia.[1]

[R. de Piles, *Abrégé de la vie des peintres*, 1699, trans. 1750]

Jan Gossaert, called Mabuse (fl. c. 1503, d. 1532) and the Damask Costume

Mabuse was for a few years in the service of the Marquis van der Voren. This nobleman, about to receive a visit from Charles v, dressed all the members of his court in white silk damask. Mabuse had frequently to think about means of obtaining money for rather low pleasures. He sold the damask which had been given him for the making of a special costume, and spent the money thus received. What should he do? The time for the festive reception was approaching. He took a piece of beautiful, white paper, had a well-cut gown made of it, and decorated it with fine damask flowers and embroidered ornaments.

The Marquis also had at his court, besides the painter, a poet and a philosopher. He wanted them to pass in turn before a window of the palace, from which the Emperor could have a good view of them. When they passed in front of the window, the Marquis asked the Emperor which of them had the most beautiful damask costume. The eyes of the Emperor were mostly attracted by the costume of the painter, which was the whitest of all, and showed the most beautiful flowers. It surpassed all the other costumes in its effect. The Marquis, for he knew everything, ordered Mabuse to serve at the table. He was asked to come near, and the Emperor, touching the material, discovered the paper.

When the Emperor was told about the trick which had been played, he was highly amused and laughed a great deal. The Marquis,

1. Erasmus had published a book called *Adagia* (*Proverbs*) in 1500.

however, wished for all the amount of damask, that the painter had not played such a trick to amuse the Emperor.

[Carel van Mander, *Het schilderboek*, 1618] This is a favourite art anecdote, often repeated by later writers. Some accounts say Mabuse was imprisoned.

The Madness of Joos van Cleve (fl. c. 1511, d. 1540/1)

[Joos van Cleve] became mentally disturbed . . . he varnished his clothing, cape and bonnet with turpentine varnish, and in this glittering costume went out into the street. He painted the backs of his panels too, because, he said, even if they were placed backwards, people would still see something of his hand. Whenever he got hold of paintings he had done before, he would destroy them, pretending he was going to improve them.

[Carel van Mander, *Het schilderboek*, 1618]

The Anxieties of Marten van Heemskerk (1498–1574)

He was by nature thrifty and niggardly. He was faint-hearted and so easily frightened that, when the militia had a parade, he climbed into the upper part of the tower; so afraid was he of their shooting, he did not feel safe otherwise. Marten always had a fear that he might come to poverty in his old age, and for this reason he always carried gold crowns hidden in his clothing, till his death.

[Carel van Mander, *Het schilderboek*, 1618]

Two Sides of Pieter Brueghel the Elder (fl. c. 1551, d. 1568)

Brueghel was a quiet and able man who did not talk much, but was jovial in company, and he loved to frighten people, often his own pupils, with all kinds of ghostly tricks and pranks that he played.

[Carel van Mander, *Het schilderboek*, 1618]

William Key (c. 1515/20–68) and the Duke of Alva

William Kay, a Flemish painter, gained such reputation for portrait painting, that the Duke of Alva sat to him; but whilst he worked on the

[101]

picture, the Judge Criminal and other officers waited on the duke, to know his determinate orders in regard to the Counts Egmont and Hoorn.[1] The duke, with a terrible austerity of countenance, ordered their immediate execution. Kay was so violently affected by the piercing look and peremptory command of Alva, that he went home, fell sick, and died through the terror impressed on his mind by this transaction.

[*The Percy Anecdotes*, 1821–3]

Anthonis Mor (also Called Antonio Moro; c. 1517/21–76/7) and the King of Spain

Moro became so free in his ways with the King [Philip II of Spain] that, on a certain occasion when the King slapped him on the shoulder, the artist playfully touched the King with his mahlstick. This was a very serious action, for it was a very dangerous offence indeed to touch a Lion. This familiarity would have been most harmful to Moro, if he had not been warned by a Spanish nobleman moved by friendship and real love for the artist. The fact was that the members of the Inquisition were quite jealous of the artist. They were afraid that the artist was influencing the King regarding the policy to be followed in the Netherlands. Moro ran the risk of imprisonment. On a pretext, he went back to the Netherlands, receiving a formal leave of absence and promising to return.

[Carel van Mander, *Het schilderboek*, 1618]

Frans Floris (c. 1518–70) on Pleasure and Work

He was a man who always had a strong desire to paint. Even when he came home half or entirely drunk, he would pick up his brushes and produce a great amount of work. He seemed to catch the spirit of art under these conditions, and to take greater delight in his work in this way. He used to say: 'When I work, I am living; when I indulge in pleasure, I am dying.'

[Carel van Mander, *Het schilderboek*, 1618]

---

1. These Flemish noblemen were arrested and executed by the Duke of Alva in 1568 because of their support for religious and political liberty in the Netherlands.

Lucas de Heere (1534–84)[1] and English Fashions

Lucas, a painter in the reign of Queen Elizabeth, was employed to paint a gallery for the Earl of Lincoln, Lord High Admiral. He was to represent the habits of different nations. When he came to the English, he painted a naked man with cloth of various sorts lying by him, and a pair of shears, as a satire on their fickleness of dress. The thought was borrowed from Andrew Borde, who in his Introduction to Knowledge, prefixed a naked Englishman, with these lines:

> I am an Englishman, and naked; I stand here
> Musing in my mind what rayment I shall wear.

[*The Percy Anecdotes*, 1821–3]

The Experimental Methods of Cornelis Ketel (1548–1616)

In 1599, he conceived the idea of painting without brushes, using only his hand. Many persons think this is a ridiculous notion and not in accordance with good taste – as the cravings of pregnant women for strange food. To speak, and with some reserve, about the subject, one is surprised that he succeeded so well, and that his experiment did not bear ill-formed fruit.

. . .

Stranger yet is the fact that, in 1600, Ketel got the idea of painting only with his feet. He wanted to find out what he could do by painting this way. This method made many persons laugh; their scorn was more than before, because feet are less able than hands for such work. But they were wrong. No one could be harmed by this experiment, except the brushmaker.

. . .

When Ketel painted these subjects, he was always careful not to touch any tool and to use only one leg and foot, as he had planned to do; this can be ascertained by the testimony of many persons.

[Carel van Mander, *Het schilderboek*, 1618]

---

1. A Netherlandish painter, who worked extensively in England.

Gillis Mostaert (fl. c. 1554, d. 1560) and a Difficult Customer

Gillis painted a picture of the *Virgin Mary* for a Spaniard who did not want to pay him. Whereupon, Gillis covered the painting with a size of white and glue, and arranged the drapery of the Madonna in such a way that she looked as alluring and seductive as a courtesan. He then invited the Spaniard to his studio; he made things look as if he was not at home. The Spaniard turned the picture round; he recognized it readily by the back, as he had marked it. When he saw the new type of Mary picture, he became very angry, and went to the Margrave. This happened in the time of Archduke Ernest of Austria. Meanwhile Gillis washed over the over-painting and, when it had dried well, placed the picture on the easel. The Margrave came to Gillis and said: 'What do I hear, Gillis? I am sorry that you seem to have involved yourself in trouble. Whatever made you do such a thing?' Gillis invited him to look at the picture which looked all right. The Spaniard did not know what to say. Then Gillis made his complaint. He stated that the Spaniard would not recompense him for his work, and that, apparently, he had tried to cause him all kinds of trouble, so, in the end, he might get the piece for nothing.

[Carel van Mander, *Het schilderboek*, 1618] Van Mander also relates that Mostaert painted a *Last Judgement* in which he showed himself and one of his acquaintances playing backgammon in Hell.

Hendrick Goltzius (1558–1617) on Self-criticism

When Goltzius heard painters praising their own works and indulging in their own achievements, he said they were happy, and rich, because he who is satisfied with himself is rich. 'As for myself,' he said, 'I have never been able to get that sensation from my work.'

I have heard him say, many times, that he had never done a thing entirely to his satisfaction, or which even pleased him well. He always thought of possible improvements that he could make. This is a good sentiment: the artist who feels this way should not stray from his path, as do the Pygmalions who fall in love with their own products, and who are less than they realize.

[Carel van Mander, *Het schilderboek*, 1618]

Goltzius and the German Nobleman

Once Goltzius was invited out by some young German noblemen, one of whom wanted to have his portrait painted on a panel, and then, later, engraved. They urged Goltzius to drink, and soon they had many glasses in front of him. Goltzius asked them why they had invited him to come. They answered: 'To make a drawing.' 'Why, then, gentlemen,' he said, 'why do you ask me to drink so much? You realize I am not a beast. But suppose I did! What good would that do? How could I serve you properly?' At this, they were ashamed of themselves.

[Carel van Mander, *Het schilderboek*, 1618]

Goltzius and the Supposed Print by Dürer

He then played a funny trick with the print of the *Circumcision*, which he had done in the style of Albrecht Dürer and in which his own portrait appeared. Goltzius had the portrait and his monogram burned out with a hot coal or iron, and then had the print smoked and treated, so that it looked as if it was ancient, and had existed many years. His print, disguised in this way, was shown in Rome, Venice, Amsterdam and elsewhere. The artists and connoisseurs were amazed and pleased by it. It was sold and re-sold for high prices. The buyers were delighted to obtain a work by the great artist of Nuremberg, particularly an engraving that had been completely hidden and unknown. It was ridiculous, that the master was so much exalted. When the question was raised, as to whether or not Goltzius could have made the engraving, some critics said he was far from able, and he could not make such an engraving in a whole lifetime; and this was the best print by Dürer they had ever seen. Others said Albrecht Dürer had made a special engraving which he requested be hidden for a hundred years after his death, and then, if his work should be appreciated, the engraving should be printed; this engraving, in question, was the one.

[Carel van Mander, *Het schilderboek*, 1618] The early seventeenth century saw a strong revival of Dürer's reputation, and many imitations were made of his work.

Goltzius in Italy

Towards the end of April that same year Goltzius [travelling incognito] went from Rome to Naples with an amiable companion, Jan Mathisjen Silversmit, and a learned young nobleman, Philips van Winghen, from Brussels. The three had donned shabby looking clothing, as there was the danger of meeting outcast vagabonds in numbers that made travelling unsafe. Van Winghen, an archaeologist, described everything he saw and made notes. He was a good friend of the famous geographer, Abraham Ortelius, of Antwerp. Van Winghen showed to Goltzius many letters he had received from Ortelius saying Goltzius was in Italy. In these there was the mention of some scars on his face and of the crippled right hand. It was odd that Van Winghen was so eager to see the man who was daily before his eyes, and with whom he had enjoyed friendly relations for a number of months.

Finally it was clear to Jan Mathisjen, and he said: 'This must be Goltzius.' Forgetting about himself and, seeing Goltzius's shabby clothing, although the three looked equally shabby, Van Winghen said: 'No, Hendrik, you are not the one. I mean that engraver from Holland'. Goltzius laughed, as Van Winghen judged the man by his clothing. Goltzius asked: 'Would it not be funny, Sr. Van Winghen, if Goltzius were talking with you?' – 'No, you are not Goltzius,' replied the other again. At night, when they arrived at Velletri, they spoke again on the same subject. Van Winghen relied entirely upon his letters. Jan Mathisjen asked: 'Why do you rave so much about your letters? This *is* Goltzius.' Van Winghen became angry and refused to believe it. When Goltzius himself confirmed it, on the road, Van Winghen said: 'By God, I can't believe it'.

When they came to Terracina, the debate started again. Goltzius knew then that Van Winghen could not believe the truth, and since the man had been a good honest companion, he thought he could not leave him in the dark any longer. Goltzius extended his crippled right hand, and showed him at the same time his handkerchief marked with the same monogram he had on all his prints – an interlaced H and G. Van Winghen became silent and white in the face. He embraced Goltzius most kindly and warmly, and regretted he had not recognized him sooner.

[Carel van Mander, *Het schilderboek*, 1618]

VIII
CARAVAGGIO AND ANNIBALE
CARRACCI

৯৶

Caravaggio's fame is currently much greater than that of Annibale
Carracci. In many respects, however, they are the two sides of the
same coin, and between them they accomplished a revolution in
Italian painting.

   Both had roots in the naturalism which had long flourished in north
Italy, particularly in Lombardy. Caravaggio was influenced by Giorgione, Annibale by Correggio. Both men were outsiders, in terms of
the main Florentine–Roman tradition, which stemmed from Michelangelo and Raphael.

   After a certain point, their paths diverged. Caravaggio, though
much imitated, was not by temperament a teacher, and he was always
scornful of classical art. Carracci began to marry naturalism and
classicism, and was able to turn this marriage into a system which
could be passed on to the pupils who flocked around him.

   Anecdotes about Caravaggio show contemporaries struggling to
understand his personality, and failing. Those about Carracci are far
more sympathetic. His pithy sayings became the cherished currency of
Roman and Bolognese studios. He nevertheless revealed, towards the
end of his life, a temperamental instability which expressed itself in
melancholy withdrawal, rather than in the outbursts of violence which
marked the brief career of Caravaggio.

The Arrival of Caravaggio (1571–1609/10) in Rome

When he was about twenty, he moved to Rome, where, since he was penniless, he lived with Pandolfo Pucci from Recanati, who had a benefice at St Peter's, because there he was able to work for his room without working at anything unpleasant. However he was given nothing but salad to eat in the evening – it served as appetiser, main course and dessert. It was, as the corporal says, both accompaniment and toothpick. After a few months he left with little to show for it, calling his benefactor and master 'Monsignor Salad'.

[Giulio Mancini, *Considerazioni sulla pittura*, c. 1614–21]

Caravaggio's 'Fortune Teller'

He paid no attention to the superb marbles of ancient artists or to the famous paintings of Raphael, but despised them – nature alone became the object of his brush. When people pointed at the most celebrated statues of Phidias and Glycon[1] as models for his painting, his only reply was to point at a crowd of men, to show that nature had given him enough teachers. To prove his contention he summoned a gypsy who was passing in the street and, taking her to his lodging, showed her telling fortunes, as is the custom with these Egyptians. In this painting he also showed a youth with one gloved hand upon his sword and the other bare, held out to the woman who holds it and examines it. With these two half length figures he caught reality so well that he did indeed confirm what he had said.

[G. P. Bellori, *Vite de' pittori, scultori e architetti moderni*, 1672]

Caravaggio's 'Amore Vincitore'

For one of his patrons, Marchese Giustiniani, he painted a lifesize *Cupid* – the model was a boy of about twelve years old, seated on the globe and holding his bow above his head in his right hand. To the left were instruments of the arts of all varieties, together with books for study, and a laurel wreath lying on the books. The figure of Cupid has

---

1. The *Farnese Hercules*, then still in Rome, is signed by the Greek artist Glycon, though it is in fact of Roman date.

large brown eagle's wings, and it is drawn with such correctness, such powerful colour, cleanness of form and plasticity that it is little inferior to life itself. The picture was exhibited in a room where there were also one hundred and twenty other works by leading artists. However, it was, on my advice, covered with a curtain of dark green silk, and was only uncovered when all the other paintings had been thoroughly examined, since it would otherwise have made the other curiosities seem insignificant. This painting may, with excellent reason, be called 'the eclipse of all paintings'. A Cavalier of high rank liked it so much that he offered a thousand pistoles for it in the presence of us all. However, when I told our patron (who had an income of ninety thousand crowns annually, much of which he spent on art), and requested a reply – at the time he was suffering from gout – he smiled and said: 'Tell the noble Cavalier that, if he can find another picture with the same qualities, I will pay him double for it – that is, two thousand pistoles.'

[Joachim von Sandrart, *Teutsche Akademie*, 1675–9]

Caravaggio Criticized by Federico Zuccaro

The lifelike qualities of Caravaggio's works at San Luigi [dei Francesi] increased his reputation, all the more so because these paintings were seen side by side with those of d'Arpino,[1] whose talent was enviously acknowledged by his colleagues. Spiteful people therefore gave Caravaggio exaggerated praise. However, when Federico Zuccaro came to look, he said, whilst I was present: 'What's all the fuss about?' and added, as he carefully scrutinized the entire work: 'All I see here, in the picture of the saint called to the Apostolate by Christ,[2] is the ideas of Giorgione.' Then, smiling, and marvelling at the excitement, he shrugged his shoulders and left.

[G. Mancini, *Considerazioni sulla pittura*, c. 1614–21] The incident represents the complaints of the Mannerist Old Guard against the new naturalism and stresses Caravaggio's links to Venetian art.

1. Giuseppe Cesari, il Cavaliere d'Arpino (1568–1640), immensely prolific and successful late mannerist artist who was the standard bearer for the conservative faction in Rome.
2. *The Calling of St Matthew*, one of Caravaggio's paintings in the Contarelli Chapel, S. Luigi dei Francesi.

Caravaggio's Appearance and Temperament

Caravaggio's method of work corresponded to his features and appearance. He had a dark complexion, and dark eyes, black hair and eyebrows – this, of course, was reflected in his paintings. His early style, with its sweet and pure hues, was the best. Using this manner he achieved great things and proved himself to be an excellent Lombard colourist. Later, driven by his strange temperament, he gave himself up to the dark manner which expressed his turbulent and quarrelsome nature. Because of his temperament he was forced to leave Milan, and his native region, and later to flee from Rome and then from Malta, and go into hiding in Sicily, and live under threat in Naples, and to die at the last in misery on a deserted shore. Something must also be said about his dress and manners. He liked to dress in velvet and other fine stuffs, but, once he had put on an outfit, never changed it until it had fallen into rags. He was very neglectful of personal cleanliness, and for many years, morning and evening, used the canvas of a portrait as a tablecloth.

[G. P. Bellori, *Vite*, 1672]

Caravaggio's Opinions and Behaviour while in Rome

He thinks that all paintings are mere nothings, child's play or trifles, whatever their subject-matter or authorship, unless they have been painted from the life, and that nothing can be good and nothing better than to follow nature. Therefore he will not make a single brushstroke without close study from the life, which he copies in paint. And this surely is no bad way in which to reach a good result. Painting from drawings, even if these have been done from life, is not as reliable as confronting life itself and following Nature with all her different hues. Yet [in order to do this] one must first have achieved a degree of insight that will enable one to choose, and to distinguish amid the beauty of life what is most beautiful. However, the grain is accompanied by the chaff – that is, having worked for a fortnight he will then swagger about for a couple of months with his sword at his side and his servant following after, going from one ball game to the next,[1] always ready

1. Caravaggio was forced to flee Rome after killing a companion in a quarrel over a game of *palla a corda*, a game which was a primitive ancestor of tennis.

to get involved in a fight or argument, so that he is very hard to get along with. And all this is not compatible with our Art. Mars and Minerva have certainly never been best friends.

[Carel van Mander, *Het schilderboek*, 1618]

Caravaggio in Messina

Since Caravaggio garnered much fame, he [also] gained much money, which he squandered in escapades and revels. Once, when he was going into the church of the Madonna del Pilero in the company of some gentlemen, one of these, a most cultivated man, stepped forward to offer him some holy water. Caravaggio asked him why, and the man answered that it would wipe out any venial sin. 'It is not necessary,' Caravaggio said, 'for all my sins are mortal.'

[F. Susinno, *Le Vite de' pittori messinesi*, 1724]

Caravaggio Leaves his Mark

He went about with a black dog which was taught to do various tricks – something Caravaggio enjoyed hugely. On holidays he used to disappear, so as to follow a grammar school master named Don Carlo Pepe, who took his pupils to play at the arsenal. Galleys used to be built there, but now it is the warehouse of Portofranco. Michele went there to watch the attitudes of the boys at play, and to form his ideas. The teacher became suspicious, and wanted to know why he was always hanging around. The question so much disturbed the painter, and he became so angry that (so as not to forfeit his reputation for being a madman) he wounded the poor man in the head. Because of this, he had to leave Messina. In a word, wherever he went he would leave the mark of his madness.

[F. Susinno, *Le Vite de' pittori messinesi*, 1724]

Caravaggio's 'Raising of Lazarus' in Messina

When Caravaggio finally finished the great canvas showing the *Raising of Lazarus*, this was much anticipated by those responsible for the commission, since it had been kept secret while Caravaggio was at work. People were astonished when it was unveiled. Since all of us pride ourselves on our artistic judgement and our ability to discuss art, there were among the patrons some who had brief comments to make, not meaning to criticize Caravaggio, but wanting to seem informed. Michelangelo [i.e. Caravaggio], with his usual impetuosity, drew his dagger, which he always carried at his side, and aimed many furious blows at this admirable painting, so that it was miserably slashed. Then, having vented his anger on the innocent work, and with his spirit now apparently calmed, Caravaggio reassured these gentlemen, and told them not to worry, since he would very quickly paint a picture for them which would satisfy their taste and be still finer.

[F. Susinno, *Le Vite de' pittori messinesi*, 1724]

The 'Raising of Lazarus': Caravaggio Encourages his Assistants

Michele gave the faces of [Lazarus's] sisters wonderfully beautiful expressions; then, in order to impart a realistic air to the central figure of Lazarus, asked them to dig up a corpse already in a state of decomposition, and had it put into the arms of the workmen who, however, were hardly able to stand the smell, and wanted to abandon their work. Caravaggio, with his usual fury, raised his dagger and jumped on them, and these unlucky fellows were therefore forced to go on with the job, and nearly die, just like those miserable creatures whom the impious Maxentius[1] condemned to die tied to corpses. Similarly Caravaggio's picturesque room could be likened to the slaughterhouse of the same tyrant.

[F. Susinno, *Le Vite de' pittori messinesi*, 1724]

Annibale Carracci (1560–1609) before he Arrived in Rome

Annibale, who never wandered from his profession, to inform himself of all things necessary to it, went through Lombardy to Venice. He could not contain his raptures at the sight of Corregio's works in Parma. He wrote to Lodovico,[2] and prayed him to excite his brother Augustino[3] to come and see the wonders he had seen at Parma, saying, 'He could never find out a better school; that neither Tibaldi,

---

1. Maxentius, Roman Emperor, 306–312, persecutor of Christians. Defeated by Constantine at the Milvian Bridge.
2. Lodovico Carracci (1555–1619), Annibale's cousin.
3. Agostino Carracci (1557–1602), Annibale's brother.

Gicolini, nor even Raphael in his St Cecilia, had done any thing comparable to the extraordinary things he saw in Corregio's pictures; that all was great and graceful; that Augustino and he should with pleasure study those beautiful pieces, and live lovingly together.

[R. de Piles, *Abrégé de la vie des peintres*, 1699, trans. 1750]

Annibale Carracci and his Brother Agostino

When he came to Rome Annibale was overcome by the great knowledge which the ancients had possessed, and devoted himself to contemplation and the silent solitude of art. His brother Agostino, who arrived later, to help in the [Farnese] Gallery, was talking to several companions and was praising the ancients' great knowledge of sculpture. He praised the Laocoön at length, and, seeing that his brother remained silent, and seemed to pay little attention to what he was saying, took umbrage and scolded him as if he possessed no appreciation of such a wonderful sculpture. He then went on talking, and the bystanders continued to listen. Annibale turned and, with a piece of charcoal, drew the sculpture on the wall, exactly as if he had it in front of him ready to be copied. The others were full of admiration for what he had done, and Agostino stopped talking, admitting that his brother had demonstrated the point better than he. As Annibale left, he laughed and turned to his brother saying: 'Poets paint with words; painters speak with works.' This remark wounded Agostino in more ways than one, since he wrote verses and liked to be called a poet.

[G. P. Bellori, *Vite*, 1672]

Annibale and Agostino Carracci:
Family Differences

[Annibale] was never avaricious or mean about money. In fact, he valued money too little, and kept it quite openly in his box of paints, so that anyone could dip his hand in when he wanted. As is so often the case with artists, what kept pecuniary preoccupations at bay was his constant application to his art, and when he relaxed it was without thinking of family matters. Disregarding money, he also despised ostentation in people as well as in painting, seeking the company of plain men without ambition. He fled the pride of courtiers and of the court. Being there against his will, he did not understand that people accustomed to judge by appearances did not esteem him. He used to live shut up in his lodgings with his pupils, spending hours at his painting, which he was accustomed to describe as his mistress. Agostino's predilections did not please him – the latter was much impressed with the showiness of the courtiers, and Annibale would disdainfully see him with these people in the halls. Similarly, though Annibale dressed respectably and kept himself clean, he paid little attention to matters such as his beard and his collar, since he spent most of his time thinking about art. Sometimes, tired out by his work, he would go outdoors later just as he was in order to get some air, and be ashamed to meet his brother in the palace or in the piazzi in the company of some fine gentlemen. Thus, on one occasion, when he was going up from the gallery to his own rooms, dishevelled from work, he encountered his brother, walking (to Annibale's scorn) with several cavaliers. He drew him aside as if he had important things to discuss, and murmured in his ear: 'Agostino, remember, you are a tailor's son.' Later, in his lodgings, he took some paper and made a drawing of his father, wearing eyeglasses and threading a needle, and over this wrote his father's Christian name, Antonio, then next to the portrait drew his old mother, with her scissors in her hand. Having completed the drawing he sent it to his brother, who was so much troubled by it that this, with other causes, was the reason why he soon separated himself from Annibale and left Rome.

[G. P. Bellori, *Vite*, 1672]

Annibale Carracci and Cardinal Farnese

The Cardinal wanted to reward Annibale for creating so many works during the time he had been in Rome – a period of eight years. Yet, while Annibale hoped to taste the fruit of that prince's generosity, fortune opposed this, through the evil influence of a courtier, Don Juan de Castro, the Cardinal's favourite, a Spaniard who played a part in all his patron's doings. Don Juan added up a bill for all the food, wine and provisions provided for Annibale during the whole time he had spent in the palace, and put it to Annibale's debt, persuading the Cardinal to give him only five hundred gold scudi. The money was brought in a saucer to Annibale in his room. He was struck dumb, and could not react. What he felt showed clearly in his face: it was not a question of the money, which he did not value, but the realization that he had wearied himself without hope of respite, still to be in want of the necessities of life; and that he had been the butt of the wickedness of powerful men.

[G. P. Bellori, *Vite*, 1672] This story refers to Annibale's celebrated frescos in the Farnese Gallery.

Annibale Carracci and the Inn Sign

Among the beautiful paintings at Rome, none are more deservedly admired than those in the Farnesian Gallery. They were executed in Fresco by Annibal Caracci, and represent the amours of the gods and goddesses, with the history of Andromedes.

All the paintings are so surprisingly beautiful, that the best judges are of opinion, that no gallery in the universe can be compared to this. But merit is not always properly rewarded. Caracci experienced this; for when the gallery, which cost the labour of eight years, was finished, Pope Paul III. asked his favourite Gioseppino, otherwise Joseph d'Arpino, what it was worth? D'Arpino, who was himself a painter, and extremely jealous of Caracci's high reputation, told the Pope that two thousand crowns would do very well; though he knew, in conscience, that an hundred thousand would hardly be a sufficient equivalent. The silly Pontiff listened to his adviser; and Caracci hearing of this unjust transaction, was so enraged, that he vowed he would be revenged both of the Pope and his adviser. He set out immediately for Naples, and having no money, was obliged to travel on foot.

The first stage he stopped at was a wretched village, called Piperno, where the fatigues of his journey, and the vexations of his mind, threw him into a long and dangerous fit of sickness. To complete the poor artist's misfortunes, his landlord grew very insolent, taking every opportunity of teazing him for money. Caracci was long at a loss how to pacify his rude host; but at last thought of the following expedient, which, he apprehended, would at once satisfy the innkeeper, and his own resentment against the Pope. He had recourse to his pencil and colours, drew on a piece of a broken chest an ass of a monstrous size, magnificently accoutred, and decorated with the ignorant Pontiff's arms. The driver of this beast was proportionally large and tall, representing to the life of the envious Gioseppino.

This picture being finished, Caracci advised his landlord to set it up instead of the old sign post of his inn. This being done, the novelty of the painting drew the eyes of travellers, and occasioned a very considerable quantity of money to be spent in the house. Many of them being well acquainted with Gioseppino, soon guessed the true reason for his portrait being placed there, and unravelled the whole design of the emblem. This occasioned a great deal of mirth and laughter in Rome, at the expense of the Pope and his worthless favourite.

[*The Percy Anecdotes*, 1821–3]

Some Sayings of Annibale Carracci

To a stupid painter who showed him a large canvas which was to be prepared with white gesso and then painted, he said: 'It would be better if you painted it first and whitened it afterwards.'

Another artist of the same sort said, after detaining him a long time in order to show him drawings of work he wanted to carry out: 'If I have bothered you by showing so many of my efforts, Annibale, please forgive me.' To which Annibale answered: 'Indeed not – as I didn't see them.'

Cavaliere Giuseppe d'Arpino, hearing that Annibale had criticized something of his, wanted to fight a duel with him. Annibale seized a brush, and said: 'I challenge *you!*'

Walking through the city to San Pietro in Montorio, as he often did to look at Raphael's famous painting of the *Transfiguration*, he saw a young man at the bottom of the hall, drawing copies on the wall of some mediocre paintings by Giovanni Battista della Marca[1] and others. Annibale said: 'Don't stay down there young man, climb up the top of the mountain' – meaning, by this, the painting by Raphael. The simple boy said he first wanted to make his drawings smaller. 'Not at all, you need to be enlarged!' exclaimed Annibale.

When two paintings were made in competition by Sisto[2] and Domenichino,[3] Sisto boasted that had finished his in a few days, while Domenichino had dawdled over his for months. 'Shut up,' Annibale said. 'Domenichino worked quicker than you because he worked well.'

1. G. B. della Marca, called Lombardelli (working 1566–d. 1592).
2. Sisto Badalocchio (1581/5–1647).
3. Domenichino (1581–1641). Annibale's favourite pupil.

He used to talk intimately with Monsignor Giovanni Battista Agucchi about matters pertaining to art. One day the latter asked him what the difference was between Titian and Raphael. 'Titian painted delightfully and Raphael painted marvellously,' Annibale replied.

[G. P. Bellori, *Vite*, 1672]

Annibale Carracci and his Pupils

He instructed his pupils very lovingly, teaching them by example and demonstration rather than with words, and treated them with so much kindness that he often neglected his own work. Silently he would go from one to the other, and taking the brush from their hands would show them the rules by example, teaching all of them without fear or reserve. Generosity of this sort is the mark of an extremely fruitful genius, and it is evidence of Annibale's knowledge of art that so many and such excellent painters came from his school. Superabundant merit is more than sufficient for him who has it, and flows outward for the benefit of others. Only Raphael and his famous school had achieved such distinction previously. Michelangelo did not achieve this, being sterile rather than fruitful, while Titian was afraid of Tintoretto, and expelled him from his house – but these are matters which we will speak of elsewhere.

The casualness of Annibale's behaviour was also something that he liked to find in his pupils. When he saw a young man who had been recommended to him as a pupil, and who arrived all prinked and pranked out, he looked at him closely, but said nothing. When the boy asked for some drawings to copy, Annibale went to his room and made a drawing of him which was ridiculous but real,[1] and then said: 'Here is the drawing, learn to do well from this.' The young man was ashamed, and changed his ways.

[G. P. Bellori, *Vite*, 1672]

Bernini and Annibale Carracci

[Bernini] said that Annibale Carracci advised him, when he was young, to make drawings after the *Last Judgement* of Michelangelo for a period of at least two years, in order to understand the

---

1. Annibale Carracci is generally credited with being the inventor of caricature.

relationship between the muscles. Later, when he was drawing from life at the Academy, Scivoli [Cigoli][1] watched him and said; 'You're a thief; you are not drawing what you see – this is Michelangelo'.

[Paul Fréart de Chantelou, *Journal du voyage du Cav. Bernini en France*, 1885]

Carracci Teaches Drawing

[Bernini] also said that Annibale Carracci was accustomed to assert, when he went to draw at the academy of Signor Paolo Giordano, that the torso must be made large in proportion to the arm, just as tree-trunks are, in proportion to their branches.

A member of the academy drew a torso which was a finger's breadth too narrow on either side. When Carracci told him to make it broader, he did so merely by adding an additional couple of lines. He showed it to Annibale, who noted this, laughing, and using his characteristic mocking tone and Bolognese slang. Then Annibale sharpened his little stick of chalk, and drew a third contour between the two outlines, so as to make fun of the artist. Berni added that one of Annibale's maxims was that, when a particular concept fails to please, you have to change your theme, and go in an entirely different direction.

[Chantelou, *Journal du voyage du Cav. Bernini en France*, 1885]

Annibale Carracci's Bêtes Noires

I forgot to say that [Bernini] told us that Annibale Carracci, seeing something done in a tight and fiddling way, used to say in Bolognese dialect: 'It looks just like Pietro Perugino'. Seeing something which was done boldly and broadly, but which was badly proportioned, he used to say: 'It looks as if it's by Giorgione'.

[Chantelou, *Journal du voyage du Cav. Bernini en France*, 1885]

Annibale Carracci on Michelangelo

The Cavalière [Bernini] told how Annibale Carracci one day visited the church of S. Maria sopra Minerva in the company of several members of his school. One, a Florentine, very ready to praise a

1. Ludovico Cardi, Il Cigoli, (1559–1613), Florentine painter.

compatriot, said: 'Well now, Signor Annibale, what do you have to say about this statue of Christ?' – 'By God,' said Annibale, 'it's by Michelangelo. Have a good look at it, all of you. In order to understand it properly, you have to know how bodies used to be made in those days.' He was joking about the fact that Michelangelo had not followed nature.

[Chantelou, *Journal du voyage du Cav. Bernini en France*, 1885]

IX

THE ITALIAN BAROQUE

୬

The dominant artistic personality during the developed phase of the Baroque in Italy was undoubtedly the great sculptor and architect Gianlorenzo Bernini, and we are therefore lucky in being able to know him more intimately than any other Italian artist of the time, thanks very largely to the detailed diary of Bernini's visit to France in 1665 kept by Paul Fréart de Chantelou, a royal official who was also an enthusiastic collector of art – especially the paintings of his compatriot Nicolas Poussin.

The purpose of Bernini's visit was twofold – to make a portrait bust of Louis XIV, a task which he accomplished successfully, and to make designs for the completion of the Louvre. Bernini had already submitted preliminary drawings before he arrived in Paris. From the French frontier onwards he had been received with quasi-royal honours. Soon after his arrival in Paris, however, things started to go wrong. His relationships with French artists (very jealous of the attention paid to him) and with Louis XIV's civil servants were not happy. The king's chief minister Colbert, who was responsible for Bernini's invitation, soon became impatient with the sculptor's persistent criticism of everything French. An anti-Bernini cabal sprang up, and it became apparent that his architectural projects would never be carried out. Having arrived in June he left for Rome again in October, and never returned to France.

During the months of Bernini's visit Chantelou was in constant personal contact with him, and served as what would now be called a 'minder', doing his best to keep Bernini happy and productive on the one hand, and reporting on his activities to Colbert on the other. Luckily for posterity, there was real personal sympathy between Chantelou and Bernini. Chantelou's record quotes the Italian artist extensively on artistic matters, and offers anecdotes which give an intimate view of him – more intimate than is available for any other artist of his day.

The other seventeenth-century Italian artist about whose personality we know a good deal is Salvator Rosa. Rosa fancied himself as a universal man, and it is his widespread literary connections which have helped to ensure the preservation of stories about him. In the version offered by contemporaries of his life and sayings one seems to detect a further evolution of the cult of genius which had already sprung up around the personality of Michelangelo. Unlike Michelangelo, however, Salvator Rosa was self-conscious about his situation. He clearly aimed to do and say things which would bolster his claim to be someone who was wholly different from the common run of humanity.

The anecdotes collected about the successful followers of Annibale Carracci offer a less systematic vision of what the artist should be and do, but the quirks they record often seem more convincingly human than some of those described in connection with earlier artists.

Guido Reni (1575–1672) and Ideal Beauty

When Guido Reni who, as a painter, surpassed all other artists of our century, sent the picture of St Michael (done for the church of the Capuchins[1]) to Rome, he wrote to Monsignor Masani . . . 'I would like to have possessed an angel's brush and to have grasped the forms of Paradise itself in order to create the Archangel and see him in heaven. I was unable to aspire so high, and vainly looked for him on earth. Therefore I made reference to the Idea which I had set up within myself. You can also find the Idea of ugliness, but I leave it to the Devil to bring that out, since I flee from it even in thought and do not want to occupy my mind with it.' Guido thus boasted that he portrayed beauty not as he beheld it with his eyes, but as he beheld it in his mind.

[G. P. Bellori, *Vite de' pittori, scultori e architetti moderni*, 1672]

Guido Reni's Mania for Gambling

Guido returning to Bologna grew famous for the care he took in finishing his pieces: and perceiving that the persons of quality were eager to have them, he set a price upon them according to the number of figures in each picture, and every picture he valued at one hundred Roman crowns.

By these high prices Guido found himself, in a little while, very well at ease, and lived nobly, till an immoderate love of gaming seized him. He was unfortunate, and his losses reduced him to necessities that he could not go through. His friends used all imaginable arguments to dissuade him from play, but he would not give it over. He sent his pictures to be sold under-hand at a sorry rate, and took it for such as he had before refused large sums for. As soon as he had got the little money he had for them in his pocket, he immediately went to look out for his gamesters to have his revenge. At last, as one passion weakens another, his love of gaming lessened that of Painting so far, that he never thought of his reputation in what he did, but only to rid his work, and get subsistence-money.

[R. de Piles, *Abrégé de la vie des peintres*, 1699, trans. 1750]

1. Santa Maria della Concezione, Rome.

The Labours of Domenichino (1581–1641)

They were wont to call him the Ox, and said he laboured as if he was at the plow. But Annibale,[1] who knew his character better, told them, 'This ox, by dint of labour, would in time make his ground so fruitful, that Painting itself would be fed by what it produced;' a prophecy which proved very true, for there are many excellent things to be learned from Domenichino's pictures.

[R. de Piles, *Abrégé de la vie des peintres*, 1699, trans. 1750]

Domenichino's Character

He was a man of liberal and honest humour, sober in his way of living, modest and restrained in conversation. He lived a very retired life, thinking that he might thus avoid the malignity of the envious, who continued nonetheless to persecute him, although he did his utmost to avoid them. Though he could not help complaining about the ill spoken of him by other artists, he was nevertheless indifferent both in their praise and their condemnation. Since he was well aware of their evil intentions, when he heard that the painters of Naples decried what he had done in the Capella del Tesoro, instead of being upset, he responded with a sort of joy, saying that it was a proof that his work was good. One day he was told that certain painters had spoken well of some of his figures. 'I am much afraid,' he replied, 'that I have left uncorrected some strokes of the brush which are bad, and which please them.'

One of his friends tried to persuade him not to give such a high degree of finish to his work, and not to work with such precision, but to accommodate himself to the taste of others, rather than pleasing himself. 'I work for myself alone,' he said, 'and for the perfection of Art.' He was well aware that the whole merit of a work of art lies in the fact that it is equally finished in all its parts, and that the artist has taken all possible pains with it – has 'carried it as far as it will go', as the saying is. It was for this reason that he would never allow his young pupils to content themselves with making mere sketches when they were drawing, or to indicate things in painting with a few strokes of the brush instead of finishing them. He frequently told them that

1. Annibale Carracci. Domenichino was one of his most important pupils.

nothing should come from a painter's hand – no stroke of the brush and no line – which had not been fully formed in his spirit beforehand; and that they must always remember, when considering some object, that it was not enough to look at it once – they must give it prolonged attention, because it was the mind, not the eye, which was the best judge of how things should be. Before beginning work, or picking up a brush, he himself was accustomed, as I have already said, to meditate long about what he was going to do. Sometimes he meditated alone for the best part of the day about a particular subject; and when he had come to a conclusion within himself concerning the invention and disposition of the parts, he then seemed content, and rejoiced as if he had already completed the greater part of the work.

He could not understand how there could be painters who undertook ambitious projects, with so little application; and who, while they worked, continued to converse with their friends. He thought of them as workmen with no real experience or knowledge of Art. He was convinced that a painter, in order to succeed, must acquire a complete knowledge of the affections of the spirit and the passions of the soul; that he must feel them within himself and, so to speak, imitate the actions, and follow the movements, which he wished to represent – something which it was impossible to do in the midst of distractions. Thus he was sometimes heard talking to himself while he worked, either in a voice which was languishing and full of sorrow, or else agreeable and joyous, all according to the emotions he wanted to represent. In order to work thus, he withdrew to some solitary spot, so as not to be seen in these different emotional states, either by his pupils or by members of his family, since people who had seen him in this sort of state had sometimes suspected he was mad. Once, when he was young, and working on his *Martyrdom of Saint Anne* which is in S. Gregorio, Annibale Carracci came to see him, and caught him in an angry, menacing attitude. Having looked at him for a while, Annibale understood that he was making a representation of a soldier who was threatening the holy Apostle. Not being able to conceal himself any longer, he came up to Domenichino and embraced him, telling him that he had learned a great deal from him just at that moment.

[A. Félibien, *Entretiens sur les vies et sur les ouvrages des plus excellens peintres*, 1666–8]

How Guercino (1593–1666) was Named

He was nicknamed Guercino[1] of Cento, because his parents gave him to a nurse to bring up, and through the carelessness of this woman he was startled, while sleeping, by the sound of a loud voice, which woke him suddenly. As a result his eye turned round in such a way that the pupil remained for ever after stuck in the corner.

[C. C. Malvasia, *Felsina pittrice*, 1678]

Guercino is Invited to England by Charles I

For Signore Daniele Ricci he painted a *Semiramis*, which was exhibited in Bologna as a marvel of art. The painting was taken to England, to the King of that country. The King invited Guercino to his court, with very advantageous offers to pay any price asked for his paintings, to pay his expenses, and to give him an annual salary. But he did not wish to accept the opportunity, not desiring to converse with heretics, so as not to contaminate the goodness of his angelic habits, and also to avoid exposing himself to such a disastrous voyage, in a climate so remote from his own people.

[C. C. Malvasia, *Felsina pittrice*, 1678]

Bernini (1598–1680) on Portrait Sculpture

Talking about sculpture, and the difficulty he found in succeeding with it, especially his difficulties in getting a likeness in portrait busts made of marble, [Bernini] told me something remarkable (and repeated it frequently thereafter). It was this: if someone were to whiten their hair, beard, eyebrows, etc. – and even, if that were possible, they whitened the pupils of their eyes and also their lips – and if they presented themselves in this state to those who saw them daily, the latter would have difficulty in recognizing them. In proof of this, he added: 'When someone swoons, the pallor which spreads over his face – that alone – makes him almost unrecognizable. In those circumstances, people often say: "He no longer looks like himself!" For this reason – because it is all one colour – it is very difficult to get a likeness in a portrait bust made of marble.'

1. Guercino means 'the Squinter'.

He said something more extraordinary still – that sometimes, with a bust, it was necessary, in order to imitate life, to do something which is not like life. This seems paradoxical, but he explained his meaning thus. In order to represent the dark tone of the skin around the eyes (which occurs in some people), it is needful to hollow out the marble where the tone is, in order to get the colour, and to supply, by this artifice, something lacking in the art of sculpture, from which colour is absent. Realism, he said, is not the same thing as imitation.

He added another observation about sculpture, which I did not find as convincing as the preceding ones. 'A sculptor,' he said, 'wants to make a statue with one hand stretched out and the other placed on its breast. Experience tells him that the hand which is stretched out must be larger and fuller in form than the other. The reason is that the atmosphere surrounding the outstretched hand eats away part of it. That is, it reduces the fullness of the shape.'

[Chantelou, *Journal du voyage du Cav. Bernini en France*, 1885]

The Young Bernini Sculpts a Portrait

Jacopo Fois Montoja decided to adorn his tomb in the church of S. Jacopo degli Spagnuoli with his own likeness carved in marble; and gave the task to our young artist. The latter made a portrait so like life that everyone was astonished by it. When it was put in its place, many cardinals and other prelates went to see so fine a work. Amongst them was someone who said: 'This is Montoja, turned to stone'. He had no sooner said it, than Montoja himself appeared. Cardinal Maffeo Barberini, later Urban VIII, who was also there, turned to greet him and said, touching him: 'This is the portrait of Monsignor Montoja'. Then, turning to the bust: 'And this *is* Monsignor Montoja'.

[F. Baldinucci, *Notizie de' professori del disegno da Cimabue in qua*, 1681–6]

Bernini's Methods as a Painter

We spoke of different matters concerning expression – the thing which lies at the heart of painting. The Cavaliere said that, in order to try to succeed, he made use of a method he had discovered for himself. When he wanted to give expression to a figure, he took up the correct pose himself, and had himself drawn by a good draughtsman, performing the action he wanted to represent.

[Chantelou, *Journal*, 1885] See the rather similar anecdote about Domenichino (p. 124). Both stories emphasize the value Baroque artists placed on empathy with the subject.

Bernini on Women

Asked in the presence of many French ladies who were the more beautiful, the French or the Italians, he replied that all were very beautiful, but with this difference: that there was blood under the skin with the Italians, while with Frenchwomen there was milk.

[F. Baldinucci, *Vita del Cavaliere Gio. Lorenzo Bernino*, 1681, from the 1846 edition of the *Notizie*]

Bernini's Lucky Star

To [M. de Menars, Colbert's brother] he modestly said that he owed his entire reputation to his lucky star, which saw to it that he was esteemed in his own lifetime. When he died, however, this occult influence would no longer operate, and his reputation would suddenly decline and fall.

[Chantelou, *Journal*, 1885]

Bernini's Advice on Self-appraisal

The Cavaliere said . . . that two things helped artists to judge their own work. One was not to see it for some time; the other, when time pressed, was to look at it through lenses which changed the colour, or made things larger or smaller, so that it was in some way disguised, and seemed to the artist like the work of someone else. In this way one could rid oneself of the illusions caused by self-conceit.

[Chantelou, *Journal*, 1885]

Bernini Draws Louis XIV at the King's Council

From time to time he said, when the king looked at him: 'Sto rubando [I'm a thief]'. On one occasion the king replied, also in Italian: 'Si ma e per restituire [only in order to give back].' He then replied to His

Majesty: 'Pero per restituir, meno del rubato [yes, it is to give back what I have stolen].'

[Chantelou, *Journal*, 1885]

Bernini's Bust of Louis XIV

The Cavaliere said that he had been working almost entirely from imagination, and that he had only very occasionally glanced at his sketches. What he had chiefly looked at was what was in here (indicating his forehead), where he found his idea of what His Majesty was. If he had done otherwise, he would only have made a copy instead of an original. In commissioning a portrait the king could not have given him anything more difficult to do. What caused him most trouble was to make this the least bad of all the portraits he had done. In this sort of work, one had to try, not only to achieve a likeness, but to put into the portrait what was going on within a hero's mind.

[Chantelou, *Journal*, 1885]

Aspects of Likeness: Bernini Responds to Criticism

Lefebvre,[1] having looked at [the bust] from all sides, cried out, saying that it was not a likeness even when seen from the back. The Cavaliere, having heard of this, said something worthy of remark – which was that if, in the evening, one took a candle and placed it behind someone, so that his shadow was cast on the wall, one would recognize him simply from that, since everyone's head and shoulders have a different shape from that of anyone else. So, too, for all the rest: the first thing a portraitist must look at was the general shape of the sitter, before beginning to think of details.

[Chantelou, *Journal*, 1885]

Bernini's Bust of Charles I

An anecdote is related of Charles, which it would be wrong to omit. The king wished to employ Bernini the sculptor, and tried in vain to allure him into England. Not succeeding in this, and still desirous to have one of his works, he employed Vandyke to draw those inimitable

1. Claude Lefebvre (1632–75), French painter.

profiles and full face in the royal gallery, to enable the sculptor to make his majesty's bust. Bernini surveyed these materials with an anxious eye, and exclaimed, 'Something evil will befal this man; he carries misfortune on his face.' Tradition has added, in the same spirit, that a hawk pursued a dove into the sculptor's study, and, rending its victim in the air, sprinkled with its blood the finished bust of King Charles. I have also heard it asserted, that stains of blood were still visible on the marble when it was lost in the fire which consumed Whitehall.

[A. Cunningham, *The Lives of the Most Eminent Painters, Sculptors and Architects*, 1829]

Bernini and Andrea Sacchi (1559–1663)

Bernini desiring to have him see the chair of St Peter,[1] before he exposed it to public view, called on him to take him in his coach; but could by no means persuade him to dress himself: Sacchi went out with him in his cap and slippers. This air of contempt did not end here; but stepping near the window, at his entrance into the church of St Peter, said to Bernini, 'This is the principal point of view from which I will judge of your work:' and whatever Bernini could say to him, would not stir a step nearer. Sacchi, considering it attentively some time, cried out as loud as he could, 'Those figures ought to have been larger by a palm:' and went out of the church without saying another word. Bernini was sensible of the justness of his criticism, but did not, for all that, think fit to do his work over again.

[R. de Piles, *Abrégé de la vie des peintres*, 1699, English trans. 1750]
Sacchi was one of the chief upholders of the classicizing tendency in the Roman Baroque, and not likely to be friendly to Bernini's art.

The Riches of Michelangelo Cerquozzi (1602–60)

Michael Angelo surpassed all his fellow students in the goodness of his taste. He had a manner of Painting peculiar to himself. His chearful temper appeared in his pictures. He work'd up the ridicule in his pieces so well, and gave them so much force and truth, that it was impossible not to laugh at them. He was so fond of the Spaniards, that he affected

1. Bernini's Cathedra, a Baroque shrine enclosing the original throne of the Apostle, 1656–66.

their dress. He was very well made in his person, and a most delightful companion. By his pleasant manner of Painting, and the jollity of his humour, his painting room was always filled both with Romans and strangers. The quickness and facility of his pencil were so great, that on the recital of a battle, a shipwreck, or an uncommon figure, he would express it directly on his canvas. His colouring was vigorous, and his touch light. He never made designs or sketches; he only re-touched his pictures, till he had given them the utmost perfection in his power. His works were spread all over Italy. He could hardly supply the commissions he received. By this means, he grew rich apace, and heaped together so much money, that it embarrassed him. The custom at Rome of placing riches in the mount of piety, was not to his taste. The same odd turn that furnished such extraordinary thoughts for his pictures, suggested as singular means of securing his effects. In short, he resolved to bury his money. To which purpose, he set out one night from Rome on foot, to hide a large sum of money in a very retired place he had observed in the neighbourhood of Trivoli. The length of the way, and the weight of the money, prevented his getting there before day-break, which determined him to bury it under a hillock. As he was returning to Rome, the fear lest somebody should find his money, made him return to the place; and finding several shepherds there with their cattle, he kept watch all day long, till the shepherds retired, when he dug up his money, which he had much ado to carry home; where he arrived half dead, having been two nights and a day without sleeping, or taking any nourishment. This accident opened his eyes. He placed his money in the usual places, which he made use of afterwards in pious foundations. But he could never recover his health, whatever care his friends took to procure him that blessing. At the time when he had the greatest hopes of it, a violent fever seized him, and carried him off. He ended his days at Rome in the year 1660, at the age of 58. His epitaph is fixed up in the church De Orfanelli, which he had not forgot in his will.

[R. de Piles, *Abrégé de la vie des peintres*, 1699, trans. 1750]

Reflections on Salvator Rosa (1615–73)

His room was furnished with a large looking-glass, before which he placed himself in those attitudes he wanted; and this was all his study.

His friend Lorenzo Lippi,[1] finding himself at a loss in putting in the landskips to a history he had painted, Salvator took up his pallet and pencils, and in a little time laid in a piece of landskip which every body admired. After Salvator left Florence and Volterra, he fixed himself at Rome; where he took it into his head for some time, by fixing an extravagant price on his pictures, to prevent any body from buying them. He took it mighty ill to be praised as a landskip Painter; his great vanity was being esteemed excellent in history, and to have it thought that he was superior to every body in the allegorical and poetic parts of Painting. He did a great number of pictures in churches, which are certain proofs of his capacity in treating history. His manner of living was that of a philosopher, which he affected to shew in his Paintings, by giving them a moral signification. He was so fond of his liberty, that he would never enter into the service of any Prince, though often pressed: amongst others, Don Ferdinand of Austria solicited him, when he came to Florence on account of the nuptials of the son of the Grand Duke with Margaret of Orleans. As Salvator was very lively in his sallies of wit, I shall mention a few of them.

The Painters of Rome having refused to admit him into the academy of St Luke; one day, when he knew they were assembled, on account of a holy-day, in a church, where they had exposed their pictures, he sent one of himself, in which he had disguised his manner; and pointing it out to them, told them, – 'That the author of it was a surgeon, whom they had refused admission into their academy; for which certainly they were in the wrong, as they had such constant occasion for him, to set the limbs of those poor figures which they lamed every day so unmercifully.'

One day, as he was touching a bad spinet, a person who stood by, told him, it was good for nothing: 'But, says he, I will make it worth an hundred crowns;' and immediately painted so fine a piece on the cover of it, that it sold on the spot for that sum.

A certain person intending to adorn his gallery with the portraits of his friends, set Salvator to work; who made all their caricatures, in which he excelled perfectly; not forgetting his own, which prevented their resentment. His genius naturally led him to that kind of Painting which partook of satire. In finishing this Work, he was seized with a fever, so that it proved his last.

1. Lorenzo Lippi (1602–65), Florentine Baroque painter.

This Painter was exceeding generous, and worked more for reputation than to get money, as the following adventures clearly shew.

A certain rich Knight had been haggling with him for some time
about a large landskip; as he was frequently coming after it, he always
asked the price, to which Salvator, on every demand, added an
hundred crowns. The Knight mentioned his surprize. He replied, –
'You'll find it a hard matter, with all your riches, to agree with me.'
And to prevent any farther importunity, defaced the picture.

The Constable Colonna having ordered a large picture, Salvator
finished it with great care; and sent it him home, without mentioning
any thing about the price. The Constable expressed his satisfaction by
a purse of gold, which he sent in return. Salvator, charmed with his
behaviour, and finding himself greatly overpaid, painted and sent
another picture to the Constable, who made him the same return. He
afterwards sent him a third; and a fourth; for each of which, the
Constable advanced the sum: but on receiving the fifth, he sent him
two purses, and at the same time word, that the contest was by no
means equal between them; as it was not near so easy for him to fill a
purse, as it was for Salvator to paint a picture.

After a long abode at Rome, Salvator was seized with the dropsy;
during which illness he married his maid, who was a Florentine, by
whom he had had several children. He had an extreme aversion to this
marriage, as the woman, who was a mean, low creature, had behaved
more as mistress, than a servant to him; and, at the same time, had
bestowed her favours without much reserve, amongst his acquaintance. These considerations shocked him greatly, as he was a man of
nice honour; but his confessor, supported by some of his friends,
urging all the arguments their zeal could furnish, and finding that his
strongest reasons had not a proper weight, cried, – 'But, Signor
Salvator, you must marry her, if you hope to enter paradise.' He
calmly replied, – 'Then, if I cannot enter into paradise without being a
cuckold, I must do it.'

This chearfulness of temper never left him; nor did his distemper,
though tedious, ever alter it. Alluding to his name, Salvator, he looked
upon it as an earnest of his salvation, and that God would never suffer
the devil to persecute a man that bore the name of Salvator. He ended
his days at Rome, in 1673, aged 58. He was buried in the Chartreux,

over against Carlo Marat,[1] where his epitaph and representation may be seen in marble.

[R. de Piles, *Abrégé de la vie des peintres*, 1699, trans. 1750]

The Good Humour of Filippo Lauri (1623–94)

His barber hearing he had presented his apothecary with a picture, for the care of him when he was ill, flattered himself with hopes of the same favour, and begged a picture of him. Philip, who knew his intention, made his caricature, imitating the ridiculous gestures he used in talking to him; he wrote under the picture, – 'This man looks for a dupe, and can't find him;' and sent it to the barber's at a time he knew that several of his friends would meet in his shop. Every one of them was struck with the oddness of the character, and fell a laughing and joking the poor barber, whom they prevented venting his rage on the picture; and though Philip diverted himself at his expence, he never ventured to come under his hand afterward.

. . .

He would never marry, or give himself the trouble of forming disciples. His pleasure was, to amuse himself with his friends. He would, on public holidays, distinguish himself by playing off fire-works. He was always diverting himself with one merry prank or other, the sallies of his lively imagination. He loved expence, and by his mirth and good humour seemed to forget he grew old, till a distemper surprized and carried him off at Rome, in 1694, at the age of 71.

[R. de Piles, *Abrégé de la vie des peintres*, 1699, trans. 1750]

Baciccio (1639–1709) Demonstrates a Peculiar Talent

Bacici, a Genoese painter, who flourished in the seventeenth century, had a very peculiar talent of producing the exact resemblance of deceased persons whom he had never seen. He first drew a face at random, and afterwards altering it in every feature, by the advice and under the inspection of such as had known the party, he improved it to a striking likeness.

[*The Percy Anecdotes*, 1821–3]

1. Carlo Maratta (1625–1713), leading painter in Rome during the last phase of the Roman Baroque.

Luca Giordano (1632–1705) Makes Sure He Gets Paid

Two Neapolitans having sat for their pictures, never thought of sending for them when they were finished. Jordano having waited a great while without hearing from them, painted an ox's head on one, and put a Jew's cap on the other, and placed a suit of old cloths in his arms, and exposed them to view in this manner; on the news of which, they hastened away with money in their hands, and begged him to efface the ridicule that was annexed to their pictures.

[R. de Piles, *Abrégé de la vie des peintres*, 1699, trans. 1750]

Luca Giordano in Spain

He was so engaged to his business, that he did not even rest from it on holidays, for which a Painter of his acquaintance reproached him; to whom he answered pleasantly, – 'If I was to let my pencils rest, they would grow rebellious; and I should not be able to bring them to order, without trampling on them.' His lively humour, and smart repartees, amused the whole court. The Queen of Spain one day enquiring after his family, wanted to know what sort of a woman his wife was: Luca painted her on the spot, in a picture he was at work upon, and shewed her to the Queen; who was more surprized, as she had not perceived what he was about; but was so pleased, that she took off her pearl necklace, and desired him to present his wife with it in her name.

Jordano had so happy a memory, that he recollected the manners of all the great masters, and had the art of imitating them so well, as to occasion frequent mistakes. The King shewed him a picture of Bassan,[1] expressing his concern that he had not a companion. Lucas painted one for him so exactly in his manner, that it was taken for a picture of that master. The King, in return, knighted him, gave him several places, made one of his sons a Captain of horse, and nominated another Judge and President of the vicariate of Naples; one of the King's coaches attended him every evening to carry him out: nor was this all; the King carried his goodness still further; marrying his

---

1. Jacopo Bassano (1510/15–92).

daughters to gentlemen of his court, and bestowing good places on them for portions.

[R. de Piles, *Abrégé de la vie des peintres*, 1699, trans. 1750]

Luca Giordano Chooses Pearls

On one occasion, a friend who was a fellow painter was present when a jeweller brought [Luca Giordano] two pairs of pearl ear-rings, which were wonderful things. Luca asked the price, and the jeweller said three hundred doubloons for one pair and five hundred for the other. Luca replied that this was too little, and asked for something more expensive. The friend was shocked to hear an artist say this, and Giordano asked him what was the matter? Hadn't he seen the choker, or pearl necklace, that he had bought? The friend said no, so Luca produced it, and it was the most wonderful thing anyone could imagine. The pearls, quite apart from being round and white and even, were as big as the biggest chickpeas, and had cost untold gold. Luca said that it was better for him to take his money in jewels such as this than in coins. Besides being less bulky and inconvenient, they were worth much more in Italy than here [in Spain]. The friend was astonished to behold a painter who was able to spend ten or twelve thousand doubloons and not miss them.

[A. Palomino, *El parnaso espanol pintoresco laureado*, 1724]

X

FRENCH PAINTING IN THE SEVENTEENTH CENTURY

ૐ

Nicolas Poussin is the central figure in contemporary accounts of seventeenth-century French art. There were several reasons for the pre-eminence given to him. One was the combination of sheer ability with independence of spirit and an intellectual cast of mind. Another, more purely practical, was the fact that he had left France to live in Rome, where artists had become public figures. They did not become so in Paris until the advent of Charles Le Brun, Louis XIV's dictator of the arts – and even where Le Brun is concerned we have surprisingly few personal details and only one brief anecdote of any consequence.

Although he lived for nearly all of his adult life in Rome, and attracted the admiration of Bernini (as demonstrated by an extract given here), Poussin was a very different sort of artist from the Italian sculptor. The life he lived was withdrawn and private. His patrons were most often high officials back in France. Many of his paintings were made for himself (that is to say, on speculation) rather than in fulfilment of commissions. When he took commissions, these were usually quite loosely framed.

Poussin thus represents a new stage in the evolution of artistic personality in Europe. He is not a professional 'genius', like Rosa, but he does have a conscious intellectuality: he is a philosopher who expresses himself in paint. He was perceived as such by those who busied themselves with the things of the mind.

The other anecdotes included in this section are also mostly concerned with French artists who lived and worked in Rome. In this, they reflect the general bias of the sources.

Nicolas Poussin (1594–1665) in Rome

He used frequently to examine the ancient sculptures in the vineyards about Rome, and this confirmed him more and more in the love of those antiquities. He would spend several days together in making his reflections upon them by himself. It was in these retirements that he considered the extraordinary effects of nature, with respect to land-skips, that he designed his animals, his distances, his trees, and every thing which was excellent and agreeable to his gusto.

[R. de Piles, *Abrégé de la vie des peintres*, 1699, trans. 1750]

Nicolas Poussin Gathers Material for his Work

All days were for him days of study, and the moments he spent in painting and drawing were for him a recreation. He was always at work wherever he found himself. When he walked through the streets, he observed the actions of the people round him, and if he found anything worthy of remark, he made notes in a book which he carried with him. He avoided large gatherings as much as possible, and avoided his friends to seek solitude amongst the vineyards and the remotest parts of Rome, where he might at ease contemplate antique statues or agreeable views, and observe the most beautiful effects of nature. It was in these retreats, and upon these promenades that he made slight sketches of things that interested him – both notes for landscapes (terraces, trees, and beautiful effects of light); and also for figure compositions (groups of figures, details of costume, or other particular ornaments). Of these he later made a good choice, and excellent employment.

[A. Félibien, *Entretiens sur les vies et sur les ouvrages des plus excellents peintres, anciens et modernes*, 1666–8]

Poussin's Preparatory Studies

When he decided to paint a new composition [Poussin] first studied the subject carefully, then made two or three slight drawings of the general arrangement. If the painting was to contain figures, he would take a board marked out in squares, of the right proportion for this project, and would arrange upon it little nude figures made of wax, in the poses necessary to explain the action of the whole. Then, in order to represent the drapery, he clothed these figures either in wetted paper or in thin cloth, then sewed his draperies with threads which allowed him to suspend the figures at the appropriate height above the line of the horizon. It was after these models that he painted his pictures. In order to execute the pictures he also made use of living models, and took his time in studying them. Often he would begin painting, then interrupt the work in order to go for a walk – but as he walked he was still busy with serious cogitations concerning his art.

[J. von Sandrart, *Teutsche Akademie*, 1675–9]

Poussin on the Use of Intellect

Speaking of painting, [Poussin] said that as the twenty-four letters of the alphabet[1] serve to form our words and express our ideas, so too the lineaments of the human body serve to express all the different passions of the soul in order to make manifest what we have within ourselves.

No painter was a great painter if he only imitated what he saw, nor a great poet. Amongst painters there were some born with an instinct which was like that of the animals: it allowed them to reproduce easily what they saw. They were different from the beasts only in this, that they were aware of what they did and brought to it a certain variety. Able men must work with their intellects, that is, they must conceive beforehand what they wanted to do – must, for example, imagine generous, courteous Alexander, then must express this personage using a painter's means, so that his very face makes Alexander recognizable, as a man possessing the qualities attributed to him.

[A. Félibien, *Entretiens sur les vies et sur les ouvrages des plus excellents peintres*, 1666–8]

Poussin and Bishop Massimi

Bishop Massimi, who was afterwards a cardinal, visiting him on a certain time, their conversation lasted insensibly till it was night, and the prelate being about to take a coach, Poussin took the candle in his hand, lighted him down stairs, and waited on him with it to his coach. The bishop was sorry to see him do it himself, and could not help

1. The seventeenth-century French alphabet.

saying, 'I very much pity you, monsieur Poussin, that you have not one servant: And I pity you more, my lord, replied Poussin, that you have so many.' He never made words about the price of his pictures; he put down his rates on the back of the canvas, and it was always given him.

[R. de Piles, *Abrégé de la vie des peintres*, 1699, trans. 1750]

Poussin and the Antique

Though he resolved when he went from France, to copy the pictures of the greatest masters, yet he exercised himself very little that way. He thought it enough to examine them well, to make his reflections upon them, and that what he should do more, would be so much time lost; but he had another opinion of the antique figures. He designed them with care, and formed such an high idea of them in his mind, that they were his principal object, and he applied himself entirely to the study of them. He was convinced, that the source of every beauty and every grace rose from those excellent pieces, and that the ancient sculptors had drained nature to render their figures the admiration of posterity. His close friendship with two sculptors, l'Algarde[1] and Francois Flamand,[2] in whose house he lodged, strengthened, and perhaps begat his inclination: be it as it will, he never left it, and it encreased in him as he grew older, which may be seen by his works.

[R. de Piles, *Abrégé de la vie des peintres*, 1699, trans. 1750]

Nicolas Poussin's Achievement

One day I asked him how he had achieved such a high rank amongst the greatest painters of Italy. He modestly replied: 'I neglected nothing.'

[*Mélanges d'histoire et de littérature recueilles par M. Vigneul-Marville,*[3] 1699–1700]

1. Alessandro Algardi (1602–56). Bernini's nearest rival, but more classical in style.
2. François Flamand, i.e. Duquesnoy (1594–1643). A Flemish artist living and working in Rome.
3. Pseudonym of Bonaventure d'Argonne.

Poussin on Raphael

Poussin said of Raphael, 'That he was an angel compared with the modern Painters, but an ass in comparison of the ancients.'
[R. de Piles, *Abrégé de la vie des peintres*, 1699, trans. 1750]

Poussin on Caravaggio

M. Poussin . . . could not stand the work of Caravaggio, and said that he had been brought into the world in order to destroy painting.
[A. Félibien, *Entretiens sur les vies et sur les ouvrages des plus excellens peintres*, 1666–8] Poussin's attitude to Caravaggio is similar to that of Ingres to Delacroix: see p. 281.

Bernini on Poussin

[During Bernini's visit to Paris, Chantelou showed Bernini his own collection of paintings, which included the set of *Seven Sacraments* now on loan from the Duke of Sutherland to the National Galleries of Scotland.]

'If I had to choose one of these paintings I would be hard put to it,' [Bernini] said, pointing to the one by Raphael as well as to the others. 'I would not know which to choose. I have always had a high opinion of Signor Poussin, and I remember that Guido Reni was angry with me when I spoke of Poussin's *Martyrdom of St Erasmus* in St Peter's. For his taste I had exaggerated its beauties to Urban VIII, to whom I said: "Were I a painter, this painting would be a great mortification to me. He is a great genius, and on top of that his chief study is the Antique."'
Turning to me, Bernini said: 'Your Excellency must believe that I take great pleasure in these pictures; it is something I must express without restraint.'
[Chantelou, *Journal du voyage du Cav. Bernini en France*, 1885] Colbert, who had been nettled by what he took to be Bernini's anti-French attitudes, commented sourly on what Chantelou told him about this episode: 'I am happy to hear it, since at least he has now praised something in France.'

Claude Gellée, called Le Lorrain (1600–85), and his Approach to Painting

Chance at last brought him to Augustino Tasso,[1] who hired him to pound his colours, clean his pallet and pencils, look after his house, dress his meat for him, and do all his houshold-drudgery, Augustino keeping no other servant. His master, in hopes to make him serviceable to him in some of his greatest works, by little and little taught him some rules of perspective. Lorrain at first could hardly be brought to understand those principles of art; but when he began to have some notion of them, and to profit by his industry, he took heart. His soul enlarged itself, and he set about his studies with wonderful eagerness. He would be in the country from morning to night, making his observations on the effects of nature, and in painting or designing them. Sandrart relates, that being in the country with him to study together, le Lorrain made him observe, with as much nicety as if he had been well versed in physics, the causes of the diversity of the same view or prospect, explaining why it appeared sometimes after one fashion, and sometimes after another, with respect to colours, instancing in the morning dews and evening vapours. His memory was so good, that he would paint with a great deal of faithfulness what he had seen in the country, when he came home. He was so absorbed in his labours, that he never visited any body. His diversion was the study of his profession, and by mere force of cultivating his talent, he drew some pictures that got him an immortal reputation in the kind of Painting to which he took. By this we may perceive, that constancy and assiduity of working, will be too hard for the heaviness of a man's intellectuals. He did not perform without difficulty; and his performance not answering his intention, he would sometimes do and undo the same pieces seven or eight times over. There was nothing of manner in his touches, and he often gave a tenderness to his finished trees by glazing.

[R. de Piles, *Abrégé de la vie des peintres*, 1699, trans. 1750]

Claude Gellée (Le Lorrain): Figures in a Landscape

He ornamented his landscapes with figures drawn with the greatest care, but, since he could never overcome one obvious fault, which was

1. Agostino Tassi (1580–1644), painter of decorative landscapes. Artemisia Gentileschi (1597–after 1631) accused him of rape in a famous trial held in 1612.

to make them too thin, he was accustomed to say that he sold his landscapes, and made a present of his figures.

[F. Baldinucci, *Notizie de' professori del disegno da Ciambue in qua*, 1681–6]

Claude Gellée (Le Lorrain) and the Art of Landscape

He was thrifty, and studied his art very seriously and diligently, trying to understand nature by every means. He would go into the fields before dawn and be there until nightfall, to learn how to show, as exactly as possible, the red sky of morning, and sunrise, and sunset in the evening. When he had studied one or other of these in the open, he immediately mixed his colours accordingly, then went home and used them for the work he had in mind with greater naturalness than anyone had ever achieved. He pursued this difficult and burdensome method of study for many years, going daily to the fields, then walking the long way back, until finally he met me, with a brush in my hand, at Tivoli, among the wild rocks of the celebrated cascade. He found me painting from life, and saw that I frequently painted directly from nature, creating nothing imaginary. This pleased him so much that he immediately adopted the same method, and thanks to great laboriousness and long-continued exercise achieved such naturalness that his landscapes were in demand with collectors everywhere, and despite having been little esteemed to begin with were afterwards much appreciated and were sold for a hundred or more gold crowns, so that though he was never idle, he was nevertheless unable to paint enough of them.

[J. von Sandrart, *Teutsche akademie*, 1675–9]

The Integrity of Philippe de Champaigne (1602–74)

Monsieur Poncel, Counsellor in the court of Aids, who was one of his particular friends, desired him, one Sunday, to draw his daughter's picture, who the Monday following was to profess herself a sister of the Carmelites in la Rue Chapon, and after that day she was not to be seen by any lay-man; but Champagne making it a scruple of conscience on account of the day, would not touch his pencil on the Sunday, whatever his friend said or offered him in order to prevail with him to make her portrait; for he was very disinterested, as well as a good christian: a proof of which I shall give in the following relation.

Cardinal Richlieu had offered to make his, and his family's fortune, in case he would quit the queen mother's service. De Champagne always refused to desert his mistress; and the cardinal commended his fidelity, and valued him the more, because he persisted in his duty to the queen. The cardinal's chief valet de chambre, who proposed his entering into his eminency's service, added, that whatever he desired, the cardinal, he was sure, would grant him. Champagne replied, 'If monsigneur the cardinal could make him a better Painter, the only thing he was ambitious of, it would be something: but since that was impossible, he only begged the honour of the continuance of his eminency's good graces.' The valet de chambre told the cardinal de Champagne's answer, which instead of offending him, encreased his esteem of this Painter; who, though he refused to enter into his service, did not however refuse to work for him. Among other things, he drew his picture for him, at several fittings, and it is one of the best pieces he ever painted in his life.

[R. de Piles, *Abrégé de la vie des peintres*, 1699, trans. 1750]
Champagne belonged to the austere, quasi-Protestant sect of Jansenists, which was eventually suppressed by Louis XIV.

The Miniaturist Jean Petitot (1607–91) and Louis XIV

As he was a zealous protestant, at the revocation of the edict of Nantz in 1685, afraid of being taken up, he demanded the King's permission to retire to Geneva; who finding him pressing, and fearing he should escape, cruelly caused him to be arrested, and sent to Fort l' Eveque, where the Bishop of Meaux was appointed to instruct him. Yet neither the eloquence of the great Bossuet, nor the terrors of a dungeon, could prevail. Petitot was not convinced; but the vexation and confinement threw the good old man, now near eighty, into a violent fever. The King being informed of it, ordered him to be released. The Painter no sooner found himself at liberty, than, terrified at what he had suffered, he escaped with his wife, in 1685, to Geneva, after having lived at Paris thirty six years. His children, remaining in that city, and fearing the King's resentment, flung themselves on his mercy, and implored his protection. The King received them favourably, and told them, he could forgive an old man the whim of desiring to be buried with his fathers.

[R. de Piles, *Abrégé de la vie des peintres*, 1699, trans. 1750] Petitot was celebrated for his work in enamel.

Gaspard Dughet, called Poussin (1615–75)

Gaspar, to have it more in his power to design after nature, hired four houses; two in the highest quarters of Rome, one at Tivoli, and a fourth at Frescati. By the studies he made from them, he acquired a great facility, and admirable touch, and a great freshness of colouring. Poussin,[1] who often came to see him work, took great pleasure in adorning his landskips with excellent figures.

[R. de Piles, *Abrégé de la vie des peintres*, 1699, trans. 1750]

A Tribute to Eustache Le Sueur (1617–55) from Charles Le Brun (1619–90)

This excellent painter, who died at the age of thirty, was pupil to Simon Vouet,[2] but he soon surpassed his master; and though he never quitted France, became one of the first painters of his day. His contemporary, Le Brun, appears to have been very jealous of his superior talents, for on hearing of his death, he malignantly said, 'I feel now as if I had a thorn just taken out of my foot.'

[*The Percy Anecdotes*, 1821–3]

1. Nicolas Poussin. The two artists were brothers-in-law.
2. Simon Vouet (1590–1649).

XI

SPANISH PAINTING OF
THE GOLDEN AGE

ৈ

The chief, indeed almost the only, source of anecdotes about the Spanish painters of the so-called 'Golden Age' is Antonio Palomino's El parnaso español pintoresco laureado, which was not published until as late as 1724, over forty years after the death of Murillo.

Palomino's coverage of the great artistic personalities of the seventeenth century is extremely uneven. Velásquez is the undoubted hero of his book. Palomino is impressed not only by his pre-eminent skill, but by his close personal relationship with Philip IV, and the honours given to him, such as his appointment as Gentleman of the Bedchamber. In the etiquette-ridden Spanish court, Velásquez's social progress was a matter of great interest and importance. About Murillo, Palomino has much less to say, and about Zurbaran almost nothing of a personal nature. One reason for this was clearly Zurbaran's semi-eclipse and fall from fashion during the decade or so preceding his death.

The other personality which fascinated Palomino was that of Alonso Cano, not now regarded as an artist of absolutely the first rank. Cano's eccentricities, especially those prompted by the artist's obsessional anti-Semitism, occupy a good deal of space in Palomino's pages. Though Cano's quirks make him deeply unsympathetic to any modern audience, Palomino's account has a vividness and a ring of authenticity which makes us feel he must have been in contact with a good source. The fact that we would much rather know more about Zurbaran is, in the circumstances, beside the point.

[147]

Luis de Morales (?c. 1509–?c. 1586) and Philip II

Morales, a disciple of Raffael, from his constant choice of divine subjects, and the extreme delicacy of his pencil, acquired the appellation of El Divino, and is known to the present age by no other name than El Divino Morales. All his paintings are upon wood or copper, and almost generally heads of the crucified Saviour; no instance occurring of his having executed any composition or figure at full length.

When Morales was summoned to the Escurial, by Philip II of Spain, he left Badajos at the king's command, and putting himself in the best array that his whole substance could procure, presented himself to the sovereign, more like an ambassador upon the delivery of his credentials, than a rural artist called to labour at his profession for hire. Upon the king's remarking on the unexpected splendour of his appearance, he answered with an air of national gallantry that being resolved to dedicate every thing he possessed by nature or by fortune to the service of his sovereign, he had presented himself in the best condition and attire that his means admitted, in obedience to his summons.

Morales was liberally rewarded by the king for his performances; but upon the completion of his works, he returned to Badajoz with the same spirit of extravagance; for when Philip passed through that place in 1581, on his way to take possession of the kingdom of Portugal, Morales presented himself in a far different condition, reduced by poverty and age, for he was then seventy-two years old. 'Morales,' said the king 'methinks you are grown very old since I last saw you.' 'True, sire,' replied he, 'and also very poor.' Philip turning to the city treasurer, ordered Morales two hundred ducats, telling him it was to purchase a dinner. 'And a supper too,' said Morales. 'No,' answered the king, 'give him a hundred ducats more.'

[*The Percy Anecdotes*, 1821–3]

The young Jusepe Ribera (c. 1590–1652) in Rome

[Ribera] was very poor, and kept himself through his own industry, and crumbs from the draughtsmen of the Academy [of St Luke]. He had no other support or protection. One day, when he was making a drawing after one of those paintings that embellish the streets of Rome [on the facades of the palaces] a cardinal who was passing in his carriage happened by chance to see him. Inspired by pious and noble thoughts he looked at this boy (so absorbed in his drawing and so much neglected by Fortune that he scarcely had a rag to cover him), then called him over and sent him to his house. There he gave him clothes and showed him so much favour that pampering did what necessity had been unable to accomplish: Ribera started to become spoiled and to forget the goal which had led him to leave his home and his native region. However, because it came naturally to him to do what others do against their will, he came to his senses and (without even saying goodbye) left the house and comforts he had been enjoying, and returned to his original way of living and studying. When the cardinal found him again, he berated him for this and for his bad behaviour, calling him an ingrate and a thankless little Spaniard. However, when he had been satisfied as to the purity of Ribera's motives, he praised him and admired his uncommon virtue, for having preferred his studies to the comforts of his [the cardinal's] house.

[A. Palomino, *El parnaso espanol pinturesco laureado*, 1724]

Ribera's Subject-matter and the Pregnant Woman

Ribera did not like painting sweet, devout subjects so much as harsh and horrifying ones – for instance, old men with dry, wrinkled, skinny bodies and gaunt and withered faces, all painted accurately from the model with extraordinary skill, vigour and elegance of technique. This can be seen in his *Martyrdom of St Bartholomew*, where the saint is being flayed and the anatomy of the arm is revealed, and also in his *Tityus*, whose entrails are being eaten by a vulture as a punishment for his wanton audacity, and in the torments of Sisyphus, Tantalus and Ixion. Portraying the last of these, Ribera vividly expresses the torment of being tied to the wheel, upon which Ixion was forever lacerated and wracked, showing him constricting his fingers to help bear the pain. So much so that when the painting was in the house of Jacoba van Uffel in Amsterdam[1] at a time when she was pregnant, she gave birth to a child with withered fingers, like those in the picture. Because of that the painting was taken to Italy, and afterwards, with the three others in the series and many more, transferred to Madrid, to the Buen Retiro Palace.

[A. Palomino, *El parnaso espanol*, 1724]

1. There was a brisk trade between Naples, where Ribera was based, and the Low Countries. One of the greatest collectors in Naples, Gaspar Roomer, was a Flemish merchant and shipowner.

The Early Paintings of Velásquez (1599–1660)

Understanding that Titian, Dürer and Raphael had already caught the
wind in their sails and had pulled away, their fame being all the more
alive now that they were dead, [Velasquez] made use of his own capacity
for invention and began to paint rustic subjects with much dash and
with unusual lighting and colour. He was reproached for not representing with more delicacy and beauty themes where he might hope to
emulate Raphael of Urbino. His polite answer was that he would rather
be 'first in this sort of coarseness than second in delicacy'.

   [A. Palomino, *El parnaso espanol*, 1724]

The Honours Received by Velásquez from Philip IV

It is hard to credit the liberality and friendliness which so great a king
manifested to our Velasquez. He was ordered to set up his studio in the
palace, in what is called the North Wind gallery. His Majesty had the
key to this, and had a chair put there so as to watch him paint at leisure –
just as Alexander regularly watched Apelles paint, honouring him with
the signal favours Pliny describes in his *Natural History*, and just as His
Imperial Majesty Charles V, though occupied with many wars, liked to
watch the great Titian, and Philip II, the Catholic King, liked to see
Alonso Sanchez Coello, favouring him with signal marks of affection.
Thus too did His Majesty honour Velasquez, imitating and even
surpassing his great predecessors.

   He gave him the position of Gentleman of the Wardrobe, one of
the most esteemed appointments in the royal household, and honoured
him too with the key to his bedchamber, which was something that
many Knights of the Orders[1] would have liked to have. His
advancement continued, and Velasquez was finally made Gentleman of
the Bedchamber, though he could not exercise the office until 1643.

   [A. Palomino, *El parnaso espanol*, 1724]

---

1. The Spanish royal orders, such as the Order of Santiago. According to legend,
Philip IV himself painted the cross of this order on Velasquez's doublet, in the self-
portrait which forms part of *Las Meninas*.

Velásquez as Royal Confidant

Don Diego Velasquez was held in such respect by His Majesty that he confided in him more than a king usually confides in a subject, and discussed difficult matters with him, especially during those intimate hours when the noblemen and other courtiers had retired. A proof of it is the following: it so happened that the son of a great nobleman, because of the impetuosity of youth, said some rather intemperate things to Velasquez because the latter refused to relax the formalities of his office. He told his father, thinking he had done something amusing. His father said: 'Have you fallen out with a man whom the king holds in such high esteem, and who spends hours together talking to His Majesty? Go, and unless you get him to accept your apologies and regain his friendship, do not show yourself to me again.'

[A. Palomino, *El parnaso espanol*, 1724]

Velásquez's Portrait of Admiral Pulido Pareja

In the same year Velasquez finished a portrait of Don Adrian Pulido Paresa, Admiral of the King's fleet in New Spain: This officer was under orders for repairing to his command, when Philip, upon entering the chamber of Velasquez then at work upon this portrait, mistaking it for the Admiral himself, entered into sudden expostulation with him for staying at Madrid beyond his time; declaring to Velasquez after discovering his mistake, that it was so perfect a counterpart of the Admiral, that with no light in the room but what struck immediately upon the figure, he had for some time actually believed it to be the person himself, and was surprized at finding him there in disobedience to his orders.

[R. Cumberland, *Anecdotes of Eminent Painters in Spain*, 1787]

Velásquez's Equestrian Portrait of Philip IV

He did another portrait of His Majesty in armour, mounted on a fine horse, and when he had finished it with his usual care, he inscribed on a rock:

Philippus magn. Hius nom. IV
Potentissimus Hispaniarum Rex.
Indiar. Maxim. Imp.
Anno Christ. xxv Soeculi xvii
Era xx. a.

Then he made an imitation of a rather crumpled piece of paper, stuck to a small stone with sealing wax, also painted from life with some care, as the thing itself demonstrates. This was for his own signature, after the painting had been exhibited for everyone's criticisms and opinions and after he had thought about what ever faults had been found, because he regarded the public as being more discerning judges then he was himself. He offered the work for public criticism, and the horse was damned for breaking the rules of art, but the judgements were so contradictory that it was impossible to reconcile them. Irritated, Velasquez effaced the greater part of his work and, in place of his signature, put (since he had expunged what he had done): *Didacus Velasquius, Pictor Regis, expinxit.*

[A. Palomino, *El parnaso espanol,* 1724]

Velásquez's 'Las Meninas'

When Charles the IId of Spain shewed this picture to Lucas Jordan,[1] he exclaimed with rapture and surprize, *Señor esta es la Theologia de la Pintura* [Sir, this is the theology of painting].

[R. Cumberland, *Anecdotes,* 1787]

Alonso Cano (1601–67) and a Niggardly Client

A Counsellor of Grenada having refused to pay the sum of one hundred pistoles for an image of San Antonio de Padua which Cano had made for him, he dashed the Saint into pieces on the pavement of his academy, whilst the stupid Counsellor was reckoning up how many pistoles per day Cano had earned whilst the work was in hand: You have been five-and-twenty days carving this image of San Antonio, said the niggardly arithmetician, and the purchase-money demanded being one hundred, you have rated your labour at the exorbitant price of four pistoles

1. Luca Giordano (1632–1705).

[153]

per day, whilst I, who am a Counsellor and your superior, do not make half your profits by my talents – Wretch, cried the enraged Artist, to talk to me of your talents – I have been fifty years learning to make this statue in twenty-five days, and so saying he flung it with the utmost violence upon the pavement.

[R. Cumberland, *Anecdotes*, 1787] Compare similar anecdotes related by Vasari.

Alonso Cano's Anti-Semitism

Cano hated Jews. In Granada those condemned by the Holy Office to wear the penitent's cloak or sackcloth peddle linen and other things in the street. Most of the streets are very narrow, and Cano therefore took great care that the penitents' garments should not touch his own – he either changed over to the other pavement, or stepped into an entryway. If it so happened that, when he was turning a corner or stepping out of a house, his clothes were touched by these people, he would immediately go into an entryway and take off his mantle or cassock and send home for another. Whatever a Jew had touched Cano gave to his servant, not for his own use but to sell; if he discovered the servant wearing the garment in question, he kicked him out of the house. For this reason his servant, who was a bit of a rogue, would slyly take the opportunity to say to him, when there was some question whether a Jew had touched something or not, that it was just a touch, nothing to worry about. 'What do you mean?' Cano would cry. 'In matters such as this, there *are* no trifles.' And thus the servant got a new mantle.

On one occasion, when Alonso was absent, his housekeeper, who was new to the job and did not know his nature, called one of the penitent Jews who happened to be passing into the house, so as to buy some linen. Just at that instant the master returned, saw the Jew and roused the whole house with his cries. He looked for something to hit him with so as to get rid of him without having to touch him, so that the poor man scurried to pick up his bundle of cloth and get out of there with a whole skin. Afterwards he confronted his servant, and she took refuge in a neighbour's house. Though she sent many people to intercede on her behalf, she was not allowed back until she had undergone a period of quarantine. Meanwhile Cano made diligent enquiries as to whether her blood was pure, and also whether she might not have some kind of friendship, relationship or kinship with this or any other Jew. Until she was cleared of these suspicions he would not take her back. And he did more – he discarded the shoes he had had on, and would never wear them again, in case he had stepped where the Jew had trodden. Nor was that the end of it – he had the pavement and bricks removed and then replaced, wherever he thought the Jew had walked.

Such was his mania (one may really call it that) where these people were concerned that the following happened during his last illness. At that time he was living at Albacin, in the parish of Santiago, where the Inquisition's prison is, so the parish priest went to see him and, seeing how sick he was, told him that whenever he wanted to confess and receive the viaticum, he should send for him. Very calmly, Alonso asked him if he also gave the sacrament to the penitent Jews and the priest said yes. 'Well, then, Master, go with God and do not come back here, for a man who gives the sacrament to penitent Jews is not going to give them to me.' Then he sent a message to the Vicar to send the priest of San Andres (the neighbouring parish) to come and give him the sacraments, and that was what was done.

[A. Palomino, *El parnaso espanol*, 1724] In sixteenth- and seventeenth-century Spain, *conversos* – or converted Jews – laboured under many disadvantages, and the sincerity of their conversion remained under suspicion.

Alonso Cano's Death

When Cano was already dying, the priest took him a carved crucifix (not the work of a good artist) so as to exhort him with its help. Cano told him to remove it. The priest was so alarmed by this that he was about to exorcise him and said: 'My son, what are you doing? Look, this is the Lord who has redeemed and will save you!' And Cano replied: 'Father, I do so believe. But am I to get angry because this is so poorly done, and thus let the devil take me? Give me a bare cross, and with the help of my faith I will then venerate and reverence Him there, as He is in essence, and as I behold Him in my mind.' And so it was done, and Cano made an exemplary end, to the edification of those present, in 1676, aged seventy-six years.

[A. Palomino, *El parnaso espanol*, 1724] The same story is told, much less plausibly, about Antoine Watteau.

Velásquez's Slave, Juan de Pareja (c. 1610–70)

Don Juan de Pareja, a half-breed native of Seville and man of colour, was Don Diego Velasquez's slave. And although his master, for the honour of art, never allowed him to occupy himself with painting or drawing or anything to do with these, but only to bring colours and prepare canvases and do other things for the service of art and the household, he was so talented that, behind Velasquez's back and by going short of sleep, he was able to produce paintings which were worthy of much esteem. Forseeing that Velasquez would certainly be displeased by this, he devised an ingenious strategem. He had noted that whenever Philip IV came down to the lower rooms to watch Velasquez at work, and saw a painting leaning with its face to the wall, he would either turn it itself or have it turned round so as to see what was on the canvas. Pareja placed a little picture of his own so that it casually faced the wall. As soon as the king saw it, he went to turn it and Pareja, ready and waiting for this, flung himself at his feet and begged him very humbly to protect him from his master, without whose leave he had learned the art, and made this painting himself. The king, magnanimously, was not content simply to do what Pareja begged for but, turning to Velasquez, said: 'Not only must you say no more about this, but you must note that so skilled a man should not remain a slave.'

[A. Palomino, *El parnaso espanol*, 1724]

The Death of Murillo (1617–82)

Murillo was so modest it is possible to say that decorousness killed him. He was up on a scaffold, in order to paint a very large picture of St Catherine for the Capuchin convent in Cadiz, and he stumbled, climbing it. His intestines were ruptured and came out,[1] and, because he did not want to show physical weakness or permit himself to be examined, he died as a result of this unexpected accident in the year 1685, aged seventy-two years, more or less.[2]

[A. Palomino, *El parnaso espanol*, 1724]

---

1. i.e., he suffered a hernia.
2. Both date of death and age are inaccurate.

XII

SEVENTEENTH-CENTURY ART
IN NORTHERN EUROPE

ॐ

The contrasting central personalities in this section are Rubens and Rembrandt. Rubens was a man whom contemporaries found it easy to admire. They were impressed by his facility, his energy, his cultivation and his ability to mingle on easy, almost equal, terms with the great. This last characteristic he shared with his pupil Van Dyck.

Rembrandt they found it hard to assess and even harder to assimilate. It was not that he remained in obscurity, like Vermeer. There are three early biographies – one by Sandrart (not cited here), one by Filippo Baldinucci, and a third by the Dutchman Arnold Houbraken. Houbraken's account, the longest, is also the latest in date – it was not published until 1718, fifty years after Rembrandt's death.

All of Rembrandt's early biographers seem to have been puzzled by his personality and artistic aims. In this he resembled Caravaggio. Another link was the fact that they were both regarded as extreme proponents of naturalism. In Rembrandt's case, as in Caravaggio's, what upset contemporary chroniclers was his lack of stylistic propriety combined with an apparently farouche lifestyle. His early biographers did, however, regard him as an important artist, though they found it hard to analyse the reasons for this importance.

In our own time, writers on Rembrandt have found it difficult to deal with one aspect in particular of the biographical tradition – the idea that Rembrandt was by nature avaricious. This springs not only from reluctance to accept something which seems to cast a shadow on the nature of their hero, but from incomprehension of the way in which artists worked and earned their living.

In the Low Countries the medieval tradition of apprenticeship seems to have been more strictly maintained than it was in Italy. We can see this clearly in the stories concerning the relationship between Adriaen Brouwer and his master Frans Hals, who is also described as

[157]

avaricious. Essentially, the situation was that whatever the apprentice produced could be sold for the profit of the master, and generally under the master's name. It was for commercial reasons that Rembrandt himself at one period maintained a large studio. His pupils and apprentices enabled him to satisfy an eager demand for 'Rembrandts'.

Most of the stories which have come down to us about the artists of the Low Countries originate in the closed world of studio gossip. Rubens was exceptional in having a taste for intellectual company. In Holland, in particular, most art was produced speculatively, rather than on commission. It was offered for sale as a finished commodity. Many young apprentices must have felt they were exploited, and nourished a certain resentment towards their masters. It is this attitude which is reflected in the studio tradition I have referred to.

The biographical tradition about Adriaen Brouwer not only reflects the conflict of interest between master and apprentice, but adds fresh touches to the image of the 'Bohemian' artist. The fact that Brouwer, who began his career as a pupil of Hals, later became the protégé of Rubens, is a useful reminder of the continuing links between Dutch and Flemish art, despite the religious and political divide imposed on the region in the sixteenth century.

The Daily Routine of Peter Paul Rubens (1577–1640)

Though there seemed to be a good deal of dissipation in his life, his way of living was nevertheless strictly regulated. Each morning he rose at four. His rule was to begin the day by hearing mass, at least when he was not prevented from doing so by gout, from which he suffered greatly. After this he began work, having always at his side a reader, paid to read some improving book aloud – usually Livy, Plutarch or Seneca.

Since he greatly enjoyed painting, he lived so that he could work easily, without damage to his health. For that reason he ate little at dinner, so that the vapour of what he ate should not prevent him from applying himself, and so that labour should not impede digestion. He continued work until five in the evening, then went out on horseback to take the air – either in the countryside or on the ramparts – or else he chose some other form of relaxation.

Returning from his ride, he normally found friends at his house, who came to take supper with him, and who added to the pleasures of his table. He had nevertheless a great dislike of excessive drinking or eating – also of gaming. His greatest pleasure was to mount a fine Spanish horse, to read a book, to look at his medals, or his agates, cornelians and other engraved gems, of which he possessed a fine collection, which now belongs to the King of Spain. Since he painted everything from nature, and often had occasion to represent horses, he had in his stables the finest and fittest to be painted.

[R. de Piles, *Dissertation sur les ouvrages des plus fameux peintres*, 1681]

Frans Hals (1581/5–1666) and Anthony Van Dyck (1599–1641)

Anthony Van Dyck, the phoenix of his day, having entered the service of Charles 1 and being about to sail to England, wanted to see Frans Hals before he left. He went to Haarlem and called at Hals's house, but it took a while to find the latter in the taverns, since he never left before he had finished his ale. Van Dyck stood waiting patiently and did not give his name, saying merely that he was a stranger who wanted to have his portrait painted, and that the present moment was the only convenient one. Hals agreed promptly, took the first canvas that came to hand and set to work. Van Dyck did not speak much while posing, lest he be recognized and his identity discovered. The portrait was soon complete, and Hals asked him to get up and see how he liked it. Van Dyck praised it, and talked to Hals for a while, but still in such a way as to conceal his identity. Among other things he remarked: 'So this is how one paints? Perhaps I could do likewise.' Then taking an unpainted canvas which he found there, he placed it on the easel and invited Hals to sit. Frans saw immediately, from the way he held the palette and brushes, that this was no novice, and realized that this Ulysses in disguise would soon reveal himself. Nevertheless he had no notion that this was Van Dyck; he thought it was some prankster who wanted to declare himself by providing a sample of his art. Soon enough, Van Dyck told him to get up and take a look at the work. As soon as he saw it, Hals said; 'You are Van Dyck; no one but he could do this.' And he fell on his neck and kissed him.

. . .

Van Dyck is said to have gone to great lengths to entice Hals to come to England, but Hals would not listen – he liked his dissolute ways too much. Van Dyck had great respect for Hals's art, saying later that if he had blended his colours a bit more delicately and thinly he would have been one of the greatest masters. He had no equal in his control of the brush, or in his ability to conceive a portrait and give a correct rendering of its essential features, what was salient and what receded, with a touch of the brush, without compromise or change.

It is said that it was Hals's custom to lay on [the paint] in his portraits thick and wet, then to apply the [visible] brush-strokes later with the words: 'Now to give it the master's touch.'

[A. Houbraken, *De groote schoubergh der Nederlantsche Konstschilders en schilderessen*, 1718–21]

Frans Hals and his Pupils

Frans usually got drunk every evening. His pupils, however, greatly respected him, and the older ones agreed that they would take it in turns to keep an eye on him, and convey him to and from the tavern, in case he fell into the water or suffered some other mishap. Having duly brought him home, they removed his shoes and stockings and helped him to bed.

All these pupils noticed that, no matter how drunk he was, Hals always stumbled out a prayer when he went to bed, which ended with this request: 'Dear Lord, carry me soon up to your high heaven.' They wondered amongst themselves if their master was in earnest about this, and thought of a way to put matters to the test. Privy to the plan were a certain Adriaen Brouwer, a pupil of Hals and a practical joker from his boyhood, and Dirck van Delen[1] . . . The Four [conspirators] swore that they would not give one another away. They cut four holes in the ceiling above Hals's bed, and led down strong ropes which they tied to its corners. The next night, when they had helped him to bed, 'full-brimmed and sweet', as the saying has it, and had taken the lamp from the room, they went upstairs in their stockinged feet, without Hals noticing, ready for action. They listened eagerly to him mumbling his evening prayer, which he concluded as usual with the request: 'Dear Lord, carry me soon up to your high heaven.' Then, all together, they started to pull up the bed. Drunk as he was, Hals noticed this, and was convinced that heaven had answered him. As he felt himself going up, he changed his tone and said: 'Not so fast, Lord, not so fast, not so fast,' and so on. So then they gently lowered him again and he remained unaware of the trick that had been played on him. They neatly undid the ropes as he lay there snoring, and neither they nor he spoke of what had happened until many years afterwards. However, from that day onwards Frans abandoned his prayer, and they often laughed when they no longer heard him pining for heaven.

[A. Houbraken, *De groote schoubergh*, 1718–21] Accounts of Brouwer's life (see pp. 164–5) give a less idyllic version of his relationship with Hals.

The Death of Pieter van Laer (1592/5–1642)

The Italians gave him the name of Bamboccio, on account of his extraordinary figure: his legs were long, his body short, and his head sunk into his shoulders;[2] but the beauty of his mind more than made amends for the deformity of his body, and his good nature and good manners hid the disagreeableness of his person. He died at threescore years old by an accident, falling into a ditch near the city of Haerlem,

1. Dirck van Delen (1604/5–1671), Dutch architectural painter, specializing in church interiors and fantastic Renaissance palaces.
2. *Bamboccio*: a rag doll. Another reason for his nickname may have been the fact that his paintings contained numerous small figures.

in which he was drowned. It appears by the manner of his death, that divine vengeance pursued him for a crime he was guilty of at Rome while he lived there. He was one Lent taken three or four times, with five Dutchmen of his acquaintance, eating flesh on the banks of the Tiber, without having any necessity for it. A divine, who had advised them often not to do so, surprized them at it once more, and seeing that fair means would not do, threatened to put them into the Inquisition: and both the priest and the Dutchmen being very much exasperated, they threw him into the river. It is observable, that all these five Dutchmen died by water.

[R. de Piles, *Abrégé de la vie des peintres*, 1699, trans. 1750]

Anthony Van Dyck as a Pupil of Rubens

Whilst he lived with this master, there happened a passage which not a little contributed to his reputation: Rubens having left a picture unfinished one night, and going out, contrary to custom, his disciples made use of that opportunity to sport and play about the room; when one, more unfortunate than the rest, striking at his companion with a maul-stick, chanced to throw down the picture, which receiving some damage, as not being dry, the young men were not a little alarmed at it, well knowing how very angry their master would be when he came to find his work spoiled. This made them use their best endeavours to set things right again; but finding all ineffectual, they had recourse, as their last remedy, to Vandyck, who was then working in the next room, entreating him by all means that he would touch up the picture anew. He complied with their request, and having touched up the piece left it upon the easel. Rubens, coming next morning to his work again, first stood at a distance to view his picture, as is usual with Painters, and having contemplated it a little, suddenly cried out, he liked his piece far better than the night before, the occasion of which being afterwards talked of, it not a little redounded to the honour of Vandyck, and encreased his esteem with his master.

[R. de Piles, *Abrégé de la vie des peintres*, 1699, trans. 1750]

Van Dyck in England

He was indefatigable, and keeping a great table, often detained the persons who sat to him, to dinner, for an opportunity of studying their countenances and of retouching their pictures again in the afternoon. Sir Peter Lely[1] told Mrs. Beale,[2] that Laniere[3] assured him he had sat seven entire days to him, morning and evening, and that notwithstanding Vandyck would not once let him look at the picture till he was content with it himself. This was the portrait that determined the king to invite him to England a second time.

[H. Walpole, *Anecdotes of Painting in England*, 1780]

Van Dyck's English Court Portraits

He was so much employed in drawing the portraits of the royal family, and the lords of the court, that he had no time to do any history-pieces. He did a prodigious number of portraits, about which he took a great deal of care at first; but at last he ran them over hastily, and painted them very slightly. A friend of his asking him the reason of it, He replied, 'I worked a long time for my reputation, and I do it now for my kitchen.'

[R. de Piles, *Abrégé de la vie des peintres*, 1699, trans. 1750]

Van Dyck's Method of Work

It is said that he always painted his portraits in a single session. He began work in the morning, and then, so as not to interrupt his work with a long hiatus, kept to dinner those whose portraits he was doing. They remained the more willingly, however high in rank they were, because they were so well looked after and entertained during the meal. After dinner he again started to paint, and worked so rapidly, and with so much intelligence that he was able to produce two portraits per day – only needed some retouching was required, and then they were finished.

[A. Félibien, *Entretiens sur les vies et sur les ouvrages des plus excellens peintres*, 1688]

---

1. Sir Peter Lely (1618–80).
2. Mary Beale (1633–97). English portrait painter.
3. Nicholas Lanier (1588–1665). Painter and collector. He was also Master of the King's Music and Charles I's chief agent in the formation of the royal collection. Lanier sat to Van Dyck in Antwerp in 1630. The painting is now in the Kunsthistorisches Museum, Vienna.

Van Dyck and Charles I

Charles I took great pleasure in talking with this artist. One day, as he was making the king's portrait, the latter complained in a low voice to the Duke of Norfolk about the state of his finances. Noting that Van Dyck had overheard this, the king asked him, laughing: 'And you, Chevalier, do you know what it is to lack 6000 guineas?' The painter replied: 'Yes, sire – an artist who keeps open house for all his friends, and opens his purse to his mistresses, only too often experiences the problem of empty coffers.'

[J. B. Descamps, *La Vie des peintres flamands, allemands et hollandais*, 1754]

Van Dyck and Henrietta Maria

He made another witty response to Queen Henrietta Maria, when he was painting her. She had very beautiful hands. Van Dyck excelled in portraying these extremities. Noting that he had paused for a long time, the princess coyly asked him why he took more trouble with her hands than with her head. 'Ah, madame,' he said, 'it is that I expect from those hands a reward worthy of their owner.'

[J. B. Descamps, *La Vie des peintres flamands*, 1754]

Adriaen Brouwer (1605/6–38) and Frans Hals

Having joined Hals, Brouwer worked with great energy. He was separated from the other pupils of the artist and shut up in an attic. This separation aroused the curiosity of his fellows, who took the chance, during the master's absence, of finding out what he was doing. Climbing up, turn by turn, to a small window, they were surprised to see that this apprentice, poor and despised, was an accomplished artist, who made very fine paintings.

One of the youngsters made a proposition to Brouwer – that he should paint a set of the Four Senses, for four sols apiece. These succeeded so well that another asked for the Twelve Months of the Year, at the same price. Brouwer agreed, and did well here too. They persuaded him to work more hours, promising to raise the price. Brouwer was happy to do so, and thought himself lucky to be able to sell these little pictures made in his moments of leisure.

However, the profit they made from his work prompted Hals and his wife to watch him so closely that he no longer had a single moment to himself. In addition, the wife, not content with crushing him with work, was ready to let him die of starvation. He hardly looked like a living man; his whole appearance, even his clothing, proclaimed his miserable condition. Adriaen van Ostade, his friend, and pupil to the same master, was touched by compassion and advised Brouwer to leave the house and seek his fortune elsewhere. He ran away and wandered through the town, without knowing where to go or what would become of him. He halted at a gingerbread seller, and found food for the day, then hid beneath the organ in the great church. While he was wondering how to procure a less miserable existence for himself, he was recognised by someone who visited Hals often, and who deduced, from his appearance and his clothes, at least part of his troubles. He therefore asked what was the matter. Brouwer, who was as unsophisticated as it is possible to be, poured out his troubles, stressing the excessive greed of Hals and his wife who, not content with the profit they made from his work, left him hungry and almost naked. His pallor and his rags lent conviction to the recital. He won the sympathy of his interlocutor, who said that he would take him back to his master but promised him better treatment.

The poor young man followed his protector to Hals's house. Hals, enraged by having searched in vain throughout the town, and by his chagrin at having lost such a lucrative apprentice, greeted Brouwer with threats. But the man who had accompanied him remonstrated, and these remonstrances had their effect. The next day the master greeted his pupil kindly, and gave him new clothes (of the cheapest sort, naturally). The young artist thought himself very fortunate in comparison and worked with renewed energy, but always for the benefit of his host, who sold for large sums the paintings that cost him so little.

[J. B. Descamps, *La Vie des peintres flamands*, 1754]

Brouwer's Character

Brouwer's fellow apprentices enlightened him [about the way in which he was being exploited], and he once again managed to escape. He went directly to Amsterdam and there, by chance, found lodgings with an innkeeper called Hendrick van Soomeren, who had tried painting in his youth, and whose son was a good painter of the figure, of landscapes, and of flowers. Brouwer was better fed and less confined, and recovered strength and courage. He produced several small paintings which surprised van Soomeren and awoke his generosity – he made Brouwer a present of a copper plate.

On this plate Brouwer painted a gambler's quarrel between soldiers and peasants. The combatants attack one another; cards are scattered and tables overturned. The composition was excellent, well drawn and coloured, with vividly rendered facial expressions. The painter whose work Hals had been selling so dear was recognized. The collector M. de Vermandois had been searching for him for a long time. He made an offer for the painting on copper, giving 100 ducatoons for it very willingly. Brouwer was astonished. He rubbed his eyes and feared it might be a dream, then spread out the money on his bed and rolled on it, to enjoy it more palpably. Then he gathered it up and went off without saying a word. He came back, gay and singing, several days later. People asked what had become of the money, 'God be praised,' he said, 'I've got rid of it, and feel much happier for that.'

[J. B. Descamps, *La Vie des peintres flamands*, 1754]

Brouwer is Arrested as a Spy

Brouwer lived . . . at Amsterdam for some time, earning a great deal, spending everything he got, and paying none of his bills. He got rid of his debts by running out on them. He secretly left the city and took the road for Antwerp. However, he was less *au courant* with world affairs than he was with events in tap-rooms, and he was unwise enough to appear at the gates of Antwerp without a passport, at a time when the Dutch were at war with Spain. He was arrested as a spy and imprisoned in the citadel.

Luckily for him, he found the Duke of Aremberg there, who had been detained on the orders of the King of Spain. He mistook the Duke for the governor of the fortress and told him, tears in his eyes, about his misfortunes, saying that he was a painter who had left Amsterdam to practise his profession at Antwerp, and that he could give proof of this if provided with brushes and a palette. That same day the Duke sent to Rubens to ask for what was necessary, saying that he wanted to provide work for an artist who seemed to be in some danger of losing his life, if someone didn't take the trouble to save it for him.

Brouwer was given artist's materials and a canvas. Some Spanish soldiers were playing cards and throwing dice in the courtyard, in view of the painter's cell. He made a sketch of the group, representing, with great accuracy, the appearance of the different players. Behind them he showed an old man squatting on his heels — the umpire of their disputes. The physiognomy of this individual was striking — with two teeth only remaining in a large mouth. Brouwer's customary brilliance, to be found in all his works, was especially marked in this one. When he saw the painting the Duke burst out laughing, and sent to ask Rubens to come and see if the work done by this dauber was worth keeping.

Rubens arrived, and hardly had he clapped eyes on the painting than he cried: 'It's by Brouwer! He's the only one who can paint subjects of this sort, with this kind of strength and beauty'. When the Duke saw Rubens examining and praising the painting, he asked him to put a price on it. Rubens offered 300 ryksdaelers. The Duke replied: 'You know very well it is not for sale. I want it for my own collection, both for the adventure it commemorates and for its own merits.'

The painting can still be seen with the descendants of this illustrious house; it is a little damaged and flaking because the preparation of the canvas was done with chalk and glue.

Rubens went to the Governor of Antwerp to ask that the painter should be set at liberty; he told the whole story and gave something of the character of the man. The governor had the supposed spy brought before him; the artist admitted that he had arrived at Antwerp without a passport, but said his only reason for going there was in order to paint. Rubens scolded Brouwer, obtained his freedom, took him to his own house, fed and lodged him, and tried to drag this gifted man out of the mire — but Brouwer, incapable of responding to such generous treatment, soon left him, sold his clothes, spent everything he possessed, and said that he found Rubens's house less tolerable, because of its regulated way of life, than the prison in the citadel.

[J. B. Descamps, *La Vie des peintres flamands*, 1754]

Brouwer's New Clothes

One day, having been stripped by robbers, and deprived of his last sou, he came into Amsterdam and made himself a suit and cloak out of canvas. He painted flowers on them, put some glue over the paint and, dressed in this fashion, went a-promenading, and then to the theatre to see a play. He attracted the attention of women above all – they wanted to know where such fine Indian stuff could be got. So Brouwer took a sponge and some water and the flowers disappeared – but he astonished them still more by his matter-of-fact attitude. The conclusion was that he was a good painter but a ridiculous individual.

[J. B. Descamps, *La Vie des peintres flamands*, 1754]

Rembrandt (1606–69) and his Working Methods

He could have painted many portraits, thanks to his prestige in Holland as a colourist (his colour was, however, better than his drawing). But when it became commonly known that whoever wanted to be painted by him had to sit for three or four months, few came forward. The cause of his slowness was that, immediately after his first work had dried, he took it up again, repainting with great and small strokes, so that at times the pigment was more than half the thickness of a finger. This extravagance of manner was on a par with Rembrandt's mode of life, since he was extremely temperamental and despised everyone. To the ugly, plebeian face nature had been unkind enough to give him, he added untidy and dirty clothes, since it was his custom, when at work, to wipe his brushes on himself, and do things of a similar nature. When he worked he would not have granted an audience to the greatest monarch in the world, who would have had to come back again and again till he found him no longer at work. He often went to public auction sales, and there bought clothes which were old-fashioned and disused, just so long as they struck him as being bizarre and picturesque. Despite the fact that these were sometimes downright dirty, he hung them on the walls of his studio among the beautiful curiosities he also took pleasure in possessing: every kind of old and modern arms – arrows, halberds, daggers, sabres, knives and so forth – plus vast quantities of drawings, engravings and medals, and everything else that he thought a painter might on some occasion need. He deserves praise for one virtue, though he took it to extravagant lengths – because of the high esteem in which he held his art, he would, whenever things to do with it were offered at auction, and notably when paintings and drawings by important local artists were offered, bid so high from the very outset that no one else came forward to contest the bid. He said that he did this in order to emphasize the prestige of his profession. He was also very generous in lending studio props and items from his collections to any other painter who might need them for some project of his own.

[F. Baldinicci, *Notizie de' professori del disegno da Ciambue in qua*, 1681–6]

A Scandal in Rembrandt's Studio

These commissions flowed to him from all quarters, and so did a throng of pupils, for whom he rented a house on the Bloemengracht, where he gave each a room to himself, often divided from that of others simply by paper and canvas, so that each, without disturbing anyone else, could draw from life. Young people, especially when there are many of them together, will frequently get into mischief, and so it happened here. One, needing a female model, took her into his room. This aroused the curiosity of the others who, so as not to be heard, stood in their socks, one after the other, to look through a chink in the wall which they had made for the purpose. It happened to be a warm summer's day, and both the painter and his model stripped stark naked. The merry jokes and words which passed between the two of them could easily be recalled by the spectators of this comedy. Soon afterwards Rembrandt arrived to see what his pupils were doing, and, according to his custom, to instruct them one after the other. In due course he came to the room where the two naked figures were sitting next to one another. The doors were closed, but Rembrandt, having been told what was happening, watched their pranks for a while through the chink that had been made, until, among other words, he also heard them say: 'Now we are exactly as Adam and Eve were in paradise.' Whereupon he knocked on his door with his mahlstick and called out, to the terror of them both: 'Because you are naked you must depart from paradise.'

[A. Houbraken, *De groote Schoubergh der Nederlantsche Konstschilders en Schilderessen*, 1718–21] As Professor Svetlana Alpers points out, in her book *Rembrandt's Enterprise* (1988), the Rembrandt studio was a commercial venture, not merely in the sense that the painter was paid to instruct pupils, but because the pupils' products were sold under the 'Rembrandt' brand-name. Among these products were a number of so-called self-portraits of Rembrandt – a fact which helps to confuse our whole notion of artistic identity.

The Death of Rembrandt's Monkey

One day he was working on a large portrait group, in which a man and his wife and children were depicted. When he had half-completed it, his monkey happened to die. As he had no other canvas available for the moment, he portrayed the dead ape in the aforesaid picture. Naturally the people concerned would not tolerate the idea that the disgusting dead ape should appear alongside them in the picture. But no: he so adored the model offered by the dead ape that he would rather keep the unfinished picture than obliterate the ape in order to please the people portrayed by him. The picture in question subsequently served for a long time as a dividing wall for his pupils.

[A. Houbraken, *De groote schoubergh*, 1718–21] The number of stories about painters and pet apes suggests a hidden metaphor – in the Western tradition, painting a picture is a form of 'aping'.

Rembrandt's Technique

For years he was so overwhelmed with orders that people had to wait a long time for their pictures, although, especially in the last years of his life, he worked so fast that his pictures, when examined from close by, seemed as though they had been daubed with a bricklayer's trowel. For this reason visitors to his studio who wanted to look at his works were frightened away by his saying, 'The smell of the colours will bother you'. It is said that he once painted a portrait in which the colours were so heavily applied that you could lift it from the floor by the nose.

[A. Houbraken, *De groote schoubergh*, 1718–21] Perhaps the origin of the proverbial saying, 'Pictures are meant to be looked at and not to be smelt.' To some readers the final sentence may recall the work of the contemporary British artist Frank Auerbach.

Rembrandt's Prints: Manipulating the Market

Thanks to his engravings he achieved great riches and this bred a proportionate pride and self-conceit. Since it now seemed to him that his prints did not sell for the prices they deserved, he thought he had found a method of making everyone want them. At intolerable expense he had them bought back all over Europe, wherever he could find them, at any price. Among others he bought one for 50 *scudi* at an auction sale in Amsterdam – the subject was the *Raising of Lazarus*. He purchased it when he himself still possessed the copper plate engraved by his own hand.[1]

[F. Baldinucci, *Notizie de' professori del disegno*, 1681–6]

The Demand for Rembrandt's Prints

These works [prints] brought him fame and no small advantage, in particular through the device of slight changes and small and unimportant additions, which he made on his prints, thanks to which they could be sold again as fresh ones. Nay, the demand was at that time so great that people were not considered true amateurs who did not possess the *Juno* with and without the crown, the *Joseph* with the light and the dark head and so on. Indeed, everyone wanted to have the *Woman by the Stove* – as it happened, one of his least important etchings – both with and without the stove-key, in spite of the fact that he sold the etching through his son Titus, as if it were too unimportant for himself.

[A. Houbraken, *De groote schoubergh*, 1718–21]

Rembrandt's Avarice

Such was his love of money (I will not say craving for money) that his pupils, who had noticed this, would play tricks on him. They would paint pennies, twopenny pieces and shillings on the floor and elsewhere, at places where he was bound to pass. He often stretched out his hand in vain to pick these up, and tried to avoid notice as he was embarrassed by his mistake.

[A. Houbraken, *De groote schoubergh*, 1718–21]

Rembrandt's Final Years

In the autumn of his life he kept company mostly with common people and such as practised art. And he gave this reason for it: 'If I want to give my mind diversion, then it is not honour I seek, but freedom'.

[A. Houbraken, *De groote schoubergh*, 1718–21]

---

1. i.e. Rembrandt was in a position to go on producing copies of the same image. The concept of the limited edition print did not yet exist.

The Hard-working Gerard Dou (1613–75)

The common height of his pictures did not exceed a foot, and his price was sometimes six hundred, sometimes eight hundred, and sometimes a thousand livres each picture, more or less, according to the time he spent about it, reckoning after the rate of twenty sols an hour. His painting-room was open a-top, for the light to enter, that he might have the better opportunities for his shadows, and it was built on the side of a canal to avoid dust. He pounded his colours on crystal. He locked up his pallet and pencils when he had done work, and when he began it he rested himself a little till the dust was laid. In fair weather he generally went abroad in the fields to take the air, and repair the loss of his spirits, for he was so indefatigable in his labour, that it consumed him very much.

[R. de Piles, *Abrégé de la vie des peintres*, 1699, trans. 1750]

Nicholas Berchem (1620–83) and his Wife

His wife, the daughter of John Wills,[1] one of his masters, through her avarice allowed him no rest: as industrious as he was at his business, she usually kept herself under his painting room, and when she neither heard him sing or stir, she struck upon the ceiling to rouse him: she got from him all the money he earned by his labour, so that he was obliged to borrow from his scholars, when he wanted money to buy prints that were offered him, which was the only pleasure he had; and his collection of this kind was found considerable after his death.

[R. de Piles, *Abrégé de la vie des peintres*, 1699, trans. 1750]

A Landscape by Paulus Potter (1625–54)

The prince's dowager Amelia, countess of Solmes,[2] ordered him to paint a picture for a chimney piece for one of the fine apartments of the old court: This picture represented a beautiful landskip, in which he painted a cow staleing; a favourite courtier insinuated that it was an unseemly object to be continually in the view of a princess, and dissuaded her from taking it; so that Potter was obliged to take his

1. Jan Wils (c. 1600–66).
2. Amelia van Solms, widow of William of Orange.

picture back again. This trifling absurdity gave the picture a reputation; the curious bid upon one another for it, and it has past
successively into some of the best cabinets in Flanders.

[R. de Piles, *Abrégé de la vie des peintres*, 1699, trans. 1750]

Artist and Model: Melchior Hondecoeter (1636–95)

Melchior Hondekoeter was celebrated for his skill in painting domestic fowls, which he described in a variety of elegant actions and
attitudes. He gave to every animal he painted, such truth, such a degree
of force, expression, and life, as seemed to equal nature itself; and the
feathers of his fowls were expressed with such a swelling softness, as
might readily deceive the eye of any spectator. It is said, that
Hondekoeter had trained up a cock to stand in any attitude he wanted
to describe, and that it was his custom to place the bird near his easel;
so that at the motion of his hand, it would fix itself in the proper
posture, and continue in that particular position, without the smallest
perceptible change, for several hours at a time.

[*The Percy Anecdotes*, 1821–3]

Frans Hals's Pupil Pieter Roerstraten (c. 1630–1700)

Was born at Haerlem, and disciple of Frans Hals, whose manner he at
first followed, but afterwards falling into still-life, and having performed an extraordinary piece, that Sir Peter Lely shewed to king
Charles, and which his majesty approved, he was encouraged to
pursue that way, which he continued to his dying day. He was an
excellent master in that kind of Painting, viz. in gold and silver plate,
gems, shells, musical instruments, &c. to all which he gave an unusual
lustre in his colouring, and for which his pictures bear a good price. It
is said, that one day promising to shew a friend a whole-length of his
master Frans Hals, and through a little delay, his friend growing
impatient to see it, he suddenly called up his wife (his master's
daughter, whom he had married) and told him she was a whole-length
of that master.

[R. de Piles, *Abrégé de la vie des peintres*, supplement to the English
translation, 1750]

The Courtship of Pieter van Slingeland (1640–91)

A widow who sat for her picture, tired out with his tediousness, and vexed that her portrait was in so little forwardness; after much time spent in sitting, rallied him on his slowness: It is a much easier matter to love you, madam, replied Slingelandt, than to paint your likeness; I find so many graces to represent, so many charms to copy, that my pencil is confounded in the attempt; but in loving you, I should follow my inclination, which if it meet with the least incouragement, I should think myself the happiest man breathing. The lady was not insensible to his declaration, with which she was both charmed and surprized, the person of the Painter did not displease her, and he had the character of worth and probity; she made no answer but let him finish the picture, and when rising from the last fitting, she asked him if he would take the original in payment for the copy; he accepted the condition, and soon after married the lady, whose estate being considerable, made him easy for the remainder of his life.

[R. de Piles, *Abrégé de la vie des peintres*, 1699, trans. 1750]

The Plain-spoken Gottfried Schalcken (1643–1706)

Delicacy was no part of his character. Having drawn a lady who was marked with the small-pox, but had handsome hands, she asked him, when the face was finished, if she must not sit for her hands. 'No,' replied Schalken, 'I always draw them from my housemaid.'

[H. Walpole, *Anecdotes of Painting in England*, 1780] On the subject of painting hands, compare Van Dyck's courtly reply to Queen Henrietta Maria.

Mother and Daughter: Maria Sibylla Merian (1647–1717)

At the age of eleven, Sibylla Merian[1] could not be persuaded to renounce her taste for painting, despite the reproaches of her mother, whose ill-treatment Sibylla bore with steadfast fortitude. Thanks to her stubbornness, she was allowed to abandon the needle for the brush. Her father-in-law, Jacques Murel, persuaded the mother of this learned woman to allow her daughter to follow the talent given to her

1. Maria Sibylla Merian (1647–1717), German natural-history painter.

by nature. This obstinacy on the daughter's part caused the mother to remember that when she was pregnant she had suffered from a kind of malady – a constant desire to look at insects and other curiosities of nature. She had made a collection of caterpillars, butterflies, shells and fossils, most of all during her pregnancy, when it was her chosen amusement. This seems to be yet another example of the way in which mothers impress their tastes upon their children. In any event, Sibylla Merian's liking for making imitations of natural curiosities was preceded by her mother's obsessive taste for the same researches.

[J. B. Descamps, *La Vie des peintres flamands*, 1754]

XIII
ARTISTS IN SEVENTEENTH-
CENTURY ENGLAND

৯

The scanty harvest of stories from seventeenth-century England indicates the minor role played by the visual arts. Many of the chief figures, such as Lely and Kneller, were foreign born. These anecdotes make it plain that the main business of the artist, so far as English patrons were concerned, was to produce portraits, and the majority of the anecdotes in this section therefore concern the relationship between artists and eminent sitters.

The Well-ordered Life of Sir Peter Lely (1618–80)

Lely lived in a grand manner, in imitation of his predecessor Van Dyck. His table was laid for twelve courses, and, in the next room to the dining room, a group of musicians played during the meal. Although the cost was considerable, it did not exceed his resources, because, while making as much money as Van Dyck, he kept fewer mistresses, and never wasted money on will o' the wisps such as alchemy.

This artist had an inborn spirit of order, of the kind which both makes and conserves money. One of his servants kept a record of all those who came to be painted – there was no favouritism, the days and hours were marked, and those who failed to turn up were sent to the bottom of the list. Lely himself behaved with equal exactitude. He began work at nine in the morning, and continued until 12.15 p.m. He then put aside his brushes to sit at table with his friends. The rest of the day was spent in making visits and attending court. Never fawning on high personages, always affable with his equals, he won the esteem of everyone. Poets wrote verses about him, above all his friend Jean Vollenhove.

[J. B. Descamps, *La Vie des peintres flamands*, 1754]

Lely and Oliver Cromwell

Lely drew the rising sun, as well as the setting. Captain Winde told Sheffield, Duke of Buckingham, that Oliver certainly sat to him, and while sitting, said to him, 'Mr. Lely, I desire you would use all your skill to paint my picture truly like me, and not flatter me at all; but remark all these roughnesses, pimples, warts, and everything as you see me, otherwise I never will pay a farthing for it.'

[H. Walpole, *Anecdotes of Painting in England*, 1780] This story is sometimes transferred to Samuel Cooper (1609–1702), whose likeness of Cromwell in the Buccleuch Collection is the best-known image of its subject.

The Strange Projects of John Bushnell (d. 1701)

John Bushnell was an admired statuary, but is better known for his capricious character, than his works. He had agreed to complete the set of Kings at the Royal Exchange; but hearing that Cibber[1] had made interest to carve some of them, Bushnell would not proceed, though he had begun six or seven. He had previously finished statues of Charles the First and Second, and one of Sir Thomas Gresham. Some of his profession asserting, that though he was skilful in drapery, he could not execute a naked figure, he engaged in an Alexander the Great; which proved that his rivals were in the right, as to what he could not do. His next whim was to demonstrate the possibility of the Trojan Horse. He undertook to make such a wooden receptacle, and had it made in timber, intending to cover it with Stucco. The head was capable of containing six men sitting round a table; the eyes served for windows. Before it was half completed, a storm of wind overset and demolished it; and though two vintners who had contracted with him to use his horse as a drinking booth, offered to be at the expense of erecting it again, he was too much disappointed to recommence.

[*The Percy Anecdotes*, 1821–3]

The Self-admiration of Simon Verelst (1644–?1710/21)

Lord Chancellor Shaftsbury going to sit, was received by him with his hat on. Don't you know me? said the peer. Yes, replied the painter, you are my Lord Chancellor. And do you know me? I am Varelst. The king can make any man chancellor, but he can make nobody a Varelst. Shaftsbury was disgusted, and sat to Greenhill.[2] In 1680, Varelst, his brother Harman, Henny and Parmentiere, all painters, went to Paris, but stayed not long. In 1685, Varelst was a witness on the divorce between the Duke and Duchess of Norfolk; one who had married Varelst's half-sister was brought to set aside his evidence, and deposed his having been mad and confined. He was so, but not much more than others of his profession have been; his lunacy was self-admiration; he called himself the God of Flowers.

[H. Walpole, *Anecdotes of Painting in England*, 1780]

1. Caius Gabriel Cibber (1630–1700). He carved the statues of *Melancholy* and *Raving Madness* that once stood over the gate of Bedlam (the Bethlehem Mental Hospital).
2. John Greenhill (1649–76).

Sir Godfrey Kneller (1646–1723) as Justice of the Peace

Sir Godfrey, at Whitton, acted as Justice of Peace, and was so much more swayed by equity than law that his judgments accompanied with humour have said to have occasioned those lines by Pope –

> I think Sir Godfrey should decide the suit,
> Who sent the thief (that stole the cash) away,
> And punish'd him that put it in his way.

This alluded to his dismissing a soldier who had stolen a joint of meat, and accused the butcher of having tempted him by it. Whenever Sir Godfrey was applied to determine what parish a poor man belonged to, he always inquired which parish was the richer, and settled the poor man there; nor would ever sign a warrant to distrain the goods of a poor man, who could not pay a tax. These instances showed the goodness of his heart; others, even in his capacity of justice, his peculiar turn; a handsome young woman came before him to swear a rape; struck with her beauty, he continued examining her, as he sat painting, till he had taken her likeness. If he disliked interruption, he would not be interrupted. Seeing a constable coming to him at the head of a mob, he called to him, without inquiring into the affair – 'Mr. Constable, you see that turning; go that way, and you will find an ale-house, the sign of the King's head – go, and make it up.'

[H. Walpole, *Anecdotes of Painting in England*, 1780]

Godfrey Kneller on Portraiture

Kneller was one day conversing about his art, when he gave the following neat reason for preferring portraiture. 'Painters of history,' said he, 'make the dead live, and do not begin to live themselves till they are dead. I paint the living, and they make me live!' In a conversation concerning the legitimacy of the unfortunate son of James the Second,[1] some doubts having been expressed by an Oxford Doctor, he exclaimed with much warmth, 'His father and mother have sat to me about thirty-six times a-piece, and I know every line and bit of their faces. Mein Gott! I could paint King James *now* by memory. I say the child is so like both, that there is not a feature in his

1. The Old Pretender.

[181]

face but what belongs either to father or to mother; this I am sure of, and cannot be mistaken: nay, the nails of his fingers are his mother's, the queen that was. Doctor, – you may be out in your letters, but I cannot be out in my lines.'

[A. Cunningham, *The Lives of the Most Eminent Painters, Sculptors and Architects*, 1829]

Kneller and Queen Anne

Merit in art is not the only ground of success; much is done by management as well, and of this quality there are various kinds that have been practised by different painters. Kneller's was bravado; take, for instance, his little speech to Queen Anne, 'Many painters have given your Majesty the crown and cushion, but it remained for me to make you a Queen!'

[*Conversations of James Northcote with James Ward*, ed. E. Fletcher, 1901]

John Riley (1646–91) and Charles II

Charles sat to him, but almost discouraged the bashful artist from pursuing a profession so proper for him. Looking at the picture he cried, 'Is this like me? then od's fish, I am an ugly fellow.' This discouraged Riley so much, that he could not bear the picture, though he sold it for a large price.

[H. Walpole, *Anecdotes of Painting*, 1780]

John Evelyn's Meeting with Grinling Gibbons
(1648–1721)

Mr. Evelyn, author of the 'Sylva,' was the first to notice the talents of Grinling Gibbons, and introduced him to Charles II. His meeting with this admirable artist, is thus noticed in his diary: 'This day I first acquainted his majesty with that incomparable young man, Gibbons, whom I had lately met with in an obscure place, by mere accident, as I was walking near a poor solitary thatched house, in a field in our parish near Say's Court. I found him shut in; but looking in at the window, I perceived him carving that large Cartoon or Crucifix of Tintoret, a copy of which I had myself brought from Venice, where the original painting remains. I asked if I might enter? He opened the door civilly to me, and I saw him about such a work as, for the curiosity of handling, drawing, and studious exactness, I never had before seen in all my travels. I questioned him why he worked in such an obscure and lonesome place? He told me, that it was that he might apply himself to his profession without interruption, and wondered not a little how I had found him out. I asked if he was unwilling to be made known to some great man, for that I believed it might turn to his profit; he answered, he was yet but a beginner, but would not be sorry to sell off that piece: on demanding the price, he said, one hundred pounds. In good earnest the very frame was worth the money, there being nothing in nature so tender and delicate as the flowers and festoons about it, and yet the work was very strong; in the piece were more than a hundred figures of men, &c. I found he was likewise musical and very civil, sober and discreet. Of this young artist, and the manner of finding him out, I acquainted the king, and begged that he would give me leave to bring him and his work to Whitehall; for that I would adventure my reputation with his majesty, that he had never seen any thing approach it, and that he would be exceedingly pleased, and employ him. This was the first notice he had of Mr. Gibbons.'

[*The Percy Anecdotes*, 1821–3]

Michael Dahl (1656–1743) and Queen Christina

But it was more flattering to Dahl to be employed by one that had been his sovereign, the famous Queen Christina. As he worked on her picture, she asked what he intended she should hold in her hand? He replied, 'A fan.' Her majesty, whose ejaculations were rarely delicate, vented a very gross one, and added, 'A fan! give me a lion; that is fitter for the Queen of Sweden.'

[H. Walpole, *Anecdotes of Painting*, 1780] Dahl was Swedish-born but spent most of his career in England. For that reason the anecdote is placed here.

John Closterman (1660–1711) Paints the Duke and Duchess of Marlborough

He painted the Duke and Duchess of Marlborough and all their children in one picture, and the duke on horseback, on which subject, however, he had so many disputes with the duchess, that the duke said, 'It has given me more trouble to reconcile my wife and you, than to fight a battle.'

[H. Walpole, *Anecdotes of Painting*, 1780] Sarah, Duchess of Marlborough, wife of the victor of Blenheim and favourite of Queen Anne, was famous for her domineering nature and violent temper.

XIV

EUROPEAN ART IN
THE EIGHTEENTH CENTURY

৯৯

*The eighteenth century saw the publication of an increasing number of
collections of artists' lives, but these tended to be concerned with the
art of the immediate past (the sixteenth and seventeenth centuries)
rather than with the present. The most comprehensive list of artists
occurs in the extensive compilation of notes brought together by the
great connoisseur P. J. Mariette, and now known as the Abécédario.
Mariette, who knew many of the artists who were his contemporaries,
devotes little space to the majority, and only rarely gives personal
details. His fullest biography is that of the portraitist Maurice Quentin
de La Tour, whom he seems to have disliked for what he considered to
be insolence and avarice.*

*The artistic personality who attracted most attention from the
French writers of the first half of the century was Watteau. Watteau
died young, and was at the height of fashionable success at the time of
his death. His friends (and also those who stood to make a profit out of
his work) seem to have made a concerted effort to put his reputation
on solid foundations. They made an attempt at complete publication
of Watteau's drawings as well as of his paintings, reproducing them as
prints, and they put on record their reminiscences of him. Neither
Boucher nor Fragonard attracted anything like the same degree of
attention.*

*One important document, certainly in terms of what was to happen
in the future, is D'Azara's account of the pioneer Neo-classicist Anton
Rafael Mengs. At one moment we seem to get a glimpse of the very
beginnings of abstraction in art, when D'Azara visits Mengs's Roman
studio in the company of the British sculptor Christopher Hewetson:
'We found him whistling and singing alone, and demanding the*

reason, he replied, that he was practising a sonata of Corelli's, because he wished to finish this painting after the style of that great composer.'

In general, however, the impression made by the anecdotes included in this section is less focused than in previous sections. This reflects the nature of the available material.

Giuseppe Maria Crespi (1665–1747) and Marriage

Soon after that he started another portrait of his Eminence the Archbishop [Lambertini], full-length standing, and the size of life. While he was at work on this there was another amusing upset which is worth noting. It is necessary to know that my father never wanted his sons to marry. If you wished to see him in a rage, all you had to do was mention the subject. On one occasion, when the Cardinal was at our house and my father was painting him, one of my brothers came in with a letter which had come by the post from Modena. It was from another of my brothers who was there on business. Lambertini promptly took the letter, saying, as he opened it, that my father should go on painting and that he would read it out. He then rapidly read a completely fabricated letter in which this absent son, with a multitude of expressions of shame and apology, threw himself at my father's feet and begged forgiveness, explaining that he couldn't get out of an obligation to marry a certain Signora Apollonia.

When the Archbishop reached this point, my father leaped to his feet, threw aside his palette, brushes and stool, and upset the varnish, oil and everything else on his little bench, giving vent to a thousand different exclamations, all at the same time. Lambertini rose to calm him, and to tell him it was all just a joke of his own devising, and finally they returned to the morning's work. But thereafter, whenever His Eminence came to visit, he would always joke before he got out of his carriage, and assure my father that he did not have Signora Apollonia with him.

[L. Crespi, *Felsina Pittrice*, 1769] G. M. Crespi is better known as a genre-painter than he is as a portraitist.

How Rosalba Carriera (1675–1757) Took up Painting

Vleughels,[1] a friend of Rosalba, told me that, before she [Rosalba] took up painting, her trade was making designs for the kind of lace called Point de Venise. The fashion for this having passed, she found herself in a difficult situation, as neither she nor her family, had the means to live. When she was thus embarrassed a French artist called

1. Nicolas Vleughels (1668–1737). A minor artist, also a friend of Watteau.

Jean Steve came to Venice. He was a painter of snuffboxes, then increasingly fashionable, and advised her to follow the same trade. As she already knew about design and colour, she followed his advice and found it good. It is thus that great things follow from little ones.

[P. J. Mariette, *Abécédario*, 1851–3, written first half of eighteenth century] Rosalba made an immense reputation throughout Europe with her portraits in pastels, generally considered superior to those of either La Tour or Liotard. Her celebrity outstripped that of any other Venetian artist of her time, including G. B. Tiepolo.

Jean-François de Troy (1679–1752) in Rome

M. de Marigny,[1] or as he was then still called, M. de Vandières, made a tour of Italy when M. de Troy was Director [of the French School in Rome]. He stayed in the French Embassy and M. de Troy treated him with all due respect. At first, everything went well on both sides. There were various entertainments: the students gave a ball and all the high nobility in Rome were invited; M. de Vandières was grateful to the director for all his kind attentions.

Unfortunately, the latter had a mistress, the wife of a doctor, who was extremely pretty. He was madly in love with her. It is one of the weaknesses of old men to carry passion to excess and be extremely jealous. M. de Troy fell victim to this. It seemed to him that his guest was attracted by this pretty woman; he could not contain himself, lost his self-possession, and was insolent to his superior. He said things which were heard and not liked. From that moment his ruin was certain. For some time he had been requesting his own recall – this was perhaps a game: head over heels in love as he was he would have been very vexed to be taken at his word. Having had no reply, he no doubt thought the whole thing had been forgotten. But here he was in error. His successor had been appointed. At the moment when he least expected it, his replacement arrived and left him no hope of keeping his place. He remained in Rome, still the captive of the woman who had ensnared him; he temporized but finally had to take his leave. M. de Nivernois, our ambassador in Rome, had obtained permission to return to France. A frigate from Marseilles was waiting to carry him home. M. de Troy received orders to depart, and to make use of this

1. Brother of Mme de Pompadour, mistress of Louis XV.

opportunity. He was at the opera with his mistress when the news was given to him and he was told the appointed day, which was only a little way off. The news came like a thunderclap. Completely shattered, but making an effort to conceal his feelings, he went home. He immediately succumbed to a fever. A sore throat, which was attributed to the cold air he had met when coming away from the theatre, threatened him with quinsy. The doctors were called, and the illness soon went to his chest, so that he died within a few days.

[P. J. Mariette, *Abécédario*, 1851–3]

Antoine Watteau (1684–1721) works as a Copyist

Knowing little, and having no one to help him, the Pont Notre-Dame[1] provided him with a means of livelihood which he was only too happy to discover. This miserable business of making copies a hundred generations removed from the original, with crude colours applied without modulation, and in even worse taste than the coloured up prints which at least retain the outlines of the original, did not sit well with the feelings nature had already implanted in him. However, necessity is a hard taskmaster. To give an idea of his talent and natural disposition, I can tell the following story.

Watteau had been working for some time in the house of a dealer in this species of work, to whom chance had directed him. The genius of painting, which helps us to sustain adversity through the exercise of the imagination, and which sometimes seasons misfortune with a touch of humour, inspired him to play a trick which consoled him, at least for the moment, for the boredom of having to paint the same thing over and over. He worked at daily rates. At noon, one day, he had not yet come to ask for what was called, by courtesy, 'the original' – the mistress of the establishment took great care to lock this away every evening. She noted his absence and called for him, shouting several times, without effect, to get him to come down from the attic where, from morning, he had been at work, and where, in fact, he had already done the painting in question from memory. When she had finished shouting, he came downstairs, and, with perfect coolness, combined with a gentleness which was natural to him, asked for the model, in order to paint (so he said) the spectacles. The painting was, I

1. Where the cheapest picture-dealers had their shops.

think, an old woman after Gerard Dou, looking at her account book —
a kind of composition which was much in fashion at that time.

[Comte de Caylus, *La Vie d'Antoine Watteau*, reprinted in P. Champion,
Watteau, 1921]

Antoine Watteau and the Académie Royale

The extraordinary fashion in which he became a member of the
Académie Royale des Beaux Arts did much honour to him. He wanted
to go to Rome in order to study the great masters, above all the
Venetians, whose colour and composition he loved. He could not
afford to make the journey without help, and for this reason applied
for a grant from the king. To achieve this aim, he had two paintings
which he had sold to my father-in-law taken to the Académie. Having
neither friends nor protectors other than these works, he had them put
on view in a room which was usually crossed by the members. They all
saw the paintings, and admired them without knowing who the artist
was. M. de La Fosse,[1] an artist well known at that time, stopped in
front of them even longer than his colleagues, astonished by their
quality. Going into the Academie's own room, he enquired who had
done them. The vigorous colouring and harmony of tones seemed to
suggest that they were the work of an Old Master. He was told that
they were the work of a young man who had come to ask the
academicians to intervene on his behalf, so he might be given a royal
grant to go and study in Italy.

M. de La Fosse, surprised, ordered that the artist should be brought
in. Watteau appeared. There was nothing imposing about him. He
explained modestly the reasons for his manoeuvre and begged earnestly for a grant, if he was thought worthy of it. 'My dear friend,' M.
de La Fosse said gently, 'you do not know your own talent, and are
uncertain of your powers. Believe me, you know more than we do; we
think you capable of honouring our academy. Go through the
necessary procedures; we already think of you as one of ourselves.'
Watteau withdrew, made his official visits, and was immediately
elected.

[E. F. Gersaint, *Catalogue du feu M. Quentin de Lorangère*, reprinted in
P. Champion, *Watteau*, 1921]

1. Charles de La Fosse (1636–1716).

Watteau Takes Advice

Reading was his great relaxation. He knew how to make use of what he read, and in general he perceived and wittily repaid the stupidity of those who came to interrupt him. However, as I have already said, he was much too easy-going, and people quickly took advantage of him.

This characteristic gave rise to an imbroglio with a miniature painter whose name I will not give here. This man talked well, but much too much, about painting. But apparently he knew how to keep quiet on the day he visited Watteau – or else the latter, in order to shorten his importunities, had been only too anxious to be rid of him. In any case, he succeeded in getting a picture . . .

This miniaturist was so much persuaded of his own merits, that he arrogated to himself the success of all the best paintings, asserting this was due to the advice he gave their authors, and to the way in which he had helped with the harmony, the tonality and the disposition of the figures. He chose the wrong company in which to show off: his subjects were de Troy,[1] Largillière[2] and Rigaud,[3] all then at the height of their powers. I was young then, and with me he was incautious – he had no idea I was interested in painting. One day, with all the enthusiasm and false confidence of a braggart who has a good audience, he talked for two hours about the way in which he had corrected these great men, and the deference they had shown to his good taste. I was irritated by his overweening conceit, but, sound as the grounds for defence were, I did not dare to contradict him – I did not feel confident enough, and I did not wish, by my own defeat, to enhance the triumph he was already enjoying thanks to his self-assurance and the ignorance of those listening to him.

Several days later, talking to Watteau about the way in which artists are unjustly criticized, and how they often suffer from the wrong impressions given to the foolish and ignorant people who are always in the majority, I told him about this conversation, and named the culprit. 'If I'd known he was like that,' said Watteau, 'I wouldn't have given him a painting the other day.' He then told me of his experience with the same man, resolved now to learn from it.

A little later, the miniaturist came to see Watteau, to thank him for

1. Either François de Troy (1645–1730) or Jean-François de Troy (1679–1752).
2. Nicolas de Largillière (1656–1746).
3. Hyacinthe Rigaud (1659–1743).

the magnificent present. He praised the picture to the skies, but nevertheless added that, having looked at it carefully, he had noted several improvements which he deemed necessary. Inwardly delighted to see him digging his own grave, Watteau said that he would make the changes with pleasure. The man replied, that if Watteau would make these in his presence, he would tell him what needed to be done. Watteau agreed.

Delighted by a docility which perhaps he had not anticipated when he arrived, the miniaturist pulled the painting from under his coat. Watteau, coolly, took some oil, and in a twinkling had completely cleaned off the canvas. The man started to be angry, but Watteau spoke to him firmly, and thus revenged the great men whose superiority he now brought home, telling him that it was not his place to speak about them as he did.

[Comte de Caylus, *La Vie d'Antoine Watteau*]

Watteau and the Wig-maker

A wig-maker brought Watteau a wig *au naturel* which had nothing to recommend it, but which nevertheless delighted the artist. It seemed to him a masterly imitation of nature. Certainly not of nature in curlers — I can see it now, all long and lank. Watteau asked the price, but the wig-maker, shrewder than he, said that he would be happy to make an exchange for something by the artist. A couple of drawings would have satisfied him. Watteau thought he had never made so good a bargain, and, apportioning his gift to the pleasure he got from his new possession, gave the man a pair of small paintings, perhaps the most delightful he had made. I arrived soon after the conclusion of this exchange. Watteau was still feeling scruples about it. He wanted to do yet another painting for the wig-maker, and it was with some difficulty that I managed to quieten his conscience.

[Comte de Caylus, *La Vie d'Antoine Watteau*]

Watteau's Trees

But there is one fault of Watteau for which till lately I could never account. His trees appear as unnatural to our eyes as his figures must do to a real peasant who had never stirred beyond his village. In my late journeys to Paris the cause of this grievous absurdity was apparent to me, though nothing can excuse it. Watteau's trees are copied from those of the Tuileries and villas near Paris – a strange scene to study nature in! There I saw the originals of those tufts of plumes and fans, and trimmed-up groves, that nod to one another like the scenes of an opera. Fantastic people! who range and fashion their trees, and teach them to hold up their heads, as a dancing-master would, if he expected Orpheus should return to play a minuet to them.

[H. Walpole, *Anecdotes of Painting in England*, 1780]

Watteau's Appearance and Character

Watteau was of medium height and had a weak constitution; his mind was lively and penetrating, his sentiments were elevated; he spoke little, but well – it was the same when he wrote. He was always meditative, a great admirer of nature and of all the masters who have copied nature. Labour had made him melancholic; he had a cold and somewhat distant manner, which made things difficult for his friends, and sometimes for himself. His only fault was indifference and love of change.

[P. J. Mariette, *Abécédario*, 1851–3]

The Death of Watteau

The curate of the village who attended him in his sickness, presented him the crucifix according to custom. Watteau observing it all carved, desired him to take it away, saying, Remove that crucifix; it grieves me to see it; is it possible that my master is so ill serv'd?

[R. de Piles, *The Art of Painting*, 1750] The same story is told of Alonso Cano and others.

An Assessment of Jean-Baptiste Pater (1695–1736)

The defect of this painter was that he did not know how to put a figure together and possessed a heavy brush. His sole occupation was to make money and to hoard it. The poor man never gave himself a moment of relaxation; he denied himself necessities and his only pleasure was counting his money. I have never seen anyone who lived such a miserable life.

[P. J. Mariette, *Abécédario*, 1851–3]

G. B. Tiepolo (1696–1770) and Anton Raffael Mengs (1728–79)

Don José de Ribera of Madrid has communicated to us the following anecdote concerning Tiepolo's residence at the Court of Spain, which he found in a manuscript in his possession, entitled *Vidas de los pintores*:

The enmity which existed between Mengs and Tiepolo, at the time when both were in Spain, is well enough known. In a letter written to Guibal on 23rd December 1761 Mengs stated that his two rivals were Tiepolo and Corrado Giaquinto.[1]

With two strokes of the brush Tiepolo could obtain effects which Mengs was far from being able to procure, even with much labour; Tiepolo had a wonderful fluency which Mengs was in no way able to imitate. The impossibility of rivalling our painter so weighed upon his spirit that he thought of defeating him by illicit methods.

When Tiepolo was going from the Escorial to San Ildefonso, Mengs entrusted two *satadores de caminos* (bandits) with the job of intercepting the painter and giving him a good beating, so as to put him out of action for enough time for Mengs to get the upper hand over him. Mengs himself climbed a tree to watch the effect of the beating.

Tiepolo was going in the direction of San Ildefonso, mounted on a mule, which was led by his muleteer. The two bandits duly emerged from the undergrowth where they had concealed themselves, ready to carry out their instructions. All of a sudden the tree where Mengs had stationed himself broke, and he fell senseless to the ground. The bandits abandoned their prey and ran to Mengs's aid.

The latter, picked up with much care by Tiepolo, who even amongst Iberian clods had preserved a generous Venetian heart, was given assistance and help to transport himself on a road which was difficult for a sick man.

It seems that peace was made over flasks of Alicante, at a feast made before long by the two painters in the company of Flipart[2] and Amigoni.[3]

[G. M. Urbani, *Tiepolo e sua famiglia*, 1879]

1. Corrado Giaquinto (1699–1775).
2. Charles Joseph Flipart (1721–97).
3. Jacopo Amigoni (1675–1752).

Jean Baptiste Chardin (1699–1779) Instructs a Patron

The painter Chardin was notoriously outspoken and tough-minded. He was offended if people showed their ignorance of the art he practised, of which he himself had a high opinion. Foolish questions annoyed him with their impertinence, and once prompted him to give a sharp lesson to a noble lady. 'Monsuex, monsuex,' said this lady, in whose house Chardin was working, 'is it difficult to do what you do?' 'You just have to whistle and keep your fingers busy, Madame,' said the artist. 'It's like this,' she went on, 'My butler has been learning to paint for the past eight days – he's three-quarters of the way through his training. A few more lessons, and he ought to be able to produce a painting, don't you think?' 'On my word, Madame, he can, if you like, finish my painting, because I'm off.'

[Dusaulchoy, *Mosaique historique, literaire et politique*, 1818]

Chardin on Colour

Chardin was short, but strongly built and muscular. He was witty and, most of all, possessed much commonsense and excellent judgement. He was forceful in expressing his ideas, even where this concerned things that generally resist explanation, such as the wizardry of colour and the causes of various effects of light. His retorts were often quick and to the point. One day a painter was explaining at great length how he purified and perfected his use of colour. Chardin grew impatient at so much chatter from a man whose paintings he knew to be cold and slick. 'Since when,' he demanded, 'does one paint with colour?' 'What else does one paint with?' came the astonished reply. 'You should *use* colour, but *paint* with your feelings,' said Chardin.

[C. N. Cochin, *Essai sur la vie de M. Chardin*, 1780]

Francesco Zuccarelli (1702–88) Travels to England

It has been remarked, that among the figures which he introduced in his landscapes, he frequently represented one with a *gourd bottle* at his waist, as is often seen in Italy. This is said to have been done intentionally, as a sort of pun on his own name, *zucco* being the Italian word for a gourd.

At what time he came into England is not exactly known, but the following anecdote may serve to ascertain, that it was not till after the peace of Aix-la-Chapelle; for, as he was travelling on the Continent, upon the territories of one of the belligerent states, he was detained as a suspicious person, but obtained his release with honour, by the following candid and ingenuous appeal to those who detained him.

After declaring his profession and name, both of which he considered as sufficiently known, he offered to prove the truth of his assertion, by painting a picture, provided the necessary materials were allowed him: His proposal was granted, and his veracity was confirmed, by the production of his pencil, and he was consequently released.

[E. Edwards, *Lives of Painters who have resided or been born in England*, 1808] This parallels one of the stories told, in more elaborate form, about Adriaen Brouwer.

The Limited Talent of Jean-Etienne Liotard (1702–89)

At the Porte[1] he became acquainted with Richard second Lord Edgecumbe (who was the particular and early friend of Mr. Reynolds), and Sir Everard Fawkener, our embassador, who persuaded him to come to England. In his journey to the Levant he had adopted the Eastern habit, and wore it here with a very long beard. It contributed much to the portraits of himself, and some thought it was to attract customers. He painted both in miniature and enamel, though he seldom practised them: but he is best known by his works in crayons. His likenesses were very strong, and too like to please those who sat to him; thus he had great employment the first year and very little the second. Devoid of imagination, he could render nothing but what he saw before his eyes. Freckles, marks of the small-pox, every thing found its place; not so much from fidelity, as because he could not conceive the absence of any thing that appeared to him. Minuteness prevailed in all his works, grace in none; nor was there any ease in his outlines, but the stiffness of a bust in all his portraits. Thence his heads want air and the softness of flesh.

Reynolds gives his opinion of this artist thus: 'The only merit in Liotard's pictures is neatness, which, as a general rule, is the characteristic of a low genius, or rather no genius at all. His pictures are just what ladies do when they paint for their amusement; nor is there any

1. Constantinople.

person, how poor soever their talents may be, but in a very few years, by dint of practice, may possess themselves of every qualification in the art which this *great man* has got.' Liotard was twice in England, and staid about two years each time.

[J. Northcote, *Memoirs of Sir Joshua Reynolds*, 1813] Mariette records similar criticism of Liotard in the *Abécédario*.

The Modest Pleasures of François Boucher (1703–70)

M. Boucher hardly ever went out, and his movements were confined to periodic visits to Versailles, to Gobelins,[1] of which he was the director, to the Opera, where he was in charge of both the costumes and stage-sets, and to the homes of naturalists and amateurs interested in their work.

. . .

He was an enthusiastic collector, especially of rare minerals. The Duke of Zweickbrücken gave him a case full of these: 'Weak and decrepit though he was, he made an endless procedure of unpacking it. Every time a rare and choice piece was taken out, he cried out with joy like a child. However, from the whole case he only kept seven pieces for his own collection; the remainder was set aside to be bartered with the connoisseurs and merchants with whom he spent his life and carried on trade.'

[J. C. von Mannlich, *Memoires du Chevalier du Mannlich*, ed. J. Delage, 1948] Both extracts refer to the 1760s. However, other stories, concerning Boucher's alleged debauchery, his connection with Louis XV's Parc aux Cerfs, etc., appear to be nineteenth-century fictions, which can be traced no further than Arsene Houssaye's *Histoire de l'art français au XVIIIe siècle*, a collection of articles published in book form in 1860.

Maurice Quentin de La Tour (1704–88) and the Art of Deception

To enliven what I have written, I will tell an amusing story which I had from the painter himself. A man whom he did not know whom he never saw again, wanted his portrait done. La Tour accepted willingly. Once the portrait was done, this man, who always came alone and

1. The Royal manufactury of tapestries.

who seemed anxious to preserve his incognito, asked La Tour to glaze it and put it into the kind of frame used for a dressing table mirror. On the appointed day, he came in the morning, by himself as always, took the portrait, wrapped it in a cloth, then took it in his arms and placed it in his carriage – all this in perfect silence and without saying a word about payment. La Tour watched these operations and dared not say a word, waiting for the money to appear. To himself he kept saying: 'Is he going to carry it off without paying for it?' And after the man had gone, he said quietly: 'Well, that's just what he's done.' The strangeness of the incident silenced him; and there matters rested.

The client went home. The first thing he wanted to know was whether his wife was up yet. She was still asleep, which is what he had hoped for. He went into her room, removed the mirror from her dressing table, put his portrait in its place, and hid in a room next door. His wife, having woken, got up, and immediately went to her dressing table. Her husband took advantage of this to leave his hiding place and put himself immediately behind her chair. The wife opened up the table, saw her husband in front of her and imagined it was his image reflected in the glass. She looked behind her, and was confirmed in this opinion. No portrait ever produced such a perfect illusion. It was shattered only when the husband moved, and let the wife see that her eyes had deluded her. Well content with the success of this little scene, he went back the following day to La Tour and apologized for having given him any anxiety, told him what had passed since their last meeting (something which could only flatter the artist's amour-propre), and threw a purse on the table. 'There are a hundred louis in that,' he said. 'Take whatever you want – all, if you think it appropriate: it still wouldn't be enough to testify to my gratitude or measure up to the pleasure you have given me.' La Tour only took what he thought was his legitimately, and returned the rest of the money to his client; who went off and never reappeared. My guess is that he was an Englishman – where would one find someone French who behaved in this way?

[P. J. Mariette, *Abécédario*, 1851–3]

Maurice Quentin de La Tour and Louis XV

He sometimes took liberties of a kind hardly permissible even among equals. Once, when he was painting Mme la marquise de Pompadour, the King was present. His majesty turned the talk to the buildings he was having constructed, and spoke of them with a certain satisfaction. Suddenly La Tour began to utter – he pretended he was talking to himself. 'That's all very fine,' he said, 'but "vessels"[1] would be better.' This was just at the moment when the English had destroyed our fleet. The King turned red and fell silent; the painter congratulated himself secretly on having told the truth in a land where truth was unknown. He did not feel he had committed an imprudence which deserved only contempt.

[P. J. Mariette, *Abécédario*, 1851–3]

Pompeo Batoni (1708–87) Moved by his own 'Coriolanus'

Batoni was very kind, tender-hearted and devout. Once, when I was saying goodbye to him, he went with me to the door. His unfinished painting of *Coriolanus and His Mother* hung in the anteroom. 'Why don't you finish it?' I asked him. 'I cannot do that,' he replied. 'It moves me too much for me to do so. Just look at Coriolanus' mother, whom he has found amidst the throng of women. He goes up to embrace her, and she pushes him away and says: "You beast! You were born in Rome, Rome nourished you and gave you strength and now you want to let her die of hunger and thirst? That city, where I fed you from my breast? If you want to go to Rome, the road to it goes right through my breast."' Having said this, Batoni was so moved he started to cry bitterly and, since my own tears are not frozen into place, both of us wept in front of the painting.

[W. W. Tischbein, *Aus Meinem Leben*, 1922] A typical display of 'sensibility' in late eighteenth-century style, surprising only because associated with an artist whose rich English clients, who sat to him for portraits, regularly accused him of pride and avarice.

Pompeo Batoni and Benjamin West (1738–1830)

West used to tell how he was introduced to Battoni when he went to Rome, and of the vast consequence the latter assumed. 'Come here, young man!' said Battoni to West, 'there – stand just there!' He then dipped his pencil in the colour and laid on the canvas a single touch,

1. There is a pun in French – *bâtiment* (building) could also mean a large sailing vessel.

saying, 'Go! young man; now you have it in your power to say that you have seen Battoni paint!' And Fuseli used to tell how, in complimenting Battoni, he was waggish enough one day to say to him, 'You, Signor, far exceed Raphael, Correggio, or Titian, for you unite in yourself all their separate excellencies!' Battoni answered Fuseli with, 'But they had *their* merit! – yes, yes, they had their merit, too!'

   [*Conversations of James Northcote and James Ward*, ed. E. Fletcher, 1901]

Claude Joseph Vernet (1714–89) Paints St Jerome

Vernet relates, that he was once employed to paint a landscape, with a cave, and St. Jerome in it; he accordingly painted the landscape, with St. Jerome at the entrance of the cave. When he delivered the picture, the purchaser, who understood nothing of perspective, said, 'The landscape and the cave are well made, but St. Jerome is not *in* the cave.' I understand you, sir, replied Vernet, 'I will alter it.' He therefore took the painting and made the shade darker, so that the saint seemed to sit farther in. The gentleman took the painting; but it again appeared to him that the saint was not in the cave. Vernet then wiped out the figure, and gave it to the gentleman, who seemed perfectly satisfied. Whenever he saw strangers to whom he showed the picture, he said, 'Here you see a picture by Vernet, with St. Jerome in the cave.' 'But we cannot see the saint,' replied the visitors. 'Excuse me, gentlemen,' answered the possessor, 'he is there; for I have seen him standing at the entrance, and afterwards farther back; and am therefore quite sure that he is in it.'

   [*The Percy Anecdotes*, 1821–3]

Jean-Baptiste Greuze (1725–1805) and the Italian Princess

What did Greuze remember about this trip to Italy, which had scarcely more influence on him than the same journey had on Boucher. One memory which remained living and present in the midst of many other events, was a love story which Greuze sometimes alluded to in old age, perhaps to his own surprise, when women denied too warmly in his presence the possible idealism of the opposite sex in matters of the heart . . .

   Greuze had received letters of recommendation to the Duke of Orr

. . . who received him very kindly. The Duke was a widower and had a charming daughter who loved painting; Greuze soon became her teacher. After a few lessons, Greuze, already in love himself, divined that Laetitia (for that was her name) loved him in return. Frightened by the distance that the difference both in rank and fortune placed between them, he fled from the temptation, and no longer went to her palace. Sunk in misery, harassed by the teasing of his fellow-pensioners in Rome, in particular by the mockery of Fragonard,[1] who nicknamed him 'the amorous Cherubino' – his blond curly hair lent point to the comparison – Greuze learned that the young princess was unwell, and that the cause of her malady was mysterious. He hung around the palace, trying to get news, ready to open his heart to the patient. In the midst of all this, one day, while he was drawing in St Peter's, he encountered the duke, who carried him off home to see a painting he had just acquired – two heads by Titian. 'My daughter,' the duke added, 'wants to make a copy of them when she is better; I hope you will come and see her at work; she wants you to.' And since the duke also asked Greuze to make a copy immediately, so that he could send it to one of his relatives, the artist could not refuse – he returned to the palace, and worked there all day. Each morning, he got news of Laetitia's state of health from her nurse – the eternal nurse of the *novillieri* – who had already guessed the girl's secret, and now guessed that of Greuze himself, and hastened to take the patient assurances of the painter's love; he had not dared to declare himself (so she said) for fear of displeasing her.

The nurse sought out Greuze, she brought him secretly to the sick princess's room: she was very thin, but still had 'her beautiful looks, like Cleopatra'. After a moment's silence, the princess, urged on by the nurse, told Greuze that she loved him. 'Yes,' she continued after an instant, 'I love you! Tell me truly – do you love me too?' Greuze remained silent from sheer happiness, and she, misunderstanding the cause, buried her face in her hands and burst into tears. Then Greuze threw himself at her feet, spoke with kisses, poured out his heart. 'I can then be happy!' cried Laetitia, and clapped her pretty hands. It was the joy of a child. She ran to embrace her nurse, she reiterated her happiness, as one gets up in the morning repeating the thought that made one laugh on waking. 'Now listen, both of you; I love Greuze

1. Jean-Honoré Fragonard (1732–1806).

and I'm going to marry him.' – 'You're dreaming, my darling!' cried
the nurse. 'What about your father?' – 'My father will never agree, I
know it – he wants me to marry his eternal Casa . . . the oldest and
ugliest of men, or young Count Palleri, whom I do not know and do
not wish to know. I have a good inheritance from my mother, which I
can dispose of myself. I shall give it to Greuze whom I will marry, and
he will take me off to France and you will go with us.' Intoxicated with
dreams, she ran through all the arrangements, all the details: the kind
of life they would live together in Paris; Greuze would continue to
paint; he would become another Titian (her favourite Old Master);
her father in the end would be proud to have him for a son-in-law.
'Won't it be nice?' she said to Greuze naïvely. And her dreams became
ever madder, more intoxicating.

When Greuze saw her again, he had had time for serious reflection.
The princess teased him for his reserve and air of gravity, arguing
against him with foolish tenderness, then becoming furious, calling
him perfidious, accusing him of having pretended to be in love in order
to break her heart, weeping, tearing her hair. Greuze ended by falling
at her feet and vowing to obey her blindly. But when he left her,
commonsense, and a clearer view of things returned. He foresaw her
father's despair, his curse upon him, his vengeance, all the unhappiness
which would fall upon their union. Resolved to give in no more, to see
Laetitia no more, not to let his resolutions be swayed by her words, he
feigned illness. This sickness soon became genuine enough, and he was
three months in bed with fever and delirium.

When he had recovered, the princess was about to marry. She asked
only a word from the painter; she was ready to break off the match.
This word Greuze had the courage never to say. Seized with a terrible
jealousy of the princess's fiancé, who was young, handsome, made to
attract the love of any woman, he fled, saying adieu forever, carrying
with him Laetitia's portrait, the copy of one he had made for her
father.

[E. and J. de Goncourt, *L'Art du XVIIIe siècle*, 2me series, 1882]

Greuze's Worst Enemy

Ridicule did not reach him; irony passed him by. 'This is fine,' M de Marigny[1] said to him, as he paused in front of *La Pleureuse*. 'Monsieur, I am well aware of it. People praise me, but they don't give me work.' – 'It is because you have a swarm of enemies,' Vernet[2] told him, 'and among these enemies there is one who seems to love you passionately, and who is responsible for your ruin.' – 'And who is that?' – 'Yourself.'

[E. and J. de Goncourt, *L'Art du XVIIIe siècle*, 1882]

Greuze Responds to Criticism

Encountering the slightest criticism of his work, the artist flew into naïve and often amusing rages. Mme Geoffrin allowed herself to criticize the 'fricasée of children' in Greuze's *La Mère Bien-Aimée*, and the artist cried: 'What right has she to talk about works of art? She'd better be careful, or I'll make her immortal! I'll paint her as a schoolmistress, with a whip in her hand, and she will frighten all the children of today and those as yet unborn!'

[E. and J. de Goncourt, *L'Art du XVIIIe siècle*, 1882]

Greuze and his Wife

I love to hear [Greuze] talking to his wife. It's like a Punch and Judy show where Punch returns Judy's blows with a skill which makes his companion even more malicious. The only thing I do is to offer my own opinion sometimes in that brisk tone you are well acquainted with.

[D. Diderot, *Mémoires, correspondance et ouvrages inédits*, 1831] This extract is from a letter of 1767 to the sculptor Pierre Etienne Falconet (1741–97), who was then working in Russia.

---

1. Brother of the royal mistress Mmme de Pompadour and, as Surintendant des Bâtiments, effectively Minister of Fine Arts. Greuze was complaining of a lack of official commissions.
2. Claude Joseph Vernet (1714–89), landscape painter.

Francesco Casanova (1727–1802) on Rubens

Casanova was very witty and original. He loved gossiping, and amused us greatly, when we dined with Prince Kaunitz, by telling stories, often without a word of truth in them, which owed their comicality to his own lively, if bizarre imagination. His retorts were prompt and to the point. One day, when we were dining with the Prince, the talk turned to painting. Rubens was mentioned, and after his genius had been praised, someone said that, thanks to his cultivated mind, Rubens had been appointed an ambassador. Hearing this, an old German baroness commented: 'What? A painter–ambassador? He must have been an ambassador who painted in his spare time!' 'Not at all, Madame,' Casanova replied, 'He was a painter who was an ambassador in his spare time.'

[E.-M. Vigée Le Brun, *Souvenirs*, 1835–7] Francesco Casanova was a battle-painter and a brother of Giacomo, the author of the famous *Memoirs*.

Anton Raffael Mengs (1728–79) Paints in Tune

I now come to the last work in which Mengs deposited the very essence of his talent, and even surpassed himself. The King [Charles III of Spain] having commissioned him for three large paintings, for the new chapel at Aranjuez, he began by the principal one, which represented the Annunciation. After having laboured two months to meditate and design that painting, in the morning that he began it, I was present with Mr Hewetson,[1] a very eminent sculptor. We found him whistling and singing alone, and demanding the reason, he replied, that he was practising a sonata of Corelli's, because he wished to finish this painting after the style of the music of that great composer.

[J. N. D'Azara, *The Work of Anthony Raphael Mengs*, 1796]

Mengs Advises the Pope

Clement 14th having bought, by means of a merchant, various paintings at Venice, and wishing to have the opinion of Mengs, he told him clearly that they were worth nothing, and that he had been deceived. The Holy Father replied to him that such and such painters

1. Christopher Hewetson (1739–98), Irish Neo-classical sculptor resident in Rome.

had praised them much; to which Mengs answered, N.N. and I are two professors, the one praises that which is superior to his abilities, and the other condemns that which is inferior to his.

[J. N. D'Azara, *The Work of Anthony Raphael Mengs*, 1796]

Mengs on Invention

Of a Sculptor, who had put his name to a statue of Disinterestedness in the sepulchre of a great Pope, in this manner, N. INVENIT, Mengs said, that he was right in declaring that he had invented it, because certainly he had not taken it from anything in the world.

[J. N. D'Azara, *The Work of Anthony Raphael Mengs*, 1796]

Mengs Observed by James Northcote

Mengs also affected the great man; to be sure, the court that was paid him, even by crowned heads, might in some measure excuse it. It is usual, in Passion Week, for the tapestries from Raphael's cartoons, together with many others, to be exposed to view under the circular piazza in front of St. Peter's. Sometimes a cardinal would come to look at them, his retinue keeping behind him, and moving as he moved; if he made a step, so did they, and when he stopped, they stopped, always carefully keeping the same distance. Now I remember once seeing Mengs come along with a whole train of his pupils to see these tapestries; he marched on before, with a ridiculously pompous air, and they walked behind him just as the cardinal's attendants did.

[*Conversations of James Northcote with James Ward*, ed. E. Fletcher, 1901]

The Tentative Beginnings of Jean-Honoré Fragonard (1732–1806)

Timidity, which rules in the character of this artist, inhibits his hand. Never content with what he produces, he continually wipes things out and revises. This way of proceeding is harmful to talent, and may prevent this young artist from doing himself justice. I shall be sorry if this is the case; the efforts he makes to do well merit greater success.

[P. J. Mariette, *Abécédario*, 1851–3] Mariette wrote this note when Fragonard was at the beginning of his career. Posterity perceives his work in a completely different way.

The Fortunate Hubert Robert (1733–1808)

Robert, the landscape painter, was extremely good at painting ruins. His pictures of this type resembled those by Panini.[1] It was fashionable – something very grand indeed – to have your drawing room decorated by Robert, so he left a great mass of work behind him. Understandably, not all is equally good; Robert had a wonderful facility with the brush which might be described as both happy and fatal – he painted a picture as quickly as he wrote a letter. Yet when he put reins on his fluency his work was very good. Some of his compositions are as good as those of Vernet.

Of all the artists I have known, Robert was the one who was most at ease in good society, which in any case was something he enjoyed. A lover of all pleasures, including those of the table, he was much sought after, and I doubt if he dined at home more than thrice a year. Visits to the theatre, dances, dinners, country outings – he never refused an invitation; when he was not at work he liked to enjoy himself.

He had a natural wit, was well-read but certainly not a pedant, and the inexhaustible gaiety of his character made him welcome everywhere. He had always been famous for his physical dexterity, and even in mature years retained his youthful habits. When he was more than sixty, and had become quite stout, he remained supple and was quicker than anyone when playing prisoner's base, or tennis, or other ball games. His schoolboyish antics made us cry with laughter. For example one day, at Colombes, he drew a long line on the drawing-room parquet with a piece of chalk, then dressed himself up as an acrobat and, with a balancing pole in his hands, marched solemnly along it, giving a perfect imitation of all the gestures and movements of a tightrope walker – we had never seen anything so droll.

When he was a student at the French Academy in Rome, being then aged barely twenty, Robert bet his friends six sketchbooks made of grey paper that he would climb alone to the very top of the Colosseum. Risking his life a thousand times on the way up, the silly boy managed to do so, but, when he tried to come down, couldn't find the footholds he had used to make the ascent. Someone had to throw him a rope through one of the openings. He tied this round himself and jumped;

1. Giovanni-Paolo Panini (c. 1692–1765/8). Painter of architecture and ruins.

they succeeded in pulling him back into the interior. A mere account of this escapade was enough to make one's hair stand on end. Robert was the only person ever to try it – and all this for six sketchbooks.

It was also Robert who got lost in the Roman catacombs – Abbé Delille celebrates this episode in his poem *Imagination*. Mme de Grollier, who, like the rest of us, had had an account of the adventure from Robert himself, afterwards heard Abbé Delille's poetic version. She said: 'I enjoyed the Abbé more, but Robert's version was more thrilling.'

The good fortune that Robert enjoyed throughout his life also marked his end. This good and happy artist had no premonition of death, and suffered no pain. He seemed perfectly well, and had just finished dressing in order to go and dine in town; Madame Robert, who had just finished her own toilette went to her husband's studio to tell him she was ready, and found him there dead, struck down by a sudden fit of apoplexy.

[E.-M. Vigée Le Brun, *Souvenirs*, 1835–7]

Mme Vigée Le Brun (1755–1842) and Marie-Antoinette

One day I could not come to a sitting I had arranged with [the Queen]. I was far advanced in my second pregnancy, and was suddenly taken ill. Next day I hurried to Versailles to offer my apologies. The Queen was not expecting me; she had ordered the horses to be harnessed so as to go for a drive, and her barouche was the first thing I saw as I entered the courtyard. Nevertheless I went in to talk to the Queen's gentlemen-in-waiting. One, M. Campan, received me frostily, and said, violently annoyed, in a loud voice: 'Madame, the Queen was expecting you yesterday. Today she's going for a promenade and certainly cannot sit.' When I said that I had only come to ask Her Majesty to give me another appointment, he went in to see the Queen. She was finishing her toilette and asked me into her dressing room. She held a book in her hand; she was hearing her daughter's lesson. My heart beat fast – my fear was more than equivalent to my fault. The Queen turned, and said gently: 'I waited for you all yesterday morning. What happened?' 'Alas, Madame,' I said, 'I was so ill I could not obey Your Majesty's commands. I have come today to receive fresh orders. I will then leave at once.' 'No, no, don't go!' the Queen replied. 'I wouldn't like you to make a wasted journey.' She dismissed the carriage, and sat for me. I remember that I was so eager to demonstrate my gratitude for her kindness that I grabbed my paintbox and overturned it. All my brushes were scattered on the floor. I started to remedy the results of my clumsiness. 'Leave them! leave them!' said the Queen. 'Your condition is too advanced for you to bend down safely,' and in spite of my protests she bent and picked the brushes up herself.

[E.-M. Vigée-Lebrun, *Souvenirs*, 1835–7] This is a late but apparently authentic story that closely resembles the celebrated anecdote told about Titian and the Emperor Charles V.

The First Success of Antonio Canova (1757–1822)

At a festival, it is said, which was celebrated in the villa Falier, and attended by a numerous assembly of Venetian nobility, the domestics had neglected to provide an ornament for the dessert, without discovering the omission, till the moment it was required to be supplied. Fearing lest they should on this account incur their master's displeasure, and being in the greatest terror, they applied to Pasino, who then happened to be engaged at work in the house, accompanied by his grandson. The old man's invention could suggest no remedy; – his youthful associate, seeing the necessity of the case, desired some butter to be provided; and from this material presently carved a lion, with such skill and effect, that, on being presented at table, it excited the attention and received the applause of all present. So singular an ornament naturally produced inquiry. The servants were questioned; – the whole was disclosed, and Tonin Canova declared to be the contriver. Tonin was immediately called for; and blushing, – half reluctant, apprehensive of having done something amiss, was ushered into the brilliant assembly; – when, to his great relief, instead of rebuke, he received praises and caresses from the whole company. From this circumstance, it is stated, his talents for sculpture were first discovered by the Senator Falier, who from thenceforth resolved to encourage them, by patronizing their possessor.

[J. S. Memes, *Memoirs of Antonio Canova*, 1825]

The Young Canova in Venice

Even in walking the streets, where that exercise can be enjoyed in Venice, [his] habits of observation were not intermitted. He would often stop before the workshop of some artisan, to remark the forceful yet easy positions into which the body was thrown in different occupations. On perceiving that he was observed by those who had been the objects of contemplation, he immediately retired, saying, 'They will now endeavour to do their best, and consequently spoil all.'

[J. S. Memes, *Memoirs of Antonio Canova*, 1825]

Canova in Love

While pursuing his studies in the Farsetti Palace, on first arriving in Venice, he one day beheld a female, somewhat older than himself and very beautiful, enter the gallery accompanied by a friend or attendant, who daily departing soon after, returned again before the hour of closing, leaving the former to pursue her studies which chiefly consisted in drawing from antique heads. Chance first placed the youthful pair near each [other. The lady,] leaning on the shoulder of her companion, praised his work as being *assai bello*; – words never forgotten! though answered only by a silent obeisance, and he hoped again to attract her notice. At length the attendant again appeared – alone and habited in deep mourning; – the heart of the youth failed at the sight, but summoning courage as she passed in departing with a portfolio, he ventured to inquire for her friend. *La Signora Julia*, replied she, bursting into tears, – is dead: No more was asked, and nothing more said. Who Julia was Canova never knew: – but her name, her image, long remained engraven on his memory.

[J. S. Memes, *Memoirs of Antonio Canova*, 1825]

Canova's 'Theseus and the Minotaur' Exhibited in Rome

The group which had so long formed the subject of secret solicitude and unwitnessed labour, was now finished. On this occasion, in order to give full effect to the surprise and eclat of its first exhibition, an entertainment was given by the Venetian Ambassador to the most celebrated artists, men of letters, and other distinguished characters then in Rome. No previous intimation of a work thus carefully concealed had yet transpired; – a model of the head of his victorious hero, purposely prepared by the artist, and placed in the apartments destined for the reception of the guests, was the first announcement of the new production. This beautiful and novel object, in such an assembly naturally attracted universal attention; and the whole company by degrees had collected around it. Various were the opinions on its forms – its expression – its subject; and keen were the disputes to which it gave rise. All were agreed that the cast must have been taken from a work of Grecian sculpture, and of great merit; but they were divided on what it represented, and where the original was to be found. Some affirmed that they had seen it in such a collection; – some said it was in a different gallery; – part maintained that such a personage of antiquity was pourtrayed; – others asserted a contrary statement; – in short, the acknowledged beauty of the piece was the only common sentiment which experienced no opposition. Seizing the proper occasion, when he perceived every one to be thus deeply interested in the affair, '*Ebbene*,' said the Ambassador, '*andiamo a vederne l'originale*;' – 'Come, let us terminate these disputes by going to see the original.' All were astonished. What! the antique, about which so many conjectures had just been made, in the possession of their host! It seemed hardly credible; and they eagerly followed to where Canova's Theseus, victorious over his cruel foe, in all the brightness of recent finish, and placed to the best advantage, was disclosed to view. The effects produced by this unexpected sight, it is impossible to describe. Every feeling was absorbed in surprise, delight, and admiration.

[J. S. Memes, *Memoirs of Antonio Canova*, 1825]

Canova's Response to Criticism

About the period of which we now speak, an English nobleman had objected to the group of Theseus and the Minotaur, 'that it was too cold, at the same time bestowing just commendation on the simplicity and purity of the style; recommending to preserve the same manner in another similar performance, but to select a more impassioned subject.' To these observations the artist listened in silence, but in a short time after produced the model of that most lovely work – the group of Cupid and Psyche, in which the latter is recumbent, and the former bending over the object of his affections. To his Lordship's expressions of surprise and pleasure, the unassuming sculptor merely replied, '*Preferisco costantemente di rispondere a quanto convenevole osservato più tosto collo scarpello, che colle parole.*' 'I always prefer to answer a judicious observation rather with my chisel than by words.'*

* Or as the anecdote has been differently reported to the author, 'Amo meglio parlare colle mane che colla lingua.' 'I love better to speak with my hands than with my tongue.'

[J. S. Memes, *Memoirs of Antonio Canova*, 1825] The critic was the Earl-Bishop of Bristol, builder of Ickworth.

Napoleon Sits to Canova

His auditor, struck by the novelty or veracity of some remark, would often stop him for some moments, then motion to proceed, muttering, half aside, '*Buono, buonissimo, non siete solamente scultore;*' – 'Good, very good, that is not the saying of a mere sculptor.' It was not, however, always with calmness that Buonaparte at such times listened to observations which went near to implicate the integrity of his actions, or the humanity of his views. '*Come!*' 'how!' he would exclaim, 'Citizen Canova, *parlate senza tema,*' – 'you speak without fear:' – '*Parlo da uom sincero,*' – 'I speak without flattery,' was the laconic and unperturbed reply. These conversations chiefly took place while the Consul sat for his bust. On one of these occasions the first sketch of the intended statue was shewn to him; not seeing in this design any arms among the accessories, 'How is this,' said he, playfully addressing the artist, 'Citizen Canova, there must be a plot against me, – you have left me without defence.' – 'No, Sire,' replied the sculptor, pointing out the parazonium [dagger] suspended on the trunk which supports the figure, 'I have only hung up the sheathed sword, in sign of that peace, to which the wishes of all good men have long inclined.'

[J. S. Memes, *Memoirs of Antonio Canova*, 1825] Compare the accounts of encounters between Napoleon and J. L. David included in Part XVI.

Canova Inspects the Spoils of Napoleon's Conquests

Thus, by the particular desire of Napoleon, he examined the *Musée* of the Louvre, for the purpose of ascertaining what improvements could be effected in the disposition of those *chef-d'œuvres*, which had recently been transported from their former sites to that superb collection. Being then asked by the Consul, 'Whether they were not judiciously arranged,' he answered with admirable brevity, '*certo stavano meglio in Italia,*' – 'they certainly were better placed in Italy.'

[J. S. Memes, *Memoirs of Antonio Canova*, 1825]

Canova's Way of Life

He rose early and bent his whole attention during the day to professional labours. Mixing little in public society, he usually spent his evenings at home, having always a few chosen friends to dine with him, whom he entertained with great cordiality, but without any pomp or unnecessary display. From inclination, which habit, and the necessity of nursing a precarious state of health, had reduced almost to abstemiousness, he was extremely moderate in the enjoyments of the table. But after even these frugal repasts, a short repose was always requisite, his powers of digestion being so feeble, that the slightest exertion of body or mind materially deranged them. His friends were therefore careful to introduce after dinner light and agreeable conversation, which might amuse, without agitating his mind; and in this Canova joined with the utmost cheerfulness. If, however, any subject connected with the arts were mentioned, or of a nature otherwise calculated to interest deeply the feelings, so keen were his perceptions, and so lively his sensibility, that the system certainly suffered from this excess of mental activity. After thus spending in the bosom of friendship the close of each day, the conversation becoming gradually more serious and animated as the evening advanced, he retired before eleven to his apartment; and either immediately sought repose, or amused himself with a book, or more frequently with his pencil, and at such hours many of those beautiful sketches were composed, some of which have already been published under the title of *Pensieri*. To describe one day, is to delineate the whole life of Canova, so equable its tenor, so regular his habits, and so confirmed his industry.

[J. S. Memes, *Memoirs of Antonio Canova*, 1825]

XV

ART IN ENGLAND FROM
HOGARTH TO BLAKE

ॐ

Despite what was probably a much lower level of artistic activity, compared to the situation in Europe, anecdotal information about artists' lives and characters seems to be much more abundant in eighteenth-century England than it is in Europe.

Several reasons can be suggested for this. The two most important are: first, that writers on art in France, Holland and Italy tended to have their eyes fixed on the past (as suggested in the introduction to the last section) rather than the present. This alternative was not open to English commentators, since in seventeenth-century England art had fallen to a low level. It was the revival of painting and sculpture in England, from the time of Hogarth onwards, which provided them with a source of patriotic pride, and at the same time with subject matter which seemed worth writing about. The second reason, as the following extracts show, is that the artistic community in England was for some reason much more tightly knit together with the literary one than was the case in Europe. Artists found their friends amongst writers – a fact abundantly recorded, for example, in various accounts of Sir Joshua Reynolds. Reynolds's success, which sprang as much from his character as from his artistic abilities, established a new conception of what an artist was, and how he should behave.

Another artist, even more abundantly recorded, forms a complete contrast with Reynolds (something he himself realized). This was William Blake. Living in poverty, Blake nevertheless, in the final years of his life, attracted faithful disciples, who were eager to pass on their memories of him. Even those who were less committed found him sufficiently singular to wish to record their observations. Eventually Blake became the subject of one of the best nineteenth-century biographies – a work of art in its own right. In Alexander Gilchrist's Life, the subject clearly powered the book – to read the earlier biography of Etty by the same author leaves no doubt on the matter.

Hogarth (1687–1764) and his Habit of Sketching

It was Hogarth's custom to sketch out on the spot any remarkable face which struck him, and of which he wished to preserve an accurate remembrance. He was once observed in the Bedford coffee-house drawing something with a pencil on the nail of his left thumb – he held it up to a friend who accompanied him – it was the face, and a very singular one, of a person in the same room – the likeness was excellent. He had dined with some friends at a tavern, and as he threw his cloak about him to begone, he observed his friend Ben Read sound asleep and presenting a most ridiculous physiognomy: Hogarth eyed him for a moment, and saying softly, 'heavens, what a character!' called for pen and ink, and drew his portrait without sitting down: – a curious and clever likeness and still existing.

    [A. Cunningham, *The Lives of the Most Eminent Painters, Sculptors and Architects*, 1829]

Hogarth and the Naval Officer

In the year 1745, one Launcelot Burton was appointed naval officer at Dover. Hogarth had seen this gentleman by accident, and on a piece of paper, previously impressed by a plain copper-plate, he drew his portrait with a pen in imitation of a coarse etching. Mr. Burton was represented riding on a lean Canterbury hack, with a bottle sticking out of his pocket, and underneath was an inscription, intimating that he was going down to take possession of his place. The sketch was enclosed to him in a letter; and some of his friends who were in the secret, protested that the drawing was a print which they had seen exposed for sale in the print shops in London. This put him in a violent passion, and he wrote an abusive letter to Hogarth, whose name was subscribed to the work. But after poor Burton's tormentors had kept him in suspense throughout three uneasy weeks, they proved to him that it was no engraving, but merely a sketch with pen and ink. He then became so perfectly reconciled to his resemblance, that he showed it with exultation to Admiral Vernon and the rest of his friends.

    [*The Percy Anecdotes*, 1821–3]

Hogarth's Apparent Absence of Mind

His thoughts were so much employed on scenes which he had just witnessed or on works which he contemplated, that he sometimes had neither eyes nor ears for any thing else; this has subjected him to the charge of utter absence of mind. 'At table,' says Nichols, 'he would sometimes turn his chair round as if he had finished eating, and as suddenly would return it and fall to his meal again.' According to this writer – soon after our artist set up his carriage, he went to visit Beckford, who was then Lord Mayor; the day became stormy during the interview; and when Hogarth took his leave, he went out at a wrong door – forgot that he had a carriage – could not find a hackney coach, and came home wet to the skin, to the astonishment of his wife. This is a good story – and it *may* be true.

[A. Cunningham, *Lives*, 1829]

Louis François Roubiliac (?1705–62) Returns from Rome

Of Roubiliac I may here record another anecdote which took place on the return of that Sculptor from Rome, when he paid a visit to Reynolds, and expressed himself in raptures on what he had seen on the Continent – on the exquisite beauty of the works of antiquity, and the captivating and luxuriant splendour of Bernini. 'It is natural to suppose,' said he, 'that I was infinitely impatient till I had taken a survey of my own performances in Westminster Abbey, after having seen such a variety of excellence, and by G — my own work looked to me meagre and starved, as if made of nothing but tobacco-pipes.'

[J. Northcote, *Memoirs of Sir Joshua Reynolds*, 1813–15]

The Landscape Art of Richard Wilson (1714–82)

His whole heart was in his art, and he talked and dreamed landscape. He looked on cattle as made only to form groups for his pictures, and on men as they *composed* harmoniously. One day looking on the fine scene from Richmond Terrace, and wishing to point out a spot of particular beauty to the friend who accompanied him – 'there,' said he, holding out his finger, 'see near those houses – there, where the *figures* are.' He stood for some time by the waterfall of Terni in speechless admiration, and at length exclaimed, 'Well done: water, by God!' In

[216]

aërial effect he considered himself above any rival. When Wright of Derby offered to exchange works with him, he answered, 'With all my heart. I'll give you air, and you will give me fire.'

[A. Cunningham, *Lives*, 1829]

Richard Wilson's Style of Life

He was abstemious at his meals, rarely touching wine or ardent spirits – his favourite beverage was a pot of porter and a toast; and he would accept that when he refused all other things. This was a luxury of which he was determined to have the full enjoyment – he took a moderate draught – sat silent a little while, then drank again, and all the time eyed the quart vessel with a satisfaction which sparkled in his eyes. The first time that Wilson was invited to dine with Beechey,[1] he replied to the request by saying, 'You have daughters, Mr. Beechey, do they draw? All young ladies draw now.' 'No, Sir,' answered his prudent entertainer, 'my daughters are musical.' He was pleased to hear this, and accepted the invitation. Such was the blunt honesty of his nature, that when drawings were shown him which he disliked, he disdained, or was unable to give a courtly answer, and made many of the students his enemies. Reynolds had the sagacity to escape from such difficulties by looking at the drawings and saying 'pretty, pretty,' which vanity invariably explained into a compliment.

His process of painting was simple; his colours were few, he used but one brush, and worked standing. He prepared his palette, made a few touches, then retired to the window to refresh his eye with natural light, and returned in a few minutes and resumed his labours. Beechey called on him one day, and found him at work; he seized his visitor hastily by the arm, hurried him to the remotest corner of the room, and said, 'There, look at my landscape – this is where you should view a painting if you wish to examine it with your eyes, and not with your nose.' He was then an old man, his sight was failing, his touch was unsure, and he painted somewhat coarsely, but the effect was wonderful. He too, like Reynolds, had his secrets of colour, and his mystery of the true principle in painting, which he refused to explain, saying, 'They are like those of nature, and are to be sought for and

1. Sir William Beechey (1753–1839).

found in my performances.' Of his own future fame he spoke seldom, for he was a modest man, but, when he did speak of it, he used expressions which the world has since sanctioned. 'Beechey,' he said, 'you will live to see great prices given for my pictures, when those of Barret will not fetch one farthing.'

The salary of librarian rescued him from utter starvation; indeed, so few were his wants, so simple his fare, and so moderate his appetite, that he found it, little as it was, nearly enough. He had as he grew old become more neglectful of his person – as fortune forsook him he left a fine house for one inferior – a fashionable street for one cheap and obscure; he made sketches for half-a-crown, and expressed gratitude to one Paul Sanby for purchasing a number from him at a small advance of price. His last retreat in this wealthy city was a small room somewhere about Tottenham-Court Road; – an easel and a brush – a chair and a table – a hard bed with few clothes – a scanty meal and the favourite pot of porter – were all that Wilson could call his own. A disgrace to an age which lavished its tens of thousands on mountebanks and projectors – on Italian screamers, and men who made mouths at Shakespeare.

[A. Cunningham, *Lives*, 1829]

The Teaching Method of Alexander Cozens (c. 1717–86)

Alexander Cozens, by birth a Russian, was a landscape painter, but chiefly practised as a drawing master in London. He taught in a way that was new and peculiar, but which appears to have been adopted from a hint of Leonardo da Vinci. The process by Cozens, was to dash out upon several pieces of paper, a number of accidental large blots and loose flourishes, from which he selected forms, and sometimes produced very grand ideas; but they were in general indefinite in their execution and unpleasing in their colour, similar in effect to the appearance of nature, when viewed through a dark coloured lens.

[*The Percy Anecdotes*, 1821–3]

The Appearance and Character of Sir Joshua Reynolds (1723–92)

As to his person; in his stature Sir Joshua Reynolds was rather under the middle size, of a florid complexion, roundish blunt features, and a lively aspect; not corpulent, though somewhat inclined to it, but extremely active; with manners uncommonly polished and agreeable.

In conversation, his manner was perfectly natural, simple, and unassuming. He most heartily enjoyed his profession, in which he was both fortunate and illustrious, and I agree with Mr. Malone who says he appeared to him to be the happiest man he had ever known. He was thoroughly sensible of his rare lot in life and truly thankful for it; his virtues were blessed with their full reward.

It is a common, but a just observation, that virtue cannot exist where irregularity is present; and the converse is true as applied to Sir Joshua's mode of life, which was so regular as to produce correctness without degenerating into insipidity, or tediousness to his friends by unnecessary and troublesome precision.

Rising at eight o'clock in general, he was enabled to retire from the breakfast table to his painting room about ten, where, for an hour at least, he occupied himself in arranging the subordinate accessories in such of his works as he was then engaged in, or perhaps in preserving some new ideas by a sketch.

The hours dedicated to his sitters were generally from eleven to four, but not with rigid attention, as he often gave a relaxation to his mind by receiving the visits of particular friends. Yet upon the whole, his application was great, nay, in some measure, excessive; for it is very true, as he himself observed to Malone, that such was his love of his art, and such his ardour to excel, that he had often and during the greater part of his life, laboured as hard with his pencil, as any mechanic working at his trade for bread.

[J. Northcote, *Memoirs of Sir Joshua Reynolds*, 1813–15]

Reynolds's Self-contained Nature

Sir Joshua had more contempt for mankind than either Johnson or Goldsmith, for they were always thinking more of themselves, and the parts they had to play, while Sir Joshua concealed *his* talent under the garb of mildness and childlike simplicity; he listened, indeed, with such patient attention, that everyone thought he was admiring what was said. He was greatly afraid of being thought a wit, or possessing anything formidable in his disposition. I remember on some occasion, when it was stated in the newspapers that 'Dr. Johnson, Goldsmith, Sir Joshua Reynolds, and *the other wits* were there,' he exclaimed, 'What do they mean by calling me a wit? I never was a wit in all my life!' and he seemed quite annoyed by it. He well knew that to make the world afraid of him would be ruinous to him in his profession. Though he kept so much company he had no boon companion – no one had his confidence – he was an isolated being.

[*Conversations of James Northcote with James Ward*, ed. E. Fletcher, 1901]

Reynolds's Style of Entertainment

These, accounts, however, in as far as regards the splendour of the entertainments, must be received with some abatement. The eye of a youthful pupil was a little blinded by enthusiasm – that of Malone was rendered friendly by many acts of hospitality and a handsome legacy; while literary men and artists, who came to speak of books and paintings, cared little for the most part about the delicacy of their entertainment, provided it were wholesome. Take the following description of one of the painter's dinners by the skilful hand of Courteney; 'There was something singular in the style and economy of his table that contributed to pleasantry and good humour: a coarse inelegant plenty, without any regard to order or arrangement. A table prepared for seven or eight, often compelled to contain fifteen or sixteen. When this pressing difficulty was got over, a deficiency of knives and forks, plates, and glasses, succeeded. The attendance was in the same style; and it was absolutely necessary to call instantly for beer, bread, or wine, that you might be supplied before the first course was over. He was once prevailed on to furnish the table with decanters and glasses for dinners, to save time and prevent the tardy manoevres of two or three occasional undisciplined domestics. As these accelerating utensils were demolished in the course of service, Sir Joshua could never be persuaded to replace them. But these trifling embarrassments only served to enhance the hilarity and singular pleasure of the entertainment. The wine, cookery, and dishes, were but little attended to: nor was the fish or venison ever talked of or recommended. Amidst this convivial animated bustle amongst his guests, our host sat perfectly composed, always attentive to what was said, never minding what was eat or drank, but left every one at perfect liberty to scramble for himself. Temporal and spiritual peers, physicians, lawyers, actors, and musicians, composed the motley group, and played their parts without dissonance or discord. At five o'clock precisely dinner was served, whether all the invited guests were arrived or not. Sir Joshua was never so fashionably ill-bred as to wait an hour perhaps for two or three persons of rank or title, and put the rest of the company out of humour by this invidious distinction.'

Of the sluttish abundance which covered his table Courteney says enough; as to the character of the guests, we have the testimony of Dunning, afterwards Lord Ashburton. He had accepted an invitation to dinner from the artist, and happened to be the first guest who arrived; a large company was expected. 'Well, Sir Joshua,' he said, 'and who have you got to dine with you to-day? The last time I dined in your house, the company was of such a sort that by — I believe all the rest of the world enjoyed peace for that afternoon.' 'This observation,' says Northcote, 'was by no means ill applied, for as Sir Joshua's companions were chiefly men of genius, they were often disputatious and vehement in argument.'

[A. Cunningham, *Lives*, 1829]

Reynolds and Public Opinion

That Reynolds was a close observer of nature, his works sufficiently show; he drew his excellence from innumerable sources; paid attention to all opinions; from the rudest minds he sometimes obtained valuable hints, and babes and sucklings were among his tutors. It was one of his maxims that the gestures of children, being all dictated by nature, are graceful; and that affectation and distortion come in with the dancing-master. He watched the motions of the children who came to his gallery, and was pleased when he saw them forget themselves and mimic unconsciously the airs and attitudes of the portraits on the wall. They were to him more than Raphael had ever been. 'I cannot but think,' he thus expresses himself in one of his memorandums, 'that Apelles's method of exposing his pictures for public criticism was a very good one. I do not know why the judgment of the vulgar, on the mechanical parts of painting, should not be as good as any whatever; for instance, as to whether such or such a part be natural or not. If one of these persons should ask why half the face is black or why there is such a spot of black or snuff as they will call it, under the nose, I should conclude from thence that the shadows are thick or dirtily painted, or that the shadow under the nose was too much resembling snuff, when, if those shadows had exactly resembled the transparency and colour of nature, they would have no more been taken notice of than the shadow in nature itself.' Such were the sound and sagacious opinions of this eminent man when he sat down to think for himself and speak from practice.

He had a decided aversion to loquacious artists; and spoke little himself whilst he was busied at his easel. When artists love to be admired for what they say, they will have less desire to be admired for what they paint. He had, in truth, formed a very humble notion of the abstract meditation which art requires, and imagined it to be more of a practical dexterity of hand than the offspring of intellect and skill. He assured Lord Monboddo that painting scarcely deserved the name of study; it was more that sort of work (he said) which employed the mind without fatiguing it, and was thereby more conducive to individual happiness than the practice of any other profession.

[A. Cunningham, *Lives*, 1829]

Reynolds and True Criticism

Sir Joshua being in company with a party of ladies and gentlemen, who were viewing a nobleman's house, they passed through a gallery of portraits, when a little girl, who belonged to one of the party, attracted the particular attention of Sir Joshua by her vivacity and the sensible drollery of her observations; for whenever the company made a stand, to look at each portrait in particular, the child, unconscious of being observed by any one, imitated, by her actions, the air of the head, and sometimes awkward effect of the ill disposed position of the limbs in each picture; and this she did with so much innocence and true feeling, that it was the most just and incontrovertible criticism that could be made on the picture.

[J. Northcote, *Memoirs of Sir Joshua Reynolds*, 1813–15]

Reynolds's Attitude to his own Work

Sir Joshua Reynolds, like many other distinguished persons, was never satisfied with his own efforts, however well they might satisfy others. When the ingenious M. Mosnier,[1] a French painter, was one day

1. Jean-Laurent Mosnier (1733/4–1808)

praising to him the excellence of one of his pictures, he replied, 'Ah! Monsieur, je ne fais que des ebauches, des ebauches.' Alas! sir, I can only make sketches, sketches.

[*The Percy Anecdotes*, 1821–3]

Reynolds's Use of Fugitive Colours

One of these critics, who passed for a great patron of the art, was complaining strongly to a judicious friend of Sir Joshua's 'flying colours' and expressing great regret at the circumstances as it prevented him from having his picture painted by the president. To all this his friend calmly replied, that he should reflect that any painter who merely wished to make his colours stand, had only to purchase them at the first colour shop he might come to; but that it must be remembered that 'every picture of Sir Joshua's was an experiment of art made by an ingenious man, – and that the *art advanced by such experiments, even where they failed.*'

In fine, what Gainsborough said of the President is strictly true: that in his opinion Sir Joshua's pictures in their most decayed state were better than those of any other artist when in their best.

[J. Northcote, *Memoirs of Sir Joshua Reynolds*, 1813–15]

Reynolds's Retort to Northcote on the Subject of his Fugitive Colours

I remember he looked on his hand and said 'I can see no vermilion in flesh.' I replied, 'but did not Sir Godfrey Kneller always use vermilion in his flesh colour,' when Sir Joshua answered rather sharply, 'What signifies what a man used who could not colour. But you may use it if you will!'

[J. Northcote, *Memoirs of Sir Joshua Reynolds*, 1813–15]

Reynolds and Mrs Siddons

He was skilful in compliments. When he painted the portrait of Mrs. Siddons as the Tragic Muse, he wrought his name on the border of her robe. The great actress conceiving it to be a piece of classic embroidery, went near to examine, and seeing the words, smiled. The artist bowed and said, 'I could not lose this opportunity of sending my name to posterity on the hem of your garment.' He painted his name, in the same manner, on the embroidered edge of the drapery of Lady Cockburn's portrait. When this picture was taken into the exhibition room, such was the sweetness of the conception, and the splendour of the colouring, that the painters, who were busied with their own performances, acknowledged its beauty by clapping their hands. Such eager admiration is of rare occurrence amongst brothers of the trade.

[A. Cunningham, *Lives*, 1829]

Reynolds's Portrait of Haydn

When Haydn was in England, one of our princes commissioned Sir Joshua Reynolds to take his portrait. Haydn went to the painter's house, and sat to him, but soon grew tired. Sir Joshua, careful of his reputation, would not paint a man of acknowledged genius, with a stupid countenance; and deferred the sitting till another day. The same weariness and want of expression occurring at the next attempt, Reynolds went and communicated the circumstance to his royal highness, who contrived the following strategem. He sent to the painter's house a pretty German girl, in the service of the queen. Haydn took his seat for the third time, and as soon as the conversation began to flag, a curtain rose, and the fair German addressed him in his native language, with a most elegant compliment. Haydn, delighted, overwhelmed the enchantress with questions; his countenance recovered its animation, and Sir Joshua rapidly seized its traits.

[*The Percy Anecdotes*, 1821–3]

Reynolds's Portrait of Dr Johnson

In this year [1775] was painted that portrait of his friend Dr. Johnson, which represents him as reading and near-sighted. This was very displeasing to Johnson, who when he saw it, reproved Sir Joshua for painting him in that manner and attitude, saying, 'It is not friendly to hand down to posterity the imperfections of any man.' But, on the contrary, Sir Joshua himself esteemed it as a circumstance in nature to be remarked as characterizing the person represented, and therefore as giving additional value to the portrait.

Of this circumstance Mrs. Thrale says, 'I observed that he would not be known by posterity, for his defects only, let Sir Joshua do his worst:'

and when she adverted to his own picture painted with the ear trumpet, and done in this year for Mr. Thrale, she records Johnson to have answered, 'He may paint himself as deaf as he chooses; but I will not be *blinking Sam*.'

[J. Northcote, *Memoirs of Sir Joshua Reynolds*, 1813–15]

Reynolds and Lord Holland

This unfinished look which some of Reynolds's pictures had when they were first sent home caused occasional disappointment; and it is said that Lord Holland when he received his portrait, could not help remarking that it had been hastily executed; and making some demur about the price, asked Reynolds how long he had been painting it, the offended artist replied, 'All my life, my Lord.'

[W. Cotton, *Sir Joshua Reynolds and his Works*, 1856]

Reynolds and Mme Vigée-Le Brun

He was questioned by Northcote on the merits of two French portraits, by Madame Le Brun, which were then exhibited in London: 'Pray what do you think of them, Sir Joshua?' Reynolds: 'That they are very fine.' Northcote: 'How fine?' Reynolds: 'As fine as those of any painter.' Northcote: 'As fine as those of any painter! – do you mean living, or dead?' Reynolds, sharply: 'Either living or dead.' Northcote: 'Good God! what, as fine as Vandyke?' Reynolds: 'Yes, and finer.' Reynolds had seen – as men see now – the wreck of high hopes and lofty expectations; he rated vulgar popularity at its worth, and disdained to interfere with the brief summer of Madame Le Brun.

[A. Cunningham, *Lives*, 1829]

George Stubbs (1724–1806) in Rome

It does not appear that while in Rome Stubbs ever copied a picture, designed any composition in the grand style, or made a single drawing or model from the antique, although he, undoubtedly, executed many landscape sketches of Italian scenery. His motive for the voyage, according to his own account, was mainly to decide if Nature were superior to Art, whether that art were Greek or Roman, ancient or contemporary. There is an old debate, as we know, concerning the

[225]

relation of nature and art, and it says much for Stubbs's ingenuousness that he should have undertaken such a voyage to clear up his doubts in the matter. Once convinced in his own mind he immediately resolved, with characteristic promptitude to leave Rome. Very characteristic too was it, as we read, that 'whenever he accompanied students in Rome to view the palaces of the Vatican, Borghese, Colonna etc., and to consider the pictures there, he differed always in opinion from his companions, and when it was put to the vote, found himself alone on one side and his friends on the other'.

[W. Gilbey, *The Life of George Stubbs R.A.*, 1898]

Gainsborough (1727–88): Stolen Pears and Stained Glass

When Gainsborough resided at Sudbury, both himself and his neighbours were ignorant of his genius; till seeing a country fellow looking wistfully over his garden wall at some pears, he caught up a bit of board, and painted him so inimitably well, that the board being placed upon the wall, several of the neighbouring gentry, farmers, &c. immediately recognized the figure who had paid so many unwelcome visits to their gardens; and being by the means of this likeness charged by one of them with the robbery of his orchard, he acknowledged it, and agreed to go into the army, to avoid a worse fate.

When Mr. Jarvis made an exhibition of some beautiful stained glass at a room in Cockspur Street, Gainsborough visited it, and was so much struck with the effect of what he saw, that upon his return home, he immediately began to construct an apparatus that should diffuse splendour on his pencil, and produce an effect similar to the stained glass which he admired.

This machine consisted of a number of glass planes, which were moveable, and presented paintings by himself of various subjects, chiefly landscapes. They were lighted by candles at the back, and viewed through a magnifying lens; by which means the effect produced was truly captivating, especially in the moonlight pieces, which exhibited the most perfect resemblance of nature.

[*The Percy Anecdotes*, 1821–3]

Gainsborough and Music

Among his amusements, music was almost as much his favourite as painting. This passion led him to cultivate the intimacy of all the great musical professors of his time, and they, by their abilities, obtained an ascendancy over him, greater than was perhaps consistent with strict prudence. Of his powers in the science, no better description can be given, than what has been already written by that able musician, Mr. Jackson of Exeter, who, in one of his publications, has furnished some pleasant anecdotes of his friend, from which the following extract is selected:

Gainsborough's profession was painting, music was his amusement. Yet there were times when music seemed to be his employment, and painting his diversion. As his skill in music has been celebrated, I will, before I speak of him as a painter, mention what degree of merit he possessed as a musician.

When I first knew him he lived at Bath, where Giardini[1] had been exhibiting his then unrivalled powers on the violin; his excellent performance made Gainsborough enamoured of that instrument, and conceiving, like the servant maid in the Spectator, that the music lay in the fiddle, he was frantic until he possessed the *very instrument* which had given him so much pleasure, but seemed surprised, that the music of it remained behind with Giardini.

He had scarcely recovered this shock, (for it was a great one to him) when he heard Abel on the viol-di-gamba; the violin was hung on the willows. Abel's viol-di-gamba was purchased, and the house resounded with melodious thirds and fifths, from morn till dewy eve. Fortunately my friend's passion had now a fresh object, Fischer's hautboy!

The next time I saw Gainsborough, it was in the character of King David; he had heard a performer on the harp at Bath; the performer was soon left harpless.

In this manner he frittered away his musical talents, and though possessed of ear, taste, and genius, he never had application enough to learn his notes; he scorned to take the first step, the second was, of course, out of his reach, and the summit became unattainable.

His conversation was sprightly, but licentious; his favourite subjects were music and painting, which he treated in a manner peculiarly his own; the common topics, or any of a superior cast, he thoroughly hated, and always interrupted by some stroke of wit or humour.

[E. Edwards, *Lives of Painters who have resided or been born in England*, 1808]

---

1. Felice Giardini (1716–76), French violinist and composer of Italian descent.

Gainsborough's Methods and Style of Life

Like Reynolds, he painted standing, in preference to sitting; and the pencils [brushes] which he used had shafts, sometimes two yards long. He stood as far from his sitter as he did from his picture, that the hues might be the same. He generally rose early, commenced painting between nine and ten o'clock, wrought for four or five hours, and then gave up the rest of the day to visits, to music, and to domestic enjoyment. He loved to sit by the side of his wife during the evenings, and make sketches of whatever occurred to his fancy, all of which he threw below the table, save such as were more than commonly happy, and those were preserved, and either finished as sketches or expanded into paintings. In summer he had lodgings at Hampstead, for the sake of the green fields and luxury of pure air; and in winter he was often seen refreshing his eyes with light at the window, when fatigued with close employment.

He was an admirer of elegant penmanship, and looked at a well-written letter with something of the same pleasure as at a fine landscape. His love of music was constant; and he seems to have been kept under a spell by all kinds of melodious sounds.

[A. Cunningham, *Lives*, 1829]

A Visit to Gainsborough

Upon our arrival at Mr Gainsborough's, the third west division of Schomberg-house, Pall Mall, the artist was listening to a violin, and held up his finger to Mr. Nollekens as a request of silence. Colonel Hamilton was playing to him in so exquisite a style, that Gainsborough exclaimed, 'Now, my dear Colonel, if you will but go on, I will give you that picture of the boy at the stile, which you have so often wished to purchase of me.' Mr. Gainsborough, not knowing how long Nollekens would hold his tongue, gave him a book of sketches to choose two from, which he had promised him. As Gainsborough's versatile fancy was at this period devoted to music, his attention was so riveted to the tones of the violin, that for nearly half an hour he was motionless; after which, the Colonel requested that a hackney-coach might be sent for, wherein he carried off the picture. Mr. Gainsborough, after he had given Mr. Nollekens the two drawings he had selected, requested him to look at a model of an ass's head which he had just made. – *Nollekens*. 'You should model more with your thumbs; thumb it about, till you get it into shape.' – 'What,' said Gainsborough, 'in this manner?' having taken up a bit of clay; and looking at a picture of Abel's Pomeranian Dog which hung over the chimney-piece – 'this way?' – 'Yes,' said Nollekens, 'you'll do a great deal more with your thumbs.'

Mr. Gainsborough, by whom I was standing, observed to me, 'You enjoyed the music, my little fellow, and I am sure you long for this model; there, I will give it to you'; – and I am delighted with it still. I have never had it baked, fearing it might fly in the kiln, as the artist had not kneaded the clay well before he commenced working it, and I conclude that the model must still contain a quantity of fixed air.

Colonel Hamilton above-mentioned, was not only looked upon as one of the first amateur violin-players, but also one of the first gentlemen pugilists. I was afterwards noticed by him in my art as an etcher of landscapes; and have frequently seen him spar with the famous Mendoza in his drawing-room, in Leicester-street, Leicester-square.

[C. T. Smith, *Nollekens and his Times*, 1828]

Gainsborough's Failures as a Portraitist

Amongst those who sat to him was the Duchess of Devonshire – then in the bloom of youth, at once the loveliest of the lovely, and the gayest of the gay. But her dazzling beauty, and the sense which she entertained of the charms of her looks, and her conversation, took away that readiness of hand, and hasty happiness of touch, which belonged to him in his ordinary moments. The portrait was so little to his satisfaction, that he refused to send it to Chatsworth. Drawing his wet pencil across a mouth which all who saw it thought exquisitely lovely, he said, 'Her Grace is too hard for me.' The picture was, I believe, destroyed. Amongst his papers were found two sketches of the duchess – both exquisitely graceful.

He had customers who annoyed him with other difficulties than those of too radiant loveliness. A certain lord, whom one of our biographers, out of compassion for rank, calls an *alderman*, came for his portrait; and that all might be worthy of his station, he had put on a new suit of clothes, richly laced, with a well-powdered wig. Down he sat, and put on a practised look of such importance and prettiness, that the artist, who was no flatterer either with tongue or pencil, began to laugh, and was heard to mutter, 'This will never do!' The patient having composed himself, in conformity with his station, said, 'Now, sir, I beg you will not overlook the dimple on my chin!' 'Confound the dimple on your chin,' said Gainsborough – 'I shall neither paint the one nor the other.' And he laid down his brushes, and refused to resume them. Garrick, too, and Foote, also came for their likenesses; he tried again and again, without success, and dismissed them in despair. 'Rot them for a couple of rogues,' he exclaimed, 'they have everybody's faces but their own.'

[A. Cunningham, *Lives*, 1829]

Gainsborough and Sheridan

Though Gainsborough was not partial to the society of literary men, he seems to have been acquainted with Johnson and with Burke; and he lived on terms of great affection with Richard Brinsley Sheridan. He was also a welcome visitor at the table of Sir George Beaumont, a gentleman of graceful manners, who lived in old English dignity, and was, besides, a lover of literature and a painter of landscape. The latter loved to relate a curious anecdote of Gainsborough, which marks the unequal spirits of the man, and shows that he was the slave of wayward impulses which he could neither repress nor command. Sir George Beaumont, Sheridan, and Gainsborough, had dined together, and the latter was more than usually pleasant and witty. The meeting was so much to their mutual satisfaction, that they agreed to have another day's happiness, and accordingly an early day was named when they should dine again together. They met, but a cloud had descended upon the spirit of Gainsborough, and he sat silent, with a look of fixed melancholy, which no wit could dissipate. At length he took Sheridan by the hand, led him out of the room, and said, 'Now don't laugh, but listen. I shall die soon – I know it – I feel it – I have less time to live than my looks infer – but for this I care not. What oppresses my mind is this – I have many acquaintances and few friends; and as I wish to have one worthy man to accompany me to the grave, I am, desirous of bespeaking you – will you come – aye or no?' Sheridan could scarcely repress a smile, as he made the required promise; the looks of Gainsborough cleared up like the sunshine of one of his own landscapes; throughout the rest of the evening his wit flowed, and his humour run over, and the minutes, like those of the poet, winged their way with pleasure.

[A. Cunningham, *Lives*, 1829]

Gainsborough, Reynolds and Wilson

Gainsborough was a natural gentleman; and with all his simplicity he had wit too. An eminent counsellor once attempted to puzzle him on some trial about the originality of a picture by saying, 'I observe you lay great stress on the phrase, the *painter's eye*; what do you mean by that?' 'The painter's eye,' answered Gainsborough, 'is to him what the lawyer's tongue is to you.' Sir Joshua was not fond of Wilson, and said at one of the Academy dinners, 'Yes, Gainsborough is certainly the best landscape-painter of the day.' 'No,' replied Wilson, who overheard him, 'but he is the best portrait-painter.' This was a sufficient testimony in Gainsborough's favour.

[W. Hazlitt, *Conversations of James Northcote, Esq, R.A.*, 1830]

Reynolds on Gainsborough

Of Gainsborough, he said, that he could copy Vandyke so exquisitely, that at a certain distance he could not distinguish the copy from the original, or the difference between them.

His manner he considered as peculiarly his own, and as one producing great effect and force; and one day whilst examining a picture of his with considerable attention, he at length exclaimed, 'I cannot make out how he produces his effect!'

[J. Northcote, *Memoirs of Sir Joshua Reynolds*, 1813–15]

Gainsborough's Death

About a year after the promise obtained from Sheridan to attend his funeral, he went to hear the impeachment of Warren Hastings, and sitting with his back to an open window, suddenly felt something inconceivably cold touch his neck above the shirt collar. It was accompanied with stiffness and pain. On returning home he mentioned what he felt to his wife and his niece; and on looking they saw a mark, about the size of a shilling, which was harder to the touch than the surrounding skin, and which he said still felt cold. The application of flannel did not remove it, and the artist, becoming alarmed, consulted one after the other the most eminent surgeons of London – John Hunter himself the last. They all declared there was no danger; but there was that presentiment upon Gainsborough from which none perhaps escape. He laid his hand repeatedly on his neck, and said to his sister, who had hastened to London to see him, 'If this be a cancer, I am a dead man.' And a cancer it proved to be. When this cruel disease fairly discovered itself, it was found to be inextricably interwoven with the threads of life, and he prepared himself for death with cheerfulness and perfect composure. He desired to be buried near his friend Kirby in Kew churchyard; and that his name only should be cut on his gravestone. He sent for Reynolds, and peace was made between them. Gainsborough exclaimed to Sir Joshua, 'We are all going to heaven, and Vandyke is of the company,' and immediately expired – August 2d, 1788, in the sixty-first year of his age. Sheridan and the President attended him to the grave.

[A. Cunningham, *Lives*, 1829]

Nollekens (1737–1823) in Rome

Nollekens, who wished upon all occasions to save every shilling he possibly could, was successful in another manoeuvre. He actually succeeded as a smuggler of silk stockings, gloves, and lace; his contrivance was truly ingenious, and perhaps it was the first time that the Custom-house officers had ever been so taken in. His method was this: All his plaster busts being hollow, he stuffed them full of the above articles, and then spread an outside coating of plaster at the back across the shoulders of each, so that the busts appeared like solid casts. I recollect his pointing to the cast of Sterne, and observing to the late Lord Mansfield: 'There, do you know, that busto, my Lord, held my lace ruffles that I went to Court in when I came from Rome?'

His mode of living when at Rome was most filthy: he had an old woman, who, as he stated, 'did for him', and she was so good a cook, that she would often give him a dish for dinner, which cost him no more than threepence. 'Nearly opposite to my lodgings,' he said, 'there lived a pork-butcher, who put out at his door at the end of the week a plateful of what he called cuttings, bits of skin, bits of gristle, and bits of fat, which he sold for twopence, and my old lady dished them up with a little pepper, and a little salt; and, with a slice of bread and sometimes a bit of vegetable, I made a very nice dinner.' Whenever good dinners were mentioned, he was sure to say: 'Ay, I never tasted a better dish than my Roman cuttings.'

[J. T. Smith, *Nollekens and his Times*, 1828] Nollekens, successful as a portrait sculptor, also made a reputation as a miser. Many of Smith's anecdotes about him concern his avarice, which was equalled by that of his wife.

Nollekens and Dr Johnson

Dr. Johnson, upon hearing the name of an eminent Sculptor mentioned, observed: 'Well, sir, I think my friend Joe Nollekens can chop out a head with any of them.' When the Doctor sat to Mr. Nollekens for his bust, he was very much displeased at the manner in which the head had been loaded with hair, which the Sculptor insisted upon, as it made him look more like an ancient poet. The sittings were not very favourable, which rather vexed the artist, who, upon opening the street-door, a vulgarity he was addicted to, peevishly whined: 'Now, Doctor, you *did* say you would give my busto half an hour before dinner, and the dinner has been waiting this long time.' To which the Doctor's reply was: 'Bow-wow-wow!'

[J. T. Smith, *Nollekens and his Times*, 1828]

Nollekens and his Female Sitters

Most of his sitters were exceedingly amused with the oddity of his manner, particularly fine women, who were often gratified by being considered handsome by the Sculptor, though his admiration was expressed in the plainest language. I remember his once requesting a lady who squinted dreadfully, to 'look a little the other way, for then', said he, 'I shall get rid of the shyness in the cast of your eye': and to another lady of the highest rank, who had forgotten her position, and was looking down upon him, he cried, 'Don't look so *scorney*; you'll spoil my busto; and you're a very fine woman; I think it will be one of my best bustos.'

[J. T. Smith, *Nollekens and his Times*, 1828]

Nollekens's Miserliness

When Mr. Jackson[1] was once making a drawing of a monument at the Sculptor's house, Nollekens came into the room and said: 'I'm afraid you're cold here.' – 'I am, indeed,' said Jackson. 'Ay,' answered the Sculptor, 'I don't wonder at it; why, do you know there has not been a fire in this room for these forty years!'

[J. T. Smith, *Nollekens and his Times*, 1828]

Benjamin West (1738–1830)
Executes the Philadelphia Salute

There are minor matters which sometimes help a man on to fame; and in these too he had his share; West was a skilful skater, and in America had formed an acquaintance on the ice with Colonel – afterwards too well known in the colonial war as General Howe; this friendship had dissolved with the thaw, and was forgotten till one day the painter having tied on his skates at the Serpentine, was astonishing the timid practitioners of London by the rapidity of his motions and the graceful figure which he cut. Some one cried 'West! West!' it was Colonel Howe. 'I am glad to see you,' said he, 'and not the less so that you come in good time to vindicate my praises of American skating.' He called to him Lord Spencer Hamilton and some of the Cavendishes, to whom he introduced West as one of the Philadelphia prodigies, and requested him to show them what was called 'The Salute.' He performed this feat so much to their satisfaction, that they went away spreading the praises of the American skater over London. Nor was the considerate Quaker insensible to the value of such commendations; he continued to frequent the Serpentine and to gratify large crowds by cutting the Philadelphia Salute. Many to their praise of his skating added panegyrics on his professional skill, and not a few, to vindicate their applause, followed him to his easel, and sat for their portraits.

[A. Cunningham, *Lives*, 1829]

1. John Jackson (1778–1831).

Benjamin West in Paris

He certainly had a very lofty notion of himself, and his account of the stir which he excited in Paris, marks a mind amiably but extravagantly vain. 'Wherever I went,' he said, 'men looked at me, and ministers and people of influence in the state were constantly in my company. I was one day in the Louvre – all eyes were upon me; and I could not help observing to Charles Fox, *who happened to be walking with me*, how strong was the love of art, and admiration of its professors, in France.'
    [A. Cunningham, *Lives*, 1829]

Benjamin West's Vanity

Ah, happy West! – he, for instance, was so entrenched in his own conceit that nothing could touch him; his port-holes were all shut. He used to say, 'When my pictures come into the Exhibition, every other painter takes his place as if a sovereign had come in.'
    [*Conversations of James Northcote with James Ward*, ed. E. Fletcher, 1901]

Benjamin West, George III and the Bishops

'West used to tell an interesting anecdote which I shall be glad to relate to you. He had been commissioned by the old King to paint a series of Scripture subjects, and a certain day was appointed upon which he was to take his sketches for these pictures to the King for his inspection. He accordingly went down with them one day to the Palace, but he was a good deal startled, upon being shown into a room there, to find it filled with bishops, who had been specially sent for – he soon discovered – to attend on this particular occasion. The King, who was very punctual, soon came into the room in his usual hurried manner. He commanded West to explain to the bishops his intentions in those sketches, and his various reasons for them – a thing that West was mighty capable of doing, for he was fond of talking. The King kept smiling whilst the painter was speaking, and, at the conclusion, said, with an air of triumph, 'You see how well *he* understands these things, for whilst you bishops have been spending your time amongst heathen fables, he has been studying his Bible!'

[*Conversations of James Northcote with James Ward*, ed. E. Fletcher, 1901]

Benjamin West and Cardinal Albani

When he went to Rome to study, he was introduced to the old Cardinal Albani, who was blind, and who, upon being told that he was from America, fancied he must be an aboriginal Indian, and consequently a savage, for he asked if he spoke any language. Upon being told that West spoke English, the blind old Cardinal was greatly pleased, and, calling upon him to approach near to him, he passed his hand over his features, and exclaimed, in Latin, 'Ah, fair young man! handsome fellow!'

[*Conversations of James Northcote with James Ward*, ed. E. Fletcher, 1901]

James Hamilton Mortimer (1740–79) and Richard Payne Knight

Mr. Knight[1] happening to call upon Mortimer at his house in Church-court, Covent Garden, expressed his uneasiness at the melancholy mood in which he found him. 'Why, Sir,' observed Mortimer, 'I have many noble and generous friends, it is true; but of all my patrons, I don't know one whom I could now ask to purchase an hundred guineas' worth of drawings of me, and I am at this moment seriously in want of that sum.' 'Well, then,' observed Mr. Knight, 'bring as many sketches as you would part with for that sum to me to-morrow, and dine with me.' This he did, and enjoyed his bottle. Mr. Knight gave him two hundred guineas, which he insisted the drawings were worth; and on this splendid reception, Mortimer, who was no starter, took so much wine, that the next morning he knew not how he got home. About twelve o'clock at noon, his bedside was visited by the late 'Memory Cooke', who, after hearing him curse his stupidity in losing his two hundred guineas, produced the bag! 'Here, my good fellow!'

---

1. Payne Knight was a celebrated collector, especially of Greek and Roman antiquities.

cried Cooke, 'here is your money. Fortunately you knocked me up, and emptied your pockets on my table, after which I procured a coach and sent you home.'

[J. T. Smith, *Nollekens and his Times*, 1828]

James Barry (1741–1806)

Mr. Barry was extremely negligent of his person and dress, and not less so of his house, in Castle-street, Oxford Market, in which he resided nearly twenty years, and until the time of his death it had become almost proverbial for its dirty and ruinous state. In this mansion he lived quite alone, and scarcely ever admitted any visitor.

He was more than once invited to dine by some of his friends, who respecting his abilities, wished to treat him with kindness; and as a favour to them he accepted their invitation. But such was his inconsistent pride, that after dinner it was his custom to deposit eighteen pence upon the table, observing, that he always dined for that sum, and therefore could not think of being obliged to any man for a meal.

[E. Edwards, *Lives of Painters*, 1806]

James Barry's Sleeping Habits

A little before his illness, he had, with much persuasion, been induced to pass a night at some person's house in the country. When he came down to breakfast the next morning, and one asked how he had rested, he said, remarkably well: he had not slept in sheets for many years, and really he thought it was a very comfortable thing.

[A. Cunningham, *Lives*, 1829]

Barry Entertains Edmund Burke (1729–97)

His own character and whole system of in-door economy, were exhibited in a dinner he gave Mr. Burke. No one was better acquainted with the singular manners of this very singular man than the great statesman; he wished, however, to have ocular demonstration how he managed his household concerns in the absence of wife or servant, and requested to be asked to dinner. 'Sir,' said Barry, with much cheerfulness, 'you know I live alone – but if you will come and help me to eat a steak, I shall have it tender and hot, and from the most classic market in London – that of Oxford.' The day and the hour came, and Burke arriving at No. 36, Castle Street, found Barry ready to receive him; he was conducted into the painting room, which had undergone no change since it was a carpenter's shop. On one of the walls hung his large picture of Pandora, and round it were placed the studies of the Six Pictures of the Adelphi. There were likewise old straining frames – old sketches – a printing press, in which he printed his plates with his own hand – the labours too of the spider abounded, and rivalled in extent and colour pieces of old tapestry.

Burke saw all this – yet wisely seemed to see it not. He observed too that most of the windows were broken or cracked, that the roof, which had no ceiling, admitted the light through many crevices in the tiling, and that two old chairs and a deal table composed the whole of the furniture. The fire was burning brightly; the steaks were put on to broil, and Barry, having spread a clean cloth on the table, put a pair of tongs in the hands of Burke, saying, 'Be useful, my dear friend, and look to the steaks till I fetch the porter.' Burke did as he was desired: the painter soon returned with the porter in his hand, exclaiming, 'What a misfortune! the wind carried away the fine foaming top as I crossed Titchfield Street:' they sat down together – the steak was tender and done to a moment – the artist was full of anecdote, and Burke often declared, that he never spent a happier evening in his life.

[A. Cunningham, *Lives*, 1829]

Barry and Joseph Nollekens

Barry, the historical-painter, who was extremely intimate with Nollekens at Rome, took the liberty one night, when they were about to leave the English coffee-house, to exchange hats with him; Barry's was edged with lace, and Nollekens's was a very shabby plain one. Upon his returning the hat the next morning, he was requested by Nollekens to let him know why he left him his gold-laced hat: 'Why, to tell the truth, my dear Joey,' answered Barry, 'I fully expected assassination last night, and I was to have been known by my laced hat.' This villainous transaction, which might have proved fatal to Nollekens, I have often heard him relate; and he generally added: 'It's what the Old Bailey people would call a true bill against Jem.'

[J. T. Smith, *Nollekens and his Times*, 1828]

Henry Fuseli (1741–1825)

Fuseli left Rome in 1778. He was not very partial to the modern Italians, who, he said, 'were lively and entertaining, but there was the slight drawback of never feeling one's life safe in their presence.' He then related: 'When I was one day preparing to draw from a woman selected by artists for a model, on account of her fine figure, on altering the arrangement of her dress, I saw the hilt of a dagger in her bosom, and on inquiring with astonishment what it meant, she drew it, and quaintly answered, 'Contre gl' impertinenti.'

. . .

Fuseli was, at no time of his life, an admirer of West. At his re-election to the chair of the Royal Academy, in 1803, after a secession of twelve months, the votes for his return to the office of President were unanimous, except one, which was in favour of Mrs. Lloyd (Miss Moser) then an academician. Fuseli was taxed by some of the members with having given this vote, and answered, 'Well, suppose I did; she is eligible to the office, and is not one old woman as good as another?'

. . .

One day, when Fuseli was dining out, a gentleman of the company called to him from the other end of the room, 'Mr. Fuseli, I have lately purchased a picture of yours.' Mr. F. 'Did you? what is the subject?' Gent. 'I really don't know.' Mr. F. 'That's odd enough: you must be a strange fellow, to buy a picture without knowing the subject.' Gent. (a little nettled) 'I don't know what the devil it is.' Mr. F. 'Perhaps it is the *devil*; I have often painted him.' Gent. 'Perhaps it is.' Mr. F. 'Well, you have *him* now; take care that he does not one day have *you!*'
   [J. Timbs, *Anecdotes from the Lives of William Hogarth, etc.*, 1865]

Benjamin Robert Haydon (1786–1846)
Meets Fuseli for the First Time

Fuseli had a great reputation for the terrible. His sublime conception of Uriel and Satan had impressed me when a boy. I had a mysterious awe of him. Prince Hoare's apprehensions lest he might injure my taste or hurt my morals, excited in my mind a notion that he was a sort of gifted wild beast.

My father had the same feeling, and a letter I received from him, just before my calling, concluded with these words: 'God speed you with the terrible Fuseli.'

This sort of preparation made everything worse, and I was quite nervous when the day arrived. I walked away with my drawings up Wardour Street. I remembered that Berners Street had a golden lion on the right corner house and blundered on, till without knowing how or remembering why, I found myself at Fuseli's door! I deliberated a minute or two, and at last making up my mind to see the enchanter, I jerked up the knocker so nervously that it stuck in the air. I looked at it, as much as to say: 'Is this fair?' and then drove it down with such a devil of a blow that the door rang again. The maid came rushing up in astonishment. I followed her into a gallery or showroom, enough to frighten anybody at twilight. Galvanised devils – malicious witches brewing their incantations – Satan bridging Chaos, and springing upwards like a pyramid of fire – Lady Macbeth – Paolo and Francesca – Falstaff and Mrs. Quickly – humour, pathos, terror, blood, and murder, met one at every look! I expected the floor to give way – I fancied Fuseli himself to be a giant. I heard his footsteps and saw a little bony hand slide round the edge of the door, followed by a little white-headed lion-faced man in an old flannel dressing-gown, tied round his waist with a piece of rope, and upon his head the bottom of Mrs. Fuseli's work-basket.

[B. R. Haydon, *The Autobiography and Journals*, 1853]

Fuseli as Keeper of the Royal Academy

The students were constantly amused with Fuseli's oddities. He heard a violent altercation in the studio one day, and inquired the cause. 'It is only those fellows the students, sir,' said one of the porters. 'Fellows,' exclaimed Fuseli; 'I would have you to know, sir, those *fellows* may one day become Academicians.' The noise increased – he opened the door and burst in upon them, exclaiming, 'You are a den of wild beasts.' One of the offenders, Munro by name, bowed, and said, 'And Fuseli is our keeper.' He retired smiling, and muttering, 'The fellows are growing witty.'

A student, as he passed, held up his drawing, and said confidently,

'Here, sir, I finished it without using a crumb of bread.' 'All the worse for your drawing,' replied Fuseli; 'buy a twopenny loaf, and rub it out.'

[J. Timbs, *Anecdotes*, 1865]

Fuseli and the Royal Academy

'What do you see, Sir?' he said one day to a student, who, with his pencil in his hand and his drawing before him, was gazing into vacancy. 'Nothing, Sir:' was the answer. 'Nothing, young man,' said the Keeper emphatically, 'then I tell you that you ought to *see something* – you ought to see distinctly the true image of what you are trying to draw. I see the vision of all I paint – and I wish to heaven I could paint up to what I see.'

He reserved a little of his wit and satire for his elder brethren of the easel and the modelling stool. He had aided Northcote and Opie[1] in obtaining admission into the Academy, and when he proposed himself for Keeper naturally expected their assistance – they voted against him, and next morning went together to his house to offer an explanation. He saw them coming – he opened the door as they were scraping their shoes, and said, 'Come in – come in – for the love of heaven come in, else you will ruin me entirely.' – 'How so?' cried Opie. 'Marry, thus,' replied the other, 'my neighbours over the way will see you, and say, "Fuseli's *done* – for there's a bum-bailiff," he looked at Opie, "going to seize his person; and a little Jew broker," he looked at Northcote, "going to take his furniture" – so come in I tell you – come in!' On Northcote especially he loved to exercise some of the malevolence of rival wit. He looked on his friend's painting of the angel meeting Balaam and his ass. 'How do you like it,' said the painter. 'Vastly, Northcote,' said Fuseli, 'you are an angel at an ass – but an ass at an angel.' A person who desired to speak to the Keeper of the Academy followed so close on the porter, whose business it was to introduce him, that he announced himself with an expression which the inimitable Liston has since rendered proverbial. 'I hope I don't intrude.' – 'You do intrude,' said Fuseli, in a surly tone. 'Do I?' said the visitor; 'then, Sir, I will come tomorrow, if you please' – 'No, Sir,'

---

1. John Opie (1761–1807).

replied he, 'don't come to-morrow, for then you will intrude a second time: tell me your business now.'

Fuseli spared no one: on Nollekens he was often very merciless; he disliked him for his close and parsimonious nature, and rarely failed to hit him under the fifth rib. Once at the table of Mr. Coutts the banker, Mrs. Coutts, dressed like Morgiana, came dancing in presenting her dagger at every breast: as she confronted the sculptor, Fuseli called out, 'Strike – strike – there's no fear: Nolly was never known to bleed.' When Blake, a man infinitely more wild in conception than Fuseli himself, showed him one of his strange productions, he said, 'Now some one has told you this is very fine.' – 'Yes,' said Blake, 'the Virgin Mary appeared to me, and told me it was very fine: what can you say to that?' – 'Say?' exclaimed Fuseli, 'why nothing – only her ladyship has not an immaculate taste.'

[A. Cunningham, *Lives*, 1829]

Fuseli's Advice to Haydon

My incessant application was soon perceived by Fuseli, who, coming in one day, when I was at work and all the other students were away, walked up to me and said in the mildest voice: 'Why, when de devil *do* you dine?' and invited me to go back with him to dinner. Here I saw his sketches, the sublimity of which I deny. Evil was in him; he knew full well that he was wrong as to truth of imitation, and he kept palliating it under the excuse of 'the Grand Style.' He said a subject should interest, astonish, or move; if it did none of these it was worth 'noding, by Gode.' He had a strong Swiss accent and a guttural energetic diction. This was not affectation in him. He swore roundly, a habit which he told me he had contracted from Dr. Armstrong. He was about five feet five inches high, had a compact little form, stood firmly at his easel, painted with his left hand, never held his palette upon his thumb but kept it upon his stone, and being very near-sighted, and too vain to wear glasses, used to dab his beastly brush into the oil, and sweeping round the palette in the dark, take up a great lump of white, red, or blue, as it might be, and plaster it over a shoulder or face. Sometimes in his blindness he would put a hideous smear of Prussian blue in his flesh, and then, perhaps, discovering his mistake, take a bit of red to deaden it, and then prying close in, turn round to me and say: 'By gode, dat's a fine purple! it's vary like Corregio, by Gode!' and then, all of a sudden, he would burst out with a quotation from Homer, Tasso, Dante, Ovid, Virgil, or perhaps the *Niebelungen*, and thunder round to me with 'Paint dat!' I found him the most grotesque mixture of literature, art, scepticism, indelicacy, profanity, and kindness. He put me in mind of Archimago in Spenser. Weak minds he destroyed. They mistook his wit for reason, his indelicacy for breeding, his swearing for manliness, and his infidelity for strength of mind; but he was accomplished in elegant literature, and had the art of inspiring young minds with high and grand views. I told him, that I would never paint portrait – but devote myself to High Art. 'Keep to dat!' said Fuseli, looking fiercely at me: 'I will, sir.' We were more intimate from that hour. He should have checked me, and pointed out that portrait was useful as practice, if kept subordinate, but that I was not to allow myself to be seduced by the money that it brought in from making High Art my predominant object. This would have been more sensible.

[B. R. Haydon, *Autobiography and Journals*, 1853]

Fuseli's Accomplishments

His vigour of conversation continued to the last. His acquirements were great. He wrote Latin, spoke Italian, German, French perfectly well, and read Homer, but his knowledge of Greek was not solid. He could not argue, but illustrated everything by brilliant repartee; Horne Tooke was the only man who was an overmatch for him.

'He was fond of praise, and if you did not praise anything he was about, he would praise it himself; but if you praised it beyond truth, he would be severe in censuring it. It seemed a reflection on his genius if you did not praise, and a contempt for his understanding if you praised too much: in either case he resented.

'He was an intense egotist, as all mannerists must be. If you acknowledged the supremacy of his style, no man was more fatherly; if you disputed his infallibility, he heard you with irritation.

'On the whole Fuseli was a great genius, but not a sound genius, and failed to interest the nation by having nothing in his style in common with our natural sympathies.'

[B. R. Haydon, *Autobiography and Journals*, 1853]

Fuseli's Wish to Appear Erudite

It pleased Fuseli to be thought one of those erudite gentlemen whom
the poet describes –

Far seen in Greek – deep men of letters;

and he loved to annoy certain of his companions with the display of his
antique lore. He sometimes composed Greek verses in the emergency
of the moment, and affect to forget the name of the author. He once
repeated half-a-dozen sonorous and well-sounding lines to Porson,[1]
and said 'With all your learning now you cannot tell me who wrote
that.' The Professor, 'much renowned for Greek,' confessed his
ignorance, and said 'I don't know him.' 'How the devil could you
know him?' chuckled Fuseli – 'I made them this moment.' When
thwarted in the Academy, and that was not seldom, his wrath aired
itself in a polyglott. 'It is a pleasant thing and an advantageous,' said
the painter, on one of those occasions, 'to be learned. I can speak
Greek, Latin, French, English, German, Danish, Dutch, Icelandic, and
Spanish, and so let my folly or my fury get vent through nine different
avenues.'

[A. Cunningham, *Lives*, 1829]

James Northcote on Fuseli

Northcote said, there were people who could not argue. Fuseli was one
of these. He could throw out very brilliant and striking things; but if
you at all questioned him, he could no more give an answer than a
child of three years old. He had no resources, nor any *corps de reserve*
of argument beyond his first line of battle. That was imposing and
glittering enough.

[W. Hazlitt, *Conversations of James Northcote, Esq, R.A.*, 1836]

Fuseli and the Two Fat Men

One day, Fuseli's attention was attracted by a serpent with its tail in its
mouth, a common-place emblem of eternity, which was carved upon
an exhibited monument. 'It won't do, I tell you,' said Fuseli to the

---

1. Richard Porson (1759–1808), a celebrated Greek scholar.

sculptor, 'you must have something new.' The *something new* startled a man whose imagination was none of the brightest, and he said, 'How shall I find something new?' 'Oh, nothing so easy,' said Fuseli, 'I'll help you to it. When I went away to Rome I left two fat men cutting fat bacon in St. Martin's-lane; in ten years time I returned, and found the two fat men cutting fat bacon still: twenty years more have passed, and there the two fat fellows cut the fat flitches the same as ever. Carve them! if they look not like an image of eternity I wot not what does.'

This anecdote is related by Cunningham: it is told with a slight error, which does not, however, affect the point of its absurdity. The two fat men were the brothers who, for many years, kept the ham and beef shop in St Martin's *court*; where rounds of beef were often cooked for the royal table, and conveyed to Carlton House in the days of the Regency.

[J. Timbs, *Anecdotes*, 1865]

Angelica Kauffmann (1741–1807)
Deceived by a Fortune Hunter

Angelica, before she married Mr. Zucchi,[1] the artist, was most artfully deceived by a discarded servant of Count Horn, who had imposed himself upon her smiles with the title of his late master; and, being a very fine handsome fellow, she was determined to show her friends, with whom she had flirted, that she had at last made a good hit, and therefore, without the least hesitation, immediately gave her hand to the impostor. The next time Angelica attended at Buckingham-house upon the Queen, who was pleased by seeing her paint, she communicated her marriage to her Majesty, upon which she received the most condescending congratulations, with an invitation to her husband to come to Court; who, however, was cunningly determined to keep himself within the house, from the sight of every one, until his baggage had arrived, which he expected every day. At last Count Horn himself came to England, and when at the levee, was much surprised by being complimented upon his marriage. Angelica, who soon received the mortifying information from the Queen, was for a time inconsolable; but at last, her friends prevailed upon the fortune-hunter

1. Antonio Zucchi (1726–95).

to leave England upon a pension, and Angelica, who resumed the name of Kauffmann, which she retained till her death, was fortunately never troubled with him afterwards.

[J. T. Smith, *Nollekens and his Times*, 1828]

Angelica Kauffmann's Character

The reader will probably recollect the manner in which Angelica Kauffmann was imposed upon by a gentleman's servant, who married her under the name of Count Horn, and the way in which his treachery was discovered; as related in the early part of the present volume. Angelica, however, was universally considered as a coquette, so that we cannot deeply sympathize in her disappointment; and as a proof how justly she deserved that character, I shall give an anecdote which I have often heard Mr. Nollekens relate. When Angelica was at Rome, previously to her marriage, she was ridiculously fond of displaying her person, and being admired; for which purpose she one evening took her station in one of the most conspicuous boxes of the Theatre, accompanied by Nathaniel Dance[1] and another artist, both of whom, as well as many others, were desperately enamoured of her. Angelica, perhaps, might have recollected the remonstrance of Mrs. Peachum, where she says,

> Oh, Polly! you might have toy'd and kiss'd:
> By keeping men off you keep them on:[2]

However, while she was standing between her two beaux, and finding an arm of each most lovingly embracing her waist, she contrived, whilst her arms were folded before her on the front of the box over which she was leaning, to squeeze the hand of both, so that each lover concluded himself beyond all doubt the man of her choice.

[J. T. Smith, *Nollekens and his Times*, 1828]

James Northcote (1746–1831) Paints one of Reynolds's Maidservants

In the early part of the time that I passed with Sir Joshua as his scholar, I had, for the sake of practice, painted the portrait of one of the female

---

1. Nathaniel Dance (1735–1811), English portrait painter.
2. Quoted from Gay's *The Beggar's Opera*.

servants; but my performance had no other merit than that of being a strong likeness.

Sir Joshua had a large macaw, which he often introduced into his pictures, as may be seen from several prints. This bird was a great favorite, and was always kept in the dining parlour, where he became a nuisance to this same house-maid, whose department it was to clean the room after him; of course, they were not upon very good terms with each other.

The portrait, when finished, was brought into the parlour, one day after dinner, to be shown to the family, that they might judge of the progress I had made. It was placed against a chair, while the macaw was in a distant part of the room, so that he did not immediately perceive the picture as he walked about on the floor; but when he turned round and saw the features of his enemy, he quickly spread his wings, and in great fury ran to it, and stretched himself up to bite at the face. Finding, however, that it did not move, he then bit at the hand, but perceiving it remain inanimate, he proceeded to examine the picture behind, and then, as if he had satisfied his curiosity, left it, and walked again to a distant part of the room; but whenever he turned about, and again saw the picture, he would, with the same action of rage, repeatedly attack it. The experiment was afterwards repeated, on various occasions, in the presence of Edmund Burke, Dr. Johnson, Dr. Goldsmith, and most of Sir Joshua's friends, and never failed of success; and what made it still more remarkable was, that when the bird was tried by any other portrait, he took no notice of it whatever.

[J. Northcote, *Memoirs of Sir Joshua Reynolds*, 1813–15]

William Beechey (1753–1839) at Court

'I was recently introduced,' observed Ward, 'to Sir William Beechey, and I was somewhat surprised at my not finding him the fine gentleman I had expected in a "Sir William"'.

'Oh, no,' said Northcote, laughing; 'he is not that, certainly. His manners are coarse, but I have always considered Beechey to be a very honest man, and he is a very good-natured man, too. He has fought his way in the world exceedingly well, and brought up a family in a manner very creditable to himself; but having risen from a low station – I don't know if he was not a house-painter at first – he is not very polished. He amused the Royal Family, when painting their portraits, by his total ignorance of Court etiquette; they were every hour amused with his blunders in that respect, which seemed, however, to give him no concern; he was so totally concerned with what he was about, that he seemed to think such things of no moment whatever. When Queen Charlotte was sitting to him, he entertained the Court ladies by the homely way in which he conversed. One day, after the Queen had sat very still, and Beechey had been working hard for a long time, she said, "Now, Mr. Beechey, we will rest a little!" and, leaning back in her chair, she took a pinch of snuff. Beechey, upon seeing the box, exclaimed, "God bless your Majesty! I have been dying for a pinch this last hour!" and took a good pinch from the box at once, without the least ceremony.'

[*Conversations of James Northcote with James Ward*, ed. E. Fletcher, 1901]

William Beechey and George III

'I myself can also tell you,' said Ward, 'a story with regard to the free-and-easy manner that Beechey adopted in the presence of Royalty. The King was once sitting to him, and the conversation turned upon Sir Joshua, whom Beechey much adored. The King, in his hurried manner, shouted out, "I don't like that Reynolds! I don't like Reynolds!" "Oh! why, your Majesty?" responded Beechey. "Because," the King replied, "he paints *red* trees! paints *red* trees!" Beechey did his best to assure his Royal sitter that some kinds of trees turn very red indeed in the autumn. "No! never *red*, never *red*!" ejaculated his Majesty, hastily, and Beechey made no reply. But, taking his quiet walk in the evening through the park, Beechey discovered a branch that was almost as red as vermilion. He brought back with him a cutting from the branch, and laid it down in the painting-room, and then retired in the hope that early on the morrow his Majesty would be convinced that his favourite Sir Joshua had done nothing but what Nature had authorised him to do. Upon entering the painting-room the following morning, the eyes of the King immediately rested on the *red* branch lying there on the table. He turned, however, upon Beechey such a look of displeasure that the painter was afraid to utter, either then or afterwards, another word about it.'

[*Conversations of James Northcote with James Ward*, ed. E. Fletcher, 1901]

William Blake (1757–1827) as a Student

The specific value of the guidance to be had by an ingenuous art-student from the venerable Moser,[1] then a man of seventy-three, is suggestively indicated by a reminiscence afterwards noted down in Blake's manuscript commentary on Reynolds's *Discourses*. 'I was once,' he there relates, 'looking over the Prints from Rafael & Michael Angelo in the Library of the Royal Academy. Moser came to me & said: "You should not Study these old Hard Stiff & Dry, Unfinish'd Works of Art – Stay a little & I will shew you what you should Study." He then went & took down Le Brun's and Rubens's Galleries. How did I secretly Rage! I also spoke my Mind . . . I said to Moser, "These things that you call Finish'd are not Even Begun; how then can they be Finish'd?" The Man who does not know The Beginning cannot know the End of Art.'

[A. Gilchrist, *The Life of William Blake*, 1863]

William Blake on the Importance of Outline

His love of a distinct outline made him use close and clinging dresses; they are frequently very graceful – at other times they are constrained, and deform the figures which they so scantily cover. 'The great and golden rule of art, (says he,) is this: – that the more distinct and sharp and wiry the bounding line, the more perfect the work of art; and the less keen and sharp this external line, the greater is the evidence of weak imitative plagiarism and bungling: Protogenes and Apelles knew each other by this line.[2] How do we distinguish the oak from the beech; the horse from the ox, but by the bounding outline? How do we distinguish one face or countenance from another, but by the bounding line and its infinite inflexions and movements? Leave out this line and you leave out life itself: all is chaos again, and the line of the Almighty must be drawn out upon it before man or beast can exist.'

[A. Cunningham, *Lives*, 1829]

1. George Michael Moser (1704–83), first Keeper of the Royal Academy.
2. See p. 4.

Blake's Character

William Blake was of low stature and slender make, with a high pallid forehead, and eyes large, dark, and expressive. His temper was touchy, and when moved, he spoke with an indignant eloquence, which commanded respect. His voice, in general, was low and musical, his manners gentle and unassuming, his conversation a singular mixture of knowledge and enthusiasm. His whole life was one of labour and privation, – he had never tasted the luxury of that independence, which comes from professional profit. This untoward fortune he endured with unshaken equanimity – offering himself, in imagination, as a martyr in the great cause of poetic art; – *pitying* some of his more fortunate brethren for their inordinate love of gain; and not doubting that whatever he might have won in gold by adopting other methods, would have been a poor compensation for the ultimate loss of fame. Under this agreeable delusion, he lived all his life – he was satisfied when his graver gained him a guinea a week – the greater the present denial, the surer the glory hereafter.

[A. Cunningham, *Lives*, 1829]

Blake's Manner of Life

Last shillings were, at all periods of Blake's life, a frequent incident of his household economy. For, while engrossed in designing, he had often an aversion to resuming his graver, or to being troubled about money matters. It put him out very much when Mrs Blake referred to the financial topic, or found herself constrained to announce: 'The money is going, Mr Blake.' 'Oh, d— the money!' he would shout: 'it's always the money!' Her method of hinting at the odious subject became, in consequence, a very quiet and expressive one. She would set before him at dinner just what there was in the house, without any comment until, finally, the empty platter had to make its appearance: which hard fact effectually reminded him it was time to go to his engraving for a while. At that, when fully embarked again, he was not unhappy; work being his natural element.

As every slightest anecdote of Blake has its degree of personal value, I may give the following one. A historical painter of the class endlessly industrious yet for ever unknown, was one day pointing out to a visitor some favourite specimen of hopeless hugeness, and said: 'Mr

Blake once paid me a high compliment on that picture. It was on the last occasion when the old gentleman visited me, and his words were, "Ah! that is what I have been trying to do all my life – to paint *round* and never could."' This may be taken as an instance of the courteous care with which Blake would find some agreeable word for an inoffensive inferior in art. Had such a charge been brought against himself by an aggressor, how instant a spark would have been struck from him!

Allan Cunningham has talked of Blake's living on a crust. But in these latter years he, for the most part, lived on good, though simple fare. His wife was an excellent cook – a talent which helped to fill out Blake's waistcoat a little, as he grew old. She could even prepare a made dish,[1] when need be. As there was no servant, he fetched the porter for dinner himself, from the house at the corner of the Strand. Once, pot of porter in hand, he espied coming along a dignitary of art – that highly respectable man, William Collins, R.A.,[2] whom he had met in society a few evenings before. The academician was about to shake hands but, seeing the porter, drew up and did not know him. Blake would tell the story very quietly, and without sarcasm. Another time, Fuseli came in and found Blake with a little cold mutton before him for dinner; who, far from being disconcerted, asked his friend to join him. 'Ah! by G—!' exclaimed Fuseli, 'this is the reason you can do as you like. *Now I can't do this.*' His habits were very temperate. It was only in later years he took porter regularly. He then fancied it soothed him, and would sit and muse over his pint after a one o'clock dinner. When he drank wine, which, at home, of course, was seldom, he professed a liking to drink off good draughts from a tumbler, and thought the wineglass system absurd: a very heretical opinion in the eyes of your true wine drinkers. Frugal and abstemious on principle, and for pecuniary reasons, he was sometimes rather imprudent, and would take anything that came in his way. A nobleman once sent him some oil of walnuts he had had expressed purposely for an artistic experiment. Blake tasted it, and went on tasting, till he had drunk the whole. When his lordship called to ask how the experiment had prospered, the artist had to confess what had become of the ingredients. It was ever after a standing joke against him.

1. A fancy dish made from a number of ingredients and requiring some skill from the cook.
2. William Collins (1788–1847).

In his dress there was a similar triumph of the man over his poverty to that which struck one in his rooms. Indoors he was careful, for economy's sake, but not slovenly: his clothes were threadbare, and his grey trousers had worn black and shiny in front, like a mechanic's. Out of doors he was more particular, so that his dress did not, in the streets of London, challenge attention either way. He wore black knee breeches and buckles, black worsted stockings, shoes which tied, and a broad-brimmed hat. It was something like an old-fashioned tradesman's dress. But the general impression he made on you was that of a gentleman, in a way of his own.

[A. Gilchrist, *Life of Blake*, 1863]

Blake and Thomas Lawrence (1760–1830)

Blake, however, was rich in the midst of poverty. 'They pity me,' he would say of Lawrence and other prosperous artists, who condescended to visit him; 'but 'tis they are the just objects of pity: I possess my visions and peace. They have bartered their birthright for a mess of pottage.'

[A. Gilchrist, *Life of Blake*, 1863]

Blake's Courtesy

'He was equally polite (and that is rare indeed) to men of every age and rank; honouring all men.' In which he resembled Flaxman,[1] who addressed his carvers and workmen as 'friends,' and made them such by his kindness. Of this spontaneous courtesy to all, the following is an instance: Once, while his young friend Calvert[2] was with him in Fountain Court, a man brought up a sack of coals, knocked at the door, and asked: 'Are these coals for here?' 'No, sir,' answered Blake, in quiet, courteous tones, as to an equal; 'but I'll ask whose they are.'

[A. Gilchrist, *Life of Blake*, 1863]

Blake Visited by Henry Crabb Robinson (1775–1867)

. . . I called on him in his house in Fountain's Court in the Strand. The interview was a short one and what I saw was more remarkable than

1. John Flaxman (1755–1826), English Neoclassical sculptor.
2. Edward Calvert (1799–1883), English painter and engraver, a disciple of Blake.

what I heard – He was at work engraving in a small bedroom, light, and looking out on a mean yard – Everything in the room squalid and indicating poverty except himself. And there was a natural gentility about and an insensibility to the seeming poverty which quite removed the impression – Besides, his linen was clean, his hand white and his air quite unembarrassed when he begged me to sit down, as if he were in a palace – There was but one chair in the room, besides that on which he sat – On my putting my hand to it, I found that it would have fallen to pieces if I had lifted it, So, as if I had been a Sybarite – I said with a smile, will you let me indulge myself? and I sat on the bed – and near him and during my short stay there was nothing in him that betrayed that he was aware of what to other persons might have been even offensive not in his person, but in all about him.

His wife I saw at this time – And she seemed to be the very woman to make him happy – She had been formed by him – Indeed, otherwise, she could not have lived with him; Notwithstanding her dress which was poor, and dirty, she had a good expression in her countenance – and – with a dark eye had remains of beauty in her youth – She had that virtue of virtues in a wife an implicit reverence of her husband: It is quite certain that she believed in all his visions. And on one occasion, not this, day, speaking of his Visions she said – 'You know, dear, the first time you saw God was when you were four years old and he put his head to the window and set you a-screaming . . .'

[H. Crabb Robinson, *Reminiscences*, quoted here from Gilchrist's *Life*, 1863]

William Blake Described by Samuel Palmer (1805–81)

His knowledge was various and extensive, and his conversation so nervous and brilliant, that, if recorded at the time, it would now have thrown much light upon his character, and in no way lessened him in the estimation of those who know him only by his works.

In him you saw at once the Maker, the Inventor; one of the few in any age: a fitting companion for Dante. He was energy itself, and shed around him a kindling influence; an atmosphere of life, full of the ideal. To walk with him in the country was to perceive the soul of beauty through the forms of matter; and the high, gloomy buildings between which, from his study window, a glimpse was caught of the Thames and the Surrey shore, assumed a kind of grandeur from the man dwelling near them. Those may laugh at this who never knew such an one as Blake; but of him it is the simple truth.

He was a man without a mask; his aim single, his path straightforwards, and his wants few; so he was free, noble, and happy.

His voice and manner were quiet, yet all awake with intellect. Above the tricks of littleness, or the least taint of affectation, with a natural dignity which few would have dared to affront, he was gentle and affectionate, loving to be with little children, and to talk about them. 'That is heaven,' he said to a friend, leading him to the window, and pointing to a group of them at play.

Declining, like Socrates, whom in many respects he resembled, the common objects of ambition, and pitying the scuffle to obtain them, he thought that no one could be truly great who had not humbled himself 'even as a little child.' This was a subject he loved to dwell upon, and to illustrate.

[Letter from Palmer to Alexander Gilchrist, 23 August 1855, reproduced in Gilchrist's *Life of Blake*, 1863]

Samuel Palmer Visits Blake

On Saturday, 9th October, 1824, Mr Linnell called and went with me to Mr Blake. We found him lame in bed, of a scaled foot (or leg). There, not inactive, though sixty-seven years old, but hard-working on a bed covered with books sat he up like one of the Antique patriarchs, or a dying Michael Angelo. Thus and there was he making in the leaves of a great book (folio) the sublimest designs for his (not superior) Dante. He said he began them with fear and trembling. I said 'O! I have enough of fear and trembling.' 'Then,' said he, 'you'll do.'

[A. H. Palmer, *The Life and Letters of Samuel Palmer*, 1892]

Palmer's Pen-portrait of Blake

His eye was the finest I ever saw: brilliant, but not roving, clear and intent, yet susceptible; it flashed with genius, or melted in tenderness. It could also be terrible. Cunning and falsehood quailed under it, but it was never busy with them. It pierced them, and turned away. Nor was the mouth less expressive; the lips flexible and quivering with feeling. I can yet recall it when, on one occasion, dwelling upon the exquisite beauty of the parable of the Prodigal, he began to repeat a part of it;

but at the words, 'When he was yet a great way off, his father saw him,'[1] could go no further; his voice faltered, and he was in tears.

[Letter of 23 August 1855, reproduced in Gilchrist's *Life of Blake*, 1863]

Blake's Visionary Heads

He was requested to draw the likeness of Sir William Wallace[2] – the eye of Blake sparkled, for he admired heroes. 'William Wallace!' he exclaimed, 'I see him now – there, there, how noble he looks – reach me my things!' Having drawn for some time, with the same care of hand and steadiness of eye, as if a living sitter had been before him, Blake stopt suddenly, and said, 'I cannot finish him – Edward the First has stept in between him and me.' 'That's lucky,' said his friend, 'for I want the portrait of Edward too.' Blake took another sheet of paper, and sketched the features of Plantagenet; upon which his majesty politely vanished, and the artist finished the head of Wallace. 'And pray, Sir,' said a gentleman, who heard Blake's friend tell his story – 'was Sir William Wallace an heroic-looking man? And what sort of personage was Edward?' The answer was: 'there they are, Sir, both framed and hanging on the wall behind you, judge for yourself.' 'I looked (says my informant) and saw two warlike heads of the size of common life. That of Wallace was noble and heroic, that of Edward stern and bloody. The first had the front of a god, the latter the aspect of a demon.'

The friend who obliged me with these anecdotes, on observing the interest which I took in the subject, said, 'I know much about Blake – I was his companion for nine years. I have sat beside him from ten at night till three in the morning, sometimes slumbering and sometimes waking, but Blake never slept; he sat with a pencil and paper drawing portraits of those whom I most desired to see. I will show you, Sir, some of these works.' He took out a large book filled with drawings, opened it, and continued, 'Observe the poetic fervour of that face – it is Pindar as he stood a conqueror in the Olympic games. And this lovely creature is Corinna, who conquered in poetry in the same place. That lady is Lais, the courtesan – with the impudence which is part of her profession, she stept in between Blake and Corinna, and he was

1. Luke 15:20.
2. Sir William Wallace, Scottish patriot captured and executed by Edward I.

obliged to paint her to get her away. There! that is a face of a different stamp – can you conjecture who he is?' 'Some scoundrel, I should think, Sir.' 'There now – that is a strong proof of the accuracy of Blake – he is a scoundrel indeed! The very individual task-master whom Moses slew in Egypt. And who is this now – only imagine who this is?' 'Other than a good one, I doubt, Sir.' 'You are right, it is the Devil – he resembles, and this is remarkable, two men who shall be nameless; one is a great lawyer, and the other – I wish I durst name him – is a suborner of false witnesses. This other head now? – this speaks for itself – it is the head of Herod; how like an eminent officer in the army!'

He closed the book, and taking out a small panel from a private drawer, said, 'this is the last which I shall show you; but it is the greatest curiosity of all. Only look at the splendour of the colouring and the original character of the thing!' 'I see,' said I, 'a naked figure with a strong body and a short neck – with burning eyes which long for moisture, and a face worthy of a murderer, holding a bloody cup in its clawed hands, out of which it seems eager to drink. I never saw any shape so strange, nor did I ever see any colouring so curiously splendid – a kind of glistening green and dusky gold, beautifully varnished. But what in the world is it?' 'It is a ghost, Sir – the ghost of a flea – a spiritualization of the thing!' 'He saw this in a vision then,' I said. 'I'll tell you all about it, Sir. I called on him one evening, and found Blake more than usually excited. He told me he had seen a wonderful thing – the ghost of a flea! And did you make a drawing of him? I inquired. No, indeed, said he, I wish I had, but I shall, if he appears again! He looked earnestly into the corner of the room, and then said, here he is – reach me my things – I shall keep my eye on him. There he comes! his eager tongue whisking out of his mouth, a cup in his hand to hold blood, and covered with a scaly skin of gold and green; – as he described him so he drew him.'

These stories are scarcely credible, yet there can be no doubt of their accuracy. Another friend, on whose veracity I have the fullest dependence, called one evening on Blake, and found him sitting with a pencil and a panel, drawing a portrait with all the seeming anxiety of a man who is conscious that he has got a fastidious sitter; he looked and drew, and drew and looked, yet no living soul was visible. 'Disturb me not,' said he, in a whisper, 'I have one sitting to me.' 'Sitting to you!' exclaimed his astonished visitor, 'where is he, and what is he? – I see no one.' 'But I see him, Sir,' answered Blake haughtily, 'there he is, his name is Lot – you may read of him in the Scripture. *He* is sitting for his portrait.'

[A. Cunningham, *Lives*, 1829]

Blake and the Ghost of a Flea

This spirit visited his [Blake's] imagination in such a figure as he never anticipated in an insect. As I was anxious to make the most correct investigation in my power, of the truth of these visions, on hearing of this spiritual apparition of a Flea, I asked him if he could draw for me the resemblance of what he saw: he instantly said, 'I see him now before me.' I therefore gave him paper and a pencil, with which he drew the portrait, of which a facsimile is given in this number. I felt convinced by his mode of proceeding that he had a real image before him, for he left off, and began on another part of the paper to make a separate drawing of the mouth of the Flea, which the spirit having opened, he was prevented from proceeding with the first sketch, till he had closed it. During the time occupied in completing the drawing, the Flea told him that all fleas were inhabited by the souls of such men as were by nature blood-thirsty to excess, and were therefore providentially confined to the size and form of insects; otherwise, were he himself, for instance, the size of a horse, he would depopulate a great portion of the country.

[Quoted in A. Gilchrist, *Life of Blake*, 1863]

Blake and the Fairy Funeral

He often saw less majestic shapes than those of the poets of old. 'Did you ever see a fairy's funeral, madam?' he once said to a lady, who happened to sit by him in company. 'Never, sir!' was the answer. 'I have,' said Blake, 'but not before last night. I was walking alone in my garden, there was great stillness among the branches and flowers and more than common sweetness in the air: I heard a low and pleasant sound, and I knew not whence it came. At last I saw the broad leaf of a flower move, and underneath I saw a procession of creatures of the size and colour of green and gray grasshoppers, bearing a body laid out on a rose leaf, which they buried with songs, and then disappeared. It was a fairy funeral.'

[A. Cunningham, *Lives*, 1829]

Blake Describes his Visions to Henry Crabb Robinson

As he spoke of frequently seeing Milton, I ventured to ask, half ashamed at the time, which of the three or four portraits in *Hollis's* Memoirs (vols. in 4to) was the most like – He answd. 'They are all like, At different ages – I have seen him as a youth and as an old man with long flowing beard. He came lately as an old man – he said he came to ask a favour of me – He said he had committed an error in his Paradise Lost, which he wanted me to correct in a poem or picture; but I declined. I said I had my own duties to perform' – It is a presumptuous question, I replied – Might I venture to ask – what that could be – He wished me to expose the falsehood of his doctrine taught in the Paradise Lost that sexual intercourse arose out of the Fall . . . At the time that he asserted his own possession of the gift of Vision, he did not boast of it as peculiar to himself; all men might have it if they would.

. . .

I asked him in what language Voltaire spoke – His answer was ingenious and gave no encouragment to cross questioning 'To my sensations it was English. It was like the touch of a musical key – he touched it probably French, but to my ear it became English.'

[H. Crabb Robinson, *Reminiscences*, quoted here from Gilchrist's *Life of Blake*, 1863]

Blake and the Ancient of Days

Smith tells us that Blake 'was inspired with the splendid grandeur of this figure,' *The Ancient of Days*, 'by the vision which he declared hovered over his head at the top of his staircase,' in No. 13 Hercules Buildings, and that he has been frequently heard to say that it made a more powerful impression upon his mind than all he had ever been visited by.' On that same staircase it was Blake, for the only time in his life, *saw a ghost*. When talking on the subject of ghosts, he was wont to say they did not appear much to imaginative men, but only to common minds, who did not see the finer spirits. A ghost was a thing seen by the gross bodily eye; a vision, by the mental. 'Did you ever see a ghost?' asked a friend. 'Never but once,' was the reply. And it befell thus. Standing one evening at his garden door in Lambeth, and chancing to look up, he saw a horrible grim figure, 'scaly, speckled, very awful,' stalking downstairs towards him. More frightened than ever before or after, he took to his heels, and ran out of the house.

[A. Gilchrist, *Life of Blake*, 1863]

Blake's Last Work

The Ancient of Days was such a favourite with Blake, that three days before his death, he sat bolstered up in bed, and tinted it with his choicest colours and in his happiest style. He touched and retouched it – held it at arm's length, and then threw it from him, exclaiming, 'There! that will do! I cannot mend it.' He saw his wife in tears – she felt this was to be the last of his works – 'Stay, Kate! (cried Blake) keep just as you are – I will draw your portrait – for you have ever been an angel to me' – she obeyed, and the dying artist made a fine likeness.

[A. Cunningham, *Lives*, 1829]

John Opie (1761–1807) and James Northcote

Opie, I remember, used to argue, that there were as many different sorts of taste as genius. He said, 'If I am engaged in a picture, and endeavour to do it according to the suggestions of my employers, I do not understand exactly what they want, nor they what I can do, and I please no one: but if I do it according to my own notions, I belong to a class, and if I am able to satisfy myself, I please that class.' You did not know Opie? You would have admired him greatly. I do not speak of him as an artist, but as a man of sense and observation. He paid me the compliment of saying, 'that we should have been the best friends in the world, if we had not been rivals.' I think he had more of this feeling than I had; perhaps, because I had most vanity. We sometimes got into foolish altercations. I recollect once in particular, at a banker's in the city, we took up the whole of dinner-time with a ridiculous con-troversy about Milton and Shakespeare; I am sure we neither of us had the least notion which was right – and when I was heartily ashamed of it, a foolish citizen who was present, added to my confusion by saying – 'Lord! What would I give to hear two such men as you talk every day!' This quite humbled me: I was ready to sink with vexation: I could have resolved never to open my mouth again.

[W. Hazlitt, *Conversations of James Northcote, Esq., R.A.,* 1830]

George Morland (1763–1804): Beginnings

His father stimulated him by praise and by indulgences at the table, and to ensure his continuance at his allotted tasks, shut him up in a garret, and excluded him from free air, which strengthens the body, and from education – that free air which nourishes the mind. His stated work for a time was making drawings from pictures and from plaster casts, which his father carried out and sold; but as he increased in skill, he chose his subjects from popular songs and ballads, such as 'Young Roger came tapping at Dolly's window,' 'My name it is Jack Hall,' 'I am a bold Shoemaker, from Belfast Town I came,' and other productions of the mendicant muse. The copies of pictures and casts were commonly sold for three half-crowns each; the original sketches – some of them a little free in posture, and not over delicately handled, were framed and disposed of for any sum from two to five guineas, according to the cleverness of the piece, or the generosity of the purchaser. Though far inferior to the productions of his manhood, they were much admired: engravers found it profitable to copy them, and before he was sixteen years old, his name had flown far and wide.

But long before he was sixteen, he had begun to form those unfortunate habits by which the story of his life is to be darkened. From ten years of age, he appeared to have led the life of a prisoner and a slave under the roof of his father, hearing in this seclusion the merry din of the schoolboys in the street, without hope of partaking in their sports. By-and-bye he managed to obtain an hour's relaxation at the twilight, and then associated with such idle and profligate boys as chance threw in his way, and learned from them a love of coarse enjoyment, and the knowledge that it could not well be obtained without money. Oppression keeps the school of Cunning; young Morland resolved not only to share in the profits of his own talents, but also to snatch an hour or so of amusement, without consulting his father. When he made three drawings for his father, he made one secretly for himself, and giving a signal from his window, lowered it by a string to two or three knowing boys, who found a purchaser at a reduced price, and spent the money with the young artist. A common taproom was an indifferent school of manners, whatever it might be for painting, and there this gifted lad was now often to be found late in the evening, carousing with hostlers and potboys, handing round the quart pot, and singing his song or cracking his joke.

[A. Cunningham, *Lives*, 1829] There is a close resemblance to the stories told concerning Brouwer's early career (see Part XII).

A First Introduction to George Morland

It may be safer to select a few anecdotes from Hassell, his intimate friend. This person's first introduction to Morland was in character. 'As I was walking (he says) towards Paddington on a summer morning, to inquire about the health of a relation, I saw a man posting on before me with a sucking-pig, which he carried in his arms like a child. The piteous squeaks of the little animal, and the singular mode of conveyance, drew spectators to door and window; the person however who carried it minded no one, but to every dog that barked — and there were not a few — he set down the pig, pitted him against the dog, and then followed the chase which was sure to ensue. In this manner he went through several streets in Mary-le-bone, and at last, stopping at the door of one of my friends, was instantly admitted. I also knocked and entered, but my surprise was great on finding this original sitting with the pig still under his arm, and still greater when I was introduced to Morland the painter.'

[A. Cunningham, *Lives*, 1829]

Morland's Love of Horseflesh

During this period Morland lived at Paddington, where he was visited by the popular pugilists of the day, by the most eminent horse-dealers, and by his never-failing companions the picture merchants. He was a lover of guinea-pigs, dogs, rabbits, and squirrels; he extended his affection also to asses. At one time he was the owner of eight saddle horses, which were kept at the White Lion; and, that the place might be worthy of an artist's stud, he painted the sign where they stood at livery with his own hand. He wished to be thought a consummate judge of horseflesh and a dealer in the article. But he was taught that his wisdom did not lie in that way by two or three sagacious horse-jockies, and began to find that all the cunning of the island was not monopolized by the picture dealers. For indifferent horses he paid with excellent pictures; or, what was worse, with bills which he was not always, if ever, prepared to take up; and when due, purchased an extension of the time by the first picture he had ready. His wine-merchant too was in the discounting line, and obtained sometimes a picture worth fifty pounds for similar accommodation. 'He heaped folly upon folly,' says Hassel, 'with such dire rapidity, that a fortune of ten thousand pounds per annum would have proved insufficient for the support of his waste and prodigality.'

[A. Cunningham, *Lives*, 1829]

An Appreciation of Sir Thomas Lawrence (1769–1830)

January 9th. – Lawrence is dead: to portrait-painting a great loss. Certainly there is no man left who thinks it worth while, if he were able, to devote his powers to the elevation of commonplace faces.

He was suited to the age, and the age to him. He flattered its vanities, pampered its weaknesses, and met its meretricious taste.

His men were all gentlemen, with an air of fashion, and the dandyism of high life; his women were delicate, but not modest; beautiful, but not natural. They appear to look that they may be looked at, and to languish for the sake of sympathy. They have not that air of virtue and breeding which ever sat upon the women of Reynolds.

Reynolds' women seem as unconscious of their beauty as innocent in thought and pure in expression, as if they shrank even from being painted. They are beings to be met with reverence, and addressed with timidity. To Lawrence's women, on the contrary, you feel disposed to march up like a dandy, and offer your services, with a cock of your hat, and a 'D—e, will that do?' Whatever characteristics of the lovely sex Lawrence perpetuated, modesty was certainly one he entirely missed.

As an artist he will not rank high in the opinion of posterity. He was not ignorant of the figure, but he drew with great incorrectness, because he drew to suit the fashion of the season. If necks were to be long, breasts full, waists small, and toes pointed, Sir Thomas was too well-bred to hesitate. His necks are therefore often hideously long, his waists small, his chests puffed, and his ancles tapered. He had no eye for colour. His tint was opaque, not livid, his cheeks were rouged, his lips like the lips of a lay-figure. There was nothing of the red and white which Nature's own sweet and cunning hand laid on. His bloom was the bloom of the perfumer. Of composition he knew scarcely anything.

As a man Sir Thomas Lawrence was amiable, kind, generous and forgiving. His manner was elegant, but not high-bred. He had too much the air of always submitting. He had smiled so often and so long, that at last his smile had the appearance of being set in enamel. He indulged the hope of painting history in his day, but, as Romney[1] did, and Chantrey[2] will, he died before he began; and he is another proof, if proof were wanting, that creative genius is not a passive quality that can be laid aside or taken up as it suits the convenience of the possessor.

[B. R. Haydon, *Autobiography and Journals*, 1853, a passage written in 1830]

Lawrence Tries to Deceive George IV

Lawrence had brought his portfolio for Royal inspection, and among his drawings was one of Napoleon's son, the young Duc de Reichstadt, who is said to have been poisoned. Lawrence had taken it from life, I think in Germany.

'Lawrence,' said the king, 'I must have this.' Lawrence bowed low in acquiescence. 'If your Majesty will permit me, as it is not quite finished, I will return with it in the morning.' The fact was, Lawrence had no inclination to part with it, and on getting home, began a copy. This he carried to the king the next day. 'It is not the same,' said the king, in a passion; and setting his nails into it as if he had been a cat, drew them deeply across the face. After this, Lawrence was in disgrace.

[The Rev. W. Trimmer, quoted in W. Thornbury, *The Life of J. M. W. Turner, R.A.*, 1862]

1. George Romney (1734–1802), portrait painter, especially celebrated for his portraits of Emma, Lady Hamilton.
2. Francis Chantrey (1781–1841), sculptor and founder of the Chantrey Bequest.

XVI

DAVID TO COURBET

&

It was Jacques-Louis David who completed the process begun by
Denis Diderot – that of turning the visual arts (in France at least) into a
subject for passionate intellectual debate. At the same time, David was
directly involved in politics. He was a member of the Revolutionary
Convention, voted for the death of Louis XVI, and himself only
narrowly escaped execution at the fall of Robespierre, with whom he
had become closely associated. In addition to all this, he exercised a
powerful direct influence as an educator – the leading painters of the
next generation, such as Girodet, Gros and Guérin were all his pupils,
and so was Ingres, who helped David with the details of his celebrated
portrait of Mme Recamier.

Ingres was even more pedagogic by instinct than David himself, and
his attitudes, expressed in memorably pithy aphorisms, continued to
influence French art almost throughout the whole of the nineteenth
century. As can be seen from some of the extracts given here, Degas
remained a lifelong admirer.

Delacroix, the standard-bearer of the Romantic Movement as it
expressed itself in French art, left behind him a journal which offers
glimpses of his most intimate thoughts and feelings – something
denied to us in the case of Ingres. On the other hand, he seems to have
provided material for many fewer anecdotes largely because, unlike
Ingres, he did not teach, and remained throughout his life extremely
reserved and fond of his privacy. The young Odilon Redon supplies a
vivid snapshot of Delacroix in old age, but it is noticeable that there is
no dialogue between them. Redon simply spies on Delacroix's
solitude.

Stories of a more conventional and expected kind attached themselves to the ebullient and egotistical personality of Gustave Courbet,
and it is with some glimpses of Courbet's personality that this section
ends.

The Early Career of Jacques-Louis David (1748–1825)

Among David's drawings of this epoch, there is one which the artist gave to Etienne [i.e. to Délecluze himself], and which the latter preserved the more carefully because David, in presenting it to him, added an interesting commentary. The drawing shows two heads. One is that of a young officiant at a sacrifice, crowned with laurels. This, faithfully copied from the antique, has the tranquil feeling which the ancients imparted to figures whose moral dignity they wanted to express. 'See, my friend,' said David, 'here is what I call antiquity in its raw state. When I had carefully and laboriously copied this head, I went home and "put some modern sauce on it", as I used to say in those days. I made the brow a little knitted, I pushed up the cheekbones, I opened the mouth a bit. Finally I gave it what the moderns called *expression* – what is now (this was in 1807) called a grimace. Do you understand, Etienne?' – 'Yes' – 'Nevertheless we still have problems with the critics of our own time. Because we do precisely what the ancients did, they describe the result as cold.'

[E. J. Délecluze, *Louis David: Son Ecole et son temps*, 1855]

David and Robespierre

One day when this same Gérard[1] was with David in his studio at the Convention, David had this to say:

'Look, my dear fellow, what Robespierre likes about me is my civic spirit – my love, my enthusiasm for the Revolution! He cares nothing for painting or painters! And in fact, my dear fellow, what are paintings or painters, put beside a man like Robespierre!'

[J. Gigoux, *Causeries sur les artistes de mon temps*, 1885]

David During the Terror

It is related of that French painter, David, that he attended the execution of his friends, Danton and Camille Desmoulins, as a spectacle connected with his improvement in the art of painting; and that at the time of the massacre of the prisoners at La Force, in

1. François Gérard (1770–1837), a pupil of David.

September, 1792, he was composedly making sketches from the dying and the dead. Reboul asked him what he was doing. He coolly replied, 'I am catching the last convulsions of nature in these scoundrels.'
[*The Percy Anecdotes*, 1821–3]

David at the Waxworks

[David's] sang-froid, his impassive manner, sometimes took on the lineaments of courage. During one of the long walks he made with Etienne, they chanced, returning from the Jardin des Plantes, to follow the Boulevard du Temple, where they halted to take a casual look at the mountebanks' booths, the food stalls and the bird sellers who had set up shop there. They arrived at Curtius's waxwork show, and having gazed for a few moments at the Turk and the Grenadier of the Imperial Guard on either side of the doorway, David, smiling at the noisy exhortations of the barker employed to attract the curious, turned to Etienne and said: 'Well then, shall we go in? . . . Come along, Etienne – it's my treat!' And in they went.

Whilst the attendant with his pointer explained the 'Tragic History of Holofernes' and the 'Coronation of Napoleon', David told his pupil to have a look at several masks in wax which had obviously been moulded from life; and could not resist drawing a comparison between these and others which were evidently the product of the sculptor. These led him to make a number of remarks about the imperfect nature of all imitations. During the exchange to which this topic gave rise, the demonstrator, having put an end to his explanations because he perceived that no one was listening, leant on the railing to eavesdrop on the conversation between the two visitors, who soon turned to leave.

However, thanks to what he had overheard, the attendant perceived that here were two customers from whom he might draw some extra profit. Coming over to David, with an air which was simultaneously knowing and respectful, he said: 'I see, sirs, that you are knowledgeable people. We have several curious items which are not shown to everyone. I think,' he added, with a deep bow, 'you would be very interested in some additional things which I can show you.' Both David and Etienne thought at first that they were being offered some pornographic spectacle, and refused. The attendant understood what they were thinking from the manner of their refusal, and affirmed that 'the establishment' did not have anything of that sort, and 'they would be happy' with what he had to show. With this, he led them to an alcove in which there stood a sort of chest, and threw open the lid. Inside, suspended from a metal rod, were wax moulds of the heads of Hébert, Robespierre and several others guillotined during the same epoch. 'You see, sirs,' said the attendant, reciting his well worn patter, 'that's Hébert, called Père Duchêne, whose crimes brought him to the scaffold; there's Robespierre – please note the bandage holding his jaw together. He tried to shoot himself when . . .' David, with unruffled calm, made a small gesture, to show that this explanation had been unnecessary. He looked for a long time, and with close attention, at these heads, which still displayed in minute detail the marks and injuries which were the result of the execution. Then he turned away, putting some money into the attendant's hand, and, without addressing either him or Etienne directly, remarked: 'Yes, it's well done. Really, it's extremely well done.'

[E. J. Délecluze, *Louis David*, 1855]

David on the Italian Art Treasures Brought to Paris by Napoleon

Only one man was against all this, and had the courage to make known his opinion: David. Several days after the ceremony at the Champ de Mars, when those sixty wagons passed, filled with the statues and paintings that had been carried off, David expressed, to the pupils gathered in his studio, the regret he felt that these objects had been removed from Italy. Since he had only spoken about the subject in a general way, without giving reasons for his opinion, his words, publicly reported, were interpreted in a painful manner, and detractors of the great artist did not hesitate to say that he had been motivated by envy – by fear that direct comparison would make obvious the inferiority of his own work. Others thought that he had been motivated by a different kind of jealousy – that he would have liked these brilliant spoils to have been gathered by the Revolutionary Convention rather than the Directory.

Etienne, to whom David had begun to show special openness, felt the same astonishment as the public in general at the strange regrets expressed by his master. He resolved to question him. 'You must understand, my dear Etienne,' David said, 'that people do not naturally love the arts in France; it is a factitious taste. You may be quite sure that, despite the lively enthusiasm now being expressed for the masterpieces brought from Italy, they will soon be considered no more than curiosities. The actual location of a work, the distance one has to travel in order to admire it, make an important contribution to the appreciation of its merits. The paintings in particular, which were made to adorn churches, will lose a great part of their effect when they are no longer in the places for which they were made. The accessibility of these masterpieces may create scholars, such as Winckelmann, but not artists.'

[E. J. Délecluze, *Louis David*, 1855]

David and Bonaparte on the Subject of Heroic Defeat

The power of the First Consul was still far from being what Bonaparte desired; he gave time to many projects which were only to be realized later. His popularity and influence were soon affirmed by the victory of Marengo. On his return to Paris he thought, seriously this time, of having his portrait painted by David. He sent for the artist and interviewed him in the presence of his brother Lucien Bonaparte, Minister of the Interior.

'What are you doing now?' he asked.

'I am working on my painting of *Thermopylae*.'

'Too bad. You are wrong, David, to bother with painting the defeated.'

'But, Citizen Consul, the defeated, in this case, were also heroes who died for their country. Despite their defeat, they pushed the Persians out of Greece for a hundred years.'

'No matter – only the name of Leonidas has come down to us. Everything else is lost to history.'

'Everything,' David interrupted, 'but this noble resistance to a numberless army. Everything! Except the customs, the austere morality of the Spartans. It is useful to remind your soldiers of those.'

[E. J. Délecluze, *Louis David*, 1855]

David and Bonaparte Discuss Portraiture

After this first interview, Napoleon made it known to David that he wished the artist to paint his portrait. David had long awaited the opportunity; he accepted at once, and intimated that he wanted to begin as soon as possible. He asked the First Consul to let him know the day when he would come to pose. 'Pose?' said Bonaparte, who had already made it clear that he disliked this kind of constraint. 'What's the good of that? Do you think that the great men of antiquity whose likenesses have come down to us posed for their portraits?'

'But I am painting you for your own century, for men who have seen and known you. They want to see something which is like you.'

'Likeness? It is not exactitude in copying every feature – a little spot on the nose – which creates a likeness. What you must paint is the character of the physiognomy, the thing that animates it. One doesn't preclude the other. Quite certainly Alexander never posed for Apelles. No one bothers whether the portraits of great men are like them or not. It is enough if their genius lives.'

'You are teaching me how to paint,' said David in response.

'You are making fun of me. Why?'

'I feel that I have not as yet looked at painting from this angle. You are right, First Consul – and yes, you need not pose. Let me get on with it; I will paint you without that.'

David left Napoleon's study with the latter's brother Lucien, who returned to the subject of the painting of *Thermopylae*, saying to the artist: 'You must understand, my friend, that he only likes national subjects, because he thinks they serve a purpose. It happens to be his predilection – he doesn't get annoyed if one discusses it.'

On several occasions Bonaparte said to David that, if he was going to be painted, he wanted to be shown 'calm, upon a fiery horse'. The artist combined this motif with Bonaparte's crossing of the Alps, and thus arrived at the composition of the equestrian portrait of this celebrated personage.

[E. J. Delécluze, *Louis David*, 1855]

David at Work on his Portrait of Bonaparte

On one occasion Ducis, Alexandre and Langlois, David's pupils, who later made an extremely good copy of the equestrian portrait of Bonaparte, were present in David's studio together with their master. So too was Etienne. They were all standing round the lay-figure which was dressed in Bonaparte's clothing, looking with keen interest at his epaulettes, hat, uniform and sword – deaf-and-dumb witnesses of the celebrated Marengo campaign. Each had something more or less just, more or less witty to say, until David, whose own hands and feet were delicately made, noted the small size of Bonaparte's boots, and remarked that great men usually had extremely refined extremities. This observation, which could be flatteringly applied to the painter himself, was vehemently approved by his pupils. One of them added: 'And they usually have large heads.' David, whose good nature had its childish side, took up Napoleon's hat and said: 'Yes, you are right; let's have a look.' Whereupon he put it on his own head, which was extremely small, and burst out laughing when he discovered it fell over his eyes.

[E. J. Délecluze, *Louis David*, 1855]

David's Portrait Napoleon for the Earl of Douglas

A little later, an Englishman, the Earl of Douglas,[1] asked for a full-length portrait of Napoleon, shown in his study, in ordinary dress. David, who . . . had been only too conscious of the impediments created by imperial costume, seized upon this chance to make a simple, natural likeness. In the painting, which is $6\frac{1}{2}$ ft high, the Emperor is shown standing in his study, wearing a green uniform coat with a general's epaulettes. He is beside his desk, which is piled with papers, and he has obviously been working throughout the night. Dawn is breaking, and, so as to show this, the painter has represented several candles which are about to gutter out in their candelabrum.

The painting is perhaps a little soft. David was not bold enough to realize the central idea with sufficient candour. Napoleon's head – only a moderately close likeness – has the defect of being rendered in too ideal a way. While still preserving the indefatigability proper to the subject's character, it should also have been possible to express the weariness of the moment – weariness is usually the product of nocturnal labours. This was, indeed, the only way of bringing out the poetry inherent in such a theme.

Napoleon heard about the portrait, and was no doubt secretly flattered to learn that it had been commissioned by an Englishman. He wanted to see it. It is said that he was delighted and, having examined

1. Later Duke of Hamilton.

the picture attentively, said to his chief painter: 'You have understood me, my dear David; at night I work for the happiness of my subjects; by day I labour for their glory.'

[E. J. Délecluze, *Louis David*, 1855]

Napoleon Visits David's Studio during the Hundred Days

Linked to him by gratitude, by his own oaths of loyalty, and indeed by the immediate danger threatening Napoleon and his partisans [after the return from Elba], David went to see the Emperor, and the Emperor, despite his difficulties and cares, announced his intention of coming to see David's *Leonidas at Thermopylae* – a painting whose subject-matter he had once condemned, but which he now wished to see despite what he had said.

On this occasion Napoleon's visit to the studio lacked the formal pomp of the one made at the height of his power, to see the *Sacre*.[1] Nevertheless, his appearance there had more the character of an act of state than that of the capricious impulse of a lover of art. He imbued the occasion with the reserve and brevity which circumstances demanded. As soon as he came in, he said that he knew the painting without having seen it, and had heard it much praised. Then, after looking at it, he, who had always supposed that it would show the Persian attack and the vigorous resistance of the Spartans, gave vent to his astonishment at the scene David had chosen. The artist, still full of his earliest thoughts on the matter, explained in detail the way in which he had conceived the work. Napoleon, however, could not be reconciled to David's idea, for the latter, instead of painting the battle itself, had chosen the moment which preceded it.

Nevertheless the Emperor expressed his satisfaction and said, as he departed: 'David, continue to make France illustrious through your work. My hope is that copies of this painting will soon be hanging in our military schools. They will remind the students of the virtues of their calling.'

[E. J. Délecluze, *Louis David*, 1855]

---

1. David's painting of Napoleon's coronation as Emperor in 1808 – or, more precisely, of Napoleon crowning Josephine.

Pierre-Paul Prud'hon (1758–1823) and David

During his own lifetime Prud'hon had only a small number of admirers. Among those who had adopted the doctrines of antique art, he was seen as a painter whose taste was bad; they compared him with the artists of the period of decadence [i.e. the Rococo painters of the eighteenth century]. David, always impartial, said of Prud'hon: 'He had his own genre. He is the Boucher or Watteau of our time. Let him alone; what he does will do no harm in the present condition of the French School. He is on the wrong track, but it is not given to everyone to pursue it as he does. He has undoubted talent.' – 'What I can't forgive him,' David added smiling, 'is for having always painted the same heads, the same arms, the same hands. All his figures have the same expression; that expression is always an identical grimace. It is not thus that we should envisage nature, we others, disciples and admirers of the ancients.'

[E. J. Délécluze, *Louis David*, 1855]

Girodet-Trioson (1767–1824) at Work

Prodigal and economical with money, both to excess, he built himself a huge house which was never decorated, or even finished properly. There he piled up wonderful furniture by Boulle, Chinese vases, books, antique arms – but the walls had no hangings, the fireplaces no chimney-pieces, and in the room where he kept his wretched bed he spent his time at a round table covered with written notes and drawings, all torn and in a state of disorder. When he was at home, his old and tattered clothing gave him a totally uncivilized air; but when he sallied forth his toilette had a certain affectation, even fastidiousness – he went so far as to use perfume.

Of all his tics, the strangest was the charlatanism he employed when he was about to complete a composition. Pretending it was all a special favour, he admitted members of high society, plus a few artists, to his studio. Girodet was not the kind of man who would show a new work without having re-examined and corrected it twenty times, and his colleagues were not duped by the trap which he set for them. What happened was that you found yourself introduced mysteriously into his sanctuary, where a numerous company was already assembled. The picture was on the easel, beside it an open box of colours, a palette all prepared and a mahlstick. From time to time, as if he had been seized by some sudden idea, Girodet would make his excuses to those present, asking them to forgive him if he added just a few more touches – just a few! – at a point where a little attention was needed. Then, seizing a brush, which he agitated over his palette, he moved it lightly over the contours as if trying to endow them with additional purity and softness. This little manoeuvre generally had its greatest success with Parisian fine ladies, who later told the story of how they had seen Girodet at work, and that it wasn't surprising that his work was so perfect because he continued to correct 'right up to the last moment'. This was the little comedy which the artist played when he arranged a private view of his *Galatea* – it seemed clear the he was aware of the work's weaknesses, because he took so much trouble to ensure its success.

[E. J. Délecluze, *Louis David*, 1855]

The Bons Mots of Antoine-Jean Gros (1771–1835)

Gros's familiar talk was often very picturesque – most of all when with his pupils in his own studio, or with the students at the Ecole des Beaux Arts. Here are some of his sayings – either long familiar to us or recently reported. One day Gros said to a student making a poor copy; 'Pay attention – you are looking for midday at two in the afternoon. If you carry on this way, you'll never arrive on time.' On another occasion, he said to a student who was making the trees in a warm-toned landscape too dark: 'Do be careful – you are about to burn your roast.' Yet again, to a third student: 'That man isn't running properly. If you follow his example, you'll never get there.' . . . One day Gros was talking to us about contemporary painting: 'Nowadays,' he said, 'where painting is concerned we no longer speak French; it's the Tower of Babel – everyone speaks his own dialect.' – 'Am I on the right road?' one of his students asked. 'Yes, if you are going to Charenton.'[1] . . . When Gros saw a palette with too many colours on it, he said: 'Put on still more. We no longer make Spartan [i.e. thin] broth, why should we make Spartan paintings?' Gros said to a student who preferred to paint rather than draw: 'So you want to make drawing follow colour.

1. The famous asylum.

You're out of your mind – you are putting the cart before the horse. Go on, do it your own way if you insist; you will be no better at painting than at driving a cart.' – 'Never be mad about success; madmen only do things badly.' – 'Never worship any master. Admire other painters, profit from their examples, from seeing their work, but remain yourself.' On another occasion, wishing to give expression to the same thought: 'Be very careful about putting the ideas of others in place of your own, for that will be your ruin. You will fall into chaos and darkness. Yet dare to be yourself, and you will soon see your way clear, and find the light and success.' – 'Always work without too much anxiety about the result, and always be the master of your picture, as the horseman must be master of his steed.' – 'Don't blind yourself, by looking and looking and wishing to do better. Yes, wake up, and don't fall flat on your face on the canvas in your desire to give it finish. You'll only make a mess of both.' – 'Never forget David and his work – he is the light which we must follow if we are not to go astray.' – 'A painting should never look sickly; leave that, if necessary, to the personage it represents.' – 'It is the beauty of the formal arrangement which creates beauty of drawing; it is this beauty which makes the real draughtsman.' Some time after 1830, when the Romantics had just appeared, Gros was with several members of the Académie, discussing things of interest at the time. Naturally talk turned to the new school; everyone had his say and formulated his opinion. Gros listened attentively, but had not yet offered his judgement of Romanticism. Someone said: 'Well, Gros, what do you think?' He replied with some subtlety: 'Me? I think that, not being able to do things better, they choose to do them differently.'

[J. Tripier Le France, *Histoire de la vie et de la mort de Baron Gros*, 1880]

Baron Gros Reproaches himself

The fact that people could now see and study the monuments of French art, in the museum set up at the Petits-Augustins, had already set in train a reaction against the works of antiquity, and this direction was confirmed by the appearance of the first three or four paintings by Gros . . . From this very moment, it must also be said, date the eternal battlepieces and ceremonial scenes commissioned by Bonaparte, carried out under the supervision of his Director of Fine

Arts, Vivant Denon[1]. It was also the time when genre painting, properly so called, returned to a place of honour, and when the excessive fashion for it which came a few years later first began to manifest itself.

This opinion was that of Gros himself. He expressed it so frankly, and upon such a solemn occasion that it is a good thing to set down here how this great artist reproached himself for having harmed the doctrines professed by his master David, and how he accused himself of having brought about the decline of the grand style in France.

On the day of Girodet's funeral, at the moment when all the members of the Institut, and all the most skilful artists were assembled in the dead man's room, waiting to carry his mortal remains to the cemetery, the conversation naturally turned on Girodet's merits and on the irreparable loss suffered by the French School at the very moment when this needed a powerful hand to draw it back from the slippery slope of Romanticism. Gérard,[2] despite his grief, tried to make a speech in praise of his old comrade, regretting that Girodet would no longer be there to inspire young artists with his good example.

'It is you who must replace him, Gérard,' said one of his colleagues. 'You must stand up and put art on the right path, since David is in exile.' – 'It is indeed what I should do,' said Gérard, 'but I do not have the strength. I cannot do it.' – 'As for me,' cried Gros, whose eyes were red, and whose voice was quite changed, 'not only do I lack the authority to give the French School a direction, but I must accuse myself of having been one of the first to offer the bad example which has since been followed, both by failing to choose subjects which were sufficiently severe, but by lacking that stringency of execution which our master recommended, and which he has never ceased to demonstrate in his own work.'

[E. J. Délécluze, *Louis David*, 1855]

Gros and Richard Parkes Bonington (1801/2–28)

Bonington was the pupil of M. Gros. Here is a nice story which I have from several of those who were his contemporaries in Gros's studio.

1. Dominique-Vivant Denon (1747–1825), artist and bureaucrat. He accompanied Napoleon on the Egyptian campaign and made a record of Egyptian antiquities.
2. François Gérard (1770–1837): see also p. 267.

At this time, Gros, having done his most important work, often amused himself by strolling round the town. One day he came into the pupils' studio (where they were all very fond of him) and said:

'You are not sufficiently concerned with colour, my dear sirs. Yet it's colour which gives poetry, life and charm – no painting can come to life without it. When I was walking around, I saw in the windows of some of the picture dealers some paintings and watercolours which were absolutely glowing with colour. Go and look, study them – they're wonderful. They are signed Badington, Bonnington . . . I don't know the name exactly. In any case, that man is a master!'

While this was being said, poor Bonington hung his head, and blushed, there in the midst of his friends, without daring to utter a word.

[J. Gigoux, *Causeries sur les artistes de mon temps*, 1885]

Gros's Pastime

Married, and in the possession of a fine fortune which would have allowed him to surround himself, not merely with friends, but with distinguished personages who would have felt honoured to be admitted to his society, he lived in the strangest manner, spending almost all his leisure time playing cards with the obscure habitués of a café.

[E. J. Délecluze, *Louis David*, 1855]

Jean-Auguste-Dominique Ingres (1780–1867) to One of his Students

'You've studied anatomy? Oh yes! ah well! And now see what this horrible science leads to! I cannot think of it without disgust. If I had had to learn anatomy – yes, I, my dear sirs, I would never have become a painter. Copy nature quite simply and naïvely, and you are already on the road to something.'

[P. Amaury-Duval, *L'atelier d'Ingres*, 1878]

Ingres and the House-painter

Ingres stopped on the pavement at the corner of the rue d'Assas and the rue Vavin. He watched transfixed the motions of a large brush, dipped in a brownish colour, which a house-painter was moving, with regular and rhythmic gestures, across the wooden fascia of a grocer's shop.

'*Cher maître*, what are you doing here?' asked a colleague at the Institute, one E. Signol,[1] who happened to be passing, and who was intrigued by what he saw.

Ingres's only response was to point to the workman: 'Look at him,' he said. 'See how admirable he is – he is taking up *just what is needed.*'

[Boyer d'Agen, *Ingres, d'après une correspondance inédite*, 1909]

Renoir (1841–1919) on Ingres's Method of Drawing

When I was about twelve or thirteen years old, my employer, the potter, sent me to the National Library one day to trace a portrait of Shakespeare which was to be painted on a plate. In looking about for a seat, I came to a corner of the room where several gentlemen were gathered, among them the architect who designed the library. I noticed in the group a short man with impatient gestures who was busy doing a portrait of the architect. It was Ingres. He had a block of paper in his hand, and he would make a sketch, throw it away, begin another. Then all at once he made a drawing as perfect as if he had worked on it for a week.

Ingres must have appeared very tall when he was seated, but when he stood up, his knees seemed right next to his feet.

[A. Vollard, *Renoir, an Intimate Record*, 1925]

Ingres at a Dinner Party

In the course of conversation someone said that there was in Paris an artist called Ducornet who, having lost his hands, used his feet with great skill to wield the brush and paint pictures. M. Ingres, who until that moment had held his peace, said in a tight voice, with the air of someone in pain: 'A man who paints with his feet?' – 'Yes, monsieur, and it seems not badly.' – 'A man who paints with his feet,' Ingres retorted loudly, 'a monster who ought to be done away with!'

Everyone present was astonished by this savage riposte, and some

---

1. Emile Signol (1804–92), painter, pupil of Baron Gros and winner of the Prix de Rome in 1830; an arch-conservative.

people protested. However, M. Ingres, his jowls trembling with horror, remained silent, and seemed ill-at-ease for the rest of dinner.

[A. Barbier, *Souvenirs personnels*, 1863]

Ingres's Portrait of M. Bertin

M. Bertin himself . . . told me about the sittings, and Ingres's desperation. 'He used to weep,' he said, 'and I spent my time comforting him. At last it was agreed that he would begin all over again. One day Ingres came here to dinner, and we took our coffee in the open air, at this very spot, just as we are doing today. I was chatting to a friend, and I had assumed, so it seems, the pose you see in the portrait. Ingres got up, came close to me, and speaking almost in my ear, said: "Come and sit tomorrow, your portrait is done." The next day, I started to pose for him again. The sittings did not last long. In a month, the portrait was finished.'

[P. Amaury-Duval, *L'Atelier d'Ingres*, 1878]

M. Bertin on Ingres

I will never forget Ingres's indignant expression when someone said to him: 'I don't believe Raphael could have painted a finer portrait than that . . .' Ingres leaped to his feet, swung round and said: 'I will not allow a name such as Raphael's to be used in the presence of one of my own works. I will not allow anyone to compare me with this divine being, nor with any other of the great masters. I am nothing at all, sir, beside these giants . . . I am (and here he bent down and put his hand just a little above the floor), only *this* high (and here his hand sunk still lower). I am invisible, sir . . . But as for my contemporaries, that is something altogether different.' Then drawing himself up so as to lose not even an inch of his minimal height, and knocking on the floorboards with his heels: 'I am up there on my high horse . . . I'm not afraid of them!'

[P. Amaury-Duval, *L'Atelier d'Ingres*, 1878]

Ingres on Poussin

Ingres replied as follows to one of my friends. M. Button, a pension-naire at the French Academy in Rome, who had asked permission to go to Naples in order to study nature in that region of Italy: 'Nature at her most beautiful is to be found in Rome. Poussin, master of us all, knew well enough how to find her here, and therefore you have no need to leave the city.'

[A. Barbier, *Souvenirs personnels*, 1863]

Ingres and Théodore Géricault (1791–1824)

M. Ingres did not like Géricault. It seems that Géricault visited Ingres one day when the latter was living in Florence, and admired without reservation his drawings after nature. Ingres was delighted at the appreciation of such a talented artist. However, when he showed his paintings, Géricault uttered not one word. I have always believed that this was what Ingres held against him.

[J. Gigoux, *Causeries sur les artistes de mon temps*, 1885]

Ingres and Eugène Delacroix (1798–1863)

When passing in front of one of Delacroix's paintings, [Ingres] used to cover his eyes and say: 'I've no need to know how not to do it.'

[A. Barbier, *Souvenirs personnels*, 1863]

Ingres on Delacroix's Election to the Academy

This election [in January 1859] was that at which Delacroix was named a member of the Academy. When the result of the vote was known, Ingres cried aloud: 'They have let the wolf into the sheepfold!'

[P. Amaury-Duval, *L'Atelier d'Ingres*, 1878]

Delacroix on Ingres

Guillemet[1] told me [Vollard] also what Delacroix said one day, while he was walking with Chasseriau[2] in the Ingres room at the Hotel de Ville where he was then doing his own decorations: 'It's good, very good. Of course Ingres has his limitations; Lord, so have I. My work is full of faults too, Heaven knows. When we are both dead, I suppose

1. Antoine Guillemet (1843–1918), academic artist.
2. Théodore Chassériau (1819–56), a pupil of Ingres.

we'll stay in Purgatory a while for those faults. But if you were to give Ingres the job of doing my painting, and me his – well, I'll wager that I would come out ahead!'

[A. Vollard, *Renoir, an Intimate Record*, 1925]

Ingres and Chassériau

Ingres, who easily ran to hyperbole, predicted a wonderful future for [Chassériau], calling upon everyone to look at a triumph by his pupil, a successful study after nature; 'Come and see, messieurs, come and see! This child will be the Napoleon of painting.'

[G. Geffroy, *La vie artistique*, 1900]

Corot (1796–1875) on Ingres

Guillemet once asked Corot what he thought of Ingres. Corot answered: 'Lots of talent, but he got into a deplorable rut; he thought that life was to be found in outlines, but the truth is that outlines always elude the eye.'

[A. Vollard, *Renoir, an Intimate Record*, 1925]

Edgar Degas (1834–1917) Shows his Work to Ingres

[Degas] went to see Ingres another time . . . in the company of Valpinçon,[1] and carrying a portfolio under his arm. Ingres looked through the studies this portfolio contained, then shut it, saying: 'Very good! Never after nature, young man! Always after your memory of the masters, and after their prints.'

[P. Valéry, *Degas, Danse, Dessin*, 1938]

Ingres's Aphorisms

On every possible occasion [Degas] recalled the aphorisms of the Master of Montauban:

'Drawing is not outside the line, but inside it.'

---

1. Paul Valpinçon, amateur artist, school-fellow of Degas at the Lycée Louis-le-Grand in Paris and a lifelong friend.

'One must go after the modelling like a fly crawling over a piece of paper.'

'The muscles – those are my friends, but I have forgotten their names.'
  [P. Valéry, *Degas, Danse, Dessin*, 1938]

Degas Defends Ingres

Degas did not allow contradiction when it came to M. Ingres. When someone said to him that the great man created figures made of zinc, he replied: 'Perhaps! . . . but then he was a zinc-worker of genius.'
  [P. Valéry, *Degas, Danse, Dessin*, 1938] The French word *zingueur* means both zinc-worker and plumber, as the two occupations were often combined. A more accurate rendering (which loses the pun) might be 'a plumber of genius'.

Ingres and Degas

A little later I [Degas] saw M. Ingres. One day he organized a small exhibition in his studio, in Old Master fashion. I didn't know him, but went there with a friend who did and was able to get him talking. Among the things on view were three paintings. One showed Hermes with another figure – I don't know what, but the master explained the subject. My friend congratulated him on the perceptive way in which he had translated antiquity. The master accepted the compliment, but remained unmoved. Other compliments, anent the portrait of Mme Moitessier . . . were equally acceptable. Then, spotting a circular version of *The Turkish Bath*,[1] my companion cried: 'Now, that's something different!' 'But,' said M. Ingres, 'I do paint with several brushes.'
  [E. Moreau-Nélaton, 'Deux heures avec Monsieur Degas, 26 decembre 1907', *L'Amour de l'art*, July 1951]

1. The circular version is the *only* version of *The Turkish Bath* (1859), though Ingres produced other paintings of female bathers.

The Apprenticeship of Géricault (1791–1824)

What visibly disquieted Guérin[1] was the extraordinary influence Géricault soon began to exercise over his fellow pupils [in Guérin's studio]. 'Why,' said Guérin to these, 'do you try to imitate him? Let him alone – he has the stuff to make three or four painters; it is not the same with you.'

[Charles Clément, *Géricault*, 1868]

Géricault's Attempted Suicide

It was Charlet[2] who told the story of Géricault's attempted suicide when he was in London – a story unknown till then to anyone else. 'Charlet came back to their hotel late at night,' said M. de la Combe, 'and discovered that Géricault had not been seen all day, and that there were fears that he had some sinister project in mind. He went straight to his room, knocked without getting an answer, knocked again; then, since there was no response, burst the door open. Just in time. A brazier was still burning; Géricault was unconscious, stretched out on his bed, but was restored to life.'

'Charlet made everyone go away, and sat himself down beside his friend. "Géricault," he said, with the gravest air possible, "you have tried this several times; it's an impulse you have, no one can stop you. In future, you can do as you like, but permit me to give you a little advice. I know you are religious; you are well aware that, when you die, you will have to appear before God and answer for your sins. What are you going to say, you wretch, when you are questioned . . . Just that you hadn't had dinner?"'

'Géricault burst out laughing at this sally, and solemnly promised that this suicide attempt would be his last.'

[C. Clément, *Géricault*, 1868]

Corot at Seventy

One day, when I was wandering around not far from the pond and the white house where Corot lived for part of the summer, I saw the old

1. Pierre-Narcisse Guérin (1774–1833), French Neoclassical painter, pupil of Jacques-Louis David.
2. Nicolas Toussaint Charlet (1792–1845), French draughtsman.

man at work, clad simple in a blue smock, and bareheaded. I approached him quietly and stood at a respectful distance. I was naïvely astonished to see that, instead of painting the little field surrounded by birch-trees which was actually before my eyes, he had replaced the grass with a pond. I couldn't help saying to him:

'But, M. Corot, can one just put a pond in place of a field, when one is doing a picture?'

'Young man,' the old man replied, without turning round, 'I've been here since morning, and now it's ten a.m. and the sun is getting hot. I felt the need for a little refreshment, and that's why I've put some water into my picture!'

[J.-F. Raffaelli, *Promenades au Musée du Louvre*]

Dante's Boat by Delacroix

Having finished his painting, Delacroix had to have it framed — otherwise it would have been ineligible for the Salon. To purchase a frame of such a size was a financial impossibility at that moment. To order one on credit meant plunging into debt to an extent that terrified him. In the house where he lived there was a carpenter who had a liking for him. This fine fellow made him a present of four planks of raw wood. Delacroix coated these with fish glue, and sprinkled them with a kind of yellow powder — he thought it made a good enough effect, like matt gold. Framed thus, the picture went off to the Salon.

One can readily imagine the feverish impatience which seizes upon a poor artist at moments like these. How can he fail to lose sleep when his whole future hangs on a casual 'yes' or 'no' — spoken by a group of men who can hardly focus their attention, so worn out and beaten down are they by having to look at hundreds of paintings at a single sitting.

Finally the Salon opened its doors. Delacroix rushed there, and ran round the galleries until he was out of breath, looking for his frame. Failing to find it, he sank down upon a bench, despair in his heart.

At that point one of the attendants, who happened to know him, came up to him smiling, and said: 'I think you must be very pleased?' — 'Pleased? With what? With being refused?' — 'Haven't you seen your painting in the Salon Carré, with a magnificent frame that Baron Gros got the administration to put on it? Your own frame, I'm afraid, arrived in pieces.' *Dante's Boat* had in fact been hung in a place of honour! Delacroix couldn't believe his eyes. And all this was due to the painter of the *Plague House at Jaffa* and the *Battle of Aboukir* – to the man whom Géricault regarded as the greatest master of the French School. Probably no artist has ever sustained a greater shock.

[C. Blanc, *Les artistes de mon temps*, 1876]

Delacroix on the Difference between Antiquity and the Renaissance

One morning, after we had been on guard duty together [1830], we went back to my place, and I showed him a marble head of one of the Twelve Caesars which I had brought back with me from Italy several weeks previously.

'It's very fine,' I said to him, 'but I doubt if it's ancient.' He looked at it carefully, then replied:

'No, my dear friend – it's Renaissance. In antiquity they thought in terms of mass; in the Renaissance, in terms of line. Look here! . . .'

And with this he seized a pen and drew a series of ovals on a piece of paper – large, middling and small. Then, with a quick line, very cleverly (as will be obvious), he joined the tops of these ovals – these egg-shapes, if you like – added a few extra strokes here and there – and a horse, rearing, pawing the ground, appeared as if by magic. In terms of movement and life it left nothing to be desired. He drew five or six horses like this, in different poses; then, since I was interested, and since the exercise amused him as much as it did me, he drew a human figure – seen from the front, from behind, seated, upright, etc. He covered a dozen large sheets of paper, using an identical procedure.

While this was going on, my housekeeper served breakfast. Having spent the night on the planks of a camp bed, appetite was not lacking. Meanwhile Delacroix went on talking about these egg shapes with all the verve of his most enthusiastic period.

'Tell me, how did you find all this out?' I asked.

'Oh, it's like this: M. Gros got it from the Greeks; Géricault got it from M. Gros; then, not content with that, I went back to the Greeks and the Etruscans.'

[J. Gigoux, *Causeries sur les artistes de mon temps*, 1885]

Delacroix's Uncertainty

As I have said previously, Delacroix felt uncertain about his own art. When his demon of enthusiasm carried him off, he deformed his figures, broke their limbs, elongated them or shrank them. Nothing mattered — save that the actual brushwork should be good and the principal figure firmly in place. For him, the background had more importance than the figures.

Everyone knows his *Entry of the Crusaders into Constantinople* at Versailles. In this huge canvas, all the personages are in the right place, and actually seem alive. It seems as if a window to the past has been thrown open. You have been whisked away by magic to the shores of the Bosphorus; you see the city with its narrow white streets. In the foreground, a brutal crusader maltreats a senator, perhaps the Palaeologus himself. The old man clings to the porphyry columns; a kneeling woman implores mercy; to the right there is a group of warriors on horseback. But does the crusader who strikes down that old man in his robes of purple and gold have his front or his back to you? The question is impossible to answer. The same is true of the Moroccan I mentioned earlier — so much so that Ricourt, a great admirer of Delacroix's work, one day made this witty reply to someone who asked: 'Is that his chest or his back?' The retort was: 'Neither the one nor the other — it's painting.'

Delacroix was keenly aware of these things, but to him they weren't a joke. One day when my friend Francais was giving the finishing touches to a lithograph after *Dante's Boat*, he asked Delacroix to take a look at what he had done.

The latter was horrified by the defects he found in his own picture, and said:

'What am I supposed to do about it now? There's a shoulder seen in profile and a torso seen frontally! There's a man dying of hunger in the midst of the sea, and I've made him all plump and rosy! It's got no sense at all! How can I have done that?'

'Can't you retouch it a bit?'

'Retouch it? There's too much to do. I was in full flight when I did that. How can I change it now? Do your best. Did Audran[1] make a

---

1. Jean Audran (1657–1756).

literal copy of Lebrun?[1] No, he did things over again. So do me over again, too!'

'But, Monsieur Delacroix . . .'

'No, no, do it over. You do wonderful things every day!'

[J. Gigoux, *Causeries sur les artistes de mon temps*, 1885] The reference to 'the Palaeologus' is fanciful. The Byzantine emperor when Constantinople fell to the crusaders in 1204 was Alexius V, a connection by marriage of the dynasty of the Angeli, which had ruled since 1185. The Palaeologi did not come to the throne until 1259, with the accession of Michael VIII.

Delacroix Compared to Victor Hugo

One day, when he had organized a dinner with a lot of old friends, [Delacroix] arrived a little later than the rest and made his excuses thus:

'I'm so sorry to have made you wait, but I had people with me I couldn't get rid of – chaps I used to know in the old days. They praised me to the skies, convinced that I would be delighted with what they had to say. You'll never guess what the real, crowning compliment was: "You are the Victor Hugo of painting! . . ." Think how pleased I must have been when I heard that!'

And with this, he burst out laughing.

[J. Gigoux, *Causeries sur les artistes de mon temps*, 1885] The frequent vulgarities of the Romantic poet and dramatist Victor Hugo would have made him antipathetic to Delacroix, who was in many respects conservative.

Odilon Redon (1840–1916) Sees Delacroix at a Ball

When I saw Delacroix in 1859, he was as handsome as a tiger: the same pride, the same subtlety, the same strength.

It was at a ball given at the Prefecture, where I had been told I would see him. My brother Ernest went with me – he knew Delacroix no more than I did, but pointed him out instinctively: a short, aristocratic man, standing in front of a group of women who were seated in the ballroom. Long black hair, sloping shoulders, rather stooping. We

1. Charles Lebrun (1619–90).

moved discreetly closer to him, and the master – yes, it was really he – turned upon us that slightly narrowed gaze, unique to himself, which glittered brighter than the lustres. His manner was of the greatest distinction. He wore the Grand Cross of the Legion of Honour on his tight, high collar, and several times glanced down at it. Auber came up, and introduced him to a young Bonaparte princess – 'who wishes,' he said, 'to see a great artist.' He shuddered, bowed, gave a slight smile and said: 'You see, he's not very big.'

He was of middle height, thin and nervous. We watched him all evening, there in the midst of the throng, and left when he did, hard on his heels. We followed him. He crossed nightime Paris alone, head bent, walking the pavements with the delicacy of a cat. A poster which said 'paintings' attracted his eye; he went up to it, read it, and departed wrapped in his dream, one might say with his *idée fixe*. He crossed the town till he reached the entrance to an apartment in the rue de la Rochefoucauld where he no longer lived. Perhaps it was habit which led him astray. He tranquilly retraced his steps, still deep in thought, until he reached the little rue Furstenberg, the silent street he lived in at that time.

[*Lettres d'Odilon Redon*, 1923]

Delacroix and Gros

Gros said of Delacroix's *Massacre at Chios*: 'It is the massacre of painting.'

Renoir and Ambroise Vollard Discussing Delacroix

R.: I don't mean to compare myself with Delacroix, but do you remember that phrase of his, 'Give me some mud, and I will paint you a woman's flesh'?

V.: But by that he meant it to be understood that the complementaries should be added, did he not? At least so the critics say.

R.: Please don't ascribe things to Delacroix that he never even thought of! If he spoke of complementaries, it was probably when he was making experiments for a ceiling which had to be looked at from a distance. In that case, perhaps, you might reasonably speak of colours mixing in the eye of the beholder. The only thing I remember from the Journal of Delacroix, is that he is forever talking about red-brown. At

the very mention of passing for an innovator, Delacroix would have
. . . why, when he was painting the ceiling of the Chamber of Deputies,
an employé of the library tried to compliment him by saying:

'Master, you are the Victor Hugo of painting.'

And Delacroix returned dryly:

'You don't know what you're talking about, my dear friend! I am a
classicist, pure and simple.'

V.: Did you know that his distrust of innovations in art also
extended to music? Guillemet asked Corot one day what he thought of
Delacroix. Corot replied:

'A great artist! He's the greatest of them all! But there is one thing we
have never been able to agree upon, and that is music! He doesn't like
Berlioz – revolutionary music he calls it – and I feel very sorry for him.'

[A. Vollard, *Renoir, an Intimate Record*, 1925]

J. F. Millet (1814–75) Visits Delacroix

Saturday, April 16 [1853]

In the morning someone brings Millet to see me. He talks about
Michelangelo and about the Bible – the latter is, he says, more or less
the only book he reads. This provides an explanation for the rather
ambitious look he gives to his peasants. In any case, he is a peasant
himself, and glories in it. He belongs to that galaxy or platoon of
bearded artists who were the makers of the revolution of 1848, or who
applauded it – believing, apparently, that there would be an equality of
talent as well as of wealth. Yet I think Millet the man rises a bit above
this, and that in the small number of paintings I have been able to see
(not very different from one another) there is deep though ostentatious
emotion struggling with a technique which is either dry, or else
muddled.

[E. Delacroix, *Journal*, 1893–5]

Honoré Daumier (1808–79), Gavarni (1804–66) and Corot

Daumier was the opposite of Gavarni. The latter dreamed of being a
painter all his life and never even managed to finish his famous
Batonnistes, whereas Daumier painted every day. When a picture 'got
stuck', he left it where it was. However little work he did on a canvas,

there was always something unexpected about it which reflected his qualities of mind and heart.

One must note, nevertheless, that his figures lacked variety. No doubt without being aware of it, he continually painted himself. It was always Daumier's nose – shaped like a comma! And it was always his little eyes, sharp and bright as diamonds!

Poor Daumier – he made no provision for the future. Towards the end, when he was almost blind, and could no longer pay the rent for the place he had in the country, Corot got wind of the situation – he bought the house and gave Daumier the deeds on his birthday.

The moment was deeply moving for them both. Daumier threw himself into Corot's arms, eyes full of tears, and said: 'Oh Corot – you are the only one from whom I could take a gift like this and not feel humiliated!'

[J. Gigoux, *Causeries sur les artistes de mon temps*, 1885]

The Young Gustave Courbet (1819–77)

I took [Champfleury's] arm, and we went to the rue Mazarine, then crossed the place de l'Ecole de Medicine. When we arrived at our destination, a tall young man with magnificent eyes moved forwards to confront us. He was very thin, pale, yellow, bony, gawky (yes, Courbet was like that in those days). He nodded his head without addressing a word to me. Then he returned to his easel, upon which was a painting which I discovered for myself by walking behind him. I never remember getting such an unexpected shock. The canvas now exposed to our gaze, treated, like its subject, with rustic informality, showed a masterly insouciance, a brilliance rooted in experience. Its dark tonality, its technique, did not recall any known style. 'With such a rare and marvellous gift,' said I, 'why aren't you already famous? No one has ever painted like this before!'

'Pardie,' he replied, in his rustic franche-comtois accent, 'me, I paint like the Good Lord!'

[F. Wey, *Memoirs*, in *Courbet, raconté par lui-même et ses amis*, 1948]

Courbet's Character

He wasn't frightened of a good meal – he had kept the old habits of the Franche Comté, which involved remaining six hours at table. With him, one was never bored.

'When you pour a drink, what do you think of?'

He talked about everything. His artistic theories were designed to make supporters of the classic tear their hair; he was no less mischievous on the subject of politics. When you got to religion, he felled his adversary with his own *Retour de la Conférence*.

He was the most carefree human being it was possible to find. When he got to Salins, the plan was to stay two or three days – three months later he was still there. His baggage consisted of his donkey and cart, a shirt and two pairs of socks. The rest of his clothes were what he had on his back. When the cold weather came, he bought a blanket from a Jewish peddler, at a fair. He made a hole in the middle so that he could put his head through it, and that was his winter overcoat.

Castagnary came to find him, to take him to Ornans. Without that, who knows how long he might not have remained there? . . . His father also turned up a couple of times, to see what he was up to. Courbet said of him: 'He doesn't make paintings, as I do, but he has invented a carriage with five wheels.'

[M. Claudet, *Souvenirs, Gustave Courbet*, 1878]

Courbet's Competitiveness

The first painting which attracted notice to Courbet's work, in artistic circles – and this was as late as 1848 or thereabouts, showed three men seated at a table. The man in the middle, with his back to the spectator, was placed on a whitewood chair.

Charles Blanc, who was then Director of the Beaux-Arts, asked Courbet what the price was.

'Monsieur, whatever you like,' Courbet replied. He would have sold it, very willingly, for three hundred francs. Then, in the course of the conversation, he asked Blanc how much he had paid for a painting by another artist. 'Three thousand francs,' was the reply.

'Then,' said Courbet immediately, 'I want three thousand francs for mine, or you shan't have it.'

The whole of the man's character is to be found in this story.
[J. Gigoux, *Causeries sur les artistes de mon temps*, 1885]

The Exhibition of 1849 in the Tuileries:
Reactions to Courbet

Eugène Delacroix, whom I ran into there, took me by the arm and with his usual enthusiasm drew me towards the *Après-Diner a Ornans*. 'Have you ever seen anything as strong as that, uninfluenced by anyone? Here's an innovator, a revolutionary; he's appeared all of a sudden, with no precedents – someone totally unknown.'

When Delacroix had left me, I saw Ingres approaching. 'Look,' he cried, 'how nature manages to ruin her own creations! She has endowed this young man with the rarest gifts. Born with qualities which others hardly ever acquire, he makes them felt with the first touch of his brush. The preliminary stroke has a masterly bravado at all the most difficult points. The rest, which is art, escapes him entirely. He has been given everything and gives nothing of himself. What values lost! What gifts sacrificed! It's wonderful and it's desolating. No composition, no drawing – exaggeration, almost to the point of parody. This young man is an *eye*; he sees, with a perception peculiar to himself, with a harmony whose tonality is a convention. He improvises a nature which is more vigorous in appearance than reality itself, and what he presents us with is, in artistic terms, a perfect nullity. This revolutionary sets a dangerous example.'

[F. Wey, *Memoirs*, in *Courbet, raconté par lui-même et ses amis*, 1948]

Renoir talking to Vollard about Courbet

V.:   Did you know Courbet?

R.:   Yes, quite well. He was the most astounding man you can possibly imagine. I shall never forget an incident at his exhibition of 1867. He had built a kind of balcony or *soupente*, on which he slept and from which he could watch his exhibition. When the first visitors arrived, he was just getting dressed. In order not to miss any of the public's enthusiasm, he came down in his flannel undershirt, not even taking time to put on the rest of his clothes, which he still carried in his hand. There he stood, in grave contemplation of his own pictures, and exclaimed: 'How beautiful! How magnificent! It's incredible! It's enough to take your breath away!'

And he kept repeating: 'Incredible! Incredible!'

At some exhibition where his pictures had been hung near the entrance, he is said to have remarked: 'How stupid of them! There's such a crowd, you can't even get in!'

[A. Vollard, *Renoir, an Intimate Record*, 1925]

Courbet on Delacroix

When one got him to talk seriously, he did not deny the talent of Delacroix, but he doubted his inspiration. 'M. Delacroix paints angels. I don't understand about angels. What about you? As for me, I've never seen them. How am I supposed to make a judgement about something which represents an imaginary being? The wings make it absurd and deformed. To paint human beings, and paint them well – that's the really difficult thing.'

[J. Castagnary, *Fragments d'un livre sur Courbet*, 1911] Courbet is said to have made the same comment about Manet's *Dead Christ Supported by Angels*.

Courbet and 'Killing the Ideal'

Another time, we were at Mazières.

In the middle of the meal, Courbet, who had remained silent, folded his napkin and took himself off. We didn't bother about him till we reached dessert.

It was one of those heavy October evenings, when the only way to be at ease is to throw off coat and waistcoat and go and stand in the doorway in one's shirtsleeves, to catch a breath of air.

We were in the garden. The painter, as always holding his pipe, was leaning against an oak. Eye wide, gaze fixed, he stood and looked.

The sun had just set. The landscape was covered with dark hues. It was like a huge charcoal drawing, a symphony in black – a retort to Gautier.

Courbet studied the way in which things changed as the light faded – fresh observations for new compositions.

We came up to him.

He began to talk. First he called our attention to the pure, vibrant lowing of the cattle near the river.

Then he turned to his favourite subject, discoursing at length on the question of colour.

He pointed out to us a small cloud which, darker than the rest, stood out against the surrounding mass. He asked us to study its edges, and minute by minute, in wonderful terms, he described the different tones through which these passed, before intermingling with the mist surrounding them.

He did the same with other objects.

Pointing them out at random – a tree, an old house – in a brief moment he made us see multiple transformations which our own poor brains would have been hard put to it to imagine.

A few drops of rain began to fall, so we went in, and he said to us; 'Now you understand why I wanted to kill off that horrible thing, the Ideal.'

[E. Gros-Kost, *Courbet: Souvenirs intimes*, 1880]

Courbet and his Father

A comical detail: the father loved to advise his son when the latter was at work.

He would come creeping up behind him and look over his shoulder. His eyes went from the canvas to the landscape, from the landscape back to the canvas. His brow darkened; his lower lip projected, and finally his indignation burst forth and he began to berate the painter.

'You think you know how to draw! Oh yes, you think you know! Just look at this. Is it supposed to be a rock? And this. Is it supposed to be a tree. You ought to be ashamed of yourself. Your grass is absurd. My cattle wouldn't want anything to do with it. As for your water, why bother to talk about it? It doesn't look like anything at all. Your gravel shows no commonsense. Your sky's like an umbrella.'

Exasperated by these remarks, Courbet would slowly put down his palette and knock out his pipe. Then, little by little, he would turn himself around. Beard pointed, face pale, neck stiff, he would stare at his critic.

The latter would continue: 'If I were you, do you know what I would do? I'd take a little of that green there and put it over here. Yes, right there, on that hazel-thicket. That would look splendid. Don't you

[295]

agree? Just take a little of that green, I say, and put it over there – there, on the hazels . . .'

'In God's name,' bellowed the Realist, 'just leave me alone!' And he gathered up all his accoutrements, shut his paint-box, picked up his camp-stool, and made off, scattering curses to the four winds.

This is why, when he wanted to paint, he would go off as far away as he could, into the very depths of the forest. If he had to remain in the studio, he locked himself in.

Knock! Knock! 'Gustave, are you there?' the father would cry, banging at the door.

'Damn it, no, Papa,' the son would reply. 'Gustave is not here.'

[E. Gros-Kost, *Courbet: Souvenirs intimes*, 1880]

Courbet and the Earth-closet

Dr Nelaton used to boast that the instrument required went in so easily the effect was almost caressing. Courbet did not think so when the good doctor treated his piles. Nevertheless, the painter was cured – more or less. Thenceforward, three-quarters of an hour were enough.

Three-quarters of an hour! A whole century wasted for a working man. A century without a drink! Without being able to talk! Without being able to look at the world! Without being able to paint!

If only, in order to mitigate this long wait, he could – leaving the door open – contemplate this splendid valley full of leaves and light which his analytic gaze never tired of. That would have halved the woe and given him patience – allowed him to forget . . . But alas, this was not possible.

At that moment, he was the guest of an old friend.

The earth-closet belonging to the little villa was cleverly concealed by a curtain of fir trees. Several times a day it received within itself the most restless, the most active, the most impatient painter of landscapes that any such bourgeois facility had ever contained.

Things couldn't go on that way. In the end Courbet had to act.

That day I was strolling in the garden with the son of the household. At a certain moment we heard a saw, working away in a thicket. Its unexpected note, coming from where it did, surprised us. We quickened our steps, made our way along the paths, pulled aside branches. And what did we see? The Realist busy cutting down the firs. Sleeves rolled up, leaning forward, eyes glittering, he was sawing away.

[296]

'*Maître*, what are you doing?' cried my companion, a young painter who had recently received a medal at the Salon.

'You can see for yourself – cutting down fir trees.'

'Did you ask my father?'

'No, I didn't.'

'Then why are you destroying his trees?'

'Why? Why? You ask me *why*? Oh well, you aren't my pupil. I want to be able to work while I'm in there – *work*, with the door open. I'll never be one of those miserable people who are content to spend a whole hour in a little hut like that, surrounded by spiders' webs, breathing fetid air, arms crossed, eyes idle – *unable to look at nature!*'

[E. Gros-Kost, *Courbet: Souvenirs intimes*, 1880]

Courbet's Near-Illiteracy

'I made a mess of everything at school,' Courbet used to say. The truth is, he worked very little.

He left knowing how to read and write – more or less, and he despised both these talents.

The sight of a book would throw him into a rage. An inkwell made him shy away. He limited himself to reading those articles in which he was mentioned – something which gives the measure of his vanity.

As for spelling, no use talking about it. For him it didn't exist. Ideas were to be expressed in images, not through words.

When he was released from prison,[1] the public started to take a new interest in his work. There were requests for paintings from everywhere. The picture dealers left Paris to pursue him in his retreat.

'My work is worth four times what it used to be,' he cried – and it was true.

One day he got a letter from a M. Hollander, of Brussels, wanting some pictures. He refused. The problem was he thought he wouldn't be paid.

A reply had to be made to the request – that was another problem.

Usually he had a friend somewhere around, to provide him with a soupçon of grammar: a loan he was incapable of repaying. As ill luck would have it, no friend was available. He had to struggle on his own with the piece of paper.

1. Courbet was imprisoned and condemned to pay an indemnity for his participation in the Commune of 1871, and for his role in the demolition of the Vendôme Column.

Some months went by. 'Just think of Hollander's face!' he crowed one day, between two puffs of his pipe. But just then Castagnary had some bad news for him.

Hollander had friends in Germany, who put out an art magazine called *Le Salon*. Underhandedly, he gave them the epistle. After a savagely critical article, they printed a facsimile of the manuscript.

Countless errors – and what errors! *Toile* [canvas] was spelt with two *l*s. One of the painter's oldest friends was thunderstruck: 'How can you write a letter like that? Don't you know how much harm it does? Why must you make yourself ridiculous?'

'I am never ridiculous. In any case all great men spell badly. Take Napoleon – to conceal his errors, he used to write illegibly.'

'Then, write illegibly yourself. Don't let it be seen that you, a painter, spell the word *toile* with two *l*s.'

'I'll give it three next time! The dictionary is a stupid old thing and I want nothing to do with it. In any case, the only real errors are at the beginning and end of words – the first letter and the last are the only indispensable ones. Between the two one can put anything one likes . . .' And he filled another pipe.

Five minutes later, he added: 'We're equal, anyway, in this business. Hollander is more put out than I am!'

[E. Gros-Kost, *Courbet: Souvenirs intimes*, 1880]

A Genuine Courbet

A painter, a follower of Courbet, gave painting lessons for a living at the house of a great personage.

He valiantly defended his master against the attacks of the head of the household, a writer with great influence over the government in artistic matters. By reputation, he was a competent and infallible critic.

Poor Courbet was mocked and scorned as you may suppose.

One Sunday he had been lined up and shot, treated as a vulgar dauber, condemned for empty boasting. Next day the young professor [the painter] arrived with an unsigned picture.

A friend, he said, had discovered it in an auction. It had cost him several hundred francs, but the quality seemed very high.

The art critic looked at the portrait and said: 'Not merely excellent – admirable! It is the work of a master. This portrait was painted centuries ago. It belongs to the Spanish School. Leave it with me. I'll ask X to come (here he named an illustrious name), and we will find an attribution for this masterpiece.'

He kept the painting for a week. There were consultations on the subject. Then the young professor returned and asked for the painting back.

'Do you know who did it?' he enquired.

'X and I are inclined to think it's by Velasquez.'

'You are quite wrong, sir. The artist's name is not Velasquez – it is Gustave Courbet!'

[J. Valles, *L'Evènement*, 11 March 1866]

XVII

GIRTIN, TURNER AND
CONSTABLE

❧

C. R. Leslie's biography of Constable enjoys a classic status in the literature of art which has been denied to Walter Thornbury's A Life of J. M. W. Turner. *Yet it is the latter book which is by far the richer in anecdotal material. As extracts printed here show, neither Constable nor Turner was what is called an 'easy' personality. David Roberts, famous for his views of Egypt and the Near East, found Constable antipathetic: 'ever talking of himself and his works, and unceasing in his abuse of others'. Delacroix seems to have recoiled from Turner, on the one occasion he met him.*

It is nevertheless clear from the legacy of stories about Turner that he possessed an endlessly fascinating, alluring personality, of a kind denied to Constable. There is an almost surrealist quality about the encounter which took place between the ageing Turner and the young Pre-Raphaelite Ford Madox Brown, when they met by chance at an inn. Brown was tempted to follow Turner, and watch him at work. Like others who caught a glimpse of Turner painting or drawing, Brown found that there was something bizarre, not only about the man's personality, but about his artistic procedures.

Here and there, in the stories about Turner, there are hints of a resemblance to Rembrandt. Both had a reputation for avarice. Both used to bid up their own work at auction. Both tended to retire into the shadows as they grew older, and to avoid the company of intellectuals. Turner went so far as to construct a whole double life, details of which still remain mysterious.

Yet Turner, thanks to his devotion to the Royal Academy, remained 'clubbable', very much at the centre of the artistic life of London. Constable, on the other hand, had to struggle for acceptance by his peers, and this was one of the things that embittered him. The two artists seem to exchange places before our eyes — in terms of personality, neither is quite what we think or wish him to be.

The Apprenticeship of Thomas Girtin (1775–1802) to Edward Dayes (1763–1804)

Girtin was in early life apprenticed to Dayes, an architectural draughtsman, who had no sympathy for his genius, and treated him as a mere means of making money. Dayes was a conceited, jealous man, who eventually got embarrassed and committed suicide, it was supposed, from envy at the progress of his contemporaries – Turner and his old pupil. His works ('Tour in Yorkshire' and 'Art-Biographies') were published after his death for the benefit of his widow.

Girtin, naturally bold and reckless, began soon to find that he was more than paying back by work the premium paid for his apprenticeship. He refused to wash in any more skies for Dayes, and demanded in justice the cancelling of his indentures. Dayes refusing, and finding Girtin obdurate, had him up before the City Chamberlain and committed to Bridewell [prison] as a contumacious apprentice.

Here Girtin amused himself by covering the walls of his cell with chalk-landscapes. The turnkey was at once delighted and astonished with these works of the imprisoned genius. He told all his friends about them, and brought many of them to see the frescoed cell. Amongst others, some lord or other; and the Earl of Essex happened to hear of the prison landscapes. He came and was delighted. He went at once to Dayes, bought up the indentures, and burning them before Girtin's eyes, obtained his release, and took him down to the almost regal luxury of Cashiobury, where Girtin, free and happy, produced some of his greatest works; as Fra Lippo Lippi escaped from slavery by means of the portrait he took of the Moor his master, so Girtin, the contumacious apprentice, escaped from Bridewell by decorating the white walls of his cell with chalk landscapes.

[W. Thornbury, *The Life of J. M. W. Turner, R.A.*, 1862]

Turner (1775–1851) in Rome

Mr. Rippingille, when he was at Rome, inquired about Turner; he says: 'No other country appears to have felt his kind of merit as it was felt at home, and in this we see the clue to Turner's great success and popularity. I do not find that in foreign countries Turner was at all esteemed. In a subsequent portion of his life Turner was in Rome, and there exhibited pictures which (no disgrace, I must say) won him no credit. At the time he was in the 'Eternal City', an English tradesman was living there, who made a great to do, and sold English mustard; and when his namesake came and exposed his wares, the Romans, who are a peculiar class of jokers, proclaimed that one sold mustard, and the other painted it. Some intelligent Romans, with whom I talked, wondered that the English could be so devoid of taste as to admire and tolerate such extravagant productions.

[W. Thornbury, *Life of J. M. W. Turner*, 1862]

Turner's Secretiveness

Turner was tenacious in not disclosing any of his secrets as to how he obtained breadth and depth in his water-colour painting. He generally painted with his door locked, if he was at a stranger's house; and if any one approached him, or idlers tried to overlook him, he covered his drawing. He had no special secrets to hide; for Turner's colours were of little use to men who had not Turner's brain. But he had been accustomed, as a boy, to paint up in his bed-room, and he could not change his solitary habits. He did not like imitators, and he did not wish absurd stories spread of his mechanical artifices. Moreover, this habit of secrecy gratified his love of mystery, and his natural fondness of concealment. Yet once at Edinburgh he communicated all he knew to a struggling artist, at a time when the secret of his modes of sponging and his bistre washings was worth 100*l.* to any one.

[W. Thornbury, *Life of J. M. W. Turner*, 1862]

Turner's Mysterious Carpet-bag

Cowley Hall is about fifteen miles from London. This distance he generally walked, coming in heated and tired, carrying a small carpet-bag, which was kept like a sealed book, never allowing the key to go out of his possession. The ladies tried various means to induce him to give up its possession, ostensibly to arrange his articles of clothing which they presumed it contained, though it must be confessed that female curiosity was the predominating cause; but he clung as tenaciously to his key as a miser to his gold. On one occasion, on his returning from fishing, he came in wet and tired – a sudden shower of rain having fallen, his umbrella having been metamorphosed into a fishing-rod – the servant was sent to the bedroom for his slippers; only one was to be found. Here was an opportunity not to be missed; the ladies ordered the servant to bring down the carpet-bag, hoping, doubtless, to obtain a glimpse of its contents; but a sly look from our friend, with a peculiar shrug of his shoulders, and the two monosyllables 'No, no,' effectually put to flight their hopes; as a *dernier ressort*, one then offered to take his key and bring down the slipper. To that he replied, 'I never give it up'; and they never learnt its contents. 'The man with the carpet-bag' was not then known, or doubtless he would have obtained that *sobriquet*. The name, however, by which he was known at our house was certainly not very euphonious; how it was obtained I can scarcely surmise, unless it was his manner and figure, which was short and thick; but it was a common expression on seeing him approach the entrance, to cry 'Here comes Old Pogey'.

[Story told by 'a Mr. W. Rose of Jersey', quoted in W. Thornbury, *Life of J. M. W. Turner*, 1862]

Turner at Petworth

Turner was intensely obstinate. I think it was during a visit to Petworth that a discussion ensued between Lord Egremont and Turner as to whether carrots could float in water. I suppose Turner had introduced some in one of the Petworth pictures.

'Carrots don't swim.'

'They do.'

'They don't.'

'They do.'

Lord Egremont rings the bell, and calls for a bucket of water and some carrots. The water is brought, the carrots are thrown in. The obstinate painter is right; they *do* swim after all.

[W. Thornbury, *Life of J. M. W. Turner*, 1862]

Turner at an Exhibition of his own Watercolours

Many years ago, two of Turner's friends were standing at the door of an exhibition where some of his water-colours were on show, and were debating about the entrance-fee. Suddenly a little man dashed up to the astonished custos, snatched two tickets from the man, gave them to the applicants, and was off instanter. It was Turner, who had that morning met them in the street, and asked them if they would like to see the drawings.

[W. Thornbury, *Life of J. M. W. Turner*, 1862]

Turner's Agent in the Auction Room

Turner generally bought in his own works when they were put up for auction. If time pressed, and he was unable to attend in person, he would sometimes, but rarely, entrust his commission to the auctioneer; his ordinary practice was to send some agent, with written instructions, to bid in his behalf, and he was not always very fastidious in his selection. At the sale of the pictures of Mr. Green, the well-known amateur of Blackheath, two pictures by Turner were among the most attractive lots, though neither important in size nor of his best time. In those days their market value might have been about eighty guineas each. They would, however, have been knocked down for considerably less, but for the impetus given to the biddings by one of Mr. Turner's agents, whose personal appearance did not warrant the belief that he was in search of pictures of a very high order. He was, in fact, a clean, ruddy-cheeked butcher's boy, in the usual costume of his vocation, and had made several advances, in five-guinea strides, before anything belonging to him, excepting his voice, had attracted Mr. Christie's notice. No sooner, however, did the veteran auctioneer see what kind of customer he had to deal with, than he beckoned him forward, with a view, no doubt, of reproving him for his impertinence. The boy, however, nothing daunted, put a small piece of greasy paper into his hand – a credential, in fact, from the painter himself. The auctioneer smiled, and the biddings proceeded. Both pictures brought high prices, and the object of the painter was as successfully achieved as if Count D'Orsay had been his representative.

[W. Thornbury, *Life of J. M. W. Turner*, 1862]

Turner's Regard for his own Work

Of the jealous guard he kept over his fame, there is a good story told.

A curious instance of the value he attached to the merest trifle from his own hand, and the dislike he had to any one trading by chance with it, was related by an eminent printseller, into whose shop he once walked, to purchase, if possible, an engraving made many years before from one of his pictures. His description of the subject he aided by a few rude lines, scrawled with a pen on a loose piece of paper, which blew behind the counter in turning over the portfolios to look for the print. The painter ultimately got his print, and, missing the scrap of paper, eagerly demanded it of the unconscious printseller, whose confusion redoubled Turner's anxiety, which was only appeased when the scrap of paper was recovered from a dark corner, and carefully wrapped with the engraving.

[W. Thornbury, *Life of J. M. W. Turner*, 1862]

Turner Delivers a Painting to a Patron

A friend of Sir Thomas Lawrence's, who resided at Clapham-common, commissioned the amiable President to order of Turner a picture at a most liberal price. When the picture was finished, Lawrence and Turner were invited to dinner, to see it hung; but the former was summoned to Windsor on the morning of the appointed day. Turner, however, arrived with the picture, which was greatly admired; and when the ladies retired after dinner, the gentleman, seeing Turner fidgety, said, 'We will now to business. Excuse me a moment, while I write you out a cheque.' The cheque was written and handed to Turner, who, instead of putting it into his pocket, kept turning it over, first eyeing the gentleman, then the cheque. Seeing something was wrong, the gentleman said, 'I have made it guineas, I believe? It was to be guineas, was it not?' 'Yes, the guineas are right enough,' said Turner, in his gruff manner; 'but I paid six shillings for the coach: that's not down!' The six shillings were paid.

[W. Thornbury, *Life of J. M. W. Turner*, 1862]

Turner and his 'Ulysses Deriding Polyphemus'

His friend, the Rev. Mr. Judkins, who is neither a busybody nor a dilettante, but a friend of Constable's, and a very clever landscape artist, was one day dining with Turner at a large party. A lady sitting next to the clerical artist, with the curiosity traditionally supposed to be peculiar to her sex, was full of the glories of the 'Polyphemus,' the wonder of the last Exhibition. It was one perpetual whisper.

'Wine? No, thank you; but oh, Mr. Judkins, do you – What do you think of Mr. Turner's great picture? And – a very little, if you please. Don't you now think it is a sweet picture?' &c., &c.

Turner, glum and shy, opposite, is watching all this. He sees where the lady's eyes fall after she addresses her whispers to Mr. Judkins. His little beads of eyes roll and twinkle with fun and slyness. Across the table he growls –

'I know what you two are talking about, Judkins – about my picture.'

Mr. Judkins suavely waves his glass and acknowledges that it was. The lady smiled on the great man.

'And I bet you don't know where I took the subject from; come now – bet you don't.'

Judkins blandly replied –

'Oh! from the old poet, of course, Turner; from the "Odyssey", of course.'

'No,' grunted Turner, bursting into a chuckle; ' "Odyssey!" not a bit of it. I took it from Tom Dibdin. Don't you know the lines –

He ate his mutton, drank his wine,
And then he poked his eye out.'

The lines may be in Dibdin – I never could find them; but such is the mystifying fun Turner was so fond of.

[W. Thornbury, *Life of J. M. W. Turner*, 1862]

John Hammersley Visits Turner's Studio

In a few weeks after Ritchie made the proposal, I received a short note from Turner, to the following effect –

Dear Sir, – Mr. L. Ritchie intimates to me that you desire to see my pictures. The weather is fine, and if you will call here either on Thursday or Friday this week, not earlier than eleven o'clock, I shall be glad to see you.

Your obedient servant,
J.M.W. TURNER

Thursday was not very fine, but I found it quite impossible to wait until Friday. I wrote a note to Turner, in due acknowledgment of his communication, and precisely at eleven o'clock I found myself at his door. I left the door, walked across the street, looked at the house, gained breath, for I had nearly run all the way from Somerset House, and, foolish as it *will* appear, I could have worshipped the dirty windows that let in light enough to one whose soul saw at all times the whole brilliancy of nature. After a short time I became steady enough and calm enough to walk to the door again. I rang, and tardily enough the well-known old housekeeper opened the door to me, and I was placed in what I suppose was Turner's dining-room. I waited there for a short time, all eyes, all ears, when I heard a shambling, slippered footstep down a flight of stairs – slow, measured, yet as of one who was regardless of style or promptitude – what the world calls shambling, in fact. When the door opened, I, nobody, stood face to face with, to my thinking, the greatest man living. I shall attempt no description; you know how he looked. I saw at once his height, his breadth, his loose dress, his ragged hair, his indifferent quiet – all, indeed, that went to make his *physique* and some of his mind; but, above all, I saw, felt (and still feel) his penetrating grey eye!

Remaining only a moment longer in the cold and cheerless room, at his request I followed him into his gallery, which you, doubtless, remember well. The room was even less tidy than the one we had left – indeed, was an art chaos, all confusion, mouldiness, and wretched litter – most of the pictures, indeed all those resting against the wall, being covered with uncleanly sheets or cloths of a like size and character. Turner removed these protections to his pictures, and disclosed to my wondering and reverent observation many of those works which are now known so generally; among them, and the most prominent, being the 'Opening of the Walhalla'. I make no remark about any of the pictures which I found in the gallery; far abler hands than mine have given to the world a whole body of the noblest criticism, based upon the great painter's labours; it merely rests with me to detail any traits of character presented to my observation. Turner and I walked many times from end to end of the apartment, he occasionally giving brief descriptions of the pictures, and asking after my proceedings at the institution with which I was connected. Generally, I may say, that he was taciturn, though still sufficiently chatty to remove all idea of inattention or discourtesy. After we had been so occupied for, say five minutes, he turned somewhat quickly towards me and said, 'Mr. Hammersley, this gallery is cold; pray keep your hat on.' I moved in acknowledgment of his solicitude, but did not obey him; I kept it off quite involuntarily, I am sure, and, I trust, as a perfectly natural action. In a few minutes he turned to me again, reiterating his request, when, quite honestly and naturally also, I told him that I 'could not think of being covered in his presence'. He looked at me very steadily for a few seconds, and then said, 'Mr. Hammersley, I shall feel much more comfortable myself if you will comply with my wishes in this respect'. I put on my hat at once, seeing that he believed in my sincerity, and feeling how undoubtedly he was speaking his real wishes. This is but a small matter; but it seems pregnant to me of a kindly and most considerate mind, and, as so much evidence that way, is worth preservation.

[Quoted in W. Thornbury, *Life of J. M. W. Turner*, 1862]

Turner's Attitude and Methods

He never rhapsodized about scenery, but set hard at work at some distance from Mr. Munro, silent, concentrated (and generally a good deal higher), so as to obtain more distance and more of a bird's-eye view. He took quick sketches, and then finished them afterwards quietly (by help of his tremendous memory) at the inn. He had a horror of what he said Wilson called 'being too mappy'. If you bore with his way, it was easy to get on very pleasantly with him; indeed, there was a sort of half resolution come to that Turner and Mr. Munro should visit the East together.

Turner used no maul-stick, his touch was so sure and decisive; his materials were of the rudest: brushes worn away to single hairs, and now trebly as valuable as when new. Turner's way of showing a kindness was peculiar; he seemed to put on a certain roughness, to conceal his real feelings. One day (I believe near Sallenche) he found Mr. Munro (who, by-the-bye, is an artist himself of the most refined taste) in some difficulty with a sketch. He did not appear to notice it, but growlingly took up a new drawing-pad that was lying near (the paper he himself used was of a rough kind, and generally wrinkled in the most uncomfortable way by repeated washes), and off he went to 'see what he could do with it'. He returned in about two hours with the paper squared into four sketches, each in a different stage of completion. This was evidently his rough, kind way of showing an amateur friend the way of pushing forward a sketch. These sketches I have seen, and to me they seem invaluable. There are first rude pencilling loops for trees, and lines marking the horizon and chief masses. Then come brown dabs of marking-out colour, then washes for sky and water, till in the last sketch sapphire hills and touches of heaven seem breaking through the chaos, and every inch of colour is radiant with knowledge and beauty.

'I can't make anything of your paper,' he said, and threw the four sketches down to his friend.

Some days after Turner either thought he had made too light of his own present, or remembered some special memorandum in it which he valued, or else was led astray by his love of accumulating; for he growlingly asked for the finished sketch back. Mr. Munro gave it, and rebought it in some way or other some years after. Perhaps, after all, he had never meant to give it, and delicacy had only kept him for a time from saying so.

[W. Thornbury, *Life of J. M. W. Turner*, 1862]

John Ruskin (1819–1900) Describes Turner Painting a Watercolour

Speaking of Turner's rapidity, Mr. Ruskin tells the following interesting story:

'There is a drawing in Mr. Fawkes's collection of a man-of-war taking in stores; it is of the usual size of those of the England series, about sixteen inches by eleven. It does not appear one of the most highly-finished but is still farther removed from slightness. The hull of a first-rate occupies nearly one-half of the picture on the right, her bows towards the spectator, seen in sharp perspective from stem to stern, with all her portholes, guns, anchors, and lower rigging elaborately detailed. There are two ships of the line in the middle distance drawn with equal precision, a noble breezy sea dancing against their broad bows, full of delicate drawing in its waves; a store-ship beneath the hull of the larger vessel, and several other boats, and a complicated cloudy sky. It might appear no small exertion of mind to draw the detail of all this shipping, down to the smallest ropes, from memory, in the drawing-room of a mansion in the middle of Yorkshire, even if considerable time had been given for the effort. But Mr. Fawkes sat beside the painter from the first stroke to the last. Turner took a piece of blank paper one morning after breakfast, outlined his ships, finished the drawing in three hours, and went out to shoot.'

[Quoted in W. Thornbury, *Life of J. M. W. Turner*, 1862]

Ford Madox Brown (1821–93) Encounters Turner

Into the bar of an inn, where Madox Brown, after the day's work, sat chatting with the host, a burly elderly man entered. He had all the air of an *habitué*, but spoke hardly at all, and then only upon indifferent subjects. After a time he took his candle and retired for the night.

On Madox Brown's inquiring the old gentleman's name, he was informed that it was also Brown, and that he was an artist, or something of the sort. Turning the matter over in his mind, and ruminating over the artists of his acquaintance, Madox Brown remembered a story that was current at that day, that Turner had taken a house at Chelsea in order to be able to survey the fireworks at Cremorne Gardens without paying the shilling for entrance fee, and that amongst the watermen at the inns where he usually drank a glass of toddy Turner adopted the pseudonym of 'Old Brown'.

Under these circumstances, the features of the Brown who had just passed from the room began to form themselves into those of the great R.A. as they remained in Madox Brown's mind from the portraits he had seen. On inquiring more closely into the habits of his namesake, Madox Brown learnt that it was the other Brown's habit to be called at the very break of day, and then to make a sortie from the inn with a large roll of cartridge-paper under his arm, after which he disappeared from the ken of the innkeeper. With almost pardonable curiosity Madox Brown determined to ascertain from personal observation as much as he could of the movements of the other Brown.

He arose betimes, not until the other had already gone out of the inn, but, tracing him circumspectly, he saw him seated on the dewy ground in front of an open gateway, through which a large herd of cows was being driven.

On the large sheet of paper, placed flat before him on the ground, Turner was making what Madox Brown styled 'extraordinary, hiero-glyphic, shorthand notes' of the cows as they passed.

'What's more,' he would say, 'he was holding the pencil in his fists, downwards, as if it was a dagger, instead of in his fingers, as anyone else would have done.'

[F. M. Hueffer, *Ford Madox Brown: A Record of his Life and Work*, 1905] Hueffer misdates the incident, placing it in a chapter devoted to the years 1852–6. Turner, however, died in 1851.

Turner and Fuseli

Turner had sent a canvas to Somerset House, with a subject so undefined that it caused considerable speculation among the Royal Academicians, when they assembled on the morning of the first varnishing day, as to what he intended to represent. It was a 'Moonlight' with one, and with another a 'Storm'; at last, Howard suggested it might be an 'Allegory'. 'Yes,' said Fuseli, 'the allegorie of blazes at a *déjeuner à la fourchette*, wid molten lead!' Turner, who had entered in time to hear the keeper's remark, said, 'No, that's Limbo; where they are going to send your "Sin and Death"' (a celebrated picture). Fuseli threw himself into an attitude of mock terror, saying, 'Gentlemen, we are ondone; we all know *Tourner* to be an imp of de old one transformed into an angel of light by his double shadow.' 'Yes,' put in Beechey; 'but Turner's shadows are only double when he sees double.' 'Ah!' added Fuseli, with an affected sigh, 'gentlemen, it is what Turner sees dat concerns us, now he is in his fader's confidence, and he tells him all about de beesiness in his great fire-office below.' The picture was altered, but Turner never again ventured on a joke with Fuseli.

[W. Thornbury, *Life of J. M. W. Turner*, 1862]

Turner and Constable (1776–1837)

In 1822, when Constable exhibited his 'Opening of Waterloo Bridge', it was placed in the School of Painting, one of the small rooms at Somerset House. A sea piece by Turner was next to it – a grey picture, beautiful and true, but with no positive colour in any part of it. Constable's picture seemed as if painted with liquid gold and silver, and Turner came several times into the room while he was heightening with vermilion and lake the decorations and flags of the city barges. Turner stood behind him, looking from the 'Waterloo' to his own picture; and putting a round daub of red lead, somewhat bigger than a shilling, on his grey sea, went away without a word. The intensity of the red lead, made more vivid by the coolness of his picture, caused even the vermilion and lake of Constable to look weak. I came into the room just as Turner left it. 'He has been here,' said Constable, 'and fired off a gun.' On the opposite wall was a picture, by Jones,[1] of 'Shadrach, Meshach, and Abednego in the Furnace'. 'A coal,' said Cooper,[2] 'has bounced across the room from Jones's picture, and set fire to Turner's sea.' The great man did not come again into the room for a day and a half; and then, in the last moments that were allowed for painting, he glazed the scarlet seal he had put on his picture, and shaped it into a buoy.

In finishing the 'Waterloo Bridge', Constable used the palette knife more than the pencil. He found it the only instrument by which he could express, as he wished, the sparkle of the water.

This is a matchless story. The fact was, Turner did not much like Constable, and was not going to let himself be checkmated. What knowledge, too, it showed to suddenly alter the whole plan of his picture, and yet not to spoil it. Constable was secretly very severe on Turner's pictures, and in his violent sarcastic way would sometimes pretend to spit in disgust when they were mentioned. Leslie, his worshipper, acquired somewhat of the same prejudice; but his strong good sense soon mastered it. Once, Constable was pacing impatiently before a picture, the effect of which somehow or other did not please him. It was true to rules, but still there was something wanting (perhaps a mere red cap, a blue apron, or a tree stem); yet what it was he could not for the life of him tell. There was a line too much or too little in the composition, that was certain. A speck of colour redundant or deficient, that was evident. At that moment Turner entered.

'I say, Turner,' cried Constable, 'there is something wrong in this picture, and I cannot for the life of me tell what it is. You give it a look.'

Turner looked at the picture steadily for a few moments, then seized a brush, and struck in a ripple of water in the foreground.

That was the secret – the picture was now perfect, the spell was completed. The fresh, untired eye of the great magician had seen the want at a glance.

[W. Thornbury, *Life of J. M. W. Turner*, 1862]

Turner and Constable at Odds

Turner, though kind to younger men, could frown, and show his contempt fearlessly for those whom he considered unworthy his

1. George Jones (1786–1869).
2. Abraham Cooper (1787–1868), animal painter.

friendship. He was ever modest of his own abilities, and I never remember him uttering a word of disparagement of others. Of a contrary disposition was Constable, ever talking of himself and his works, and unceasing in his abuse of others. We had met one night at the General's, shortly after the hanging of the Royal Academy. Constable was, as usual, lavish of the pains he had taken and the sacrifices he had made in arranging the Exhibition. But, most unfortunately, he had, after placing an important work of Turner's, removed it, and replaced it by one of his own. Turner was down upon him like a sledge-hammer; it was of no use his endeavour to persuade Turner that the change was for his advantage, and not his own. Turner kept at it all the evening, to the great amusement of the party, and I must add, he (Constable) richly deserved it, by bringing it on himself.

[Story told by David Roberts (1796–1864) to Walter Thornbury, quoted in *Life of J. M. W. Turner*, 1862]

Turner and Edward Bird (1772–1819)

When Bird, the son of a Wolverhampton clothier, about 1811, first sent a picture to the Royal Academy – it might have been 'Good News', or 'Choristers Rehearsing', or some other of those early anticipations of Wilkie[1] and Webster[2] – Turner was one of the 'Hanging Committee', as it was opprobriously called. Every one said the picture of the new man had great merit, but there was no place fit for it left unoccupied. Here was a desirable guest, but the inn was full. The R. A.'s looked stolidly content, as people inside an omnibus on a wet day do when the conductor looks in at the window and begs to know 'if any jintleman would like to go outside and make room for a lady.' The R. A.'s joke and talk. The days of chivalry are past. Turner growls, and is disturbed; he up and says, 'that come what may, the young man's picture must have a place.' All the others cry 'impossible', and go on talking about other things.

But can you stop the lion in mid-leap? Can you drive off a shark by shouting when his teeth have closed on your flesh. This is not a doll man of wax and sawdust. This is not one of those committee creatures whom lords and ministers pull with a red-tape string, so that it says 'yes' and 'no', and rolls its eyes at the required moment. This is a

1. Sir David Wilkie (1785–1841), Scottish genre painter.
2. Thomas Webster (1800–66), English genre painter.

Nemean man, a real, stern, honest man, stanch as an English bull-dog, and almost as pertinacious and indomitable.

All this time he is examining the picture, right, left, surface, clear-obscure, touch, colour, character, carefully; he sees it is good, he cries out again and hushes the buzz of voices –

'We must find a good place for this young man's picture.'

'Impossible – impossible,' says the gold spectacles again, and more oracularly this time than before.

Turner said no more, but quietly removed one of his own pictures and hung up Bird's.

[W. Thornbury, *Life of J. M. W. Turner*, 1862]

Turner and Benjamin Robert Haydon

Turner was devoted to the academy, with all its faults. It had been quick to see his genius, and to confer on him honours. He had been a student at the Academy, and was now an Academician. He felt for it the affection a child does for its mother, for his great heart was very susceptible of gratitude. There is a singular story that bears on this subject. The day poor wrong-headed Haydon ended his untoward life, Mr. Maclise called upon Turner to tell him of the horrible catastrophe. The narrator's imagination was roused to the uttermost by the suddenness and ghastliness of the event. To his astonishment Turner scarcely stopped painting, and merely growled out between his teeth,

'He stabbed his mother, he stabbed his mother.'

'Good Heavens!' said Mr. Maclise, so excited that he was prepared for any new terror. 'You don't mean to say, Turner, that Haydon ever committed a crime so horrible?'

Still Turner made no other reply, but slowly chanted in a deep, slow voice,

'He stabbed his mother, he stabbed his mother.'

Nothing but this could his startled friend wring from him, and as he left the house, 'He stabbed his mother, he stabbed his mother,' still pursued Maclise down the passage. It was not till he reached home, and before spreading the story sat down quietly to think over what Turner could mean by such a horrid charge, that he came to the true conclusion that Turner had merely figuratively alluded to the ingratitude of Haydon's attacks on the Academy that had educated him.

[W. Thornbury, *Life of J. M. W. Turner*, 1862]

Delacroix Recalls his Meeting with Turner

24 March 1855

Young Armstrong[1] came to see me and told me about Turner, who left a hundred thousand pounds sterling to found a home for sick and indigent artists. He lived like a miser, with an old servant. I remember he came to see me when I was living on the Quai Voltaire – he made rather a poor impression. He looked like an English farmer, with a black coat of coarse stuff, thick-soled shoes, and a cold, hard expression.

[E. Delacroix, *Journal*, 1893–5]

Dante Gabriel Rossetti (1828–82) on Turner

I remember that one afternoon as I sat beside him while he worked, the late Mr. Virtue Tebbs came in fresh from an exhibition of the old masters at Burlington House, and full of enthusiasm for a picture by Turner which he insisted that Rossetti must speedily go and see.

'What is it called?' asked Rossetti.

'"Girls Surprised while Bathing,"' replied Tebbs.

'Umph!' returned Rossetti. 'Yes, I should think devilish surprised to see what Turner had made of them.'

[J. Comyns Carr, *Some Eminent Victorians*, 1908]

Some Opinions of John Constable

On hearing somebody say of the celebrated collection of Raphael's drawings that belonged to Sir Thomas Lawrence, 'They inspire,' he replied, 'They do more, they inform.'

The amiable but eccentric Blake, looking through one of Constable's sketch books, said of a beautiful drawing of an avenue of fir trees on Hampstead Heath, 'Why, this is not drawing, but *inspiration*;' and he replied, 'I never knew it before; I meant it for drawing.'

'My pictures will never be popular,' he said, 'for they have no *handling*. But I do not see *handling* in nature.'

---

1. Thomas Armstrong (1835–1911), an English painter who came to Paris to study in 1853. He was only twenty when he visited Delacroix.

He was struck with a remark of Dr. Gooch, that he found 'every individual case of disease a new study.' Constable applied this to painting, and said, 'In like manner every truly original picture is a separate study, and governed by laws of its own; so that what is right in one, would be often entirely wrong if transferred to another.'

A friend of Constable expressing to him his dissatisfaction at his own progress in art, received (as he told me) the greatest encouragement to proceed he ever met with, in the following answer: 'If you had found painting as easy as you once thought it, you would have given it up long ago.'

A picture of a murder sent to the Academy for exhibition while he was on the Council, was refused admittance on account of a disgusting display of blood and brains in it; but he objected still more to the wretchedness of the work, and said, 'I see no *brains* in the picture.'

[C. R. Leslie, *Memoirs of the Life of John Constable, Esq., R.A.*, 1845]

Constable on Chiaroscuro

With Constable chiaroscuro was the one thing to be obtained at whatever cost. 'I was always determined,' he said, 'that my pictures should have chiaroscuro, if they had nothing else.' In the pursuit of this indispensable quality, and of that brightness in nature which baffles all the ordinary processes of painting, and which it is hardly possible to unite with smoothness of surface, he was led by degrees into a peculiar mode of execution, which too much offended those who were unable to see the look of nature it gave at the proper distance. In the 'Waterloo Bridge' he had indulged in the vagaries of the palette knife, (which he used with great dexterity) to an excess. The subject challenged a comparison with Canaletti, the precision of whose execution is wonderful, and the comparison was made to Constable's great disadvantage; even his friend, Mr. Stothard,[1] shook his head and said, 'Very unfinished, sir,' and the picture was generally pronounced a failure. It was a glorious failure, however; I have seen it often since it was exhibited, and I will venture to say, that the noonday splendour of its colour, would make almost any work of Canaletti, if placed beside it, look like moonlight. But such pictures ought not to be compared,

1. Thomas Stothard (1755–1824), neo-classical painter and illustrator.

each has its own excellence, and nothing can be more true than Constable's remark, that *'fine pictures neither want nor will bear comparison.'*

[C. R. Leslie, *Memoirs of the Life of John Constable*, 1845]

Constable and Nature

It has been well said of photography that it strikes nature dead. Constable's great aim was to give freshness and motion. I have seen him lying at the foot of a tree watching the motion of the leaves, and pointing out its beauty. He would also stand gazing at the bottom of a ditch, and declare he could see the finest subjects for painting.

By the French he has always been considered our best landscape-painter, and he was much admired by Louis Philippe, who purchased one of his best pictures – a waggon and three horses passing a brook, of which Constable used to tell as follows: 'That's a good picture, sir,' said the old attendant at Somerset House – 'so natural, all the frost on the trees.' It was a midsummer. People always mistook his dogdays for Christmas. Fuseli used to say, 'Where is my great-coat? I am going to see Mr. Constable's pictures.'[1] As I have heard Constable say, Do away with this crispness, and all the merit of my painting is destroyed.

[The Rev. W. Trimmer, quoted in W. Thornbury, *Life of J. M. W. Turner*, 1862]

Constable Receives a Visit from John Varley

'Varley,[2] the astrologer, has just called on me, and I have bought a little drawing of him. He told me how to *"do* landscape," and was so kind as to point out all my defects. The price of the drawing was "a guinea and a half *to a gentleman*, and a guinea only to an *artist*," but I insisted on his taking the larger sum, as he had clearly proved to me that I was no artist.'

[Letter to C. R. Leslie, quoted in *Memoirs of the Life of John Constable*, 1845]

1. Constable himself reported that Fuseli said: 'I like de landscapes of Constable; he is always picturesque, of a fine colour, and de lights always in de right places; but he makes me call for my greatcoat and umbrella' (letter to his biographer C. R. Leslie).
2. John Varley (1778–1842), painter in watercolour and dabbler in the occult, for whom Blake drew many of the visionary heads. He was enormously fat.

XVIII
THE PRE-RAPHAELITES

ৡ

A considerable literature has accumulated around the personalities who joined together to create the Pre-Raphaelite Brotherhood. Essentially, however, it is just one of them who exercises a personal fascination that has endured until the present day: the painter-poet Dante Gabriel Rossetti. Not surprisingly, many of the stories included in this section are in one way or another concerned with him.

There are certain parallels between Rossetti and William Blake, whose work Rossetti was largely responsible for rediscovering. Both were just as important as writers as they were as visual artists; in both cases, too, the visual work is often dogged by a certain technical inadequacy. But Rossetti's personality cast darker shadows than Blake's did, and perhaps the atmosphere of moral ambiguity which surrounds his career makes him even more fascinating to modern readers.

One can in fact argue that Rossetti was greater as a personality than he was in terms of his achievement as either poet or painter. His contemporaries talked about him obsessively. He attracted far more attention, for example, than the worthy Holman Hunt, who was arguably a much more gifted artist.

These attitudes are reflected in the anecdotes collected here, but I have also tried to do justice to other members of the Brotherhood and to some of their associates, most notably to Ford Madox Brown, who, though never a PRB, painted in similar style and maintained intimate friendships with the leading members of the group.

Ford Madox Brown (1821–93): Student Life
in Brussels in the 1840s

He lived *en pension* at the 'Hôtel du Pot d'Etain,' occupying a *mansarde* with his almost lifelong friend Daniel Casey. Living was not expensive, and on his weekly allowance of 20 francs he fared not at all ill.

The interests of the 'Pot d'Etain' centred largely in the cuisine. Except on those evenings when their purse would not admit of a visit to the opera, they spent little of their time at their own rooms.

The classes at the Academy began early in the morning and lasted till midday, and attendance was compulsory if the prize was to be gained. Midday was the dinner-hour. There were three rates of payment at the pension. Twenty sous a day commanded lodging, the morning's coffee, dinner, and supper. Fifteen meant ostensibly the same, but the dinner was skilfully timed to be on the table exactly two courses before the officers were released from drill-parade. They were all *'quinze-sous' pensionnaires*, and, out of deference to their feelings, it was arranged that the soup and ragout should have disappeared from the board to give place to a great bowl of potatoes which formed the third course, and arrived at the table just as the first officer dashed into the room. He would unbuckle his belt, cast it and the sword into the corner behind the door, and without further ceremony fall to, in which example he was followed by his fellow-officers. The pay of these poor fellows was little more than a franc and a half a day, and when fifteen sous had gone for board and one for the indispensable Havannah, there was a very small margin for other necessaries.

The artists returned to the atelier in the afternoon, and worked till light failed them, Madox Brown in particular being an indefatigable worker. In the evening a penny purchased a great piece of hot 'gallette', or a paper cone full of roasted chestnuts, whilst five sous gave admission to the theatre.

When the necessary centimes were not forthcoming there remained the pension supper and an evening spent in leaning out of the window smoking enormous *Studentenpfeifen* [student-pipes] filled with 'canaster' or 'varinas'.

Next door to the Pot d'Etain dwelt a blonde-haired maiden, whom the students saw from their elevated posts of observation as she returned from Vespers. 'She had very pretty small feet, I remember,'

Madox Brown was accustomed to say; 'her face I can't remember – indeed, I don't know that we ever saw it, but Casey and I plotted together and made a little scheme to draw her attention to us. We each bought a bunch of violets, and as she passed underneath to reach her doorstep, we dropped them just in front of her. But she did not deign to look up; I suppose she must have known what we were up to. She stamped on one of the bunches of violets, and that was how I came to know that she had small feet, but I don't think I ever saw her face.'

[F. M. Hueffer, *Ford Madox Brown: A Record of His Life and Work*, 1905]

The Young Ford Madox Brown Visits the German Nazarene Artists Friedrich Overbeck (1789–1869) and Peter Cornelius (1783–1867) in Rome

Overbeck I visited first. No introductions were necessary in Rome at that time. I was very young – not, I believe, above two or three-and-twenty. Overbeck was in a small studio with some four or five visitors. He was habited in a black velvet dressing-gown down to the ground, corded round the waist; on his head a velvet cap, furred, which allowed his grey curling locks to stay on his shoulders. He bore exactly the appearance of some figure of the fifteenth century. When he spoke to me it was with the humility of a saint. Being so young at the time I noticed this the more. He had some five or six cartoons on view, all of the same size, about 24 inches by 30, all sacred subjects. I noted that where any naked flesh was shown it looked exactly like wooden dolls' or lay-figures'. I heard him explain that he never drew these parts from nature, on the principle of avoiding the sensuous in religious art. In spite of this, nevertheless, the sentiment – as depicted in the faces – was so vivid, so unlike most other art, that one felt a disinclination to go away. One could not see enough of it. To-day, more than forty years afterwards, when coming suddenly on one of these designs in a print-shop window, I again experienced the same sensation. Cornelius was different: short, with red hair and keen eyes under. When I called at his studio he was showing his large cartoon of *Death on the Pale Horse*. As this large canvas was between him and the door I suppose I did not hear his summons to enter, for he came out sharply, and said petulantly, '*Mais, entrez donc.*'

He was explaining his great work to some ladies, with a stick in his hand and an old brown paletot as painting-coat. The studio was a waste, as painting-rooms were in those days, when *bric-à-brac*, Oriental rugs, or armour were not much thought of.

He was explaining his picture exactly as a showman would, and I have remembered the lesson since. Some twenty years ago I saw this cartoon again in London, and it produced on me exactly the same effect it did at first. Full of action and strange character, it was everything reverse of that dreadful commonplace into which Art on the Continent seems to be hurrying back.

But Cornelius was no commonplace being; with his small fiery eyes and his lump on his cheek, like David's,[1] he was the man of genius, the man of the unexpected emphaticality.

[F. M. Hueffer, *Ford Madox Brown: A Record of His Life and Work*, 1905]

Ford Madox Brown's Account of the Formation of the Pre-Raphaelite Brotherhood

Somewhere about then – I dare say it was in '48, as you say – Rossetti came to me laughing, or at least more or less joking, about some discovery of Hunt's. It turned out that they were the reproductions of Orcagna's frescoes at Pisa – though, by the way, they say they're not by Orcagna[2] now. I told him it was all nonsense to laugh at them, they were the finest things in the world, and he'd far better go and look at them again; and, of course, he said just what I did after he'd thought about it.

As to the name Pre-Raphaelite, when they began talking about the early Italian masters, I naturally told them of the German P.R.'s, and either it pleased them or not, I don't know, but they took it. I don't know, for one thing, whether they ever asked me to become a P.R.B.; I suppose they did; but I never would have to do with societies – they're bound to end in cliquishness; besides, I was a good deal older than they were.

Of course it was Rossetti who kept things going by his talking, or it

1. J. L. David had a tumour on his cheek which obstructed his speech.
2. Orcagna (1308?–68), Florentine painter. The frescos showing the *Triumph of Death* in the Campo Santo at Pisa are no longer attributed to him.

wouldn't have lasted as long as it did, and really he talked them into founding it.

[F. M. Hueffer, *Ford Madox Brown: A Record of his Life and Work*, 1905]

Ford Madox Brown in Old Age

His personal appearance at this period of his life was singularly prepossessing. His thick hair, which he kept always parted in the middle, and which Mrs. Madox Brown always cut, had latterly become quite white, and his beard, somewhat thinner, was of the same quality of colour. His facial hue was invariably fresh, and his face comparatively little wrinkled. Until almost the last hours of his life he preserved these characteristics intact.

His personal mannerisms were rather marked. When telling a story he made free use of his hands to emphasise the 'points.' His 'deportment,' as a rule seemed to be derived from old-fashioned sources. He had much of the elaborate courteousnes of a *grand seigneur*, but when once in the full flow of conversation his absent-mindedness rendered him oblivious of every thing but the subject under discussion.

[F. M. Hueffer, *Ford Madox Brown: A Record of his Life and Work*, 1905]

Death of Ford Madox Brown

Upon the Saturday preceding his death he worked until darkness intervened, and then, whilst cleaning his palette, pointed to his name inscribed on the upper bevelling of the frame, and laying down his brushes upon his painting cabinet, said, referring to the fact that the picture was just half-finished, 'There, I've got it all finished as far as the "X". I'm very glad, because it seems as if I was going home.'

[F. M. Hueffer, *Ford Madox Brown: A Record of his Life and Work*, 1905] The painting was a second version of his *Wicliffe on Trial*.

Holman Hunt (1827–1910) Meets a Fellow Artist

One calm morning, on arriving alone at my cliff, there was so thick a sea mist that I could not see the distance. Leaving my picture-case still closed, I spread my rug and took out a little book to read. I was disturbed by advancing footsteps, and, on looking up, a visitor, proved by canvas and portentous easel in hand to be a painter, was close upon me. As I did not wish to encourage interruption, I resumed my study. Soon my brother of the brush stood behind, challenging me with 'A fine morning!' I said, somewhat curtly, that it was not much to my taste; but my visitor remained. He inquired whether I was making a sketch of the spot in oil- or water-colour, and I returned that I was trying my hand, when the weather permitted, with oil-colours. He chattered on that many distinguished artists had been working in the neighbourhood lately. Clint[1] had only left last week. Did I know him? 'Yes, I do by name,' I replied. Tom Danby[2] had also been sketching there. 'Do you know *him*?' 'Yes; indeed, in my small and choice collection, I am happy in being the possessor of a picture by him,' I said. At this his opinion of me seemed to grow, and he talked long of other celebrated artists and of what they were doing, not at all discouraged by my show of desire to continue my reading. At last, to escape the charge of being a downright bear, I remarked that painters recently appeared to make a greater point of working direct from Nature. 'Yes,' he responded, 'all but the Pre-Raphaelites.' 'Oh! I have been given to understand,' I said, 'that they make a principle of doing everything from Nature.' 'That's their humbug; they try to make ignorant people believe it; but, in fact, they do everything in their own studios.' At this I looked fully up from my book and said, 'Well, I have been assured positively that, whatever their failings and incapacity, they do give themselves the chance of getting at truth by going to the fountain-head, so your statement to the contrary surprises me. May I ask whether you speak this from hearsay or from your own knowledge? For indeed,' I added, 'I was really made to believe that Millais and Holman Hunt, with Collins,[3] were living together last summer in Surrey, and that there they painted the "Ophelia," "The Huguenot," and "The Hireling Shepherd", which were in the Academy this year.' 'Not a word of truth in it,' he said; 'you have been entirely imposed upon. I know them as well as I know myself.' 'Personally?' I asked, looking fixedly at him. 'Yes,' he said, 'and they are all thorough

1. Alfred Clint (1807–93).
2. Thomas Danby (1818–86).
3. Charles Allston Collins (1828–73).

charlatans. Don't you know how they do their landscapes? I will tell you. I've seen them do it. When they want to paint a tree they have one single leaf brought to them, and a piece of the bark, and they go on repeating these until they have completed their Brummagem[1] tree. They paint a field in the same manner, repeating one single blade of grass until the whole space is covered; and they call that Nature. Once, indeed, I did see the root of a tree fresh from the ground taken into Millais' studio.' 'By Jupiter!' I ejaculated, 'I am quite surprised to learn they they are such barefaced impostors.' Whereupon my visitor wished me 'good morning,' saying that he was glad he had been able to undeceive me; and called out as he walked away to a cottage up the glen, where he was painting, 'You may take my word for that.' His word for it! It was at first-hand too, and quite as good as 'the very best authority,' quoted often then and now for enforcement of conclusions! I never saw him any more, or I might have become a wiser man. In sending him away without explanation, which might have entailed much trouble upon me, as I had still to return daily to the spot for several weeks, I felt a singular satisfaction in the thought of the pleasant quarter of an hour he would pass in seeing my picture at the Royal Academy Exhibition of the succeeding May.

[W. Holman Hunt, *Pre-Raphaelitism and the Pre-Raphaelite Brotherhood*, 1905] This took place in 1852. Hunt was painting *Our English Coasts*, also known as *Strayed Sheep*.

Holman Hunt's 'Light of the World'

In 1853, if I remember right, Holman Hunt was painting 'The Light of the World'. I found him so employed, in a small drawing-room in the corner house near the old church of Chelsea, with an elaborate arrangement of screens and curtains so as to get the dark effect he wanted. The lay figure held a lighted lantern, and Hunt, painting by good daylight in the farther part of the room, peeped into the mysterious gloom by a hole. The arrangement had a bogey effect, and the amount of exercise made it the pursuit of painting under difficulties certainly. He was at that time, however, a Hercules, though not a giant, and after an economical dinner of savoury fish and ginger beer

1. Cheap or shoddy, by analogy with decorative metalwares made in Birmingham factories using mechanical stamping processes.

which my long walk made excellent, evening coming on, we crossed the street and jumped into a wherry, the management of which he was quite accustomed to, and he pulled me up to Hammersmith and back again. The pains he took to get every point of colour, and light, and shade as true to nature, and as perfect as possible, struck me more and more the nearer I saw his ways and contrivances. He was determined to carry out his accurate method of representation even when the subject was so removed from the realities of life that an abstract treatment, a rendering of 'the idea in his mind', as Raphael is reported to have preferred, would have emancipated him from the slavery of painting lamplight in daytime, and of rendering moonlight by artificial means. The omnibus groom, taking his horses home at one o'clock in the morning, used to see him working at open window from nature when real moonlight was to be had. The picture was finished at last, and its success threw all other successes into the shade.

[W. B. Scott, *Autobiographical Notes*, 1892]

Holman Hunt Exorcises the Devil

I was on Christmas Day induced to go and work at the studio because I had prepared a new plan of curing the twisted surface [of a panel], and, till I could find it to be a practicable one, it was useless to turn to work which I had engagements to take up on the following days. When I arrived it was so dark that it was possible to do nothing, except with a candle held in my hand along with the palette. I laboured thus from about eleven. On getting to work I noticed the unusual quietness of the whole establishment, and I accounted for it by the fact that all other artists were with their families and friends. I alone was there at the group of studios because of this terrible and doubtful struggle with the devil, which, one year before, had brought me to the very portals of death; indeed, almost, I may say, beyond these, during my delirium. Many days and nights too, till past midnight, at times in my large, dark studio in Jerusalem, had I stood with a candle, hoping to surmount the evil each hour, and the next day I found all had fallen into disorder again, as though I had been vainly striving against destiny. The plan I was trying this Christmas morning I had never thought of before the current week, but it might be that even this also would fail. As I groaned over the thoughts of my pains, which were interwoven with my calculations of the result of the coming work over my fresh

[329]

preparation of the ground, I gradually saw reason to think that it promised better, and I bent all my energies to advance my work to see what the later crucial touches would do. I hung back to look at my picture. I felt assured that I should succeed. I said to myself half aloud 'I think I have beaten the devil!' and stepped down, when the whole building shook with a convulsion, seemingly immediately behind my easel, as if a great creature were shaking itself and running between me and the door. I called out, 'What is it?' but there was no answer, and the noise ceased. I then looked about; it was between half-past one and two, and perfectly like night, only darker; for ordinarily the lamps in the square show themselves after sunset, and on this occasion the fog hid everything. I went to the door, which was locked as I had left it, and I noticed that there was no sign of human or other creature being about. I went back to my work really rather cheered by the grotesque suggestion that came into my mind that the commotion was the evil one departing, and it was for this I told you the circumstance on the day of your visit.

[Letter from Hunt to William Bell Scott, *Autobiographical Notes*, 1892]
The picture Hunt was working on was the *Shadow of Death*.

The Young Dante Gabriel Rossetti (1828–82)

When he had fairly got entangled in a new design he would refuse the attraction of home, meals, out of door engagements, or bed, and sit through the night, sleeping where he sat for an hour at the time, recommencing his work when he woke. He ate whatever was at hand when hunger suggested, and when time came for bed on the second night he would ask me to leave him; in the morning I would find him still at his engrossing task. 'The Girlhood of the Virgin' was a composition with but little intricacy in it, and therefore a penitential return to the easel soon made up for truancy. There was a special trial, however, in store not to be lightly passed by, for when he advanced to the painting of the child angel, for whom he had four or more models in succession, an untried one ever promising to be more manageable than the last, he increasingly lost patience. The unsteadiness of one mild little girl so overtried his temper that he revealed his irritation beyond bounds, storming wildly, overthrowing his tools and stamping about, until the poor child sobbed and screamed with fright, clinging to her conductress, much too alarmed to listen to any comfort he repentantly offered her. After this scene, which had raised clouds of dust and destroyed my tranquility of mind, further work that day was out of the question.

[W. Holman Hunt, *Pre-Raphaelitism and the Pre-Raphaelite Brotherhood*, 1905]

Rossetti Visits Ford Madox Brown's Studio (1856)

Mrs. Hueffer,[1] who was at the time sitting for the child in the picture of *Stages of Cruelty*, relates that whilst standing before his easel in the silence of the studio he passed the time uttering over and over again the words, 'Guggum, Guggum' – a pet name for Miss Siddall. His introduction to Mrs. Hueffer was, however, not calculated to give her a prejudice in his favour, for she relates that whilst walking in the garden she was startled by seeing a singularly hideous face peering at her through the glass door of the studio. This was Rossetti, whose powers of contriving amusement for a child do not seem in this matter to have equalled his control of the organs of his face.

[F. M. Hueffer, *Ford Madox Brown: A Record of his Life and Work*, 1905]

Rossetti, Burne-Jones (1833–98) and William Morris (1834–96) Paint Frescos at the Oxford Union

In later years Madox Brown was wont to relate weird tales of how they worked at Oxford. If they may be believed, the daily fare was roast beef, plum puddings, one to each man, and old ale. Enormous sums were spent on the mere colours for the paintings that have now disappeared beneath the dust. Rossetti, after upsetting from the top of a ladder a painter's pot full of priceless lapis lazuli ground into real ultramarine, was said to have said: 'Oh, that's nothing, we often do that.'

[F. M. Hueffer, *Ford Madox Brown: A Record of his Life and Work*, 1905]

1. Ford Madox Brown's daughter Lucy.

Rossetti and the Maidservant

In early years, when William Morris and Burne-Jones shared a studio, they had a young servant maid whose spirits were unquenchably vivacious, and whose pertness nothing could banish or check. Thinking to frighten this girl out of her complacency, Rossetti, calling one day on his friends, affected the direst madness, strutted ominously up to her with the wildest glare of his eyes, and began in his most sepulchral tones to recite the lines:

> Shall the hide of a fierce lion
> Be stretched on a couch of wood,
> For a daughter's foot to lie on,
> Stained with a father's blood?

The poet's response is a soft 'Ah, no!' but the girl calmly fixed her eyes on the frenzied eyes before her, and answered, with a swift, light accent and a merry laugh:
'It shall, if you like, sir!'
[H. Caine, *Recollections of Rossetti*, 1928]

Rossetti and Fanny Cornforth

The paradoxical conclusion that women and flowers were the only objects worth painting, was brought about by the appearance of other ladies besides Miss Siddal[1] coming within his orbit. Among these the most important was one who must have had some overpowering attractions for him, although I never could see what they were. He met her in the Strand. She was cracking nuts with her teeth, and throwing the shells about; seeing Rossetti staring at her, she threw some at him. Delighted with this brilliant *naïveté*, he forthwith accosted her, and carried her off to sit to him for her portrait.
[W. B. Scott, *Autobiographical Notes*, 1892] Fanny Cornforth later acted as Rossetti's mistress and housekeeper.

Rossetti's Method of Painting in his Later Years

Rossetti told me something of the history of 'Dante's Dream', how it had been commissioned by a friend and returned in exchange for a

1. Elisabeth Siddall (1834–62), Rossetti's wife.

replica because of its great size, which made it practically impossible to a private collection. Standing before the 'Dante' we talked of the art of painting, and I recall, with some amusement, the light way in which the author of this product of genius spoke of the gifts that had gone to produce it.

'Does your work take much out of you in physical energy?' I asked.

'Not my painting, certainly,' said Rossetti, 'though in earlier years it tormented me more than enough. Now I paint by a set of unwritten but clearly defined rules, which I could teach to any man as systematically as you could teach arithmetic.'

'Still,' I said, 'there's a good deal in a picture like this beside what you can do by rule – eh?'

I laughed, he laughed, and then he said, as nearly as I can remember:

'Conception, no doubt; but beyond that, not much. Painting, after all, is the craft of a superior carpenter. The part of a picture that is not mechanical is often trivial enough.'

And then, with the suspicion of a twinkle in his eye, he said:

'I shouldn't wonder now if you imagine that one comes down here in a fine frenzy every morning to daub canvas.'

More laughter on both sides, and then I said I certainly imagined that a superior carpenter would find it hard to paint another 'Dante's Dream', which I considered the best example I had yet seen of the English school.

'Friendly nonsense,' replied my frank host; 'there is now no English school whatever.'

'Well,' I said, 'if you deny the name to others who lay more claim to it, will you not at least allow it to the three or four painters who started with you in life – the Pre-Raphaelites, you know.'

'Not at all, unless it is to Brown, and he's more French than English. Hunt and Jones have no more claim to it than I have. Pre-Raphaelites! A group of young fellows who couldn't draw!'

With this came one of his full-chested laughs, and then quickly behind it:

'As for all the prattle about Pre-Raphaelitism, I confess to you I am weary of it, and long have been. Why should we go on talking about the visionary vanities of half-a-dozen boys? We've all grown out of them, I hope, by now.'

[H. Caine, *Recollections of Rossetti*, 1928]

Rossetti's Menagerie

The beasts upon which Dante's affections were prodigalized were the first wombat and his successor the woodchuck. The second wombat, having died immediately, counts for little. No more engagingly lumpish quadruped than the first wombat could be found, and none more obese and comfortable than the woodchuck. They were both tame, especially the woodchuck; and Dante would sit with either in his arms by the half-hour together, dandling them paunch upward, scratching gently at their cheeks or noses, or making the woodchuck's head and hind-paws meet. With the wombat no such operation was possible. Each of them was his housemate for some time, and each expired without premonition. I do not assume that my brother wept over them, but certainly 'his heart was sair'. For the wombat (not having yet seen it) he wrote from Penkill Castle the following quatrain:

> Oh how the family affections combat
> Within this heart, and each hour flings a bomb at
> My burning soul! Neither from owl nor from bat
> Can peace be gained until I clasp my wombat.

[W. M. Rossetti, *Dante Gabriel Rossetti: His Family Letters, with a Memoir*, 1895]

Rossetti's Pet Wombat

The freaks of Rossetti's menagerie formed a considerable proportion of Madox Brown's stock of anecdotes. The story of the zebu bull that 'treed' the painter in his own back garden has been frequently told. Not quite so familiar is that of the raccoon that devoured with equal equanimity the neighbours' fowls and shillingsworth's of prussic acid, and that was discovered after a long disappearance ensconced in a locked drawer with no visible means of in- or egress, or, for the matter of that, of support other than that afforded by the aforesaid neighbours' fowls.

The beast that made the greatest impression, at least on Madox Brown, was the singularly inactive marsupial known as the wombat – an animal that seems to have exercised a latent fascination on the Rossettian mind. On high days and holiday banquets it occupied a place of honour on the *épergne* in the centre of the table, where, with imperturbable equanimity, it would remain dormant. On one occasion, however, it belied its character. Descending unobserved, during a heated post-prandial discussion, it proceeded in leisurely fashion to devour the entire contents of a valuable box of cigars, achieving that feat just in time for the exhaustion of the subject under consideration and consequent attention to things mundane.

If Madox Brown may be believed, the wombat of Rossetti was the prototype of the dormouse in 'Alice in Wonderland', the author of which beloved work was a frequent visitor of Rossetti's household at Chelsea.

[F. M. Hueffer, *Ford Madox Brown: A Record of his Life and Work*, 1905]

More Incidents Concerning Rossetti's Menagerie

No one understood better than Whistler[1] why Rossetti filled his house and garden with strange beasts. It was from Whistler we heard of the peacock and the gazelle, who fought until the peacock was left standing desolate with his tail apart upon the ground; the origin, we have always believed, of the monkey and the parrot story. From Whistler, too, we had the story of the bull – the bull of Bashan – bought at Cremorne, and tied to a stake in the garden, where Rossetti would come every day and talk to him, until once the bull was so excited by this talk that he pulled up the stake and made for Rossetti, who went tearing round and round a tree, a little fat person with coat-tails flying, finally, by a supreme effort, rushing up the garden steps just in time to slam the door in the bull's face. Rossetti called his man and ordered him to tie up the bull, but he, who had looked out for the menagerie, who had gone about the house with peacocks and other creatures under his arms, who had rescued armadilloes from irate neighbours, who had captured monkeys from the tops of chimneys, struck when it came to tying up a bull of Bashan on the rampage, and gave a month's warning. From Whistler also, we first had the story of the wombat, bought at Jamrack's by Rossetti for the sake of its name. Whistler was dining at Tudor House, and the wombat was brought on the table with coffee and cigars. It was an amazing evening, Meredith[2] talking with, if possible, more than his usual brilliancy, and

1. James Abbott McNeill Whistler (1834–1903).
2. George Meredith (1828–1909).

Swinburne[1] reading aloud passages from the *Leaves of Grass*. But Meredith was witty as well as brilliant, and the special target of his wit was Rossetti, who, as he had invited two or three of his patrons, did not appreciate the jest. The evening ended less amiably than it had begun, and no one thought of the wombat until a late hour, and then it had disappeared. It was searched for high and low. Days passed, weeks passed, months passed, and there was no wombat. It was regretted, forgotten. Long afterwards, Rossetti, who was not much of a smoker, got out the box of cigars he had not touched since that dinner. He opened it. Not a cigar was left, but there was the skeleton of the wombat.

[E. and J. Pennell, *The Life of James McNeill Whistler*, 1908]

Rossetti, Whistler (1834–1903) and 'the Japanese Mania'

As to 'the Japanese mania', which has by this time half-revolutionized European art of all kinds, I hardly know what Londoner preceded Mr. Whistler and my brother. They made bids against each other in Paris as well as in London, and were possibly a little nettled to learn in Paris that there was another painter – the renowned Tissot[2] – who outstripped them both in acquisition. Rossetti gave a deal of time as well as energy to the collecting of china etc. I have seen him come home late, rather fagged from his eager pursuit, with a cargo of blue either actually in hand or ordered to arrive; and, as he dropped into an easy-chair, he called out 'Pots, pots!' with a thrilling accent. It spoke at once of achievement and of despondency. Such may have been the tone of Alexander of Macedon when he deplored that there were no more worlds to conquer.

[W. M. Rossetti, *Dante Gabriel Rossetti: His Family Letters, with a Memoir*, 1895]

Rossetti and Whistler, Remembered by Charles Conder (1868–1909)

Don't you remember, when Dante Gabriel Rossetti wrote a sonnet on a picture frame, the terrible Jimmy [Whistler] said: 'Why paint a

1. Algernon Charles Swinburne (1837–1909).
2. James Tissot (1836–1902), French painter and graphic artist.

picture – write the sonnet on the canvas instead of putting it on the frame . . . that will do'.

[J.-E. Blanche, *Portraits of a Lifetime*, 1937] Conder was Australian, and notoriously dissolute, a fact which his rather pretty-pretty paintings do not reveal. He was also a friend of Toulouse-Lautrec, who portrayed him in some of his pictures of Paris night-life.

Rossetti's Appearance and Character

His hands and feet were small; the hands quite in character for an artist or author – white, delicate, plump, and soft as a woman's. Miss Caine correctly notices that he had a rather fidgeting habit of nicking (she says 'cracking', but I think that less accurate) his right thumb-nail with the nail of the first finger; also a habit of shaking very rapidly, and for long whiles together, the foot of one leg crossed over the other. His general aspect was compact and determined, with the facial expression of a fiery and dictatorial mind concentrated into repose. Some people regarded him as eminently handsome, and no one could call him other than a well-looking noticeable man. In habit of body he was more than sufficiently indolent and lounging ('lolling about, and behaving like a seal on a sandbank', as Smetham expressively worded it), disinclined to any prescribed or trying exertion, yet not at all wanting in active promptitude whenever it suited his liking. He often seemed merely unoccupied, especially of an evening; the brain continued busy enough. A reader, to be sure, he was, but not a *great* reader.

[W. M. Rossetti, *Dante Gabriel Rossetti: His Family Letters, with a Memoir*, 1895]

A Character Description of Rossetti

Thursday, September 19. R. and I look round the furniture brokers, he buys an old mirror and several other things 'for a song,' but they will have to be done up, 'otherwise you fill your house with dinginess'. Then a walk. R. walks very characteristically, with a peculiar lounging gait, often trailing the point of his umbrella on the ground, but still obstinately pushing on and making way, he humming the while with closed teeth, in the intervals of talk, not a tune or anything like one but what sounds like a *sotto voce* note of defiance to the Universe. Then suddenly he will fling himself down somewhere and refuse to stir an inch further. His favourite attitude – on his back, one knee raised, hands behind head. On a sofa he often, too, curls himself up like a cat. He very seldom takes particular notice of anything as he goes, and cares nothing about natural history, or science in any form or degree. It is plain that the simple, the natural, the naïve are merely insipid in his mouth; he must have strong savours, in art, in literature and in life. Colours, forms, sensations are required to be pungent, mordant. In poetry he desires spasmodic passion, and emphatic, partly archaic, diction. He cannot endure Wordsworth, any more than I can S.[1] He sees nothing in Lovelace's 'Tell me not, Sweet, I am unkind'. In foreign poetry, he is drawn to Dante by inheritance (Milton, by the way, he dislikes); in France he is interested by Villon and some others of the old lyric writers, in Germany by nobody. To Greek Literature he seems to owe nothing, nor to Greek Art, directly. In Latin poetry he has turned to one or two things of Catullus for sake of the subjects. English imaginative literature – Poems and Tales, here lies his pabulum: Shakespeare, the old Ballads, Blake, Keats, Shelley, Browning, Mrs. Browning, Tennyson, Poe being first favourites, and now Swinburne. *Wuthering Heights* is a Koh-i-noor among novels, *Sidonia the Sorceress*[2] 'a stunner'. *Any* writing that with the least competency assumes an imaginative form, or any criticism on the like, attracts his attention more or less; and he has discovered in obscurity, and in some cases helped to rescue from it, at least in his own circle, various unlucky books; those, for example, of Ebenezer Jones [*Studies of Sensation and Event*] and Wells, author of *Joseph and His Brethren* and *Stories after Nature*. About these and other matters Rossetti is chivalrously bold in announcing and defending his opinions, and he has the valuable quality of knowing what he likes and sticking to it. In Painting the Early Italians with their quaintness and strong rich colouring have magnetised him. In Sculpture he only cares for picturesque and grotesque qualities, and of Architecture as such takes, I think, no notice at all.

[W. Allingham, *A Diary*, 1907]

1. Algernon Charles Swinburne (1837–1909).
2. An extravagant Gothic novel by Lady Wilde, mother of Oscar Wilde.

Rossetti's Appearance and Way of Life

About the surroundings and the way of life so much has been written that I shall pass them over quickly. The handsome old red-brick house in a row looking on the Chelsea reach of the Thames; the combined gloom and richness of its decoration, the sombre hangings, the doors and panellings painted in sombre dark-green sparsely picked out with red and lighted here and there by a round convex mirror; the shelves and cupboards laden with brassware and old blue Nankin china (in the passion for collecting which Rossetti was, if I remember rightly, an absolute pioneer); the long green and shady garden at the back, with its uncanny menagerie of wombat, raccoon, armadillo, kangaroo, or whatever might be the special pet or pets of the moment; the wilful, unconventional, unhealthy habits and hours; the rare and reluctant admission of strangers; all these things have already been made familiar by repeated descriptions to such readers as are curious about them. So have the aspect and bearing of the man himself; his sturdy, almost burly figure clad in a dark cloth suit with the square jacket cut extra long and deep-pocketed; his rich brown hair and lighter brown, shortish, square-trimmed beard, the olive complexion betraying Italian blood; the handsome features between spare and fleshy, with full, sensual underlip and thoughtful, commanding forehead in which some of his friends found a likeness to Shakespeare; the deep bar above the nose and fine blue-grey colour of the eyes behind their spectacles; and finally, the round, John-Bullish, bluntly cordial manner of speech, with a preference for brief and bluff slang words and phrases which seemed scarce in keeping with the fame and character of the man as the most quintessentially, romantically poetic of painters and writers.

[S. Colvin, *Memories and Notes of Persons and Places*, 1921]

Rossetti's Sense of Humour

I have scarcely left space to speak of the humorous, burlesque-loving elements which subsisted in Rossetti's nature alongside of the darkly passionate and mystical elements. They were somewhat singular in their kind and were often exercised frankly and light-heartedly at the expense of those about him. In writing they showed themselves chiefly in the composition of 'Limericks' on the characters of his friends. He was, at any rate while his days of tolerable health lasted, in practice a model of good friendship, somewhat masterful and domineering, it is true, among those of his inner circle, but infinitely generous withal both in word and act, loving to praise whatever he saw worthy of praise in any one's work, prompt and eager to help any one in difficulties with money or whatever form of service might be most needed – in a word, essentially *bon prince*. But at the same time he had the shrewdest eye for his friends' faults or failings, and the neatest possible knack in exposing such faults or failings in rhymes which he was apt to troll out with gusto in their hearing and never expected them to resent. For instance, he had gladly and often taken in and housed a certain prae-Raphaelite landscape-painter called Inchbold.[1] The recipient of his hospitality seeming by and by somewhat inclined to abuse it, Rossetti wrote,

> There's a troublesome fellow called Inchbold,
> With whom you must be at a pinch bold,
> Or you may as well score
> The brass plate on your door
> With the name of J. W. Inchbold.

[S. Colvin, *Memories and Notes of Persons and Places*, 1921]

John Everett Millais (1828–96) and the Phrenologist

After leaving a sufficient interval to follow Ruskin's last letter in *The Times* to make sure that we should not be influencing in any degree or manner the judgment of the writer, Millais and I [Holman Hunt] posted a joint letter to thank him for his championship. The address at Gower Street was given in the letter, and the next day John Ruskin and his wife drove to the house, they saw my friend, and after a mutually appreciated interview carried him off to their home at Camberwell and induced him to stay with them for a week.

Ruskin and his guest had their views about particular examples of art, in which they did not always concur, but they did not the less become friends; some of Turner's work Millais especially refused to approve. The pen and ink designs of modern episodes which my companion had made were highly appreciated by both Mr. and Mrs. Ruskin, and Millais' exuberant interest in human experience, as well as his child-like impulsiveness in conversation, made him in a few days

1. J. W. Inchbold (1830–88).

like an intimate of many years' duration. While my friend was there, the literary circle were in a flutter about the success of Mr. Donovan a phrenologist practising in King William Street, Strand. Tennyson, who had walked into the oracle's temple quite unknown to the High Priest of Craniology, was, after attentive examination, declared to possess powers that ought to make him the greatest poet of the age. Ruskin (weighing the suggestion that perhaps the poet was already known to the phrenologist, or that the visitor had revealed his passion for poesy by display of interest in the plaster casts of eminent men adorning the shelves of the sanctum) proposed that Millais, not being widely known in person, would be an excellent test of the Professor's ability, but my friend flatly refused to spend any of his few guineas upon the experiment. Ruskin, however, urged that it would be for *his* own particular satisfaction, and asked to pay the fee. In the end Millais yielded, and the next morning sallied out, dressed as usual in the most correct style, neatly folded umbrella in hand. As he entered the establishment the phrenologist himself was busy dusting the effigies of distinguished criminals, and of less brutal disturbers of the public peace.

'I have come to have my bumps examined,' said Millais.

'Certainly, sir,' replied Mr. Donovan. 'You shall not be delayed more than a few minutes by my present task, which I cannot trust another to perform. Excuse me, you will perceive that these heads are almost unique; they could not be replaced. Here, for instance, is the mask taken from life of Oliver Cromwell; that is Henry VII, from his tomb; that is Lord Bacon; you see the great depth of his skull. We have all kinds, you will find. That head is from the notorious murderer Greenacre, while here we have John Keats, and at the side Daniel Maclise.'

'All murderers, I assume,' said Millais.

'Oh dear no, sir. Keats was a poet, and Maclise is a celebrated artist still living, greatly admired in his work, although otherwise not quite exemplary, you understand! All denoted by the form of his head, sir.'

'Poor fellows,' said the imperturbable visitor, and pointing with his umbrella, 'Who may that old lady be?'

'Which, sir? That? Why, that is Dante Alighieri, the great Italian poet.'

'Not of a very cheery sort, I should imagine.'

'No, sir, not often gay, it is true; but now I rejoice to say,' tucking up his wristbands, 'I am quite prepared to examine your developments, and pronounce on your natural qualities.'

As the Professor with his investigating fingers searched about the *cockatoo tuft* of his patient's cranium he made encouraging comments – 'Not bad, not bad at all; good indeed,' he murmured; 'the perspective faculties decidedly well formed, the reflective faculties also very fair, Comparison good, Benevolence well built up, and Veneration quite normal, Weight and Numbers both well up to the mark, Animal faculties amply balanced, the Business organs, in fact, beyond the average. Well, sir, coming to a conclusion, I may distinctly congratulate you upon the possession of very excellent practical qualities. You may trust to your business-like powers; they should be a good security to you; much more profitable than the poetic faculties, which many aspire to gain honour by, but which often bring unhappiness in their train.'

'But what are you driving at?' said the client.

'I'll explain, sir,' said Mr. Donovan. 'Many young gentlemen on leaving college, and indeed before, often wish to be guided as to the career they should pursue; you possibly wish for such direction. Now I feel grave responsibility with youthful visitors like yourself, and I must be very candid; in a business career I feel strongly you have all the organs to secure you success; you should rise to great prosperity. On the other hand, there are pursuits in which encouragement from me would be misleading, for in them there would be no prospect of your rising; in the Church, for example, although you have religious instincts; and at the Bar, I give you caution, you would fail, for you have not the power of eloquence; and in Poetry, Literature, or in Painting, Sculpture, or Architecture you would be fighting against fate.'

'But I do draw a little,' said the amused incognito.

'Possibly it may be a pleasant accomplishment as an amateur, but you have no organ of form, none of colour, and you are deficient in ideality; for the guinea fee, however, I must apprise you that a paper will be drawn up and all your developments scientifically balanced one with the other; in the concluding remarks the general suggestions of our examination will be carefully balanced, and this may be studied much more advantageously at leisure than any words I might impulsively use now could be. If you will kindly furnish me with your name and address, I will undertake to deliver this to-morrow morning.'

'Oh!' said Millais, 'I won't trouble you. I shall be passing here to-morrow at the same time, and I will call for it.'

On the morrow Millais presented himself at the shop; all was ready, and the paper, folded up, was handed over to him by the phrenologist.

The recipient made a show of opening it. 'Pardon me, sir,' said the master, 'to perform my duty justly, I have had to draw attention to personal characteristics which should only be studied in private and with deliberation. I would rather, therefore, that you deferred reading it until you return home in quiet.'

Millais put the paper deep into his pocket.

'Now I have one favour to beg,' said Mr. Donovan, 'I keep in this book, you will see, a list of all my clients, with their addresses; it is an interesting and valuable record, and I should be glad that you should write your name and address in it.'

'Certainly,' said Millais, and he took the pen and wrote 'John Everett Millais, 83 Gower Street.'

The Professor turned the book towards him and read with undisguised attention. 'Tell me, sir, are you the son of the artist who painted a picture which attracted great attention last year, and of another this year which has excited violent discussion?'

'Oh no,' said Millais.

'Perhaps you are his brother, sir?'

'No,' said the young client, 'I am the painter himself.'

'Indeed, indeed,' he said; 'well then, I must ask you to let me have the paper again.'

'No,' said the other, 'I have paid for it, and I can't have it altered.'

'Yes,' said Mr. Donovan, 'but there are some extraordinary exceptions to the rules of our art, and you, I assure you, are one of the most remarkable, and I merely want to note it on your paper.'

'I would not part with it,' said Millais, 'for a thousand pounds,' as he walked out of the shop.

[W. Holman Hunt, *Pre-Raphaelitism and the Pre-Raphaelite Brotherhood*, 1905]

Millais, Hunt and Edward Lear

While the singer of nonsense rhymes and I were busy working, a letter from Millais announced that he would come down on Saturday night and spend Sunday with us. Lear had not seen him, but he was anxious to know what manner of man this already widely renowned one was in person. I had described him so glowingly that Lear remarked he was indeed a fit being to bring in the 'Millaisneum' of art, but he inquired, 'Is he disposed to lord it over others?' 'Well,' I replied, 'you know there are men who are good-nature itself, but who have a knack of always making others carry their parcels.' 'Oh, but I won't carry his!' said Lear. 'Yes, you will,' I returned. 'You won't be able to refuse.'

When the visitor arrived good comradeship was quickly established. The next day was perfect for a good walk, and we started early to reach Winchelsea and Rye, and take our chance for luncheon at the inn. We descended to the beach by Fairlight Cliffs, and had not walked far when we came upon cuttlefish bones lying about, clean and unbroken. Millais, when he had picked up a few, declared that he would take them home. The argument that they could be bought at any chemist's in London availed nothing, neither did the remark that with our system of painting they were scarcely wanted. Millais said he had never before seen such good ones, and that a painter never knew when he might find them essential, so he filled a large handkerchief with the spoil. At the end of ten minutes he came up to me and coaxingly said, 'I say, carry these for me now, like a good fellow, do.' Lear was already exploding with laughter, while I said, 'I am not going to spoil you. I will put them down here; no one will take them, and you can get them on our return, or carry them yourself, my dear boy.' Millais said, 'They might be trodden upon,' and could not understand why Lear laughed so helplessly, but his ardent good humour urged Millais to appeal to him, 'You carry it for me, King Lear,' he said. At which that monarch of merriment, doubled up with laughter, declared that he would take the bundle, which he did with such enjoyment that he was incapable of walking sedately while the memory of my prophecy was upon him. 'He doesn't carry his own cuttlefish' passed into a proverb amongst us.

[W. Holman Hunt, *Pre-Raphaelitism and the Pre-Raphaelite Brotherhood*, 1905]

Millais and J. F. Lewis (1805–76)

When in town Millais casually encountered John Lewis, the painter of Egyptian social scenes, near Portland Place. He was of particular interest to us because he had recently declared to Leslie, in Millais' presence, that on his return to England after seven years in Egypt he had found English art in the woefullest condition, its only hope being in the reform which we were conducting, and he had told Millais to speak to me of his appreciation of my work. Millais answered all Lewis's questions about our present occupations, and assured our new champion that when he brought his work to town he hoped that he would come and see the new background he was now painting in the country. Unexpectedly, at this point, Lewis exclaimed, 'I shall frankly tell you what I don't like in it.' Millais said he should expect him to do so, and then Lewis, who betrayed to his companion the querulous temper he was reputed to have at times, added, 'You should know that although I think your painting much better than that of most of the artists exhibiting, I am sure that oil painting could be made more delicate than either of you make it; not sufficient pains are taken to make the surface absolutely level. Why should it ever be more piled up than in water colour? But stop, I must have a cigar; come in here.' Being furnished with his usual sedative, he walked on, resuming his diatribe, 'I intend to take to oil colours myself, and, damme, I'll show you how it ought to be done. The illusion of all modern painting is destroyed by its inequality of surface. Hang, if this cigar won't draw,' and he stopped to give it attention with his penknife. 'Holbein's art and Janet's[1] paintings are as smooth as plate-glass. Why should not yours be equally even?' And then denouncing his cigar as atrocious, he went on, 'Parts of your painting are level enough, I admit, but in your deep tints there is a great deal of unseemly loading.' Stopping still, he then broke out into an unmodified oath, and threw the roll of tobacco into the road, adding, 'Everything goes wrong to-day. Good-bye, good-bye.'

[W. Holman Hunt, *Pre-Raphaelitism and the Pre-Raphaelite Brotherhood*, 1905]

1. i.e. Jean Clouet (fl. 1516–40).

The Older Millais

One Sunday afternoon he called upon me at Fulham, and at the end of his visit told me that Charles Keene,[1] the *Punch* illustrator, was seriously ill, and sinking in decline. He wanted to call upon him, but didn't know in which part of Hammersmith he lived, so I volunteered to walk with him to find Keene's house. Sallying out we went through the churchyard to the Bishop's Walk, when suddenly he stopped and said, 'You are leading me all wrong, we ought to go that way,' pointing back to town. I replied, 'Not at all. You trust me. I know the neighbourhood well.'

The fields of the Bishop's Park were full of strollers with their families. Looking around he spoke out, 'Bless my soul alive, do you mean to tell me that that's the place where, when I was a child, I used to come fishing for sticklebacks?' Still speaking, as if to the public, 'Only think, and now here am I a baronet and all that sort of thing, with a fishing of my own of several miles, and land to shoot over.' The public stared at him almost as though he were as important as the bishop himself.

[W. Holman Hunt, *Pre-Raphaelitism and the Pre-Raphaelite Brotherhood*, 1905]

Millais Speaks Up for the Taste of the Day

Millais in the eighties and the beginning of the next decade had been vigorous, hearty, and as full of passion for his painting as when he was a boy. He worked quickly, and had not endless patience for a protracted composition; but he was still, according to the original principle, a Pre-Raphaelite, and his work went to prove that our England again held a high place among the artistic nations of the world, as high as her artists could make it without a public behind them fully to appreciate the vital importance of art. Yet he had been driven to believe that a man should adapt himself to the temper of his time, and many a friendly bout occurred between him and me on this theme. I contended that reasonable limits to this necessity must not be overstepped. He accused me of adopting a too unbending attitude towards a happy-minded world. 'You argue,' he said, 'that if I paint for the passing fashion of the day my reputation some centuries hence

1. Charles Keene (1823–91).

will not be what my powers would secure for me if I did more ambitious work. I don't agree. A painter must work for the taste of his own day. How does he know what people will like two or three hundred years hence? I maintain that a man should hold up the mirror to his own time. I want proof that the people of my day enjoy my work, and how can I get this better than by finding people willing to give me money for my productions, and that I win honours from contemporaries. What good would recognition of my labours hundreds of years hence do me? I should be dead, buried, and crumbled into dust. Don't let us bother ourselves about the destinies of our work in the world, but as it brings us fortune and recognition. Let the artists of the future work for the future, they will see what's wanted. Why, you admit you can't paint more large pictures because people don't take off your hands those which you have done. Of course you can't, but isn't this proof that your system is wrong? For my part I paint what there is a demand for. There is a fashion going now for little girls in mob caps. Well, I satisfy this while it continues; but immediately the demand shows signs of flagging, I am ready to take to some other fashion of the last century which people now are quite keen on, or I shall do portraits or landscapes. You say that if the world went on this system it would never advance at all, and that all the reformers of thought, Socrates to wit, were wrong on that principle? I don't hesitate to say they were. Why should he have tried to interfere with the beliefs and religions of the day? There were priests established in connection with the temples to teach people! It was not his business to oppose them in their duties. I don't pity him, and it was quite natural that they should put him to death, otherwise he would always have gone on making mischief; he ought to have attended to his own business, and then no one would have hated him. A man is sure to get himself disliked if he is always opposing the powers that be.'

[W. Holman Hunt, *Pre-Raphaelitism and the Pre-Raphaelite Brotherhood*, 1905]

Millais's Retrospective Exhibition at the Grosvenor Gallery

When the time came for the gathered exhibition of his work in the Grosvenor Gallery, I saw Millais more often and more intimately. Day by day, as Hallé and I were engaged in arranging the pictures upon the walls, Millais would come in with his short wooden pipe in his mouth and wander round examining the rich record of his own career; sometimes elated to the verge of enthusiasm, and sometimes as frankly confessing his own dissatisfaction with this work or that. Taking me by the arm one day he drew me round the room, and pausing before the 'Knight Errant' he said:

'You know, Carr, as I look at these things there are some of them which seem to say to me, "Millais, you're a fine painter," and this is one' – pointing as he spoke to the beautiful picture before us – 'and there are others,' he added, his tones suddenly changing from triumph to dejection, 'that tell me just as plainly, "Millais, you're a damned vulgar fellow!" Oh, but there are!' he cried, as though anticipating my polite protest. 'If you don't believe me, look at that,' and he pointed to a picture I need not now name, but which he looked at with unfeigned resentment and disgust.

There was one little incident connected with that exhibition which I shall not readily forget. After many efforts, at first unsuccessful, we had at last persuaded the owner of 'The Huguenot' to lend it for the occasion; but this favourable answer to our request only reached us when the rest of the exhibition was already arranged. It so chanced that Millais had not seen the picture since the year 1852 when it was painted, and he was therefore particularly anxious that it should be included in the exhibition.

It was late in the evening when the picture arrived in its case from Preston; but Millais had waited, evidently in some trepidation as to how this first triumph of his youth would impress him when he saw it again. Its place had been reserved on the wall, and the carpenters, quickly unscrewing the case, held up the picture for the painter to see.

Millais was standing beside me as they hurried forward in their work, and I felt his arm tremble on my shoulder during the few moments that prefaced its appearance; and then, when at last it was raised to its place, he said in a voice that was half broken by emotion, 'Well, well, not so damned bad for a youngster.' And lighting his little wooden pipe hurried out of the Gallery and took his way downstairs into the street.

[J. Comyns Carr, *Some Eminent Victorians*, 1908]

Millais and the Public

Millais . . . one day said to Mr Combe: 'People had better buy my pictures now, when I am working for fame, than a few years later, when I shall be married and working for a wife and children.' It was in these later years that old Linnell[1] exclaimed to him: 'Ah, Mr Millais, you have left your first love; you have left your first love.'

[G. B. Hill, *Letters of Dante Gabriel Rossetti to William Allingham, 1854–1870*, 1897]

Edward Burne-Jones and William Morris

Sept. 26.[2] Ross[3] and Adey[4] to grub in the evening. Ross told amusing stories about W. Morris and his entourage. It seems that Morris' hardness of heart, or rather indifference, used to affect Burne-Jones, who once said: 'If I died, Topsy would be sorry as far as he is able; if he died, I should feel it frightfully.' It is curious how in human tenderness we should secretly wish even for suffering for our sake from those we love. I suppose Morris' insensibility must have been a little humbling. I remember Cockerell[5] telling me that Burne-Jones became quite unhinged at Morris' death, that he went on his knees next to the body and burst into tears, that when Walker, also deeply affected, helped him up from the ground, Burne-Jones leant forward and kissed him. Ross said that at every page in Mackail's *Life of Morris* he is at some pains to conceal the fact that Morris was hard and selfish. It seems that once at Rossetti's house, everybody in the room agreed to this, and that for once this rather impressed Morris, who forthwith decided to do a good action. The next time Morris turned up, he stamped about the room, saying: 'This is the first and last time I will do a good action. I told a man just now, "Excuse me, sir! but your fly is unbuttoned!" – "If it comes to that, sir," said the man, "so is yours!"'

[C. Ricketts, *Self-portrait, taken from the Letters and Journals collected and compiled by T. Sturge Moore*, 1939]

1. John Linnell (1792–1882).
2. 1902.
3. Robert Ross.
4. More Adey.
5. Sydney Cockerell.

'Seeing Life' with Burne-Jones

As our friendship advanced it came to be our custom to meet periodically at a little restaurant in Soho, over a quiet dinner which we boasted was to be a mere preliminary to 'seeing Life'; but these evenings nearly always ended as they began, in talk over the table – light and laughing to commence, and then drifting finally into deep and earnest discussion of the things we loved the best in Poetry and Art; until, the lights gradually extinguished, we were reminded that the closing hour had come, and that the projected visit to the music-hall, which was to constitute our vision of Life, must needs be postponed until another occasion.

And so these meetings went on from time to time, but never without a word of mock indignant protest on his part that he had been cheated of a promised debauch. Once he fired my imagination by telling me that he had made a solitary visit to the Aquarium, where he had seen 'The Last Supper' tattooed on a man's back, and this taste of blood had whetted his appetite for more salient examples of monstrosity which were at that time being exhibited in Barnum's Show.

An appointment made for the purpose I was compelled to abandon by reason of a social engagement with my wife, a circumstance which drew from him a little note of pitying sympathy:

'Carr Mio, so you have thrown me over! Well, perhaps you are right; at any rate I am wrong to have trusted. I confess I marvelled at your bravery in so openly defying woman, but knew that you must be justified in some consciousness of strength. But lo! you are even as I, who boasted not. Still, we will have Barnum another night. I *must* see the fat lady, and *will*.'

And then on the facing page he adds a monstrous portrait of that lady herself, a thing of unimagined wealth of flesh, seated on a velvet cushion before the upturned eyes of a crowded theatre.

[J. Comyns Carr, *Some Eminent Victorians*, 1908]

XIX
IMPRESSIONISTS
AND POST-IMPRESSIONISTS

&

The great Impressionists were, on the whole, extremely fortunate in those who reported on their opinions, activities and personalities. The reporters include such writers as Emile Zola and Paul Valéry, and many others of indisputable talent. In addition, they belonged to an epoch when the concept of the literary and artistic anecdote was highly developed, and there is no lack of personal material, often of a vivid and illuminating sort, about the greater names.

Nevertheless, there is some unevenness in the coverage. Amongst the founding members of the Impressionist group, Degas was the one who attracted most attention. He lived a reasonably social, urban life, and was famous – and feared – for his cutting witticisms. Manet, as an urban flâneur and a man of great personal charm, also attracted attention. Monet and Cézanne are fully recorded, but most of the stories belong to their later years. Before his death, Cézanne had already become recognized as a fascinating and unique personality, and young disciples had begun to flock to him. Monet enjoyed a couple of decades at least as a well-recognized 'great man'. There is less material about Camille Pissarro, and his own letters to his son Lucien, though full of useful details, and forthrightly expressed opinions, are not 'anecdotal' in the usually accepted sense of that adjective. The details of Sisley's life seem to have gone almost unremarked.

The two major Post-Impressionists (that is, in addition to Cézanne, who belonged to the Impressionist generation and the Impressionist social circle) are Van Gogh and Gauguin. Because Van Gogh died fairly young, and still unrecognized, people do not seem to have bothered to record stories about him. Our very full knowledge of Van Gogh's personality comes from his letters to his brother Theo, and these are not 'anecdotes' in the usual sense of the term, but the man himself, undiluted.

Gauguin, for all his gifts, was a self-serving self-publicist, and stories about him generally come straight from Gauguin himself, and often have the air of being touched up to suit the image he wanted to present. His record of Van Gogh's bout of madness in Arles, and of his own part in what happened, is too vivid to omit, but is clearly slanted – a piece of self-exculpation which strikes a distinctly uneasy note.

Manet (1832–83) as a Young Man

Manet began his career as a cadet in the French merchant marine.

He often told the story of his first efforts as a painter. 'We were coming to the end of the voyage,' he used to say, 'and we noticed that our cargo of Dutch cheeses had been damaged by the water. The rinds had become bleached, and that was a worry. I volunteered to put matters right, and, conscientiously, with a shaving brush, I touched up the pale corpses, and brought them to life again. That was my beginning as a painter.'

[J.-E. Blanche, *Manet*, 1925]

Manet Paints a Portrait

In that same studio in the rue Guyot, he painted my portrait in 1868. I thus had occasion to see at first hand the propensities and habits which guided him in his work. The little portrait showed me standing, my left hand in the pocket of my waistcoat, the right resting on a cane. I wore a grey suit and was shown against a grey background. The painting was thus almost entirely in grey. When it had been done and, as I thought, successfully completed, I noted that Manet was not happy with it. He wanted to add something. I returned to the studio one day, and he asked me to take up the original pose. He then placed a stool near me, covered in deep red, and started to paint this. Later he had the idea of placing a book on the stool, painting its bright green paper cover. Upon the stool he placed, in addition, a lacquer tray with a carafe, a glass and a knife. These objects constituted a still life of varied hues in the corner of the composition – something quite unplanned and, as far as I was concerned, unexpected. Later still, he put in something even more surprising – a lemon in the glass.

Rather astonished, I watched him make these successive additions. Asking myself why, I understood that what I was seeing in action was his instinctive and so-to-speak organic manner of seeing and feeling. Clearly, the painting did not please him in its grey and monochrome state. He needed colour, which would content his eye. Not having hit on the colours he needed at first, he added them later, in the form of a still life. His habit of using bright colours juxtaposed, the luminous 'touches' which people found rather theatrical and vulgar, and which he was accused of having adopted deliberately in order to mark himself off from others, was, in the depths of his own being, an instinctive response, the most natural reaction. My portrait was made only for himself and for me. There was no question of exhibiting it, and I could be certain that, in adding the things that he did, he was acting only in order to satisfy himself, with no thought of what might be said about it.

[T. Duret, *Histoire de Edouard Manet et de son oeuvre*, 1906]

Manet and the Model

Guillemet,[1] pointing to the *Olympia*: 'But Victoire, the one who posed for this – she was a good sort. And so funny!'

One day she arrived at Manet's studio: 'Listen, Manet, I know a really nice girl, the daughter of a colonel. You must use her, the poor thing is in the soup. The one thing, you see, is that she was brought up in a convent; she knows nothing about life. You've got to treat her like a lady – none of your usual filth in front of her.' Manet promised to behave himself. Next day Victoire arrived with the colonel's daughter, and said to her, straight off: 'Come on now, darling, show the gent your twat.'

[A. Vollard, *En Ecoutant Cézanne, Degas, Renoir*, 1938]

Manet and Ernest Meissonier (1815–91)

[In the Franco-Prussian War of 1870] Manet became a staff-officer. Over him was Meissonier, who was his colonel. There had never been any relationship between the two men, placed as they were at opposite poles artistically.[2] Now military service suddenly threw them together, and put one, a young and controversial artist, under the orders of the other, who was very celebrated and superior in rank and age. Manet, whose old-fashioned French urbanity was bred in the bone, was offended by Meissonier's chilly manner. The latter treated him with cold courtesy, but any notion of confraternity was banished. Meissonier never gave any sign that he was aware that Manet was a painter. Manet remembered the treatment meted out to him, and

---

1. Antoine Guillemet (1842–1918), French painter.
2. Meissonier was a celebrated academic painter.

several years later he responded. Meissonier was exhibiting, at the Galerie Georges Petit, his recently completed painting of the *Charge of the Cuirassiers*. Manet went to see it. His arrival aroused the curiosity of other visitors, who grouped themselves around him, curious to hear what he had to say. He gave his opinion thus: 'Yes, it's good – really, it's very good. Everything in steel – except the breastplates.' The saying made the rounds of Paris.

[T. Duret, *Histoire de Edouard Manet et de son oeuvre*, 1906]

Manet and Alfred-Emile Stevens (1823–1906)

It was obvious that anyone who knew something about art, when seeing *Le Bon Bock*,[1] might think of Hals. But these were surface resemblances, to do with the pose. In workmanship and touch the work was as personal as anything Manet had ever painted. The desire to stress any likeness which might exist between *Le Bon Bock* and Hals's topers was, where certain people were concerned, an oblique way of continuing to denigrate Manet, by hinting that he could only paint an acceptable picture by leaning on someone else. Alfred Stevens[2] made himself the spokesman for this faction by saying of Belot [the model] holding his glass: 'He is drinking the beer of Harlem.' The witticism soon spread. Stevens and Manet had long been linked. They had no influence over one another as artists, but they saw each other nearly every day at the Café Tortoni. Manet, offended at being treated in this fashion by a friend, found occasion to pay Stevens back. The latter, a while later, showed a picture he had just completed at a gallery in the rue Lafitte. A young woman in street clothes was moving past a curtain; it looked as though she meant to open it, so as to pass through into an apartment behind. Stevens had added, as an amusing touch, a feather duster beside her on the carpet. Noting the duster, Manet said: 'Oh – perhaps she has an assignation with the *valet de chambre*?' Stevens was even more offended by this remark than Manet had been by his. For a long time they were on very frosty terms with one another.

[T. Duret, *Histoire de Edouard Manet et de son oeuvre*, 1906]

1. *Le Bon Bock* was Manet's great success in the Salon of 1873.
2. Stevens was a Belgian-born painter of fashionable interiors. Manet nevertheless painted his large *Partie de Croquet* in Stevens's Paris garden shortly afterwards.

Manet and Courbet

When Manet painted his *Christ with the Angels* – what painting, by the way! what a wonderful impasto! – Courbet said to him: 'Have you ever seen an angel? How do you know whether an angel has a behind or not?'

[Story told by Renoir, quoted in A. Vollard, *Renoir, an Intimate Record*, 1925] Courbet is said to have made the same remark about a painting by Delacroix.

Manet and Honoré Daumier (1808–79)

Daumier is said to have remarked at a Manet exhibition: 'I'm not a very great admirer of Manet's work, but I find it has this important quality: it is helping to bring art back to the simplicity of playing-cards.'

[Story told by Renoir, quoted in A. Vollard, *Renoir, an Intimate Record*, 1925]

Manet on Berthe Morisot (1841–95)

Within the Impressionist movement were two women, Mary Cassatt,[1] who derived her art from Degas, and Berthe Morisot, who derived hers from Manet. Berthe Morisot married Manet's brother, and there can be little doubt that she would have married Manet if Manet had not been married already: I remember him saying to me once: My sister-in-law wouldn't have been noticed without me; she carried my art across her fan.

[G. Moore, *Vale*, 1914]

Degas (1834–1917) on his Fellow Artists

In the days of the Nouvelle Athènes we used to repeat Degas's witticisms, how he once said to Whistler, Whistler, if you were not a genius you would be the most ridiculous man in Paris. Leonardo made roads, Degas makes witticisms. I remember his answer when I confided to him one day that I did not care for Daumier – the beautiful

1. Mary Cassatt (1844–1926). American painter; she worked mostly in Paris.

[356]

Don Quixote and Sancho Panza that hangs on the wall I had not then seen; that is my apology, an insufficient one, I admit. Degas answered, If you were to show Raphael a Daumier he would admire it, but if you were to show him a Cabanel[1] he would say with a sigh: That is my fault – an excellent quip. But we should not attach the same importance to a quip as to a confession. Manet said to me: I tried to write, but I couldn't; and we must esteem these words as an artist's brag; I am a painter, and only a painter. Degas could not boast that he was a painter and only a painter, for he often wearied of painting; he turned to modelling, and he abandoned modelling for the excitement of collecting pictures – not for himself but for the Louvre. I've got it, he said to me in the Rue Maubeuge, and he was surprised when I asked him what he had got; great egotists always take it for granted that every one is thinking of what they are doing. Why, the *Jupiter*, of course the *Jupiter*, and he took me to see the picture – a Jupiter with beetling brows, and a thunderbolt in his hand. He had hung a pear next to it, a speckled pear on six inches of canvas, one that used to hang in Manet's studio, and guessing he was about to be delivered of a quip, I waited. You notice the pear? Yes, I said. I hung it next to the *Jupiter* to show that a well-painted pear could overthrow a God. There is a picture by Mr. Sargent in this room – one of his fashionable women. She is dressed to receive visitors, and is about to spring from her chair; the usual words, How do you do, Mary, are upon her crimson lips, and the usual hysterical lights are in her eyes, and her arms are like bananas as usual. There is in this portrait the same factitious surface-life that informs all his pictures, and, recognising fashionable gowns and drawing-room vivacities as the fundamental Sargent, Degas described him as *Le chef de rayon de la peinture. Le chef de rayon* is the young man behind the counter who says, I think, madam, that this piece of mauve silk would suit your daughter admirably, ten yards at least will be required. If your daughter will step upstairs, I will take her measure. *Vous pouvez me confier votre fille; soyez sûre que je ne voudrais rien faire que pût nuire à mon commerce.*

Any one, Degas said once to me, can have talent when he is five-and-twenty; it is more difficult to have talent when you are fifty. I remember the Salon in which Bastien Lepage[2] exhibited his *Potato*

1. Alexandre Cabanel (1823–89), academic painter.
2. Jules Bastien-Lepage (1848–84).

Harvest, and we all admired it till Degas said, The Bouguereau[1] of the modern movement. Then every one understood that Bastien Lepage's talent was not an original but a derivative talent, and when Roll,[2] another painter of the same time, exhibited his enormous picture entitled *Work*, containing fifty figures, Degas said, One doesn't make a crowd with fifty figures, one makes a crowd with five.

[G. Moore, *Vale*, 1914]

Degas on Drawing

I said to him: 'But, finally, what do you understand by "drawing"?' – he replied with his famous axiom: 'Drawing is not the form; it is the way of seeing the form.'

[P. Valéry, *Degas, danse, dessin*, 1938]

Degas on Detail

One day I was walking with him through the Grande Galerie in the Louvre. We stopped in front of an important canvas by Rousseau[3] – a magnificent representation of an avenue of enormous oaks.

After admiring it for a little while, I noted the patience and conscientiousness with which the artist, without losing the broad effect of the masses of foliage, had executed an infinity of minute details – or had provided an illusion of detail sufficient to make one believe in this infinity.

'Wonderful,' I said, 'but how boring to have to do all those leaves – it must have been horribly tiresome.'

'Oh shut up,' said Degas. 'If it wasn't tiresome, it wouldn't be amusing.'

[P. Valéry, *Degas, danse, dessin*, 1938]

Degas on Painting

To return to his general ideas about painting, he always said that art is a convention, that the word 'art' implies the notion of artifice.

1. William Bouguereau (1825–1905), the quintessential academic painter.
2. Alfred Roll (1846–1919).
3. Theodore Rousseau (1812–67). French landscape painter of the Barbizon School.

By contrast, to express the notion that art, however abstract it might be, had a need to go back from time to time to impressions received directly from nature, he rearranged the story of Antaeus to suit himself:

Hercules, having vanquished the giant, instead of crushing him completely, relaxed his grip and said: 'Live again, Antaeus,' and allowed him to make contact with the earth.

He also said: 'Painting is not difficult when one doesn't know . . . oh, but when one knows, that is something quite different.'

[P. Valéry, *Degas, danse, dessin*, 1938]

Degas's Response to his own Earlier Works

When he encountered one of his earlier works, he always wanted to put it back on the easel and change it.

My father had a delightful pastel which Degas saw constantly when he visited us. He was seized by his habitual and imperious need to retouch it. He returned constantly to the subject until, tired of guerilla warfare, my father allowed him to carry the picture off. It was never seen again.

My father often asked for news of this cherished object. Degas put him off, but finally confessed to his crime. He had totally demolished the work handed over to him for simple retouching.

My father was desolated; he couldn't forgive himself for having allowed the destruction of something so dear to him. So Degas, in compensation, one day brought him the famous *Danseuse à la bar*.

The really comic thing was that, afterwards, for years on end, Degas, passing in front of these dancers, used to say to my father: 'Oh decidedly, that watering can is idiotic. I ought to take it out.'

He was probably quite right – suppressing this object would have improved the picture. But my father, having learned from experience, never permitted him to make the attempt.

[Story told by Ernest Rouart, quoted in P. Valéry, *Degas, danse, dessin*, 1938]

Degas and Racehorses

Degas found in the thoroughbred racehorse a rare subject, which fulfilled the conditions his nature and his epoch imposed upon his range of choice. Where could he find something pure in contemporary reality? Realism and style, elegance and rigour, came together in the luxuriously pure thoroughbred. What could be more seductive for an artist as refined as Degas – an amateur of long-term preparations, exquisite selections, of the fine labour of dressage – than this Anglo-Arab masterpiece? Degas loved and knew horses to the point of recognizing the merits of artists very different from himself when he had found that they had studied the subject well. One day, at Durand-Ruel, he kept me standing for a long time in front of a statuette by Meissonier – an equestrian portrait of *Napoleon* in bronze, standing the height of one's elbow. He detailed all the beauties, or, rather, all the exactitudes which he found in this little work. Canons, pasterns, fetlocks, back, rump. I had to listen to a whole critical analysis, and finally a eulogy. He also made much of the statue of *Joan of Arc* by Paul Dubois,[1] which stood before the church of Saint-Augustin. He didn't bother with the heroine herself, even though her armour is so exact.

[P. Valéry, *Degas, danse, dessin*, 1938]

Degas and Stéphane Mallarmé (1842–98)

One day, he [Degas] told me, when he was dining at Berthe Morisot's with Mallarmé, that he had complained of the extreme difficulty of poetic composition. 'What a profession!' he cried. 'I've wasted a whole day on a damned sonnet, without making any progress . . . Yet it's not ideas that I lack . . . I'm full of them . . . I have too many . . .'

Then Mallarmé, with characteristic gentleness: 'But Degas, verses are not made with ideas . . . They are made with *words*.'

[P. Valéry, *Degas, danse, dessin*, 1938]

Mallarmé Does Degas a Favour

There were odd conflicts between Degas and Mallarmé which were invariably caused by the difficult nature of the former.

Mallarmé had the idea of getting a work by Degas purchased officially. He finally succeeded in obtaining the decision he hoped for from his friend Roujon, then rushed to see Degas.

1. Paul Dubois (1829–1905).

Degas, always thrown into extremes of fury by the very name of the 'Beaux-Arts', flew into an ungovernable rage, spitting out curses and anathemas, striding up and down the studio like a furious lion in its cage.

'The easels seemed to fly from under his fingertips,' said Mallarmé.

He added, according to the account given to me by Mme Ernest Rouart, 'that he would have liked to develop a nice rage himself, well conducted, elegantly regulated, not this gross, discordant tantrum.'

[P. Valéry, *Degas, danse, dessin*, 1938]

Degas among Writers, Recalled by Berthe Morisot

Finding himself one day at the end of a dinner-table where Goncourt, Daudet and Zola were all discussing their affairs, Degas remained silent. 'Ah well,' said Daudet, 'you feel contempt for us.'

'My contempt is that of a painter,' Degas replied.

[P. Valéry, *Degas, danse, dessin*, 1938]

William Rothenstein (1872–1945) on Degas

Although I was always somewhat excited visiting Whistler, his curiosity to know what I had been doing, whom I had been seeing, his friendly chaff, would put me at ease. With Degas, I was never quite comfortable. To begin with, nervous people are apt, when speaking in a foreign tongue, to say rather what comes into their heads, than to say what they mean. Moreover, Degas' character was more austere and uncompromising than Whistler's. Compared with Degas Whistler seemed almost worldly in many respects. Indeed, Degas was the only man of whom Whistler was a little afraid. 'Whistler, you behave as though you have no talent,' Degas had said once to him; and again when Whistler, chin high, monocle in his eye, frock-coated, top-hatted, and carrying a tall cane, walked triumphantly into a restaurant where Degas was dining: 'Whistler, you have forgotten your muff.' Again, about Whistler's flat-brimmed hat, which Whistler fancied, Degas said: 'Oui, il vous va très bien; mais ce n'est pas ça qui nous rendra l'Alsace et la Lorraine!'[1]

Degas was then making studies of laundresses ironing, and of

---

1. 'Yes, it suits you very well, but it won't give us back Alsace and Lorraine.'

women tubbing or at their toilets. Some of these were redrawn again and again on tracing paper pinned over drawings already made; this practice allowed for correction and simplification, and was not unusual with artists in France. Degas rarely painted directly from nature. He spoke once of Monet's dependence in this respect: 'Je n'éprouve pas le besoin de perdre connaissance devant la nature,'[1] he mocked.

He never forgot that he was once a pupil of Ingres. Indeed, he described at length, on one of my first visits, his early relations with Ingres; with what fear he approached him, showing his drawings and asking whether he might, in all modesty, look forward to being, some day, an artist; Ingres replying that it was too grave a thing, too serious a responsibility to be thought of; better devote himself to some other pursuit. And how going again, and yet again, pleading that he had reconsidered, from every point of view, his idea of equipping himself to become a painter, that he realised his temerity but could not bring himself to abandon his hopes, Ingres finally relented, saying 'C'est très grave, ce que vous pensez faire, très grave; mais si enfin vous tenez quand même à devenir un artiste, un bon artiste, eh bien, monsieur, faites des lignes, rien que des lignes.'[2] One of Ingres' sayings which came back to Degas was 'Celui qui ne vit que dans la contemplation de lui-même est un misérable.'[3] Degas had lately been at Montauban, Ingres' birthplace, where the greater number of his studies are preserved. He was full of his visit and of the surpassing beauty of the drawings.

[W. Rothenstein, *Men and Memories*, 1978]

Degas on Corot

Being one day at a café with the *pompiers*,[4] whom he was acquainted with more or less, because he kept a foot in all camps, one of them said to him: 'Come on! Do you really think Corot draws trees well?'

'It may astonish you,' said Degas, 'but he draws figures even better.'

[P. Valéry, *Degas, danse, dessin*, 1938]

1. 'I don't feel the need to lose myself in front of Nature.'
2. 'What you intend to do is very serious, but if you insist on becoming an artist, a good artist, make lines, nothing but lines.'
3. 'Anyone who spends all his days contemplating himself is entirely pitiable.'
4. Slang term for academic or Salon artists.

Degas and Léon Bonnat (1834–1922)

The story of [Degas's] meeting with Bonnat,[1] whom he had not seen for a long time, is quite amusing.

Having gone to Cauterets to take the waters, he found himself on an omnibus, sitting beside a gentleman who thereupon made himself known. It was Bonnat. 'Degas,' he said, 'what happened to that portrait you made of me. I'd love to have it.' – 'It's still in my studio. I'll be happy to give it to you.' – 'But you don't like my own stuff?' Bonnat ventured (no doubt he was thinking of proposing some sort of exchange). Degas, greatly put out, said: 'Oh Bonnat, what do you want? We've each chosen our own side.' And matters remained thus.

Degas did not spontaneously fulfil his promise. At Bonnat's request, my father asked for the portrait, and had to put on a certain amount of pressure. One day Degas decided to bring it to the rue de Lisbonne. He even wanted my father to keep the painting for himself. Naturally, he didn't do that.

[Ernest Rouart, quoted in P. Valéry, *Degas, danse, dessin*, 1938]

Degas on Meissonier

He said . . . of Meissonier, who was as small as his paintings, and who was then very successful: 'He is the giant of dwarfs.'

[P. Valéry, *Degas, danse, dessin*, 1938]

Degas and Gustave Moreau (1826–98)

Degas had known Gustave Moreau well, and had painted his portrait. One day Moreau accosted him: 'You claim to restore art through the dance?'

Degas replied: 'And you claim to renew it through jewellery?'

[P. Valéry, *Degas, danse, dessin*, 1938]

Degas and Renoir (1841–1919)

Degas liked to mystify people, too. I have seen him amuse himself like a schoolboy by puffing up a great reputation for some artist or other

1. Bonnat was an academic portrait painter.

whose fame, in the ordinary course of events, was certain to perish the following week.

He fooled me badly once. One day I was on the driver's box of an omnibus, and Degas, who was crossing the street, shouted to me through his hands: 'Be sure to go and see Count Lepic's exhibition!'

I went. Very conscientiously I looked for something of interest. When I met Degas again, I said: 'What about your Lepic exhibition?'

'It's fine, isn't it? A great deal of talent,' Degas replied. 'It's too bad he's such a lightweight!'

[Story told by Renoir, quoted in A. Vollard, *Renoir, an Intimate Record*, 1925] Vicomte (rather than Comte) Lepic was the subject, with his two young daughters, of a fine painting by Degas, lost in World War II.

Degas Goes to the Country

Granted the difficulty Degas found in separating himself from the studio, I was a little surprised when he announced that he was going to spend a fortnight at La Queue-en-Brie, with his friend M. Henri Rouart.

'It will make me do some landscapes. You'll come and see me?'

Of course I accepted the invitation.

I got to Queue, and following the directions given by M. Rouart's gardener, I arrived at a garden pavilion. On the threshold of this I found an old gentleman wearing canvas trousers, a straw hat and thick glasses. It could be none other than the 'terrible' M. Degas.

'I've been outside long enough,' he said. 'There's a moment or two before lunch, I'm going to work a little.'

I made as if to withdraw.

'Oh! you can come in; I'm only doing landscapes.'

I followed him into a little studio which he'd set up for himself. With his back turned to the window he began one of those extraordinary 'sketches after nature' which prompted Pissarro to say: 'That bloody Degas – he puts you in a corner even when he does landscapes.'

Nonetheless, I was astonished by this method of doing landscapes indoors.

Then Degas: 'From time to time, when I'm travelling, I put my nose out of the window of the railway carriage. No need to go out – with a bit of turf and a few old brushes stuck onto it, don't I have everything I need to paint all the landscapes in the world? It's like my friend Zakanan. One nut, a single grape, and a knife gives him enough material for twenty years' work. All he has to do is to change the position of the knife from time to time. There was Rouart, the other day, doing a watercolour on the brink of a precipice. Painting is something different from sport.'

[A. Vollard, *En Ecoutant Cézanne, Degas, Renoir*, 1938]

Degas at the Salon

We had arrived at the Salon. M. S. [an art critic] led Degas towards a portrait of a *Woman with Flowers in her Corsage*.

Degas: 'Yes, Fantin-Latour has plenty of talent, but I'm willing to bet he's never seen flowers in a woman's corsage.'

Degas never let an occasion pass to proclaim that Carrière[1] was a great painter. This time, passing the paintings in review, he came to those by Carrière and made the critic look at them.

'I don't see clearly enough nowadays.' Degas stopped in front of each picture. After a moment: 'To think that not one of these painters has ever asked himself what an artist ought to do.'

The critic: 'What ought he to do?'

Degas: 'If I knew, I'd do it. I've spent all my life trying to find out.'

Then suddenly: 'Monsieur Degas!' It was Vibert,[2] the well-known painter of cardinals. 'You must come and see our exhibition of watercolours.' Here Vibert looked askance at Degas's old Inverness cape. 'Perhaps you'll find our frames and mats a little much. But, after all, aren't paintings luxury goods?'

'Yours, perhaps, monsieur,' Degas replied. 'Ours are the necessities of life.'

[A. Vollard, *En Ecoutant Cezanne, Degas, Renoir*, 1938]

Odilon Redon (1840–1916) Meets Degas at Ambroise Vollard's Gallery

There's nothing weighty about the way Degas talks – it's all in miniature, sharp, alert, with subtle facets. He's read nothing – except some book published around 1830, with studio talk about Ingres and Delacroix. He is well informed about art – he's seen every possible

1. Eugène Carrière (1849–1906).
2. Jean-Georges Vibert (1840–1902).

painting, has looked at them all from top to bottom, and knows what they're made of. The real interest in what he says is the rage he breathes out against what is false or ridiculous. I told him how surprised and attracted I was by his sociability and willingness to communicate, which formed a contrast with his tigerish renown. He said that he cultivated his reputation for ferocity in order to be left alone.

[Letter from Redon to Fabre, 1895, from *Lettres d'Odilon Redon*, 1923]

Degas on Marriage

Several times Degas said to me, 'Vollard, you ought to get married. You don't know how lonely one gets when one gets old.'

One day I was trying to describe a little party I'd been to for the birthday of a grandfather. Oh yes! we'd sat at table for nine hours at a stretch. And no one had given grandpa his bread soup, so he was dying of hunger despite the *homard a l'americaine* and the foie gras.

Degas: 'Nine hours at table. And I'll bet there were flowers.'[1]

Me: 'Carnations scattered over the tablecloth. They'd modelled the decorations on a dinner with flowers described by Paul Bourget. And one of the little girls said: Grandpa, since it's your birthday I'm going to give you my two little dogs to hold.'[2]

'Ah yes,' said Degas, 'but I think it would be easier to get used to dogs, and maybe even to flowers on the table than to loneliness. To be always thinking of death . . .'

'But, M. Degas,' I ventured to say, 'why didn't you get married yourself?'

'Oh it's not the same thing for me. I was quite terrified that I'd finish a painting and then hear my wife say: Oh it's really very pretty, what you've done this time.'

[A. Vollard, *En Ecoutant Cézanne, Degas, Renoir*, 1938]

Degas in Old Age

When Degas was over seventy, his doctor told him that the air of the studio wasn't good for him.

'You must force yourself to go out – and then it'll take your mind off things.'

1. Degas detested cut flowers in the house.
2. He also detested dogs and all domestic animals.

'But, my dear friend, just suppose taking my mind off things bores me?'

No matter, the Faculty of Medecine had spoken. Degas decided that he must take the air sometimes. What he called taking the air consisted of leaping on the nearest bus, and, when he arrived at the terminus, jumping on to another, then on to yet a third.

Given Degas's known antipathy for flowers, one can imagine how disagreeable these sorties were to him on summer Sundays, thanks to the passion Parisians have for bringing great bunches of them back from the country. On such occasions, Degas's 'healthful outings' were made in the midst of great bouquets of lilacs and roses.

One day he told me about the sense of well-being he got from a country outing in an open carriage, breathing the fresh air.

'M. Degas,' I couldn't help saying, 'why don't you have your own carriage?'

He looked at me with stupefaction, touched with anger.

'Me? Buy a carriage? You think an artist should go about like that?'
[A. Vollard, *En Ecoutant Cézanne, Degas, Renoir*, 1938]

Degas and the Lady on the Tram

Degas, more and more solitary and morose, not knowing what to do with his evenings, had the idea of spending them, while the good weather lasted, on the top decks of trams or omnibuses. He climbed up the stairs, went to the end of the route, then, from the terminus, back to the stop nearest his house. One day he told me about an observation he had made while travelling in this fashion. It was one of those observations which, above all, paint a picture of the observer. A woman boarded, and sat not far from him. He noted the care she took in settling down and arranging herself. She ran her hands over her dress, smoothed out the creases, moved so as to adapt herself to the curvature of the seat. She pulled up her gloves so that they fitted her hands more closely, buttoned them with care, passed her tongue over her lips and bit them a little, wriggled inside her dress, so as to feel more at ease and fresher within her clothing. Finally she pulled down her veil, having given a little pinch to the tip of her nose, pushed a curl back into place with a nimble finger, and (not without a quick look to verify the contents of her handbag) seemed to conclude the cycle of operations, taking on the air of someone who has finished her labours, and, having taken all possible precautions before some enterprise, now has an easy mind, and confides the rest to fate.

The tram shuddered and moved onwards. The lady, definitely settled, remained for the best part of a minute in this perfected state. At the conclusion of this interval (which must have seemed to her eternal) Degas saw her – and he was a wonderful mimic of what I now give myself so much trouble to describe – becoming dissatisfied. She sat up straighter, moved her neck within her collar, wrinkled her nose, made a little grimace; then once again began all the processes of rectification and adjustment – dress, gloves, nose, veil. All of this 'highly individual' labour was followed by a new and apparently stable condition of equilibrium, which lasted only for a moment.

Degas, for his part, repeated the whole pantomine. He was ravished by the whole thing. His enjoyment was mingled with a certain degree of misogyny . . .

[P. Valéry, *Degas, danse, dessin*, 1938]

The Character of Henri Fantin-Latour (1836–1904)

Fantin was essentially *the contradictor*. When some friend knocked at his door, he opened the spy-hole set level with the eye, and, if he did open the door, he would begin by controverting what he supposed his friend was about to say, when often the latter was in perfect agreement with him. He was simply surly – like Degas and a host of artists, he was impossible to live with. He had such a childish horror of military uniforms that, when in the street he saw an officer coming, he immediately crossed the road. During the Franco-Prussian War he is said to have crouched under his bed, for the sound of the guns made him mad with fear.

[J.-E. Blanche, *Portraits of a Lifetime*, 1937]

Paul Cézanne (1839–1906) as a Young Man

He was afraid of women . . . He never brought girls back to his place. He always treated them like a young boy who knows nothing about them, with a painful shyness concealed by a show of roughness. 'I can't

have women around,' he used to say, 'they disturb my life too much. I don't know what they're for, and I've always been afraid to find out.'
    [From Emile Zola's notes for his novel *L'Oeuvre*, c. 1885, quoted in J. Rewald, *Cézanne*, 1939]

Renoir on Cézanne

It was that year also (1863) that I met Cézanne. At that time I had a little studio in the Rue de la Condamine in the Batignolles quarter, which I shared with Bazille.[1] Bazille came in one day accompanied by two young men. 'I've brought you two fine recruits!' he announced. They were Cézanne and Pissarro.

I came to know them both intimately later on, but it was Cézanne who made the sharpest impression on my mind. I do not believe that a case like Cézanne's is to be found in the whole history of art. Think of his living to the age of sixty-six, and, from the first day he took a brush in his hand, remaining as isolated as if he were on a desert island! And then, along with a passionate love for his art, was that strange indifference to the fate of his pictures, once they were done, even when he was lucky enough to 'realize'. Can you picture Cézanne having to wait for a purchaser to be sure of his next meal if he had not had an income? Can you imagine him forcing a complacent smile for an 'amateur' who dared disparage Delacroix? And with all that he was 'so unpractical in the ways of the world,' as he himself used to say.

One day I met him carrying a picture one end of which was dragging along the ground. 'There's not a cent left in the house!' he informed me. 'I'm going to try to sell this canvas. It's pretty well realized, don't you think?' (It was the famous *Bathers* of the Caillebotte Collection – a superb thing!) A few days later I met Cézanne again. 'My dear Renoir,' he said feelingly, 'I am so happy! I've had great success with my picture. It has been taken by someone who really likes it!'

'What luck!' I said to myself. 'He's found a buyer.'

The 'buyer' was Cabaner, a poor devil of a musician, who had all he could do to earn four or five francs a day. Cézanne had met him in the street, and Cabaner went into such ecstasies over the canvas that the painter made him a present of it.

    [A. Vollard, *Renoir, an Intimate Record*, 1925]

1. Jean-Frédéric Bazille (1841–70), early Impressionist painter. Killed in the Franco-Prussian war.

Cézanne at the Café Guerbois

When he entered the Café Guerbois, Claude Monet said, Cézanne, 'used to look around mistrustfully, examining the company. Then he'd unbutton his jacket, and with a very working-class thrust of the hips he'd hitch up his trousers and readjust the red sash he wore. After which, he'd go round shaking hands. However, when Manet was there, he'd doff his hat and smiling say, with his southern twang: "I can't shake your hand, Monsieur Manet; I haven't washed for the last week." '

[J. Rewald, *Cézanne*, 1939]

Renoir Acquires a Watercolour by Cézanne

Coming back from Italy, I went to the Midi. I looked up Cézanne and proposed that we should go to Estaque together to paint.

'Oh, don't go there!' cried Cézanne, who had just come back. 'Estaque is done for! They've put up parapets. I can't bear it!'

I went just the same, a little saddened by the thought of how they must have spoiled it; but I was encouraged when I found the same old Estaque, and if Cézanne had not told me, I would never have noticed any change. His parapets were just a few stones one on top of another.

It was on this trip that I brought back a magnificent water-colour of *Bathers* by Cézanne, the one you see there on the wall. The day I found it, I was with my friend Lauth. He had been suddenly taken with a violent diarrhœa.

'Do you see any good leaves around? No, I don't want pine-needles.'

'No, but here's some paper,' I replied, picking up a stray piece at my feet. It was one of the finest of Cézanne's water-colours; he had thrown it away among the rocks after having slaved over it for twenty sittings.

[Story told by Renoir, quoted in A. Vollard, *Renoir, an Intimate Record*, 1925]

Cézanne Paints Vollard's Portrait

For the sitting to go well, certain conditions were necessary. Not merely that Cézanne should feel satisfied with his studies in the Louvre, and that the weather should be bright but overcast. There must be silence from the 'steam-hammer factory'. This was Cézanne's name for a lift nearby. I was careful not to inform him that, when the noise stopped, it was because the lift halted for repairs. I left with the hope that 'those people' would go bankrupt. It was his firm belief that the banging stopped when trade was slow.

Another noise which Cézanne found insupportable was the barking of dogs. There was one in the neighbourhood which sometimes gave tongue, not very loudly it is true, but Cézanne had – for sounds which he disliked – extremely keen hearing. One day, as I arrived, he said to me happily: 'That man Lepine [the Prefect of Police] is a good chap! He's given orders that all dogs are to be locked up – it's in the *Croix*.' We had several good sittings; the weather was bright but overcast, and, by happy chance, both the dog and the steam-hammer factory fell silent. However, one day, just as Cézanne was repeating, yet again: 'That chap Lepine is a good fellow,' we heard a 'Bow! wow! wow!' Cézanne dropped his palette and cried, discouraged: 'The bugger! he's escaped!'

[A. Vollard, *En Ecoutant Cézanne, Degas, Renoir*, 1938]

Cézanne in the Late 1890s

Edmond Jaloux, who met Cézanne at Joachim Gasquet's, recalled the meeting thus: 'Suddenly the door opened. Someone entered with almost exaggerated prudence and discretion. He looked like a shop-keeper or a prosperous farmer – rather sly, but ceremonious too. His back was a bit bent; he was tanned, with a reddish complexion. The top of his head was bald, surrounded by long white locks; his small eyes were sharp and full of curiosity; he had a Bourbon nose, rather red, and short moustachios linked to a military goatee. This was Paul Cézanne as I saw him . . . His voice was slow, nasal, precise, with something studied and caressing about it. He talked about nature and art – with subtlety, with dignity, with profundity.'

[J. Rewald, *Cézanne*, 1939]

Cézanne in the Studio

He had there too, on a mechanical easel which he had just acquired, a large painting of nude women bathing, which was in a state of complete turmoil. The drawing seemed to me extremely distorted. I asked Cézanne why he did not use models when painting the nude. He said that at his age it was a matter of duty – he could not ask a woman to strip in order to paint her; or at best he might look for a model in her fifties, but he was pretty sure that no such person was to be found in Aix. He went to his portfolios and showed me the drawings he had made in his youth, at the Atelier Suisse. 'I have always made use of these,' he told me, 'and what I have is scarcely sufficient for the job – but needs must, at my age.' I understand that he was bound by an exaggerated sense of propriety, which was rooted in two different things – one, that he did not trust himself with women; the other, that he suffered from religious scruples, and felt that things of this kind couldn't be done, in a small provincial town, without creating a scandal.

Hanging in the studio I noted, in addition to landscapes drying, removed from their stretchers, and green apples on a shelf (every young painter of the present day has made imitations of the latter), a photograph of the *Romans of the Decadence* by Thomas Couture,[1] a little painting by Delacroix (*Hagar in the Desert*), a drawing by Daumier and one by Forain.[2] I was very much surprised to discover that he admired Couture. But he was right. I have since come to realize that Couture was a true master, who helped to form excellent students, amongst them Manet and Puvis.[3] What still pleased Cézanne about his work was the famous 'realization' about which I heard him talk for a whole month.

Our conversation having turned towards the Louvre, we began to discuss the Venetians. His admiration for these was absolute. He liked Veronese even more that Titian. I was surprised to find that he admired the Primitives less. His final conclusion was that the Louvre was an incomparable source of instruction; it was better to study there than to study nature.

[E. Bernard, *Sur Paul Cézanne*, 1922]

Cézanne on the Impressionists

Concerning the Impressionists, he said: 'Pissarro has come close to nature, Renoir can do Parisian women, Monet has defined a way of

1. Thomas Couture (1815–79).
2. Jean-Louis Forain (1852–1931).
3. Pierre Puvis de Chavannes (1824–98).

seeing – what comes after them doesn't count.' He always spoke poorly of Gauguin, whose influence seemed to him disastrous. 'Gauguin liked your own painting very much,' I said, 'and often imitated you.' – 'Ah well! then he didn't understand me!' Cézanne retorted furiously. 'I never sought, and would never accept, his lack of modelling and graduation – it's nonsensical. Gauguin's not a painter; he just makes Chinese images.'[1] Then he explained his ideas about form and colour, and about art and the education of an artist: everything in nature derived from the sphere, the cone and the cylinder; a painter must teach himself to use these very simple forms – after that he could produce whatever he wished. He said too: 'Drawing and colour are not distinct from one another. To paint is to draw. The more harmonious the colour, the more precise the drawing. When the colour has achieved its full saturation, the form has its full plenitude. Contrasts and harmonizations of tone – that is the secret of how to draw and model.' Then he pushed the point further, saying: 'One must be craftsmanlike in making art; one must learn one's method early. One must become a painter by using the qualities of paint itself – by making use of coarse, earthy materials.' When I spoke to him about the Impressionists, I sensed that, as an old comrade of theirs, he did not wish to speak ill of them (even if they had not refrained from doing so when discussing him!). But he considered that it was necessary to take things further. 'We must become classical again through nature,' he declared, 'that is to say, through the analysis of sensation.'

[E. Bernard, *Sur Paul Cézanne*, 1922]

Cézanne's Opinions about Painting and Painters

At Aix, Cézanne had a visit from the German collector Karl Ernst Osthaus. Osthaus reports as follows:

He explained his ideas in front of a number of different paintings and sketches which he produced from different corners of the house. They showed rocky masses, mountains and thickets intermingled. The chief thing in a painting – so he declared, was that it should render the distance. It was through this that one could recognize an artist's talent.

As he said this, his fingers followed the edges of the various planes in his paintings. He showed exactly where he had succeeded in suggesting

1. An allusion to *ombres Chinoises*, the French term for shadow puppets.

depth, and where the solution had not as yet been found – where the colour had remained colour without becoming an expression of distance.

Afterwards he spoke about painting in general. Was it simply politeness towards his German visitors which made him rank Holbein above all other masters? He did so, nevertheless, with so much emphasis that one could hardly doubt the sincerity of his convictions.

'But Holbein – one can't get as high as that,' he exclaimed. 'That's why I took Poussin for my model.'

Among the moderns, Cézanne spoke with much warm enthusiasm about Courbet. For him, Courbet possessed limitless talent, proof against any difficulty. 'He is as great as Michelangelo,' Cézanne said, but made one qualification: 'He lacks elevation.'

He barely mentioned Van Gogh, Gauguin and the Neo-Impressionists. 'They make the job a bit easier for themselves,' he said. Then, in conclusion, he embarked on an eulogy of those who had been his comrades in arms. Striking the kind of pose adopted by a great orator, thrusting at the air with his finger, he exclaimed: 'Monet and Pissarro – two great masters, the only two!'

[Quoted in J. Rewald, *Cézanne*, 1938] This meeting took place in 1906.

Claude Monet (1840–1926), Daumier (1808–79) and Decamps (1803–60)

Shortly before his death, Claude Monet told me that, at the beginning of his career, he had exhibited some paintings at a picture dealer's in the rue Lafitte. One day this man saw a couple – bourgeois in the extreme – pause before his shop-window. The man, confronted with Monet's paintings, could not contain himself: he came in and made a scene. He could not understand how horrors such as these could be put on view. 'I recognized him,' said the dealer, when he saw Monet again and told him this story. 'Who was it?' asked Monet. 'Daumier,' came the reply.

A little later, the same paintings were in the same shop-window, but Monet, this time, was present. An unknown man stopped, screwed up his eyes, pushed open the door and entered. 'Lovely paintings,' said he. 'Who did them?' The dealer introduced the artist. 'Ah, my dear sir, you are really gifted, etc.' Monet was profuse in his thanks. He wanted to know the name of his admirer. 'I am Decamps,'[1] the other said as he left.

[P. Valéry, *Degas, danse, dessin*, 1938]

Monet and Delacroix

Monet often used to read aloud. Delacroix's *Journal* was his favourite book. He was a great admirer of Delacroix's genius and liked to recall how, on one occasion, on the road to Fontainebleau, he had seen the great man, sick, muffled up, hobbling along between two friends. A memory from his youth was yet more vivid to him. At that time he was sharing a studio with Bazille. It was on the sixth floor, and the two painters could look down into the garden where the studio of Delacroix stood. They did not see the Master – just his hand, moving back and forth across the canvas, always active. The two friends tried to discover in this movement the nature of the spirit which filled Delacroix.

[M. de Fels, *La Vie de Claude Monet*, 1929]

Monet and Impressionism

'How did you become an Impressionist?' someone asked Monet one day. 'I did not become one,' he replied. 'Ever since I have known myself I have always been one.'

[M. de Fels, *La Vie de Claude Monet*, 1929]

Monet in Venice

Monet went to Venice twice with his wife. He lodged with Sargent's master.[2] Despite the delicacy and subtlety of his vision, Monet did not understand Italy. One day, when M. Raymond Koechlin expressed enthusiasm in front of his views of Venice, he cried: 'That? But it's quite awful. It's worth nothing at all, and I'll tell you why. I went twice to Venice with my wife. I took notes and I should have gone back there. But my wife died and I lacked the courage. So, I finished it away

1. Alexandre Decamps (1803–60), academic Orientalist painter.
2. John Singer Sargent (1856–1925) is not on record as having studied formally in Venice. He studied in Florence, then in Paris under the fashionable portrait painter Emile Auguste Carolus-Duran (1838–1917).

from its subject . . . and nature revenged herself. Look, I can do views of Paris away from the motif: nobody would notice, except myself. But with Venice, it's different!'

[M. de Fels, *La Vie de Claude Monet*, 1929]

Monet at Giverny

Monet lived like a gardener amongst his flowers, like a painter amongst his colours. He lived on terms of equality with his bit of ground; he studied it like a palette. The trees were his great friends, and he confabulated with them every morning. One day M. Raymond Koechlin saw him in his garden, his expression completely dis- composed, his gaze fixed, his clothes in disorder. He was walking up and down like an animal at bay.

'Well, my poor Monet, what's the matter?'

'Is something badly wrong?'

'But tell me! What's the matter?'

'Nothing. Nothing,' said Monet. 'I tell you – nothing.'

Finally he stopped in his tracks, and cried brusquely:

'Well, yes – there is. It's awful! There was a storm yesterday. Two trees in my garden were destroyed. You understand: two trees! Well there you are – it isn't my garden any more!'

And he once again started marching up and down, muttering: 'It isn't my garden any more! It isn't my garden!'

[M. de Fels, *La Vie de Claude Monet*, 1929]

Monet's Character

Monet was very good, very generous always – never refusing help or a handout whenever an appeal was made to him, or just spontaneously, without even needing to be asked. He helped many people, in one way or another – colleagues, relations, friends, local people, even people quite unknown to him. To put his hand in his pocket, to find some money to give to a beggar – and they were numerous in those days – was for him an entirely natural gesture. Beggars came every day to the house, which had become known to the gentlemen of the road. In this connection I recollect a story which is very much to his credit. Someone – I no longer remember who it was – seeing Monet give something to a beggar who did not seem to be really in want either from his clothes or his actual appearance, said: 'There's someone who doesn't seem really poor.' Monet replied, without a moment's hesitation: 'It's better to give something to a beggar who is perhaps not really in need of it than to refuse to give to someone who is genuinely poor on the excuse that he doesn't look as if he is.' I was then very young and it took me a moment, I must admit, to understand Monet's impulsive reply; but, however slow I was to take it in, the memory of it has always remained very vivid.

Monet did not like off-colour jokes, or improper words or *double-entendres* – in other words, anything coarse. He was usually silent and serious, but neither grave nor sententious, and never boring. Sometimes indeed, when his work was going as he wanted it to, he was extremely jolly. We often heard him sing out, when someone called the chauffeur Sylvain: 'Esprit charmant, Sylvain m'a dit: je t'aime . . .'

When things were not going well, he could fly into violent rages. These always stemmed from his own discontent with himself – not having been able to paint, so he said, in the way he wanted; or because the weather had changed, which made it impossible to go on with the motif he wanted to paint – he needed the same conditions for several more sessions in order to complete the work. His rages seemed like punishments which he inflicted upon himself.

[J.-P. Hoschedé, *Claude Monet, ce mal connu,* 1960]

Monet's Appearance

Monet's appearance was very much as Geffroy[1] has depicted it. He always wore much the same clothes. On his head was a beret; on his feet leather boots or sabots. His shirt was fine linen, never flannel, and of very special design. The pleated cuffs were much longer than his jacket sleeves, and partly covered his hands. The front fastening was concealed by a pleated frill, which meant that he could go tieless without seeming careless or untidy – very much the contrary, in fact. Throughout his life Monet remained faithful to shirts of this kind, which seemed to form part of his individuality. Without them, he would not have been Monet. For many years he wore velvet in winter, and coarsely woven linen in summer. His trousers were buttoned with several buttons at the ankle. This gave him the unsophisticated look of

1. Gustave Geffroy, critic and friend of the leading Impressionists.

a countryman. At ease in these garments, never constricted, he never followed fashion, never wore suits with lapels, but always instead with a plain collar, generally fastened at the top button. Despite this simplicity, even because of it perhaps, there was something a little dandified about his appearance. In his later years, nothing changed in his manner of dress, but now, no doubt because he was at long last in easier financial circumstances, he would go to a good tailor in Paris, and choose the materials himself, cloth or heavy linen, always in light but mingled hues – that is to say 'shot'. I never remember seeing Monet in a striped suit. In the country, he never wore a waistcoat, at least until old age. Just a shirt in summer, and a big pullover on top of it in winter. He always wore a beard, a fine, natural beard never touched by the barber's scissors. In the later years, he no longer wore a beret, or boots or sabots. In winter he now adopted a felt hat, twin to the famous hat worn by his friend Clemenceau;[1] in summer he wore a large straw hat – the straw was soft and supple. Sometimes, when making an excursion or when travelling, he wore a peaked cap – this dated from the age of the automobile. The boots were replaced by shoes from a Parisian bootmaker – always the same design, and made to measure. This was no longer a well-to-do peasant, but a fashionable country gentleman, though always discreet and with nothing showy about him. Even in the coldest weather, working out of doors in the depths of winter, Monet never wore a scarf or a muffler. He never bundled himself up, remaining faithful to his pullover. Often, when the weather was just a bit chilly, or on cool summer evenings, he would throw this across his back, over his jacket, leaving the sleeves to dangle on either side of his chest.

[J.-P. Hoschedé, *Claude Monet, ce mal connu*, 1960]

Monet at Table

Monet loved good wine. He never put water in it – that would have been sacrilege. However, one never saw him tipsy, and for good reason – though he loved wine, he never abused it. He was a gourmet, not a gourmand. For the same reason he liked only good cooking, but always simple dishes. For certain of these, however, he had special requirements. It was thus with asparagus, for instance. He liked them

1. Georges Clemenceau (1841–1929), French politician.

barely cooked; and the other diners had to be given a second dish, where the asparagus was cooked normally. He insisted on seasoning salad himself – and in what a fashion. He filled the whole of the salad spoon with whole peppercorns, crushed, with coarse salt and lots of olive oil and a little wine vinegar. He mixed these and let the mixture spill out of the spoon to sprinkle the salad abundantly, to the point where the leaves became more or less black with pepper. Dressed in this way, the salad was generally eaten only by Monet himself and by my sister Blanche – she liked everything he liked. He had similar quirks with other dishes. It was thus with ducks, for example. He took the wings off himself, at table (not in the kitchen). These were then put back on the grill after he had sprinkled them abundantly with crushed pepper, coarse salt and grated nutmeg. Then they were served sizzling hot. For lobster, Monet made a special sauce, once again with a base of crushed peppercorns, mixed with the 'cream' taken from the shell – something which is not usually eaten.

When it was an especially large meal, Monet often made a *trou normand*.[1] Similarly, every day after coffee had been served in the studio, Monet would have a 'Norwegian' glass[2] of plum eau-de-vie, made from fruit grown in the garden. He loved game, and most of all woodcock. I provided him with these in season, notably for Christmas and New Year's Day. To make sure of having them for both of these dates, I took my precautions eight or ten days beforehand – freshness did not matter, as Monet liked his woodcock well-hung.

[J.-P. Hoschedé, *Claude Monet, ce mal connu*, 1960]

Monet and Degas Meet in Old Age

M. Raymond Koechlin had come to see Monet. 'I'm off,' said the latter, holding out a piece of paper. It was a long letter from a German doctor who promised to restore his eyesight on condition that he took a course of treatment at Frankfurt. His cautious friend advised him to make some enquiries. 'What good will that do!' said Monet. 'I'm off.' However, before he went, Koechlin did some research – the doctor

1. *Trou normand*: a glass of eau-de-vie taken in the middle of the meal, to 'make a hole' for more food.
2. 'Norwegian' glass: a beaker without a foot, brought back by Monet from Norway, where glasses of this type are used on the fishing-boats because they cannot be overturned by the rolling of the vessel.

was a well-known charlatan, so it seemed. Monet's response was one of irritation: 'Why take away my last chance of a cure!'

At about this time, Degas was suffering from the same infliction. The two painters had once been very close, but had quarrelled at the time of the Dreyfus Affair. Vain attempts had been made to reconcile them. Years passed, years of pain and suffering, during which political differences were extinguished. The collector Manzi once again thought of trying to bring about a reconciliation. One day, at an exhibition, the two old men entered a gallery full of curious onlookers. With their imposing stature, they dominated the crowd. Slowly, with measured steps, they advanced towards one another, with hands held out. Both cried at the same instant:

'How are your eyes, Monsieur Degas?'

'How are your eyes, Monsieur Monet?'

[M. de Fels, *La Vie de Claude Monet*, 1929]

Monet and Cézanne

Claude Monet was one of the contemporary painters whom Cézanne rated the highest. Nevertheless, in his hatred of Impressionism, he sometimes launched this dart at the painter of the *Heures*: 'Monet is only an eye'. He immediately added: 'But, my God, what an eye!'

[A. Vollard, *En Ecoutant Cézanne, Degas, Renoir*, 1938]

John Singer Sargent (1856–1925) on Monet

In his letter to Mr. Jameson, Sargent relates that Monet had suffered from astigmatism and was therefore chronically in the state of a person with normal sight when 'in a blinding light or in the dusk or dark'. He thought the story amusingly significant that Monet, having been provided by an oculist with glasses, hurled them away after realizing their effect, saying: 'If the world really looks like that I will paint no more!'

[E. Charteris, *John Sargent*, 1927]

Degas on Mary Cassatt (1844–1926)

'I would have married her, but I never could have made love to her.'

[F. Watson, *Mary Cassatt*, 1932]

Renoir Recalls Encouraging Words from Manet

Among the pictures I painted in the Rue Saint-Georges studio, I remember a *Circus*, with little girls juggling oranges; a life-size portrait of Félix Bouchor, the poet; a pastel of Madame Cordey; and, finally, *The Wife and Children of Monet*, in Monet's garden at Argenteuil. I arrived at his house just at the moment that Manet, who was also a guest, was making preparations to do the same subject; with the models all ready, I could not let such a fine chance slip. When I had gone, Manet turned to his host and said:

'You're a good friend of Renoir; you ought to advise him to give up painting. You can see for yourself that he hasn't the ghost of a show.'

[A. Vollard, *Renoir, an Intimate Record*, 1925]

Renoir at Pont Aven

At Julia's[1] there was an American woman who dabbled a little in painting, and who had already come to me for criticism in Paris. I could be of no help to her, for she felt herself attracted more towards Puvis de Chavannes; but she held me responsible for her lack of progress. She was perpetually rummaging around in my colour-box.

'I'm positive you're hiding something from me . . .' she would say.

One day I cut myself with a palette knife. I have never been able to stand the sight of blood, my own particularly. I was afraid I was going to be sick. My 'pupil' came to the rescue, but just as she was about to wrap up my finger, she happened to glance at my palette; she dropped the bandage, and cried in a voice full of indignation:

'What! Venetian red? You never told me you used that!'

[Story told by Renoir, quoted in A. Vollard, *Renoir, an Intimate Record*, 1925]

Renoir at Home

I remember his embittered, vehement voice in the Nouvelle Athènes, and I caught a glimpse of his home life on the day that I went to Montmartre to breakfast with him, and finding him, to my surprise, living in the same terrace as Paul Alexis,[2] I asked: Shall we see Alexis

1. A local inn, popular with artists.
2. Paul Alexis, at one time Emile Zola's secretary.

after breakfast? He would waste the whole of my afternoon, Renoir muttered, sitting here smoking cigars and sipping cognac; and I must get on with my picture. Marie, as soon as we have finished, bring in the asparagus, and get your clothes off, for I shall want you in the studio when we have had our coffee.

[G. Moore, *Vale*, 1914]

Paul Gauguin (1848–1903) and Paul Helleu (1859–1927)

I still seem to see before me the little painting of a fish-pond, which Pissarro showed me in secret and which Gauguin had painted so close to me, while Helleu fluttered about on the terrace of the casino. Helleu, better informed than I about Gauguin's way of doing things, cried, when he ran across him in the streets of Dieppe: 'A magus, my dear, a tavern Symbolist. Just look at his hand – he has one of those arty rings on his finger. It's impossible to have talent and shamble around like that – he talks to himself. He looks as if he has been drawn by Albrecht Dürer.'

But Helleu knew, just as I did, that this madman was a true artist, shamble as he might, and despite the prophetic air – which he accentuated later on in Britanny, at that inn which he and his colleagues decorated with gothic trumpery. He must have possessed real quality not to have lost it under the influence of the Rosicrucian group,[1] whose literary tastes were nevertheless somewhat akin to his own. At that time – I don't know why – one of the jibes directed at any intellectual painter was to say: 'he does Quattrocento stuff'. The Italian primitives seemed to us (we were reacting against the vogue for the English Pre-Raphaelites) totally outmoded. One side of Gauguin's work – and here I must defend myself against the return of old associations of ideas – will always have for me a 'gothic' character, just as Helleu said, but intensified with an explorer's exoticism.

[J.-E. Blanche, *De Gauguin à la Revue Nègre*, 1928]

1. Rosicrucianism was a mystic doctrine supposedly derived from the teachings of a fifteenth-century visionary of doubtful historicity called Christan Rosenkreuz. In nineteenth-century France these doctrines were revived by the occultist and art critic Josephin Péladan (the Sâr Péladan, b. 1858). In 1892 Péladan launched his own Salon de La Rose Croix in opposition to the official one. The exhibition took place at the fashionable Durand-Ruel Gallery. Gauguin did not show in the Rose Croix exhibitions but did have a one-man show at Durand-Ruel in 1893.

Gauguin and Vincent Van Gogh (1853–90) at Arles

I arrived at Arles toward the end of the night and waited for dawn in a little all-night café. The proprietor looked at me and exclaimed, 'You are the pal, I recognize you!'

A portrait of myself which I had sent to Vincent explains the proprietor's exclamation. In showing him my portrait Vincent had told him that it was a pal of his who was coming soon.

Neither too early nor too late I went to rouse Vincent out. The day was devoted to my getting settled, to a great deal of talking and to walking about so that I might admire the beauty of Arles and the Arlesian women, about whom, by the way, I could not get up much enthusiasm.

The next day we were at work, he continuing what he had begun, and I starting something new. I must tell you that I have never had the mental facility that others find, without any trouble, at the tips of their brushes. These fellows get off the train, pick up their palette and turn you off a sunlight effect at once. When it is dry it goes to the Luxembourg and is signed Carolus-Duran.[1]

I don't admire the painting but I admire the man. He so confident, so calm. I so uncertain, so uneasy.

Wherever I go I need a certain period of incubation, so that I may learn every time the essence of the plants and trees, of all nature, in short, which never wishes to be understood or to yield herself.

So it was several weeks before I was able to catch distinctly the sharp flavour of Arles and its surroundings. But that did not hinder our working hard, especially Vincent. Between two such beings as he and I, the one a perfect volcano, the other boiling too, inwardly, a sort of struggle was preparing. In the first place, everywhere and in everything I found a disorder that shocked me. His colour-box could hardly contain all those tubes, crowded together and never closed. In spite of all this disorder, this mess, something shone out of his canvases and out of his talk, too. Daudet, Goncourt, the Bible fired his Dutch brain. At Arles, the quays, the bridges, the ships, the whole Midi took the place of Holland to him. He even forgot how to write Dutch and, as may be seen in his published letters to his brother, never wrote

1. Charles-Emile-Auguste Carolus Duran (1838–1917), fashionable portrait painter.

anything but French, admirable French, with no end of *whereases* and *inasmuches*.

In spite of all my efforts to disentagle from this disordered brain a reasoned logic in his critical opinions, I could not explain to myself the utter contradiction between his painting and his opinions. Thus, for example, he had an unlimited admiration for Meissonier and a profound hatred for Ingres. Degas was his despair, and Cézanne nothing but a faker. When he thought of Monticelli he wept.

One thing that angered him was to have to admit that I had plenty of intelligence, although my forehead was too small, a sign of imbecility. Along with all this, he possessed the greatest tenderness, or rather the altruism of the Gospel.

From the very first month I saw that our common finances were taking on the same appearance of disorder. What was I to do? The situation was delicate, as the cash-box was only very modestly filled (by his brother, a clerk at Goupil's, and on my side through an exchange of pictures). I was obliged to speak, at the risk of wounding that very great susceptibility of his. It was thus with many precautions and much gentle coaxing, of a sort very foreign to my nature, that I approached the question. I must confess that I succeeded far more easily than I should have supposed.

We kept a box, – so much for hygienic excursions at night, so much for tobacco, so much for incidental expenses, including rent. On top of it lay a scrap of paper and a pencil for us to write down virtuously what each took from this chest. In another box was the rest of the money, divided into four parts, to pay for our food each week. We gave up our little restaurant, and I did the cooking on a gas-stove, while Vincent laid in the provisions, not going very far from the house. Once, however, Vincent wanted to make a soup. How he mixed it I don't know; as he mixed his colours in his pictures, I dare say. At any rate, we couldn't eat it. And my Vincent burst out laughing and exclaiming: '*Tarascon! la casquette au père Daudet!*' on the wall he wrote in chalk:

> *Je suis Saint Esprit.*
> *Je suis sain d'esprit.*

How long did we remain together? I couldn't say, I have entirely forgotten. In spite of the swiftness with which the catastrophe approached, in spite of the fever of work that had seized me, the time seemed to me a century.

[P. Gauguin, *Intimate Journals*, 1923]

Van Gogh's Ear

During the latter days of my stay, Vincent would become excessively rough and noisy, and then silent. On several nights I surprised him in the act of getting up and coming over to my bed. To what can I attribute my awakening just at that moment?

At all events, it was enough for me to say to him, quite sternly, 'What's the matter with you, Vincent?' for him to go back to bed without a word and fall into a heavy sleep.

The idea occurred to me to do his portrait while he was painting the still-life he loved so much – some ploughs. When the portrait was finished, he said to me, 'It is certainly I, but it's I gone mad.'

That very evening we went to the café. He took a light absinthe. Suddenly he flung the glass and its contents at my head. I avoided the blow and, taking him bodily in my arms, went out of the café, across the Place Victor Hugo. Not many minutes later Vincent found himself in his bed where, in a few seconds, he was asleep, not to awaken again till morning.

When he awoke, he said to me very calmly, 'My dear Gauguin, I have a vague memory that I offended you last evening.'

Answer: 'I forgive you gladly and with all my heart, but yesterday's scene might occur again and if I were struck I might lose control of myself and give you a choking. So permit me to write to your brother and tell him that I am coming back.'

My God, what a day!

When evening had come and I had bolted my dinner, I felt I must go out alone and take the air along some paths that were bordered by flowering laurel. I had almost crossed the Place Victor Hugo when I heard behind me a well-known step, short, quick, irregular. I turned about on the instant as Vincent rushed toward me, an open razor in his hand. My look at that moment must have had great power in it, for he stopped and, lowering his head, set off running towards home.

Was I negligent on this occasion? Should I have disarmed him and tried to calm him? I have often questioned my conscience about this, but I have never found anything to reproach myself with. Let him who will fling the stone at me.

With one bound I was in a good Arlesian hotel, where, after I had enquired the time, I engaged a room and went to bed.

I was so agitated that I could not get to sleep till about three in the morning, and I awoke rather late, at about half-past seven.

Reaching the square, I saw a great crowd collected. Near our house there were some gendarmes and a little gentleman in a melon-shaped hat who was the superintendent of police.

This is what had happened.

Van Gogh had gone back to the house and had immediately cut off his ear close to the head. He must have taken some time to stop the flow of blood, for the day after there were a lot of wet towels lying about on the flag-stones in the two lower rooms. The blood had stained the two rooms and the little stairway that led up to our bedroom.

When he was in a condition to go out, with his head enveloped in a Basque *beret* which he had pulled far down, he went straight to a certain house where for want of a fellow-countrywoman one can pick up an acquaintance, and gave the manager his ear, carefully washed and placed in an envelope. 'Here is a souvenir of me,' he said. Then he ran off home, where he went to bed and to sleep. He took pains, however, to close the blinds and set a lighted lamp on a table near the window.

Ten minutes later the whole street assigned to the *filles de joie* was in commotion and they were chattering over what had happened.

I had no faintest suspicion of all this when I presented myself at the door of our house and the gentleman in the melon-shaped hat said to me abruptly and in a tone that was more than severe,

'What have you done to your comrade, monsieur?'

'I don't know . . .'

'Oh, yes . . . you know very well . . . he is dead.'

I could never wish anyone such a moment, and it took me a long time to get my wits together and control the beating of my heart.

Anger, indignation, grief, as well as shame at all these glances that were tearing my person to pieces, suffocated me, and I answered, stammeringly: 'All right, Monsieur, let us go upstairs. We can explain ourselves there.'

In the bed lay Vincent, rolled up in the sheets, humped up like a gun-cock; he seemed lifeless. Gently, very gently, I touched the body, the heat of which showed that it was still alive. For me it was as if I had suddenly got back all my energy, all my spirit.

Then in a low voice I said to the police superintendent: 'Be kind enough, Monsieur, to awaken this man with great care, and if he asks for me tell him I have left [for] Paris; the sight of me might prove fatal to him.'

I must own that from this moment the police superintendent was as reasonable as possible and intelligently sent for a doctor and a cab.

Once awake, Vincent asked for his comrade, his pipe, and his tobacco; he even thought of asking for the box that was downstairs and contained our money – a suspicion, I dare say! But I had already been through too much suffering to be troubled by that.

Vincent was taken to a hospital where, as soon as he had arrived, his brain began to rave again.

All the rest everyone knows who has any interest in knowing it, and it would be useful to talk about it were it not for that great suffering of a man who, confined in a madhouse, at monthly intervals recovered his reason enough to understand his condition and furiously paint the admirable pictures we know.

The last letter I had from him was dated from Anvers, near Pontoise. He told me that he had hoped to recover enough to come and join me in Brittany, but that now he was obliged to recognize the impossibility of a cure:

'Dear Master' (the only time he ever used this word), 'after having known you and caused you pain, it is better to die in a good state of mind than in a degraded one.'

[P. Gauguin, *Intimate Journals*, 1923]

Camille Pissarro (1831–1903) on Gauguin

Gauguin's present show is the admiration of all the men of letters. They are, it appears, completely enthusiastic. The collectors are baffled and perplexed. Various painters, I am told, all find his exotic art too reminiscent of the Kanakians.[1] Only Degas admires, Monet and Renoir find all this simply bad. I saw Gauguin; he told me his theories about art and assured me that the young would find salvation

1. Suoth Sea islanders.

by replenishing themselves at remote and savage sources. I told him that this art did not belong to him, that he was a civilized man and hence it was his function to show us harmonious things. We parted, each unconvinced. Gauguin is certainly not without talent, but how difficult it is for him to find his own way! He is always poaching on someone's ground; now he is pillaging the savages of Oceania.

[Letter dated November 23 1895, in C. Pissarro, *Letters to his Son Lucien*, 1980] Gauguin had recently returned from Tahiti, and the exhibition, consisting of forty paintings and two sculptures, was held at Durand-Ruel. It was not a financial success.

Manet and Gauguin

I remember Manet, too, another whom no one annoyed. Once, seeing a picture of mine (at the beginning) he told me it was very good. I answered, out of respect for the master, 'Oh, I am only an amateur!' At that time I was in business as a stockbroker, and I was studying art only at night and on holidays.

'Oh, no,' said Manet, 'there are no amateurs but those who make bad pictures.' That was sweet to me.

[P. Gauguin, *Intimate Journals*, 1923]

Degas Explains Gauguin

At my last exhibition at Durand-Ruel's (Works in Tahiti, '91–'92) there were two well-intentioned young men who could not understand my painting. As they were respectful friends of Degas', and wished to be enlightened, they asked him for his feeling about it.

With that good smile of his, paternal if he is so young, he recited to them the fable of the dog and the wolf: 'You see Gauguin is the wolf.'

[P. Gauguin, *Intimate Journals*, 1923]

Van Gogh in the Studio of Fernand Cormon (1845–1924)

When Van Gogh joined Cormon's studio [in 1886], he wanted to be known only by his forename. His surname long remained a secret. He was a good fellow, but it was better to leave him alone. As a man of the North, he did not appreciate Parisian jests, and the sharper-tongued members of the studio were careful not to tease him. They were, in fact, a bit afraid of him.

When there were arguments about 'art', he got rather worryingly stirred up if one disagreed with him, and pushed things hard. He was crazy about colour. Delacroix was his god; when he talked about him, his lips trembled with emotion. For a long time, Van Gogh was content simply to draw; his drawings had nothing especially strange about them, and did not seem to signal allegiance to any particular tendency. Then, one day, he put a canvas on his easel; for the first time he was going to make a painting in the studio.

A woman was posing on the model's platform, seated on a stool. Van Gogh rapidly sketched an outline, then took up his palette.

When he came to correct students' work, Cormon demanded that they stick to the model – that is that they copy precisely what was in front of their eyes, without changing anything. His pupils were accustomed to following this rule. Van Gogh ignored it completely. He was not content simply to make a study; he wanted to paint a proper picture.

He changed the stool into a divan; he placed the model on a blue drapery – intense, entirely unexpected in colour. Placed in opposition to the golden hue of the woman's skin, this gave a violent clash of tone, hues which made one another more brilliant. He worked with unbridled fury, throwing colour on to the canvas with feverish haste. He scooped up paint as if he was using a shovel. Rising up the length of the brush, it reached as far as his fingertips. When the model took her rest period, he did not stop painting. The violence of his work astounded the studio; the classicists were horrified by it.

When Cormon came into the studio the following Wednesday, conversation ceased. As always there was relative silence, broken only by the sounds of charcoal on paper, of the bread that was used for rubbing out, and of feet moving involuntarily.

He came to look at Van Gogh's sketch, and the silence became absolute. We all looked at our drawings and listened. What was the boss going to say?

I was placed not far from Vincent, and watched Cormon out of the corner of my eye. He regarded Van Gogh's painting impassively, without saying a word. When he spoke, he ignored the colour; his comments were only about the actual drawing.

[F. Gauzi, *Lautrec et son temps*, 1954]

Vincent Van Gogh in Paris

Winter of '86.

The snow is beginning to fall, it is winter. I will spare you the shroud, it is simply the snow. The poor are suffering. The landlords often do not understand that.

On this December day, in the rue Lepic of our good city of Paris, the pedestrians are in more than usual haste, having no desire to stroll. Among them is a fantastically dressed shivering man who is hurrying to reach the outer boulevards. He is wrapped in a sheepskin coat with a cap that is undoubtedly of rabbit-fur, and he has a bristling red beard. He looks like a drover.

Do not take a mere half-look; cold as it is, do not go on your way without carefully observing the white, graceful hand and those blue eyes that are so clear and childlike. It is some poor beggar, surely.

His name is Vincent Van Gogh.

Hurriedly he goes into a shop where they sell old ironwork, arrows of savages and cheap oil paintings.

Poor artist! You have put a fragment of your soul into this canvas which you have come to sell!

It is a small still-life, pink shrimps on a piece of pink-paper.

'Can you give me a little money for this canvas to help me pay my rent?'

'*Mon Dieu*, my friend, my trade is getting difficult too. They ask me for cheap Millets! Then, you know,' adds the shopkeeper, 'your painting is not very gay. The Renaissance is the thing nowadays. Well, they say you have talent and I should like to do something for you. Come, here are a hundred sous.'

And the round coin rings on the counter. Van Gogh takes it without a murmur, thanks the shopkeeper and goes out. He makes his way painfully back up the rue Lepic. When he has nearly reached his lodging a poor woman, just out of St. Lazare, smiles at the painter, hoping for his patronage. The beautiful white hand emerges from the overcoat. Van Gogh is a reader, he is thinking of the girl Elisa, and his five-franc piece becomes the unhappy woman's property. Quickly, as if ashamed of his charity, he makes off with an empty stomach.

A day will come, I see it as if it had already come. I enter room No. 9 at the auction gallery. The auctioneer is selling a collection of pictures as I go in. '400 francs for "The Pink Shrimps", 450! 500! Come, gentlemen, it is worth more than that!' No one says anything. 'Gone! "The Pink Shrimps" by Vincent Van Gogh.'

[P. Gauguin, *Intimate Journals*, 1923]

XX

THREE AMERICANS
AND A RUSSIAN

&

It seems illuminating to group together here a few anecdotes about four leading artists – three American and one Russian – of the late nineteenth century. They are stories which stress the contrast between 'insiders' and 'outsiders' of the period – the insiders, in this case, being paradoxically also expatriates. Whistler spent his career commuting between England and Europe. Sargent, somewhat younger, was actually born in Florence, to American parents, and did not set foot in the United States until he was nearly twenty. His reputation as an artist was first established in Paris. Afterwards, when he removed to London, he enjoyed even greater success.

Both Whistler and Sargent received widespread acceptance from British and French colleagues, but both remained a little apart from the main artistic currents of the time. They were touched by Impressionism, but never committed themselves fully to the revolutionary new movement.

Whereas Sargent is sometimes said to have been inarticulate, Whistler was one of the great wits of his time, and his epigrams and sayings were as sedulously recorded as those of his contemporary Degas.

Eakins and Repin both visited Paris as young men, and indeed worked there for a time. But each returned to his own country to make a career. The search for 'Americanness' and 'Russianness', respectively, was crucially important to each of them. Each tried to express the nature of national character, obedient to the dictates of nineteenth-century Realism. It is a pleasing coincidence that, where Eakins portrayed Walt Whitman, the greatest American poet of the nineteenth century, Repin painted Tolstoy: although he was a novelist rather than a poet, Tolstoy was in many ways Whitman's closest Russian equivalent.

Whistler (1834–1903) and 'the British Subject'

'Well, you know, it was this way. When I came to London I was received graciously by the painters. Then there was coldness, and I could not understand. Artists locked themselves up in their studios – opened the doors only on the chain; if they met each other in the street they barely spoke. Models went round silent, with an air of mystery. When I asked one where she had been posing, she said, "To Frith and Watts and Tadema". "Golly! what a crew!" I said. "And that's just what they says when I told 'em I was a'posing to you!" Then I found out the mystery: it was the moment of painting the Royal Academy picture. Each man was afraid his subject might be stolen. It was the great era of the subject. And, at last, on Varnishing Day, there was the subject in all its glory – wonderful! The British subject! Like a flash the inspiration came – the Inventor! – and in the Academy there you saw him: the familiar model – the soldier or the Italian – and there he sat, hands on knees, head bent, brows knit, eyes staring; in a corner, angels and cogwheels and things; close to him his wife, cold, ragged, the baby in arms – he had failed! The story was told – it was clear as day – amazing! – the British subject!'

[E. R. and J. Pennell, *The Life of James McNeill Whistler*, 1908]

Whistler in Rome

'Rome was awful – a hard sky all the time, a glaring sun and a strong wind. After I left the railway station, there were big buildings more like Whiteley's than anything I expected in the Eternal City. St. Peter's was fine, with its great yellow walls, the interior too big perhaps, but you had only to go inside to know where Wren got his ideas – how he, well, you know, robbed Peter's to build Paul's! And I like the Vatican, the Swiss Guards, great big fellows, lolling about, as in Dumas; they made you think of D'Artagnan, Aramis and the others. And Michael Angelo? a tremendous fellow, yes; the frescoes in the Sistine Chapel? – interesting as pictures, but with all the legs and arms of the figures sprawling everywhere, I could not see the decoration. There can be no decoration without repose: a tremendous fellow, but not so much in the David and other things I was shown in Rome and Florence, as in that one unfinished picture at the National Gallery. There is often elegance in the *loggie* of Raphael, but the big frescoes of the *stanze* did not interest me.'

[Whistler, quoted in E. R. and J. Pennell, *Life of Whistler*, 1908]

Whistler in Florence

'After luncheon I took him down to the Uffizi, where we had a good deal of fun in the Portrait Gallery. We seemed to be the only people rash enough to brave the awful wind, for we saw no one in the Gallery but a frozen *Guardia*. He – poor fellow – was brushed aside by a magnificent and truly awe-inspiring gesture as we approached that battered and begrimed portrait in which Velasquez still looks out upon the world which he has mastered with an expression of superbly arrogant scorn.

'It was a dramatic moment – the flat-brimmed *chapeau de haut forme* came off with a grand sweep and was deposited on a stool with the long stick, and then the Master, standing back about six feet from the picture and drawing himself up to much more than his own full natural height, with his left hand upon his breast and the right thrust out magisterially, exclaimed "*Quelle allure!*"

[J. K. Lawson, quoted in E. R. and J. Pennell, *Life of Whistler*, 1908]

Whistler and the French

When some one objected to the good manners of the French because they were all on the surface, Whistler thought, 'Well, you know, a very good place to have them.'

[E. R. and J. Pennell, *Life of Whistler*, 1908]

Whistler's Action for Libel against John Ruskin

Attorney-General: 'Can you tell me how long it took you to knock off that Nocturne?'

Whistler: 'I beg your pardon?' (Laughter.)

Attorney-General: 'I am afraid that I am using a term that applies rather perhaps to my own work.' . . .

Whistler: . . . 'Let us say then, how long did I take to – "knock off", I think that is it – to knock off that Nocturne; well, as well as I remember, about a day . . . I may have still put a few more touches to it

the next day if the painting were not dry. I had better say then, that I
was two days at work on it.'

Attorney-General: 'The labour of two days, then, is that for which
you ask two hundred guineas?'

Whistler: 'No; I ask it for the knowledge of a lifetime.'

[J. M. Whistler, *The Gentle Art of Making Enemies*, quoted in E. R. and
J. Pennell, *Life of Whistler*, 1908]

Whistler's Method of Painting

Whistler's mode of painting was most comical: he stood yards away
from the picture with his brush, and would move it as though he were
painting; he would then take a hop, skip and jump across the room,
and put a dab of paint on the canvas; he also used to wet his finger, and
gently rub portions of his picture. I have often seen him take a sponge
with soap and water, and wash the *Blue Girl's* face (on the canvas, I
mean).

[Mrs Marzetti, quoted in E. R. and J. Pennell, *Life of Whistler*, 1908]

Whistler's Portrait of his Mother

Mr. Harper Pennington writes us:

'Did I ever tell you of an occasion when Whistler let me see him with
the paint off – with his brave mask down? Once, standing by me in his
studio – Tite Street – we were looking at the *Mother*. I said some string
of words about the beauty of the face and figure – and for some
moments Jimmy looked and looked, but he said nothing. His hand was
playing with the tuft upon his nether lip. It was perhaps two minutes
before he spoke. 'Yes,' very slowly, and very softly – 'Yes – one does
like to make one's mummy just as nice as possible!'

[E. R. and J. Pennell, *Life of Whistler*, 1908]

Whistler Paints Thomas Carlyle (1795–1881)

'I used to go often to Madame Venturi's – I met Mazzini there, and
Mazzini was most charming – and Madame Venturi often visited me,
and one day she brought Carlyle. The *Mother* was there, and Carlyle
saw it, and seemed to feel in it a certain fitness of things, as Madame
Venturi meant he should – he liked the simplicity of it, the old lady

sitting with her hands folded on her lap – and he said he would be painted. And he came one morning soon after that, and he sat down, and I had the canvas ready, and the brushes and palette, and Carlyle looking on, said presently: "And now, mon, fire away!" I was taken aback – that wasn't my idea of how work should be done. Carlyle realised it, for he added: "If ye're fighting battles or painting pictures, the only thing to do is to fire away!" One day he told me of others who had painted his portrait. "There was Mr. Watts, a mon of note. And I went to his studio, and there was much meestification, and screens were drawn round the easel, and curtains were drawn, and I was not allowed to see anything. And then, at last, the screens were put aside and there I was. And I looked. And Mr. Watts, a great man, he said to me, 'how do ye like it?' And then I turned to Mr. Watts, and I said, 'Mon, I would have ye know I am in the hobit of wurin' clean lunen!'"

. . .

Before the portrait was finished, Whistler had begun to paint Miss Alexander, and another story, often told, is of a meeting at the door of No. 2 between the old man coming out and the little girl going in. 'Who is that?' he asked the maid. Miss Alexander, who was sitting to Mr. Whistler, she said. Carlyle shook his head. 'Puir lassie! Puir lassie!' and, without another word, he went out.

. . .

William Allingham wrote in his diary of the sittings:
    'Carlyle tells me he is sitting to Whistler. If C. makes signs of changing his position, W. screams out in an agonised tone: "For God's sake, don't move!" C. afterwards said that all W.'s anxiety seemed to be to get the coat painted to ideal perfection; the face went for little. He had begun by asking two or three sittings, but managed to get a great many. At last C. flatly rebelled. He used to define W. as the most absurd creature on the face of the earth.'
    [E. R. and J. Pennell, *Life of Whistler*, 1908]

Whistler's Portrait of Lady Meux

Mr. Harper Pennington, writing of this picture, says,
    'The only time I saw Jimmy "stumped" for a reply was at a sitting of Lady Meux (for the portrait in sables). For some reason Jimmy became

nervous – exasperated – and impertinent. Touched by something he had said, her ladyship turned softly towards him and remarked, quite softly: "See here, Jimmy Whistler! You keep a civil tongue in that head of yours, or I will have in some one to *finish* those portraits you have made of me!" – with the faintest emphasis on "finish". Jimmy fairly danced with rage. He came up to Lady Meux, his long brush tightly grasped, and actually quivering in his hand, held tight against his side. He stammered, spluttered – and finally gasped out: "How *dare* you? How *dare* you?" – but that, after all, was *not* an answer, was it? Lady Meux did not sit again. Jimmy never spoke of the incident afterwards, and I was sorry to have witnessed it.'

[E. R. and J. Pennell, *Life of Whistler*, 1908]

Whistler and Frederick Sandys (1829–1904)

For Sandys, Whistler had a real, if humorous, affection, though the two lost sight of each other during many years. Sandys' work never interested Whistler, but Sandys, the man, was a perpetual delight to him as the English counterpart of his friends of the Latin Quarter. Like them, Sandys was usually without a penny in his pocket, and, like them, he faced the situation with calm and swagger, but he added a magnificence they never, in their maddest moments pretended to. Accidents never separated him from his white waistcoat, though he might have to carry it himself to the laundry, or get his model, 'the little girl,' he called her, to carry it for him. You were always meeting them with the brown paper parcel, Whistler said, and at the nearest friend's house he would stop, and five minutes later come out splendid in another immaculate white waistcoat. In money matters he reckoned like a Rothschild. It was always: 'Huh! five hundred,' that he wanted. Late one afternoon, as Whistler was going to Rossetti's, he met Sandys looking unusually depressed. He stopped Whistler:

'Do, do try and reason with Gabriel, huh! He is most thoughtless. He says I must go to America, and I must have five hundred, huh! and go! But, if I could go, huh! I could stay!'

[E. R. and J. Pennell, *Life of Whistler*, 1908]

Whistler Shows his Work

Helleu,[1] Boldini,[2] and I went at the appointed time. An easel stood where the light was good. Whistling under his breath, speaking first in old-fashioned Parisian French and then with the intonation of New England, Whistler rummaged in a chest of drawers with hidden partitions, made a pretence of looking for something, a trick which strained the patience of Boldini, who was just such another comedian. At last with two finger-tips, whose nails were trimmed mandarin fashion, trembling with agitation, he pushed forward a tiny wooden panel or board, laying it down, fixing it on the shelf of the easel behind the glass of a large frame. Two Molière slippers, with heels raised inside the shoe, tripped back and forth; the locks of his hair fluttered, his lips pouted. With a strident 'Oh! oh!' he slapped Boldini's shoulder and asked for – or rather insisted on – enthusiastic approval: 'Pretty, eh?' he said. It was a cloud over the sea, a note, a nocturne, or a 'scherzo'. If you said nothing, what a Philistine you seemed. Find your way home and come no more to Tite Street – the master appeared to say.

[J.-E. Blanche, *Portraits of a Lifetime*, 1937]

Whistler and the Greaves Brothers

Whistler was not a regular attender at the Limerston Street Studio, but came occasionally, and always accompanied by two young men – brothers – Greaves by name.[3] They let out rowing boats on the Thames and Battersea Park. They simply adored Whistler, and were not unlike him in appearance, owing to an unconscious imitation of his dress and manner. It was amusing to watch the movements of the trio when they came into the studio (always late). The curtain that hung in front of the door would suddenly be pulled back by one of the Greaves, and a trim, prim little man, with a bright, merry eye, would step in with 'Good evening,' cheerfully said to the whole studio. After a second's survey, while taking off his gloves, he would hand his hat to the other brother, who hung it up carefully as if it were a sacred thing – then he would wipe his brow and moustache with a spotless handker-

1. Paul Helleu (1859–1927): see also p. 382.
2. Giovanni Boldini (1845–1931).
3. Walter Greaves (1846–1930) and Henry Greaves (1850–1900).

chief, then in the most careful way he arranged his materials, and sat down. Then, having imitated in a general way the preliminaries, the two Greaves sat down on either side of him. There was a sort of tacit understanding that his and their studies should not be subjected to the rude gaze of the general. I, however, saw, with the tail of my eye, as it were, that Whistler made small drawings on brown paper with coloured chalks, that the figure (always a female figure) would be about four inches long, that the drawing was bold and fine, and not slavishly like the model. The comical part was that his satellites didn't draw from the model at all, that I saw, but sat looking at Whistler's drawing and copying, as far as they could, that. He never entered into the conversation, which was unceasing, but occasionally rolled a cigarette and had a few whiffs, the Greaves brothers always requiring their whiffs at the same moment. The trio packed up, and left before the others always.

[J. E. Christie, quoted in E. R. and J. Pennell, *Life of Whistler*, 1908]

Whistler and Oscar Wilde (1854–1900)

After one of Whistler's brilliant sallies, Wilde said, 'I wish I had said that, Whistler.' 'You will, Oscar, you will,' was Whistler's answer.

[E. R. and J. Pennell, *Life of Whistler*, 1908]

Whistler and Lord Leighton (1830–96)

Val Prinsep[1] remembers Whistler's pressing invitation for him and Leighton to attend:

'During the time he was President of the British Artists, he and the other heads of art sometimes were asked to dine by our President (Sir F. Leighton). ("Rather late to ask *me*, don't you think?" Whistler is said to have remarked.) After dinner, he pressed Leighton and me to come to his lecture, *Ten o'Clock*, which was to be delivered a few days after. – "What's the use of me coming?" Leighton said sadly. "You know I should not agree with what you said, my dear Whistler?" – "Oh," cried Whistler, "come all the same; nobody takes me seriously, don't you know!"'

[E. R. and J. Pennell, *Life of Whistler*, 1908]

1. Val Prinsep (1836–1904).

[401]

Whistler on Lord Leighton's Accomplishments

As art was the last thing looked for in the picture of the Academician, so the artist was the last thing looked for in the Academician. The situation is summed up in Whistler's reply to a group of ladies who were praising Leighton:

'He is such a wonderful musician! – such a gallant colonel! – such a brilliant orator! – such a dignified President! – such a charming host! – such an amazing linguist!' – 'H'm, paints, too, don't he, among his other accomplishments?'

[E. R. and J. Pennell, *Life of Whistler*, 1908]

Whistler and Aubrey Beardsley (1872–98)

Then, for the first time, I learned what he thought of 'aestheticism' and 'decadence.'

'Why do you get mixed up with such things? Look at him! – he's just like his drawings – he's all hairs and peacock plumes – hairs on his head – hairs on his finger ends – hairs in his ears – hairs on his toes. And what shoes he wears – hairs growing out of them!'

[E. R. and J. Pennell, *Life of Whistler*, 1908]

Whistler and Walter Sickert (1860–1942) in the 1890s

Whistler would, on occasion, make use of Sickert's studio. Indeed, one day, seeing a half-finished canvas on the easel, he began working on it, and getting interested, he finished the canvas, carried it off, and sold it as a work of his own. But a coolness was already beginning between them at this time, while Sickert was asserting himself more and more as an independent painter.

[W. Rothenstein, *Men and Memories*, 1978]

Whistler Tries to Ride a Bicycle

His solicitor, Mr. William Webb, tried once to teach him to ride a bicycle. 'Learn it? No,' he said to us. 'Why, I fell right off – but I fell in a rose-bush!'

[E. R. and J. Pennell, *Life of Whistler*, 1908]

Thomas Eakins (1844–1916) and Rosa Bonheur (1822–99)

'He was on terms of intimacy with the entire Bonheur family,' wrote Gilbert S. Parker in 1917, 'and many were the anecdotes that he could relate concerning Rosa and her brothers.' Once when he was dining with them, he wrote to his mother, 'I took my gun & pistol around to show their cousin who was there who is a good mechanic. He said he never saw such beautiful arms & so they are. America beats the world in machinery.' Bill Sartain, who was present, recalled that 'Tom was speaking of our national mechanical skill and to illustrate his point he pulled out from his pocket his Smith & Wesson revolver – (I know of no other person in Paris who ever carried one!) – Rosa put *her* hand into her pocket and pulled out one of the same make.'

[L. Goodrich, *Thomas Eakins*, 1982]

Eakins's Tastes

'He really seemed to prefer things that are outside the range of what are usually reckoned as constituting not only the charms but even the amenities of existence,' Leslie Miller wrote. 'He declared, for example, that he preferred to ride a horse bareback rather than on a comfortable saddle with stirrups, and if you could have seen how he kept his studio and even his house, and on what terms he lived with his monkey and other pets, you would know what I mean.'

[L. Goodrich, *Thomas Eakins*, 1982]

Eakins's Recreations

Eakins read little: seldom novels, which he scorned; mostly scientific works. While in middle years not as active in scientific research as earlier, his chief mental avocation still remained the physical sciences. 'To relax his mind after painting,' Mrs. Eakins said, he would work out problems in calculus. The pianist Mary Hallock Greenewalt, who was also scientifically inclined, but on a more mystical level, said that often when she arrived to pose for him she found him reading a mathematical book, for enjoyment, as others would read a novel. She tried to interest him in the fourth dimension, but he refused to take stock in any such 'poetical mathematics,' saying, 'You can't tie a knot in the fourth dimension.' His pupil Thomas Eagan recalled his teacher walking along the street and doing mathematical problems in his head, to keep himself from 'silliness'. In the dining room hung a blackboard on which any point that came up in conversation could be illustrated. He liked to work with his hands and was a good craftsman; the top floor of the house contained a workroom with carpentry tools and Benjamin's lathe that Tom had drawn as a high-school student.

[L. Goodrich, *Thomas Eakins*, 1982]

Eakins on Whistler

In a loan exhibition at the Pennsylvania Academy in the early 1900s, the Academy's secretary saw him intently studying a painting by Whistler and inquired what he thought of it. 'I think it is a very cowardly way to paint,' he said. Asked whether he did not think that the picture had charm and beauty, he looked at it again and said that he had never thought of that. Later, in 1914, he said in an interview, 'Whistler was unquestionably a great painter, but there are many of his works for which I do not care.' (Yet in his *Music* Whistler's *Sarasate* is represented as hanging on the wall.) 'He was wont to term 'cowardly' those paintings that left much to the imagination,' Gilbert S. Parker wrote. Another phrase of disapprobation was 'no guts'; for him Italian painting had no guts, Weda Cook Addicks recalled.

[L. Goodrich, *Thomas Eakins*, 1982]

Eakins Paints Walt Whitman (1819–92)

It was probably in the spring of 1887 that Talcott Williams, associate editor of the Philadelphia *Press* and friend of both Whitman and Eakins, took the painter over to Camden, to meet the poet. Later, Whitman expressed his opinion of Eakins, recorded by Traubel: 'I asked: "Does Eakins wear well? Is he a good comrade?" W.: "He does: he is: he has seen a great deal: is not too ready to tell it: but is full, rich, when he is drawn upon: has a dry, quiet manner that is very impressive to me, knowing, as I do, its background." I asked: "Did you find him to lack the social gifts? he is accused of being uncouth, unchary, boorish." "Perhaps: I could hardly say: 'lacking social gifts' is vague: what are social gifts?" Then after further cognition: "The parlor puts quite its own measure upon social gifts: I should say, Tom Eakins lacks them as, for instance, it would be said I lack them: not that they are forgotten, despised, but that they enter secondarily upon the affairs of my life. Eakins might put it this way: first there is this thing to do, then this other thing, maybe this third thing, or this fourth: these done, got out of the way, *now* the social graces. You see, he does not dismiss them; he only gives them their place." He "remembered well" his first meeting with Eakins. "He came over with Talcott Williams: seemed careless, negligent, indifferent, quiet: you would not say retiring, but amounting to that." They left. Nothing was heard from them for two or three weeks. "Then Eakins turned up again – came alone: carried a black [obviously blank] canvas under his arm: said he had understood I was willing he should paint me: he had come to start the job. I laughed: told him I was content to have him go ahead: so he set to: painted like a fury. After that he came often – at intervals, for short sketches." I interrupted: "And that is the result" – motioning downstairs. W. at once: "Yes: and that is the result." Eakins was "no usual man," but he did "not lack the graces of friendship." He had "no parlor gallantries" but "something vastly better." At first sight "he might be taken to be negative in quality, manner, intuition" but that surface impression "wears off after a few meetings."'

[H. Traubel, *With Walt Whitman in Camden*, 1906, quoted in L. Goodrich, *Thomas Eakins*, 1982]

Whitman's Opinion of Eakins's Portrait of Him

From Traubel's record, April 16, 1888: 'I never knew of but one artist, and that's Tom Eakins, who could resist the temptation to see what they think ought to be rather than what is.'

The same day: 'W. has hung the Eakins portrait in a better light. "Does it look glum?" he inquired: "that is its one doubtful feature: if I thought it would finally look glum I would hate it. There was a woman from the South here the other day: she called it the picture of a jolly joker. There was a good deal of comfort to me in having her say that – just as there was when you said at Tom's [Harned] the other day that it made you think of a rubicund sailor with his hands folded across his belly about to tell a story."'

May 10: 'W. talked of portraits. He affects "the unceremonious – the unflattered. Of all portraits of me made by artists I like Eakins's best: it is not perfect but it comes nearest being me. I find I often like the photographs better than the oils – they are perhaps mechanical, but they are honest. The artists add and deduct: the artists fools with nature – reform it, revise it, to make it fit their preconceived notion of what it should be. We need a Millet [Whitman's favorite painter] in portraiture – a man who sees the spirit but does not make too much of it – one who sees the flesh but does not make a man all flesh – all of him body. Eakins almost achieves this balance – almost – not quite: Eakins errs just a little – a little – in the direction of the flesh" '

May 14: 'The Eakins portrait gets there – fulfills its purpose: sets me down in correct style, without feathers – without any fuss of any sort. I like the picture always – it never fades – never weakens.'

[Horace Traubel, quoted in L. Goodrich, *Thomas Eakins*, 1982]

Eakins's 'Honours'

It was probably in answer to a request from Morris[1] for biographical information, including his honors, that Eakins wrote on April 23, 1894: 'I was born in Philadelphia July 25th, 1844. I had many instructors, the principal ones Gérôme, Dumont (sculptor), Bonnat.

'I taught in the Academy from the opening of the schools until I was turned out, a period much longer than I should have permitted myself to remain there.

'My honors are misunderstanding, persecution, and neglect, enhanced because unsought.'

[L. Goodrich, *Thomas Eakins*, 1982]

Eakins Remembered by the Boxer Billy Smith

Through Cranmer and another sportswriter, Henry Walter Schlichter, Eakins got to know some of the Philadelphia fighters and persuaded them to come to the Chestnut Street studio to pose. One of them, the featherweight Billy Smith, became the central figure in two paintings. In preparation for *Between Rounds* Eakins did a head-and-bust portrait of him in the pose of the painting – not a sketch but a finished portrait – and gave it to him. When Billy sold the canvas in 1940 he wrote the Walker Galleries, who had handled the sale: 'You want to know something about Mr. Eakins, and the picture. First, as Mr.

1. Harrison S. Morris, managing director of the Pennsylvania Academy.

Eakins would say, when asked to speak of himself, My all is in my work. But, what I know. It was 1898, when Mr. Eakins came to a Boxing Club, to get a model for his first fight picture, titled, *Between Rounds*. He choose me. I posed first for the picture you just sold.

'Then, for the Between Rounds, and next for the one titled Salutat. Mr. Eakins, to me was a Gentleman and an Artist, and a Realist of Realists. In his work he would not add or subtract. I recall, while painting the portrate you just sold, I noticed a dark smear across my upper lip, I asked Mr. Eakins what it was. He said it was my mustache, I wanted it of, He said it was there, and there it stayed. You can see that he was a Realist.'

[L. Goodrich, *Thomas Eakins*, 1982]

Eakins's Attitude to Nudity

Eakins' reputation was not helped by his frankness about nudity. One of his best friends among socially solid Philadelphians was James Mapes Dodge. Mrs. Dodge told me that he once invited her and her husband to come to his studio to see a red-haired female model he and Murray had. When he admitted them, there stood the model completely nude. Mrs. Dodge said that it was the first time she had ever seen either a woman or a man nude. Eakins insisted on taking them over to examine her; he ran his hands down her side and said how fine it was ('He didn't need to do that,' Mrs. Dodge said), and took them around to admire her back. Mrs. Dodge also told of some 'lantern slides' (perhaps photographs) that he had given them, of himself and models, one or more showing him carrying a nude female in his arms – 'not the kind of thing for a respectable widow,' so she gave them to her son Kern. (I would have doubted this except that I saw one or more similar photographs in Mrs. Eakins' possession.)

[L. Goodrich, *Thomas Eakins*, 1982]

Eakins Asks a Sitter to Pose Nude

Mrs. E. Farnum Lavell, née Eleanor S. F. Pue, a pleasant, witty, rather conventional person, told me that when Eakins in 1907 asked her, then twenty, to pose for her portrait, she hesitated; people said that he had a bad reputation and might say something 'disgusting' to her. But he never did; he told a few 'broad stories' of student days in Paris, but 'he made no advances.' She said that he had 'a sensual face' and 'was like a bear – big, dirty, that thick through.' For the portrait she wore a very low-necked dress; he admired the bones of her shoulders and chest, and would poke at them with the handle of his brush and say 'beautiful bones!' He asked her to pose nude, kept on urging her, and finally went to her mother and asked her to allow her daughter to do so. 'He seemed to feel that there was something disgusting in my not being willing to.' But Mrs. Lavell felt that his interest was purely artistic.

[L. Goodrich, *Thomas Eakins*, 1982]

Thomas Eakins and the Model

September 10: 'I told him [Whitman] a story I had heard of Eakins – of a girl model who had appeared before the class, nude, with a bracelet on – Eakins, thereupon, in anger, seizing the bracelet and throwing it on the floor. W. enjoying it: "It was just like Eakins – and oh! a great point is in it, too!" '

[W. Traubel, 1889, quoted in L. Goodrich, *Thomas Eakins*, 1982]

An Unfinished Portrait by Eakins

The reason it was not completed was explained by Leslie Miller, who wrote me: 'Mrs. Gillespie refused to go near him again after he received her one blistering hot day in his studio up three or four flights of stairs in the old Presbyterian Building on Chestnut Street dressed only in an old pair of trousers and an *undershirt!* He wanted her to give him one or two more sittings but she not only refused them, but wanted me to destroy the portrait after it came into my possession, – which of course I didn't do.'

[L. Goodrich, *Thomas Eakins*, 1982] The painting represented a formidable dowager, aged about seventy-five.

Ilya Repin (1844–1930) Paints the Barge Haulers on the Volga

And so I attained the high point of my epic with the Volga barge haulers: at last I was doing a study of Kanin! What a feast for me. Before me stood my long-sought-for subject – Kanin. After fastening the strap to the barge and slipping his chest into it, he leaned into it and let his arms hang. There were not too many onlookers – only his fellow barge haulers . . .

Although it was Sunday, a free day, peasants from the nearby village of Shiriaevo did not even come close. In their eyes, something fateful, something dreadful, was happening at the barge on the shore: a man was selling his soul to the Antichrist . . . Even at a distance the women would turn their backs . . . Children were forbidden to come near us . . . There in the huts of Shiriaevo all were gripped by deadly fear, they spoke in whispers.

But here on the riverbank, I was free to lead a soul astray, contemplating and drawing the likeness of my perfect, long-wished-for hauler type.

How lucky that Kanin had not taken it into his head to go to the bathhouse or have a haircut, as happened with some models who would arrive so trimmed and shaved as to be unrecognizable. He had been instructed beforehand and, like all serious people, posed seriously. He ably held the unfamiliar pose and easily adjusted without disturbing me. . . I was absorbed and deeply impressed by Kanin as he posed in the strap. Thus it was, I thought, when Hellas lost its political independence, that the rich patricians of primitive Rome would buy for themselves, at fairs where slaves were sold, philosopher-scholars to educate their children. And so some philosopher, educated on Plato, Aristotle, Socrates, Pythagoras, and driven into a pit or cave together with runaway criminals, would be herded off to the Black Sea and would lie there in the burning sun until someone purchased him, an old man in his sixties . . .

And Kanin, with a rag on his head, with clothing patched together by his own hand and worn through again, was a man who inspired much respect: He was like a saint undergoing an ordeal.

Many years later I remembered Kanin when Leo Tolstoy, in a hempen shirt soaked with sweat, would pass before me along the furrow, following the horse-drawn wooden plow.

[I. E. Repin, *Dalekoe blizkoe (Far and near)*, translation in E. K. Valke-nier, *Ilya Repin*, 1990]

A Student of Repin's Describes him at Work

'He worked with us as a great, exceptional painter with his artistic intuition and passion . . . but not as a pedagogue who knows where and how to steer his students. Without a well-defined plan, method or knowledge, he would often contradict himself, would praise [today] what he had criticized yesterday . . . This gave us a basis not to believe in his sincerity, and only later did we understand that he was sincere and truthful on both occasions.'

It was best, she wrote, not to listen to Repin but to watch him paint: 'It's fascinating to see him work . . . His face changes completely, he sees nothing except his model [and] one feels such a power on him . . . He paints with very large brushes, but with such virtuosity! The brush obeys him magically. With it he paints both large masses of flesh and puts [a speck of] light into an eye, or outlines very fine forms. And it performs all that he wants. Somehow, his brushes are bewitched.'

[A. P. Oustroumova-Lebedeva, *Autobiograficheskie zapiski (Autobiographical writings)*, quoted in E. K. Valkenier, *Ilya Repin*, 1990]

Repin and Tolstoy, 1891

We often went bathing together, walking along a forest path some two versts to the Tolstoys' bathing place in a small river with very cold water. After leaving the estate Lev Nikolaevich would at once take off the old shoes he had made, stick them under his leather belt and walk barefoot . . . During one walk Lev Nikolaevich suddenly said:

'I'll go off by myself now.'

Seeing that I was surprised, he added:

'At times I like to stand and pray somewhere deep in the forest.'

'And may I then sketch you from somewhere behind the bushes?'

'Oh, no harm in that. Now that I am being characterized as a maiden who has lost all honor and conscience, I don't refuse anybody.'

I drew a sketch of him at prayer, barefoot. I wanted to paint him life size at this moment.

One hot August day, in the full glare, Lev Nikolaevich was getting ready after lunch to plow a widow's field. I received permission to come along. We started out at one o'clock . . . At the stables Lev Nikolaevich took two work horses, put on the work collars without breastbands, and led them by the reins . . .

We went into a wretched little yard. Lev Nikolaevich . . . walked into a little barn he knew well and dragged out a wooden plow . . . Six hours without rest he plowed the black earth, moving uphill and then descending along the slope toward the ravine. I had a sketchbook with me and, losing no time, situated myself at mid-point of his path to catch with pencil strokes the moment when the whole procession passed. That took less than one minute. In order to double the time, I walked across the plowing line to the opposite point, some twenty steps distant, and again situated myself there to await the return of the group. I verified only the contours and the relative sizes of the figures; the shadows were added later, from one vantage point, and at one moment in time.

Several times some Yasnaya Poliana peasants walked by, doffed their caps, bowed, and went on as if taking no notice of the Count's exploit. But then comes a group, evidently from farther away . . . They stop and stand for a long, long while. And a strange thing [happens]: never in my life have I seen a clearer expression of irony on a simple peasant face.

[I. E. Repin, *Dalekoe blizkoe (Far and near)*, translation in E. K. Valkenier, *Ilya Repin*, 1990]

The Appearance and Character of John Singer Sargent

So powerfully built physically, this fine looking man who could have afforded the most costly pleasures, led a life regulated like a metronome, closed in, preferring the company of his sisters, his cousins, and a few respectable ladies of their circle. He dined, far more frequently than he did at the Ritz, with daubers at an obscure club in Chelsea. We can be certain that the conversation of these professionals did not grate upon their neighbour. I saw him – he who during the war years planed over events like a swallow over an ocean in fury – break down completely when one of his charming nieces, who had married the son of André Michel, was killed at Saint Gervais by a shell from Big Bertha. He was devoted to bachelorhood. A regulated life, with no passions other than art – how many artists have not dreamed of that? But Sargent? He hated the portraitist's métier. What were his motivations? He had no needs, no ambitions. No escapades. No avarice. A monotonous existence – why did he accept it? That was his secret.

A young girl, brought up at 'John's' knee (as the saying is), once said, when her aunt, one of the painter's Egerias, had her back turned: 'What can the biographer of dear Mr. Sargent have to divulge? His letters are those of an Eton schoolboy.'

[J.-E. Blanche, *Propos de Peintre: De Gauguin à la Revue Nègre*, 1928]

Sargent in his Studio

The studio was studded with easels. 'Blanche, please don't look at that portrait.' But on reflection he asked my advice. Covering a surface with forms and lines in a definite pattern was beyond Sargent's powers; he invoked the aid of the dressmaker and the florist and filled in holes with the help of pieces of furniture; satin and velvet flowed in cascades, cushions bulged like Zeppelins on sofas, azaleas moved from vases to urns, and arum lilies added a white note to a park-like background that Marcus Stone[1] would not have rejected. The choice of a piece of furniture, of a material for a canvas for which he had an order, became a problem for him; seeing him so unhappy in not having a particular type of Louis XV armchair and a combined inlaid cupboard and writing-desk of the same style, I gave him some that I had at one time in my possession and which he was very anxious to have. In exchange he made me a gift of a sketch he had done of me at Auteuil. He used to say, 'Painting a portrait would be quite amusing if one were not forced to talk while working. What a nuisance having to entertain the sitter and to look happy when one feels wretched . . .'

[J.-E. Blanche, *Portraits of a Lifetime*, 1937]

Sargent as a Portrait Painter

It was a common experience for him, as probably for all portrait painters, to be asked to alter some feature in a face, generally the mouth; indeed, this happened so often that he used to define a portrait as 'a likeness in which there was something wrong about the mouth.' He rarely acceded, and then only when he was already convinced that it was wrong. In the case of Francis Jenkinson, the Cambridge Librarian, it was pointed out that he had omitted many lines and wrinkles which ought to be shown on the model's face. He refused to

---

1. Marcus Stone (1840–1921).

make, as he said, 'a railway system of him.' His refusal more than once led to scenes. On one occasion the lady who had taken exception to the rendering of her mouth became hysterical and fainted. Sargent was the last man in the world to cope with such a situation. A friend who happened to call found him helplessly contemplating the scene. The model was restored to sense, but the mouth remained as it was. To another lady who complained of the drawing of her nose he said: 'Oh, you can alter a little thing like that when you get it home.' To Lady Cholmondeley, of whom he did two portraits, he always called the planes of the nostrils 'the devil's own.'

A sitter has given me an account of being painted by Sargent in 1902:

At one of my sittings during which Mr. Sargent painted my hands I sat motionless for two hours. A certain way in which I had unconsciously put my hands together pleased him very much because the posture, he said, was clearly natural to me. He implored me not to move. We worked very hard – he with his magical brush, I with my determination to control fidgets and the restless instincts to which sitters are prone when forced to remain still for any length of time, for the most part we were silent. Occasionally I heard him muttering to himself. Once I caught: 'Gainsborough would have done it! . . . Gainsborough would have done it!'

He was working at fever heat, and it was so infectious that I felt my temples throbbing in sympathy with his efforts, the veins swelling in my brow. At one moment I thought I was going to faint with the sense of tension and my fear to spoil the pose which had enthused him.

At the end of two hours he declared that the hands were a failure, and he obliterated them.

'I must try again next time,' he said in a melancholy tone. At the next sitting he painted the hands quickly as they now appear a tour de force in the opinion of some, utterly unsuccessful in the eyes of others.

My husband came several times to the sittings. On one occasion Mr. Sargent sent for him specially. He rode across the Park to Tite Street.

He found Mr. Sargent in a depressed mood. The opals baffled him. He said he couldn't paint them. They had been a nightmare to him, he declared, throughout the painting of the portrait.

That morning he was certainly in despair . . . Presently he said to my husband: 'Let's play a Fauré duet.' They played, Mr. Sargent thumping out the bass with strong stumpy fingers. At the conclusion Mr. Sargent jumped up briskly, went back to the portrait and with a few quick strokes, dabbed in the opals. He called to my husband to come and look: 'I've done the damned thing,' he laughed under his breath.

My sister, on the occasion of her visit to the studio during my last sitting, remembers seeing Mr. Sargent paint my scarf with one sweep of his brush.

What appeared to interest him more than anything else when I arrived was to know what music I had brought with me.

To turn from colour to sound evidently refreshed him, and presumably the one art stimulated the other in his brain.

He used to tell of Duse[1] that she consented to give one sitting. She arrived at midday and at five minutes to one rose from her chair, saying, 'Je vous souhaite de vivre mille ans et d'avoir la gloire et beaucoup d'enfants, mais au revoir,' and he never saw her again.

[E. Charteris, *John Sargent*, 1927]

Sargent and Isabella Stewart Gardner

In his unpublished memoir of Sargent (in the Boston Athenaeum Archives), Thomas Fox, the architect who succeeded Stanford White on the murals, repeats a story concerning the brocade background of this portrait (without mentioning Mrs Gardner by name, that is). He said to his sitter he wanted a piece of Venetian brocade – ' "but unfortunately, it is on the wall of my studio in London". To which the lady replied, "Never mind that, Sargent, I knew exactly what would be the proper background for my portrait when I decided to have you paint it, and I have the other half of the piece upstairs . . ." '

[S. Olson, *John Singer Sargent: His Portraits*, 1986]

Sargent Ceases to Paint Portraits

It was about the same time that Sargent said to someone who lamented that in his painting he had veiled, and not revealed, the face of Jehovah:[2] 'You forget I have given up painting portraits.'

[E. Charteris, *John Sargent*, 1927]

Sargent's Admirations

March 6 [1902]. Rothenstein and his wife to dinner, full of amusing and malicious gossip about Sargent, etc. It seems Sargent now considers Rossetti the greatest modern artist. He also recommends to his sitters the abominable work of an Italian named Mancini,[3] who

1. Eleonora Duse (1859–1924), Italian-born actress.
2. In his decorations for the Boston Public Library.
3. Antonio Mancini (1852–1930).

plasters his paint on by the inch and has the taste of a *commis-voyageur*. Sargent gave this protagonist in paint a sketch by himself. This Mancini gave it to a really great artist, Wertheimer's French cook; the cook in turn gave it to young Wertheimer, who gave it to his father, who in turn gave it back to Sargent.

[C. Ricketts, *Self-portrait, taken from the Letters and Journals,* 1939]

XXI
THE SYMBOLISTS AND THE
FIN DE SIÈCLE

ॐ

This rather miscellaneous section contains anecdotes about artists linked either to the Symbolist Movement or to the idea of Decadence, or who in some other way seem to represent the fin de siècle *sensibility, as Sickert and Toulouse-Lautrec both did in their well-developed taste for (somewhat different) kinds of low life.*

It also demonstrates the strong links between artistic life in England and in France at this period: English artists are often seen in French settings, and vice-versa.

Pierre Puvis de Chavannes (1824–98) on Memory

Whilst M. de Chavannes was at Dieppe studying sea effects before starting on the panel he named *Vision antique*, Comtesse Greffulhe[1] was surprised to see that he was not making sketches. Seeing him on the beach one morning she said: 'Maître, where are your studies – you don't seem to be painting from nature like Monet, Renoir, Helleu, Gervex and the rest of our friends?'

'Madame,' he replied, pointing to his head that looked like a cavalry officer's, 'here are my studies, in my memory box.'

[J.-E. Blanche, *Portraits of a Lifetime*, 1937]

The Personality of Gustave Moreau (1826–98)

Aug. 30 [1901]. T. S. Moore to grub. He has met an old pupil of Gustave Moreau, now actually a landscape-painter. It seems that G. Moreau had a fascinating and affectionate personality, but was utterly devoured by self-criticism and obstinate hesitation. He suspected his work of not being entirely right, and was so morbidly conscious of coldness or indifference in others that he destroyed picture after picture and drawing after drawing. Between the ages of fifty and sixty he ceased to paint, declaring that he was not an artist. He combined great erudition in art matters with lack of balance in criticism, liking greatly, loathing greatly, and selecting from a man's work what was often not the most typical. This pupil states, and this I can quite believe, that G. Moreau had learnt his work entirely by heart, that before Nature and the antique he drew Gustave Moreau, adding the peculiarities of his type where it did not exist. This pupil was once drawing from the model in a foreshortened position; his master came up and said, 'This is wrong,' and corrected it, ignoring the foreshortening. This should possibly be taken with a grain of salt. That lack of balance in criticism seems very common in this century. I fancy that the element of competition and speculation surrounding the arts is answerable for this. Moreau loathed Whistler. This I understand. He would, however, fall in love with some stray work by an artist or pupil of his and buy it, oblivious of all the rest of the show or the man's

1. One of Proust's models for the Duchess of Guermantes in *A la recherche du temps perdu*.

work. In this he is singularly modern and wrong, for really good work is the result of a good state of things: a peach-tree produces peaches, a gooseberry-bush only gooseberries. Quality in each does not destroy kind, there are pictures by Puvis more admirable than others, but the worst is a Puvis. This is hardly true: a great man is often very bad, but an ordinary man is never really good.

Moreau was so pleased with a landscape by this pupil that he told him to do only landscapes. 'Do not do figures.' The pupil answered, 'I shall do figures also, but I shall not show them to you.' G. Moreau smiled, shook him by the shoulders, and said, 'You must show both to me.'

[C. Ricketts, *Self-portrait taken from the Letters and Journals*, 1939]

Auguste Rodin (1840–1917) Visits London as President of the International Association

Charles Cottet[1] and I used to convoy Rodin, who was always punctual, although he wore no watch and appeared to live on another planet. He used to be at the Gare du Nord in Paris an hour before the train left, fearing that he might miss it. Since at that time of the year the cold was severe, he wore a fur-lined coat with an astrakhan collar. A white silk scarf, entwined about his long fair hair that was going grey and his stream-like beard, enwrapped him up to the ears. His old re-ironed top-hat 'with eight high-lights' seemed like a shoot growing from his highly polished boots that were just visible above his snow-shoes. When the heat of the dining-car drove him to shed his coat and muffler, travellers used to be amused when they saw his frock-coat, which Poole had made for him, blossoming with the rosette of a Commander of the Legion of Honour. Turning to us he said:

'In my trunk I have my foreign orders, just in case I have to appear at Court. I always ask the Secretary at the Elysée which of them are proper to wear. Rose[2] worries me since she has found out that gentlemen have travelling suits; however, when I go to London which is an aristocratic city, I dress as when I go to garden parties at the British Embassy.'

[J.-E. Blanche, *Portraits of a Lifetime*, 1937]

1. Charles Cottet (1863–1925), French painter.
2. Rose Beuret, Rodin's long-time mistress. He married her in 1917, two weeks before her death.

Rodin in England and Germany

May 2 [1903].

Legros[1] called in afternoon to fetch me to see his new etchings. One of them is good in design: 'Le Viol'. He was better, almost himself, and told me these two stories. He had taken Rodin to see Henley and Ionides; each in his way had, after praising Rodin's work, made use of the same phrase: 'If you want to succeed in England!' Rodin ended by saying, 'What you tell me is doubtless right, but *je me contente de la journée d'un ouvrier pour faire ce que je fais.*'[2] The answer is superb. Rodin recently was in Germany, when a regiment with its band crossed his carriage. Rodin slowly got up, touched his hat, and sat down again waiting for events; he thought the band was there to meet him.

[C. Ricketts, *Self-portrait, taken from the Letters and Journals*, 1939]

Rodin Comes to Lunch with Renoir

As we were leaving the studio, we heard the sound of a motor-horn, and Rodin drove up, in high good humour.

Renoir: You haven't been able to give up your automobile either, have you? I am always complaining about mine, but I am very glad to have it when I want to go over to Nice.

Rodin: It belongs to one of my admirers, the Countess of X.

Renoir: A most remarkable woman, isn't she?

Rodin: Her heart and mind are one and the same. I must tell you her latest *bon mot*. The Countess was in the studio while I was having my hair trimmed. We were talking about the importance of proceeding with the utmost care in making restorations in cathedrals – meddling with any national property in fact, when a gentleman delegated by some of my friends came to tell me that the State was going to accept the donation of my works.

'Jules,' the Countess exclaimed to the barber, 'be careful you don't cut off too much; the Master is about to become national property!'

[A. Vollard, *Renoir, an Intimate Record*, 1925]

---

1. Alphonse Legros (1837–1911).
2. 'It's enough for me to do my day's work as an ordinary workman.'

Rodin on Food and Nature

Rodin: What handsome children, Madame! What did you feed them on?

Madame Renoir: My own milk, of course!

Rodin: If you nursed them yourself, what happened to your social duties?

Madame Renoir could hardly keep from laughing. 'We can sit down at the table now,' she said, changing the subject. 'You are going to have some olives grown on our own place, Monsieur Rodin.'

'The Greeks lived on these!' said Rodin, taking an olive between his thumb and forefinger. 'All that they needed was a piece of black bread, some goat's milk, and water from a near-by stream! How happy the Greeks were in their poverty, and what wonders they left us! The Parthenon, for instance . . . I believe I have discovered the real inspiration of their masterpieces. The secret of the Greeks lay in their love of Nature!

'Nature! On my knees before Nature I have always sculptured my finest pieces. People have often reproached me for not putting a head on my *Homme qui marche*. Does one walk with one's head?'

[A. Vollard, *Renoir, an Intimate Record*, 1925]

Rodin and Ingres

But what did that other *masked word* Beauty signify for Rodin?

'Madame,' he cried, whilst working on Mary Hunter's bust, 'as a sculptor I see you as Pallas Athanèia [*sic*], as a painter I should see you as Hélène Fourment – you resemble Rubens's portraits of her. But you are a more delicate Hélène, an Englishwoman of the period of Pericles. Your skin has the whiteness of turbot that one sees lying on the marble slabs of your amazing fishmongers; it looks as if it were bathed in milk. Ah, Madame . . .' And here he kissed Mary's hand a little too greedily. When she told me of his emotion, of his excitement, when he and she were together alone in his studio at Meudon, I reminded her of J. Dominique Ingres's frenzy in the presence of the Comtesse d'Haussonville. When he was painting her he was obliged to arrange the folds of the heavy material of the dress which obscured her form. He was so much moved that he begged her to allow him to touch her body and

Mme d'Haussonville granted him this favour. Ingres thereupon fell at her feet, weeping.

[J.-E. Blanche, *Portraits of a Lifetime*, 1937]

Rodin on Busts

'Busts have more chance to survive than memorials, whose real place is the cemetery; besides, people's taste changes. The family prefers to see the deceased as he was dressed during his lifetime. Look at the Campo Santo at Genoa – those clothes, those boatmen's hats, those fashion plates in stone. A human head is a universe and the portrait sculptor is an explorer'.

[J.-E. Blanche, *Portraits of a Lifetime*, 1937]

James Ensor (1860–1949) Plays the Piano

If literature tempted him, so did music. He composed and improvised. One day Blanche Rousseau witnessed the way in which he revenged himself by means of notes upon those who attacked him with words:

'At a wedding dinner, with a large number of prosperous middle-class people present, Ensor, pale and silent, withstood their mockery, but with constrained smiles, disdainful glances, and now and then a brief lightning flash of anger or terrifying irony. Sitting not far from him, I saw what was taking place and almost trembled. All of a sudden, one of the guests turned to him: 'Some music, James. *Your* music!' People laughed, he resisted, they insisted. He got up, went to the piano, and let loose a discordant fanfare, a tumult of topsyturvy tones, but mocking, violent, filled with unexpected and tragic irony – a sort of 'march of the bourgeois', where animal cries mingled with the din of a gong, broken by a long and sinister howling. Then he returned to his place, with his expression quite unchanged – but the others were no longer laughing.'

[E. Verhaeren, *James Ensor*, 1909]

W. R. Sickert (1860–1942): a Matrimonial Misadventure

I know not which Saturday it was after the Saturday I have just related that I brought to Vale Avenue the news that Sickert had at last succeeded in persuading the young woman to take him for better or for worse, the call of genius having proved in the end stronger than that of youth. We must give them a dinner, said I; and it was agreed that as Sickert's oldest friend I should be host. We must wear evening clothes, said Steer,[1] in deference to the bride; and Tonks[2] reminded me that a wedding feast would seem trite and commonplace if I were to forget the flowers, some floral wreaths for the table; and himself charged himself to bring a great posy to hand to Mrs. Sickert when she arrived. Or would it be better, I asked, to withhold the posy till the moment of their departure? Now, what fish would you like, Tonks? I might get a bass from Devon – Never mind the fish, but let there be champagne, for nothing makes a dinner go like champagne. And as you don't like writing letters, I'll write to tell them that we shall expect them at eight. So be it, I answered; all shall be as you wish it – champagne and flowers. We parted with restrained speech and furtive faces, and when we assembled on the balcony, our eyes set on the Victoria Street end, for they would come that way, the evening became more and more memorable, till, unable to bear the tension any further, I said: If they delay much longer my dinner will be spoilt. The ominous clock struck the half hour, and Steer asked how long we should give them, and I replied that it would indeed be disgraceful if they arrived and found us sitting at table; and Tonks, who always looks distressed if Steer's faintest suggestion is not immediately acted upon, agreed that we should wait till nine. The cabs continued to go by, and it was not till the hands of the clock pointed to the quarter that Tonks cried: Look! This driver is seeking for a number over the way, and not finding it he crosses over. He is coming towards us! He is bringing them to us! The cab stopped, and I said: Now for the pretty shoes, the silk stockings, the grey silk dress. Grey, not white, it will be; registry office brides are wedded in grey. And intense was the moment when Sickert stepped out of the cab; intenser still the next moment, for the bride did not follow him. Why has he not brought her? Where is she? I cried, leaving the balcony and running down to meet him. You shall hear presently, said Sickert, speaking almost inaudibly. She is not dead? I could not check the words. No, she is not dead, he answered; and in mournful silence and dejected mien I led my old friend into my house and up the

1. Philip Wilson Steer (1860–1942).
2. Henry Tonks (1862–1937).

staircase into the presence of Tonks and Steer, who had come in from the balcony. She married the other fellow! was all he could say, and we sat staring at each other, unable to find words, and he as dumbfounded as ourselves.

Dinner is served, sir. I'll tell you all about it after dinner, he whispered on the staircase, and our curiosity leaving us no peace we felt that we would have almost bartered the dinner for the story that was to come after dinner; and lest Sickert should change his mind and not tell it, I plied him with wine till the thought came to me that if he were to get tipsy we should not hear it, and the same thought must have been in the minds of Steer and Tonks, for the third time wine was offered to them they refused it. No more wine is needed, Mabel; we'll have coffee in the drawing-room, I said. But Mabel seemed unable to bring herself to close the drawer of the sideboard, and as I dared not ask her to leave we sat exasperated, till at last the closing of the door brought Sickert to his story. He began it in a low, stricken voice: She was always pleading for the morrow, saying that if I gave her time to get accustomed to the thought of marriage she would wed me. At last, coming to the end of my patience and unable to think of any other way out of the difficulty, I pressed her into a cab, saying: All your doubts will vanish at the sight of the registry office. The Camden Town registry office, Sickert continued, is not situated in a noble street, but she needn't have noticed it. She did, however, and guessing that it seemed paltry in her eyes, I said: We shall never see the street again. If you had any of the real affection you speak of for me, you wouldn't have asked me to marry you in so mean a street. I really would not like my people to know I was married in Camden Town. It was once a very pretty village, I replied, and with various arguments, all of them good and honest, I persuaded her to come upstairs, but she barely crossed the threshold when her courage seemed to fail her: There are no pictures on the walls! and seeing that nothing would satisfy her but her own parish, I said: You haven't given notice. She answered that she had. But we shall not get to Pimlico before the registry office closes. Why do you want to be married to-day? she asked, turning suddenly, and feeling that I could not say the right thing in any circumstance, we got into the taxi and went for a drive. Anywhere, no matter where, so long as the drive be long, I cried; and the taxi-driver, seeming to understand, took us over Hampstead Heath, and the same things were said over and over again all the way to Barnet.

Did you go as far? I asked, unable to restrain my curiosity. We were within a couple of miles of Barnet before she noticed that we were in the country, and taking fright at the fields and hedgerows, she said: We must go back, and I called to the taxi-driver to return, but he was running out of petrol and said we must go on to Barnet. At Barnet there was a long delay, for the taxi-driver had not had his dinner, and it was in the middle of Hampstead Heath that the taxi broke down. I spoke of my friends, mentioning Mr. Hammersley, but the taxi-man would not leave his machine, and she proposed that he should come inside and play gooseberry. And the three of you spent the night in the cab! I interjected. Did you sleep? No, he went off to sleep and snored, and she dozed a little on my shoulder, and when the heath began to lengthen out I asked her to come for a walk, and she answered: The taxi-man will think we want to leave without paying him; so we didn't go many yards. At eight o'cock the taxi-man began to push his machine, and as we couldn't let him push it by himself we all helped; but we couldn't get it very far, and I don't know what would have happened if we hadn't met another taxi, who took us in tow. Hammersley came down in his dressing-gown, and he heard from me that I wasn't married yet, Edith not liking to be married in Camden Town. Hammersley gave us breakfast, and by the time the taxi-man returned, his taxi mended, she told me her mind was made up. But on arriving at the registry office, she said: Look! look! There's Ernest! and she pointed to a tall fellow in a blue suit and a grey hat leaning on his cane at the door of the office. Are you going to marry him or me? I asked: and she replied: I don't know what I'm going to do now. You had better settle it between you. We agreed to leave it to her, but she said: You must settle it between you. As you can't make up your mind to marry me, I said, I suppose you had better marry him. I can't wait any longer. And I left her with Ernest, whom she married, no doubt, in the Camberwell registry office.

[G. Moore, *Conversations in Ebury Street*, 1924]

Sickert at Dieppe

One day, as we were walking on the lawns of the marine parade with Miss Ethel Sands[1] and Miss Hilda Trevelyan, Sickert proclaimed his

1. Ethel Sands (1873–1962), composer.

theories more seriously than was his custom. He asserted that anything ugly added to a building or a landscape did not really spoil the general effect; on the contrary, that the additions which every period super-imposed on buildings of a former age lent them a pictorial value. (Sickert would not have used the term 'pictorial,' but that was nevertheless what he meant to convey – at least, so we thought.)

[J.-E. Blanche, *Portraits of a Lifetime*, 1937]

Henri de Tolouse Lautrec (1864–1901) and Misia Natanson (Sert)

For Lautrec the summer ended at the beginning of the shooting season. He would put on lemon-yellow oilskins with a sailor's hat of matching material turned back from the face, and in this attire, which he considered in some way connected with hunting and shooting, he would 'open' the shooting season by an exhaustive pub-crawl through the small town. No pub was left out, however sordid it might be, and every autumn the bars of Villeneuve saw the small, frail figure faithfully reappear in its yellow oilskins to perform the opening ceremony.

There was another sport which he practised with a consummate art for my delectation. I would sit on the grass, leaning against a tree, engrossed in some entrancing book; he would squat beside me, and, armed with a paint-brush, dexterously tickle the soles of my feet. This entertainment, in which his finger sometimes played a part at propitio-us moments, sometimes lasted for hours. I was in the seventh heaven when he pretended to be painting imaginary landscapes on my feet.

We were not old, either of us, and Lautrec was always ready to improvise amusements. One morning, about seven o'clock, the house was roused by a shot, the noise of which seemed to come from his room. We rushed up the stairs in a state of panic, to find him sitting Chinese-fashion on his bed, shooting at a spider which was quietly spinning its web on the opposite wall.

[M. Sert, *Two or Three Muses*, 1953]

Lautrec Plays Bar-tender

Lautrec had just discovered the bar in the rue Royale, when one day he said to me:

'Come along to my studio this evening, after five, when I've done with the model. I'll give you an aperitif.'

I arrived at the appointed hour.

'I'm going to make a *rainbow* for you,' he said. '*Rainbow* is the English word for our *arc-en-ciel*. The Americans have named an aperitif thus. I got the recipe from the bar.'

He had provided himself with an array of silver goblets, and one of bottles containing different sorts of alcoholic liquid. On the table there were, in addition to these, a lemon, crushed ice, and two glasses.

Into a goblet filled with crushed ice, Lautrec duly poured curaçao, anisette, picon, lemon juice and a few drops of angostura bitters. He shook the mixture violently, then poured it into the two glasses. Carefully, he then placed a bit of lemon peel powdered with sugar upon each rim.

'One mustn't,' he said, 'forget the lemon and sugar. It doesn't do any thing to the mixture, but it's nevertheless indispensable. Go on, try it – it's wonderful.'

'It looks like a wonderful way of getting drunk very quickly.'

'Of course not. It has ice in it.'

I tried the mixture and congratulated him, as was only right: 'It's extremely good.'

There was still some left in the goblet – he had poured with a heavy hand. Noticing this, he said:

'Let me have your glass. You must have some more.'

'Pour away – I must do you justice. You're clearly on your way to being a real expert.'

My praise seemed to give him the greatest pleasure.

A little later, Lautrec, invited by the Natansons[1] to a party for *La Revue blanche*,[2] decided to disguise himself as a bar-tender.

Cleanshaven, wearing a little jacket made of white drill, he prepared the new drinks from America, and, thanks to this new talent, secured a well-merited and incontestable success.

He has found his second *métier*.

When I saw him next day, without his beard or moustache, his face plump and childish, his lips red and protruding beneath his big nose, I

1. The brothers Alexandre, Thadée and Louis-Alfred Natanson. Thadée was married at this period to the famous Misia, later Misia Edwards, then Misia Sert.
2. Important Symbolist periodical. The party was held in February 1893.

could not help laughing. He seemed embarrassed, rather shamefaced because of my laughter. Afraid that I might have offended him, I said:

'In whose honour have you taken your beard off? It doesn't suit you too badly, but I was surprised to see you looking like a priest.'

'Natanson asked me to his party; I disguised myself as a bar-tender, and, as you know, barmen are never bearded. So I shaved it off, but it will grow back.'

My ill-considered laughter had mortified Lautrec, and I soon discovered the reason. Dr Bourges had been given, before me, the first glimpse of Lautrec with a smooth face. When he discovered the reason, he had not been able to resist – in his capacity as friend and mentor – dressing Lautrec down and making plain to him the grotesque aspect of his behaviour, and how low he had sunk by turning himself into a flunkey.

[F. Gauzi, *Lautrec et son temps*, 1954]

Edouard Vuillard (1868–1940) and Misia Natanson

In Paris, where the Dreyfus case had provoked a reawakening of social conscience, many things were afoot, amongst others an upsurge of leagues, associations and 'movements' with more or less humanitarian aims. 'Free Bread', 'The League of the Rights of Man', 'The Education of the People through Art' – all these manifestations came into being, organised themselves and penetrated even the *salons*. They introduced a completely new jargon and a sentimental exaggeration of the condition of the lower classes.

The echoes of this agitation reached me at Villeneuve, and I decided to leave for Paris earlier than usual. Vuillard then said he wanted to take a last walk along the banks of the Yonne, and we started at dusk. Looking dreamy and grave he led me beside the river amongst the tall birches with their silvery trunks. He moved slowly over the yellowing grass, and I fell in with his mood; we did not speak. The day was closing in rapidly, so we took a short cut across a beetroot field. Our silhouettes were insubstantial shadows against a pale sky. The ground was rough, I tripped on a root and almost fell; Vuillard stopped abruptly to help me regain my balance. Our eyes met. In the deepening shadows I could see the sad gleam of his glance. He burst into sobs.

It was the most beautiful declaration of love ever made to me.

[M. Sert, *Two or Three Muses*, 1953]

Portrait of Aubrey Beardsley

During the summer of 1895, Symons and I used to see Aubrey every day. His dread of being alone drove him from his hotel and made him give up the project of doing the drawings which Smithers was expecting for the Savoy; publishers' commissions, however, were his only means of livelihood and, moreover, he was obliged to support his family. He was inclined to spend money freely. On the shore we used to meet him, carrying a morocco leather bookbinding of the Louis XIV period with gilt hinges, which he used as a holder for his sheets of drawing paper. Sometimes, as if he were forgetful of his vow as a practising Catholic, he improvised stories so daring that it would have been better had he told them in Greek. He looked like the young hero of *Marriage à la mode* by Hogarth, the skin tightly drawn over his emaciated face, his aquiline nose set between his brown eyes, and, above, his rounded forehead and flat auburn fringes. Two beauty spots on one of his cheeks looked like the patches worn by coquettes.

[J.-E. Blanche, *Portraits of a Lifetime*, 1937]

Beardsley's Illness

One day previously he had taken a stick of charcoal and sketched on a pastel canvas a conductor, beating time, cutting off poppyheads, the heads of players in the orchestra. In a state of delusion he loudly asserted that this was to be his masterpiece; he nearly tore holes into the canvas and the easel tottered. Suddenly he sank back into an armchair and blood poured from his mouth. 'This field of poppies is the field you have sown, it is like an orchestra in which the players take no notice of their conductor. Am I raving?'

From that day onwards Dr. Caron had no doubts about the seriousness of his condition.

[J.-E. Blanche, *Portraits of a Lifetime*, 1937]

XXII

THE MODERN MOVEMENT

᠙

Present-day attitudes towards the history of art are somewhat para-
doxical. Where artists before the middle of the nineteenth century are
concerned, the professional art historians, whose property they have
become, tend to play down personal details in favour of exploring the
broader socio-economic context. The popularity of the Impressionists
and Post-Impressionists with a wide public has tended to maintain
interest in the details of their lives.

This interest is insatiable when one turns to contemporary art. An
enormous amount is known about the lives of leading twentieth-
century artists, and the material has been sifted and re-sifted by
chroniclers, biographers and anthologists. A selection of anecdotes
representing all the 'best known' contemporary artists (perhaps 200 or
even 300 individuals) would certainly swamp a collection of this sort.

In order to avoid this, what I have done is to ask myself, not which
are the best or 'greatest' artists, but which seem to represent the
modern spirit most completely, and to mark the difference between
modern art and everything which preceded it. After taking some
thought, I arrived at a list of five names – Picasso, certainly the most
celebrated artist of the past hundred years; Marcel Duchamp, who
proposed that a work of art could be 'found' rather than made, and
who achieved enormous influence as a result; Jackson Pollock,
champion of subjectivity in art, and the man chiefly responsible for
shifting artistic leadership from Paris to New York; the German
sculptor Joseph Beuys, who returned art to its most primitive roots by
setting himself up as a modern shaman; and Andy Warhol, Duc-
hamp's heir, who made such adroit use of the new phenomenon of
urban mass culture. I have tried to choose stories which are not only
interesting in themselves, but which seem to sum up the particular
qualities of each of them.

Pablo Picasso (1881–1973) at the Bateau Lavoir

The studio was as hot as a furnace in summer, and it was not unusual for Picasso and his friends to strip completely. They would receive visitors half-naked, if not totally so; with just a scarf tied round the waist.

Anyway, Picasso liked wearing no clothes, and the beauty of his limbs was no secret. He had small hands and he was very proud of his Andalusian feet and of his legs, which were well-shaped though a little short. His shoulders were broad and he was generally rather stocky. He always regretted the lack of those few inches, which would have given ideal proportions to his body.

In the winter it was so cold in the studio that the dregs from the tea left in the cups from the day before were frozen by the morning. Even the cold, though, did not prevent Picasso from working without respite.

[F. Olivier, *Picasso and his Friends*, 1933, English trans. 1964]

Picasso During the Blue Period

Picasso, still unknown, was living in the place Ravignan. Someone brought along a rich collector. The collector wanted to know the price of a drawing. It was twenty francs. 'Well then,' said he, looking at the piles of drawings which were scattered around the room, 'you have a fortune here!'

[J. Cocteau, *Picasso*, 1923]

Picasso's Portrait of Gertrude Stein

One day a rich collector came to my house and he looked at the portrait and he wanted to know how much I had paid for it. Nothing I said to him, nothing he cried out, nothing I answered, naturally he gave it to me. Some days after I told this to Picasso, he smiled, he doesn't understand, he said, that at that time the difference between a sale and a gift was negligible.

[G. Stein, *Picasso*, 1938, English trans. 1959]

Kahnweiler's First Visit to Picasso, and the 'Demoiselles d'Avignon'

So one day I set off. I knew the address, 13 rue Ravignan. For the first time I walked up those stairs on the place Ravignan, which I tramped up and down so many times later, and entered that strange structure that was later named 'the laundry boat' because it was made of wood and glass, like those boats that existed then, where housewives used to come to do their washing in the Seine. You had to speak to the concierge of the adjacent building, for the house itself had none. She told me that he lived on the first flight down, for this house, hanging on the side of the hill of Montmartre, had its entrance on the top floor, and one walked down to the other floors. Thus I arrived at the door that I had been told was Picasso's. It was covered with the scrawls of friends making appointments: 'Manolo is at Azon's . . . Totote has come . . . Derain is coming this afternoon . . .'

I knocked on the door. A young man, barelegged, in shirt sleeves, with the shirt unbuttoned, opened the door, took me by the hand, and showed me in. It was the young man who had come a few days before, and the old gentleman he had brought with him was Vollard, who, of course, made one of his characteristic jokes about their visit, telling everyone he knew that there was a young man whose parents had given him a gallery for his first communion.

So I walked into that room, which Picasso used as a studio. No one can ever imagine the poverty, the deplorable misery of those studios in rue Ravignan. Gris'[1] studio was perhaps even worse than Picasso's. The wallpaper hung in tatters from the unplastered walls. There was dust on the drawings and rolled-up canvases on the caved-in couch. Beside the stove was a kind of mountain of piled-up lava, which was ashes. It was unspeakable. It was here that he lived with a very beautiful woman, Fernande, and a huge dog named Fricka. There was also that large painting Uhde had told me about, which was later called 'Les Demoiselles d'Avignon,' and which constitutes the beginning of cubism. I wish I could convey to you the incredible heroism of a man like Picasso, whose spiritual solitude at this time was truly terrifying, for not one of his painter friends had followed him. The picture he had painted seemed to everyone something mad or

1. Juan Gris (1887–1927).

monstrous. Braque,[1] who had met Picasso through Apollinaire, had declared that it made him feel as if someone were drinking gasoline and spitting fire, and Derain[2] told me that one day Picasso would be found hanging behind his big picture, so desperate did this enterprise appear. Everyone who knows the picture now sees it in exactly the same state it was in then. Picasso regarded it as unfinished, but it has remained exactly as it was, with its two rather different halves. The left half, almost monochrome, is still related to the figures from his rose period (but here they are hacked out, as they used to say, modeled much more strongly), whereas the other half, very colourful, is truly the starting-point of a new art.

[D.-H. Kahnweiler and F. Cremieux, *My Galleries and Painters*, 1961, English trans. 1971]

Picasso and the 'Demoiselles d'Avignon'

A murky atmosphere of sensuality, of that sexual excitement which Picasso needs in order to create, surrounds the inception of the picture. To start with, it was called *Le Bordel d'Avignon*, an Avignon which had nothing to do with the former city of the Popes but referred to a street in Barcelona where there was a well-known brothel. 'Avignon,' Picasso told Kahnweiler, 'has always been a name in my life. I lived two steps from the Carrer d'Avinyo, the street where I used to buy my paper and watercolours.' When this name cropped up for the first time, Max Jacob reminded Picasso that his grandmother came from Avignon and later one of the figures in the picture was jokingly called 'Max's grandma'.

[A. Vallentin, *Picasso*, 1963]

Picasso and the Invention of Camouflage

I very well remember at the beginning of the war [World War I] being with Picasso on the boulevard Raspail when the first camouflaged truck passed. It was at night, we had heard of camouflage but we had not yet seen it and Picasso amazed looked at it and then cried out, yes it is we who made it, that is cubism.

[G. Stein, *Picasso*, 1938]

1. Georges Braque (1882–1963).
2. André Derain (1880–1954).

Joan Miró (1893–1983) Visits Picasso in Paris, 1919

When I went to Paris in 1919 I went to see Picasso. He said to me, 'Listen, I'd like to see what you are doing.' I said I would be delighted, and he came to the wretched hotel where I was living in the boulevard Pasteur. He was very interested in what I was doing and said: 'Look here, you know, that's pure poetry.' I always remembered this remark. He was constantly wanting to advance beyond painting into poetry, music and other fields, not to remain stuck with pictorial art.

[Interview with P. M. Adato, 1979, for the film *Picasso: A Painter's Diary*, 1980]

Picasso in the Theatre

On the eve of the dress-rehearsal of *Antigone*, in December 1922, we, actors and author, were seated in the hall of the studio, at Dullin's. A canvas of the same blue as washing balls formed a rocky background. There were openings to the left and right; in the middle, in the air, a hole behind which the role of the chorus was to be declaimed through a megaphone. Around this hole I had hung masks of women, boys and old men which Picasso had painted, or which I had caused to be executed after his models. Under the masks hung a white panel. The question was, how to catch on this surface the sense of a fortunate decoration, which would sacrifice exactitude and inexactitude, both equally costly, to the evocation of a hot day.

Picasso was walking up and down.

He began by rubbing a stick of red chalk on the board, which, because of the evenness of the wood, became marble. Then he took a bottle of ink and traced out several motifs, with masterly effect. All at once he blackened some empty spaces, and three columns appeared. The appearance of these columns was so sudden, so surprising, that we applauded.

Once in the street, I asked Picasso if he had been calculating their approach; if he had been going toward them, or if they had taken him by surprise. He answered that they had taken him by surprise, but that one is always calculating without knowing it; that the Doric column results, like the hexameter, from an operation of thought; and that he perhaps had only now invented this column, in the same way that the Greeks discovered it.

[J. Cocteau, *Picasso*, 1923]

Vladimir Mayakovsky (1893–1930)
Visits Picasso's Studio, 1922

The first studio to be visited in Paris is, of course, that of Picasso. The range and importance of his work make him the greatest painter of the present day. A thick-set Spaniard with a sombre, energetic air, we find him in an apartment hung with paintings that have long been known to us from reproductions. Like the other artists I have met, he passionately admires Douanier Rousseau[1] . . . One question interests me particularly, that of Picasso's return to classicism. Some Russian newspapers have reproduced his latest drawings with the label 'Back to classicism' and with absurd articles to the effect that, if an innovator like Picasso had given up his crazy ideas, why was it that some cranks in Russia were still interested in planes and colours instead of straightforwardly and honestly copying nature? Picasso showed me round his studio, and I can state that the fears are groundless: he is not returning to classicism. His studio is full of the most diverse things, from realistic blue and rose scenes in classical style, all the way to constructions of tin and wire – and all of it dating from the same year. Noticing, on a table, the catalogue of the Russian exhibition in Berlin, I asked if it made him happy to decompose, for the thousandth time, a violin into a tin violin that nobody would buy, that could not be played and only served to appeal to the eye of the artist. For a long time now, our own Tatlin[2] has been saying that the important thing was not to make shiny objects of tin but to see to it that the metal, in which such tasteless constructions are now being made, should in the future be vitalized by artists. 'Why,' I asked him, 'do you not "transfer" your paintings, for instance to the side wall of the Chamber of Deputies' building? Seriously, Comrade Picasso, they would show up better.' He shook his head and was silent for a moment, then he said: 'It's all right for you, you don't have policemen or Monsieur Poincaré.' 'To hell with policemen,' I replied, 'Go along

1. Henri ('Le Douanier') Rousseau (1844–1910).
2. Vladimir Tatlin (1885–1953). Russian Constructionist.

with a pot of paint one night and decorate the walls while they aren't looking. That's what we did with the Monastery of the Passion.' I saw a glint of alarm in Madame Picasso's eye, though she didn't seriously believe it could happen.

[*Maiakovski par lui-même*, ed. C. Frioux, 1961]

Picasso and Professionalism

He was always interested in painting as a metier, an incident that happened once is characteristic. In Paris there was an American sculptress who wished to show her canvases and sculpture at the salon. She had always shown her sculpture at the salon where she was *hors concours* but she did not wish to show sculpture and painting at the same salon. So she asked Miss Toklas to lend her name for the pictures. This was done. The pictures were accepted in the name of Miss Toklas, they were in the catalogue and we had this catalogue. The evening of the *vernissage* Picasso was at my house. I showed him the catalogue, I said to him, here is Alice Toklas who has never painted and who has had a picture accepted at the salon. Picasso went red, he said, it's not possible, she has been painting in secret for a long time, never I tell you, I said to him. It isn't possible, he said, not possible, the painting at the salon is bad painting, but even so if any one could paint as their first painting a picture that was accepted, well then I don't understand anything about anything. Take it easy, I said to him, no she didn't paint the picture, she only lent her name. He was still a little troubled, no, he repeated, you have to know something to paint a picture, you have to, you have to.

[G. Stein, *Picasso*, 1938]

Picasso on Drawing

Picasso said to me once with a good deal of bitterness, they say I can draw better than Raphael and probably they are right, perhaps I do draw better but if I can draw as well as Raphael I have at least the right to choose my way and they should recognise it, that right, but no, they say no.

[G. Stein, *Picasso*, 1938]

[438]

Picasso During the German Occupation of France

Picasso was both protected by his fame and, because of it, particularly exposed. The rumour ran through occupied France that Otto Abetz himself, Hitler's ambassador in Paris and a former professor of drawing, had gone to see him and, shocked by the coldness of his studio, had offered to supply him with coal, an offer which Picasso had refused. It was also said that Abetz had been struck by a photograph of the picture *Guernica* and asked: 'Oh, it was you, Monsieur Picasso, who did that?' to which Picasso had replied: 'No, it was you.'

[A. Vallentin, *Picasso*, 1963]

Picasso Paints Françoise Gilot as 'La Femme Fleur', 1946

He began to paint the portrait of me that has come to be called *La Femme Fleur*. I asked him if it would bother him to have me watch him as he worked on it.

'By no means,' he said. 'In fact I'm sure it will help me, even though I don't need you to pose.'

Over the next month I watched him paint, alternating between that portrait and several still lifes. He used no palette. At his right was a small table covered with newspapers and three or four large cans filled with brushes standing in turpentine. Every time he took a brush he wiped it off on the newspapers, which were a jungle of coloured smudges and slashes. Whenever he wanted pure colour, he squeezed some from a tube on to the newspaper. From time to time he would mix small quantities of colour on the paper. At his feet and around the base of the easel were cans – mostly tomato cans of various sizes – that held greys and neutral tones and other colours which he had previously mixed.

He stood before the canvas for three or four hours at a stretch. He made almost no superfluous gestures. I asked him if it didn't tire him to stand so long in one spot. He shook his head.

'No,' he said. 'That's why painters live so long. While I work I leave my body outside the door, the way Moslems take off their shoes before entering the mosque.'

Occasionally he walked to the other end of the atelier and sat in a wicker armchair with a high Gothic back that appears in many of his paintings. He would cross his legs, plant one elbow on his knee and, resting his chin on his fist, the other hand behind, would stay there studying the painting without speaking for as long as an hour. After that he would generally go back to work on the portrait. Sometimes he would say, 'I can't carry that plastic idea any further today,' and then begin work on another painting. He always had several half-dry unfinished canvases to choose from. He worked like that from two in the afternoon until eleven in the evening before stopping to eat.

There was total silence in the atelier, broken only by Pablo's monologues or an occasional conversation; never an interruption from the world outside. When daylight began to fade from the canvas, he switched on two spotlights and everything but the picture surface fell away into the shadows.

'There must be darkness everywhere except on the canvas, so that the painter becomes hypnotized by his own work and paints almost as though he were in a trance,' he said. 'He must stay as close as possible to his own inner world if he wants to transcend the limitations his reason is always trying to impose on him.'

Originally, *La Femme Fleur* was a fairly realistic portrait of a seated woman. You can still see the underpainting of that form beneath the final version. I was sitting on a long, curved African tabouret shaped something like a conch shell and Pablo painted me there in a generally realistic manner. After working a while he said, 'No it's just not your style. A realistic portrait wouldn't represent you at all.' Then he tried to do the tabouret in another rhythm, since it was curved, but that didn't work out either. 'I don't see you seated,' he said. 'You're not at all the passive type. I only see you standing,' and he began to simplify my figure by making it longer. Suddenly he remembered that Matisse had spoken of doing my portrait with green hair and he fell in with that suggestion. 'Matisse isn't the only one who can paint you with green hair,' he said. From that point the hair developed into a leaf form and once he had done that, the portrait resolved itself in a symbolic floral pattern. He worked in the breasts with the same curving rhythm.

The face had remained quite realistic all during these phases. It seemed out of character with the rest. He studied it for a moment. 'I have to bring in the face on the basis of another idea,' he said, 'not by continuing the lines of the forms that are already there and the space around them. Even though you have a fairly long oval face, what I need, in order to show its light and its expression, is to make a wide oval. I'll compensate for the length by making it a cold colour – blue. It will be like a little blue moon.'

He painted a sheet of paper sky-blue and began to cut out oval shapes corresponding in varying degrees to this concept of my head: first, two that were perfectly round, then three or four more based on his idea of doing it in width. When he had finished cutting them out, he drew in, on each of them, little signs for the eyes, nose, and mouth. Then he pinned them on to the canvas, one after another, moving each one a little to the left or right, up or down, as it suited him. None seemed really appropriate until he reached the last one. Having tried all the others in various spots, he knew where he wanted it, and when he applied it to the canvas, the form seemed exactly right just where he put it. It was completely convincing. He stuck it to the damp canvas, stood aside and said, 'Now it's your portrait.' He marked the contour lightly in carcoal took off the paper, then painted in, slowly and carefully, exactly what was drawn on the paper. When that was finished, he didn't touch the head again. From there he was carried along by the mood of the situation to feel that the torso itself could be much smaller than he had first made it. He covered the original torso by a second one, narrow and stemlike, as a kind of imaginative fantasy that would lead one to believe that this woman might be ever so much smaller than most.

He had painted my right hand holding a circular form cut by a horizontal line. He pointed to it and said, 'That hand holds the earth, half-land, half-water, in the tradition of classic paintings in which the subject is holding or handling a globe. I put that to rhyme with the two circles of the breasts. Of course, the breasts are not symmetrical; nothing ever is. Every woman has two arms, two legs, two breasts, which may in real life be more or less symmetrical, but in painting, they shouldn't be shown to have any similarity. In a naturalistic painting, it's the gesture that one arm or the other makes that differentiates them. They're drawn according to what they're doing. I individualize them by the different forms I give them, so that there often seems to be no relationship between them. From these differing forms one can infer that there is a gesture. But it isn't the gesture that determines the form. The form exists in its own right. Here I've made a circle for the end of the right arm, because the left arm ends in a triangle and a right arm is completely different from a left arm, just as a circle is different from a triangle. And the circle in the right hand rhymes with the circular form of the breast. In real life one arm bears more relation to the other arm than it does to a breast, but that has nothing to do with painting.'

Originally the left arm was much larger and had more of a leaf shape, but Pablo found it too heavy and decided it couldn't stay that way. The right arm first came out of the hair, as though it were falling. After studying it for a while, he said, 'A falling form is never beautiful. Besides, it isn't in harmony with the rhythm of your nature. I need to find something that stays up in the air.' Then he drew the arm extended from the centre of the body stem, ending in a circle. As he did it, he said, half-facetiously, lest I take him too seriously, 'You see now, a woman holds the whole world – heaven and earth – in her hand.' I noticed often at that period that his pictorial decisions were made half for plastic reasons, half for symbolic ones. Or sometimes for plastic reasons that stemmed from symbolic ones, rather hidden, but accessible once you understood his humour.

In the beginning the hair was divided in a more evenly balanced way, with a large bun hanging down on the right side. He removed that because he found it too symmetrical. 'I want an equilibrium you can grab for and catch hold of, not one that sits there, ready-made, waiting for you. I want to get it just the way a juggler reaches out for a ball,' he said. 'I like nature, but I want her proportions to be supple and free, not fixed. When I was a child, I often had a dream that used to frighten me greatly. I dreamed that my legs and arms grew to an enormous size and then shrank back just as much in the other direction. And all around me, in my dream, I saw other people going through the same transformation, getting huge or very tiny. I felt terribly anguished every time I dreamed about that.' When he told me that, I understood the origin of those many paintings and drawings he did in the early 1920s, which show women with huge hands and legs and sometimes very small heads: nudes, bathers, maternity scenes, draped women sitting in armchairs or running on the beach, and occasionally male figures and gigantic infants. They had started through the recollection of those dreams and been carried on as the means of breaking the monotony of classical body forms.

When Pablo had finished the portrait he seemed satisfied. 'We're all animals, more or less,' he said, 'and about three-quarters of the human race look like animals. But you don't. You're like a growing plant and I'd been wondering how I could get across the idea that you belong to

[442]

the vegetable kingdom rather than the animal. I've never felt impelled to portray anyone else this way. It's strange, isn't it? I think it's just right, though. It represents *you*.'

[F. Gilot and C. Lake, *Life with Picasso*, 1964]

Picasso Makes a Man at Vallauris

One day we watched Picasso make a man at Les Fournas. He made him several times.

He opened the door which gave on to my field. The sun came in among the sculptures. He took some earthenware batons of various dimensions. They were the sort used to separate the pots and dishes in the kiln for firing, and were hollow like real bones. He placed them end to end on the floor, and made a recumbent man. In a mere three minutes the body was there. Once joined together, it could arise and, I was going to say, walk.

I can still see the rectangle of sunlight, it too lying on the floor of the studio. We stood quite still at the man's feet and stared at him. I was afflicted by the almost superstitious silence that always overtakes me in the heavy, tenacious, real presence of a person who is not one. This was particularly so now, for I had seen these bones, these earthenware limbs, heaped without significance in a corner of the studio.

And one could also kill this man with a kick.

Picasso went out of the door into the sunlight. We could hear him moving about in the field. He was away sometime. What could he be doing? He seemed to be searching for something. At last we saw him return and come down the step. He was holding a very long green stalk on the end of which there was a little tuft of leaves and a little flower.

I can still see the studio, the plaster casts, its inhabitants, the barred window, and Picasso coming towards us carrying the stalk.

He went up to the recumbent man and placed the stalk in his hand.

In any case, this was precisely the impression I had as I watched him do it, and the recumbent man took the stalk and closed his hand about it, and held it.

Picasso had placed the stalk in the hollow of the piece of earthenware, scarcely higher and of rather less diameter than a napkin ring, which had become the man's hand.

[H. Parmelin, *Picasso Plain*, 1963]

Picasso on Picture Frames

Frames kill, Picasso said one day, they are mourning borders to bad news. Whenever, in some house or other, he saw a canvas of his framed, he generally felt ill at ease – like the canvas itself. It had been dressed up. It had been made to wear gloves. It had been married and wreathed. It was no longer painting as such, but had become the dining-room picture.

[H. Parmelin, *Picasso Plain*, 1963]

Picasso's 'Tête de taureau'

One day his inventive eye fell on an old bicycle saddle and handlebars. Placing the handlebars at the back of the saddle in an upright position he created a bull's head with horns. The illusion was striking and the virtuosity of the transformation conferred a kind of noisy notoriety on this *Tête de taureau*. When it was exhibited after the Liberation Picasso looked at it with an amused air. 'A metamorphosis has taken place,' he said to André Warnod, 'but now I would like another metamorphosis to occur in the opposite direction. Suppose my bull's head was thrown on the rubbish heap and one day a man came along and said to himself: "There's something I could use as handlebars for my bicycle." Then a double metamorphosis would have been achieved . . .'

[A. Vallentin, *Picasso*, 1963]

Picasso and the 'Chair', 1961

Going to see Picasso one day, I found him lying in his bedroom; in front of him, by the window, was a large plywood panel with a huge piece of wrapping paper fastened to it. On this paper, before he had cut it out, he had drawn a strange form, spread out like an octopus with immobile tentacles.

'That's a chair,' said Picasso, 'and, do you see, it's an explanation of Cubism. If you imagine a chair that's been under a steamroller, it would look pretty much like that.'

The chair could certainly be seen. In its decomposed form it was more like a star than a piece of furniture, but a chair created by the brush of Van Gogh or by the spirit of Picasso is not a representation of a piece of furniture but a starting-point for thought. This chair was to become very popular.

After cutting along the lines marked in charcoal Picasso began to fold and curl the paper in such a way that it became vibrant – the *Chair* was being born. Every day, and often several times a day, I brought along the finished pieces to show him and take note of Picasso's corrections. Finally, after much manipulation the *Chair* was ready – I should call it '*Our Chair*', for, although it was Picasso's brain-child, we had helped to bring it into the world, and I believe it will be regarded as a landmark in Picasso's sculptural career.

[L. Prejger, 'Picasso découpe le fer', *L'Oeil*, no. 82, 1961]

Picasso and Self-portraiture

Picasso has painted no self-portrait for many years. When I asked him the reason he said: 'If mirrors did not exist I would not know my age,' and held a hand to his heavily lined face in explanation. But many artists have preferred to paint themselves when age has left a strongly marked individuality in their faces. I asked Picasso the date of his last self-portrait. He replied without hesitation: 'The day when Guillaume Apollinaire died.'

[A. Vallentin, *Picasso*, 1963] Picasso painted and drew many self-portraits in extreme old age, some years after Vallentin's book was written.

Picasso on Death

Brassaï was asked why Picasso did not attend Matisse's funeral:

'Because he didn't like death. He didn't like thinking about death. He didn't like going to the cemetery and to church and all that. And he thought that if he stopped working, that was death. So, that's why until his death he worked every day.'

Pignon was asked what was Picasso's attitude towards death:

'He certainly thought about it, as all men who lived to a very advanced age do. But he never spoke about it. He used to say to me from time to time, "You'll see, you'll see. Once you're older you'll see." But having said that, until his death, he had the desire to work. He used to say "I don't go out any longer in the car because some imbecile will overtake me, he'll run into me and I have still got a lot of paintings to do." That's basically it. He wanted to work more and more and you can sense that in the last canvases he did, in the four or five years before his death.'

[Interviews by Brassaï and Edouard Pignon with P. M. Adato, 1979, for the film *Picasso: A Painter's Diary*, 1980]

Marcel Duchamp (1887–1968) and the 'End' of Painting

Léger[1] has reminisced: 'Before the World War, I went with Marcel Duchamp and Brancusi[2] to the Salon de l'Aviation. Marcel, who was a dry type with something inscrutable about him, walked around the motors and propellers without saying a word. Suddenly he turned to Brancusi: "Painting is finished. Who can do anything better than this propeller? Can you?"'

[Léger in conversation with Dora Vallier, quoted in the catalogue of the Marcel Duchamp retrospective exhibition, New York Museum of Modern Art, 1973]

Duchamp at Lüchow's Restaurant, New York

It was either the second or third time I met him I (as a provincial) took him to lunch at Lüchow's. I must have been twenty-seven or twenty-eight at the time (I blush). I remember he had to borrow a waiter's tie and white jacket before they'd let him sit down. There was a Dutch painting of a sinking ship on the wall between us. Wishing to impress him I said, 'What a piece of shit that is.' The luncheon was taken up by his kindly and patiently explaining to me what was good about the painting.

[W. Copley, quoted in Duchamp exhibition catalogue, 1973]

Duchamp at the Biltmore Hotel, New York

A final sentimental anecdote. Now I think it was the second time I met him. Yes, the first time I had to send him a telegram. I got a postcard back telling me what bar to meet him in. A lot of feet on the rail and twice as many eyes glued on television.

1. Fernand Léger (1881–1955).
2. Constantin Brancusi (1876–1957).

We had agreed this time to meet in the lobby of the Hotel Biltmore. It seems that the Hotel Biltmore has lots of lobbies.

I found him after a frantic hour and was groveling with apologies. He was unruffled and incredibly not annoyed. 'I often come here just to ride the elevators,' he said.

[W. Copley, quoted in Duchamp exhibition catalogue, 1973]

Duchamp and the Dalmatian Puppy

When our new Dalmatian puppy tumbled into the living room one evening he said, 'So you have the positive! What do you suppose the negative looks like?'

[G. H. Hamilton, quoted in Duchamp exhibition catalogue, 1973]

Duchamp's Goal

But when he was sought out in 1956 by a budding aesthetician, Lawrence D. Steefel, who was then a graduate student of art history at Princeton University, he formulated his own artistic goal: 'to grasp things with the mind the way the penis is grasped by the vagina.'

[A. G. Marques, *Marcel Duchamp: Eros, c'est la vie*, 1981]

Duchamp's Epitaph

Along with his mortal remains, Duchamp had arranged to confront the citizens of Rouen with one final, impish provocation: a special dispensation had to be extracted from the cemetery authorities to permit the grave to be inscribed with Marcel's chosen epitaph: '*D'ailleurs, c'est toujours les autres qui meurent*' (Besides, it is always the others who die).

[A. G. Marques, *Marcel Duchamp: Eros, c'est la vie*, 1981]

Jackson Pollock (1912–56), John Graham (1881–1961) and Frederick Kiesler (1896–1965)

One night that January she [Lee Krasner] was walking back from Graham's apartment with Graham and Jackson when a short, 'funny man with an overcoat down to his ankles and wearing a homburg' approached them and embraced Graham 'very warmly.' Graham

introduced him – 'This is Frederick Kiesler' – then turned to introduce
Jackson. 'And *this*,' he said, searching for the right words, 'is Jackson
Pollock' – his deep voice expanded to fill the empty square – '*the
greatest painter in America*.' The sound of the phrase combined with
the frigid air to take Lee's breath away. After a long pause, Kiesler,
another of the early modernist missionaries, slowly lifted his homburg
and bowed 'almost to the sidewalk,' Lee remembers. When he
straightened up, he turned to Graham and asked in a stage whisper,
'North or South America?'

    [S. Naifeh and G. W. Smith, *Jackson Pollock. An American Saga*, 1989]
    Lee Krasner (1911–84), an Abstract Expressionist painter, married Jack-
    son Pollock in 1944.

Pollock and the 'Drip' Technique

Standing over the canvas, flinging a stream of paint from the end of a
stick, Jackson found the potency that had eluded him in real life. When
a woman asked him, 'How do you know when you're finished [with a
painting]?' Jackson replied, 'How do you know when you're finished
making love?'

    [S. Naifeh and G. W. Smith, *Jackson Pollock: An American Saga*, 1989]

Pollock on Rubens

He gave up going to museums to see the old masters because,
according to Clement Greenberg, 'he didn't want to repeat their
mistakes.' 'I showed Jackson a book of colored reproductions of
Rubens landscapes,' Greenberg recalled. 'He looked through it and
said, "I can paint better than this guy." '

    [S. Naifeh and G. W. Smith, *Jackson Pollock: An American Saga*, 1989]

Pollock's 'Stenographic Figure', Mondrian (1872–1944) and Peggy Guggenheim

Mondrian was the first of the jurors to arrive – he wanted to have
plenty of time to give every work fair consideration – and while Peggy
and Putzel rushed about with last-minute arrangements, he began to
examine the entries that Peggy had arrayed against the walls of the
gallery. Tall and professorial in a double-breasted suit and horn-

rimmed glasses, he walked slowly from painting to painting. When he came upon *Stenographic Figure*, he stopped and stroked his chin. Looking over, Peggy saw him 'rooted' in front of the Pollock and rushed to apologize. 'Pretty awful, isn't it?' she said, more as a statement than a question. 'That's not painting, is it?' Mondrian didn't reply. A few minutes later, he was still staring at the Pollock. Peggy, increasingly uneasy, felt called on to elaborate her opinion. 'There is absolutely no discipline at all. This young man has serious problems . . . and painting is one of them. I don't think he's going to be included.' Mondrian stroked his chin a few more times. 'I'm not so sure,' he finally said. 'I'm trying to understand what's happening here. I think this is the most interesting work I've seen so far in America . . . You must watch this man.'

Peggy was stunned. 'You can't be serious,' she said. 'You can't compare this and the way you paint.' Mondrian responded patiently, as if instructing a student, 'The way I paint and the way I think are two different things.'

[S. Naifeh and G. W. Smith, *Jackson Pollock: An American Saga*, 1989]
The occasion was a juried show at Peggy Guggenheim's Art of this
Century Gallery in New York.

Pollock's Wife Lee Krasner Reminisces

One thing I will say about Pollock; the one time I saw temperament in him was when he baked an apple pie. Or when he tried to take a photograph. He never showed any artistic temperament. He loved to bake. I did the cooking but he did the baking when he felt like it. He was very fastidious about his baking – marvelous bread and pies. He also made a great spaghetti sauce.

[F. Du Plessix and C. Gray, 'Who Was Jackson Pollock?', *Art in America*, May–June, 1967]

Lee Krasner on Pollock and Jazz

He would get into grooves of listening to his jazz records – not just for days – day and night, day and night for three days running until you thought you would climb the roof! The house would *shake*. Jazz? He thought it was the only other really creative thing happening in this country. He had a passion for music. He had trouble carrying a tune, and although he loved to dance he was an awkward dancer. He told me that when he was a boy he bought himself a violin expecting to play it immediately. When he couldn't get the sound he wanted out of it, he smashed it in a rage.

[F. Du Plessix and C. Gray, 'Who Was Jackson Pollock?', 1967]

Tony Smith (1912–80) on Jackson Pollock

'In many ways Jackson was a straight American boy. He wanted what most people want. Once, when he had been drinking and was pretty wild, he said, "Let's go to the Stork Club." "Come on, Jackson, we can't get in there." "Why not?" "You don't have a tie. They won't let you in." "I can get in." "On what basis?" "On the basis of my reputation".'

[F. Du Plessix and C. Gray, 'Who Was Jackson Pollock?', 1967]

Pollock's Attitudes to his own Work

You only have to see the film of him making his painting on glass to know how sure he was of himself: the way he wipes out the first start and begins over. But there were other times when he was just as unsure. A little later, in front of a very good painting – not a black-and-white – he asked me, 'Is this a painting?' Not is this a good painting, or a bad one, but a *painting*! The degree of doubt was unbelievable at times. And then, again, at other times he knew the painter he was. It's no wonder he had doubts. At the opening of the black-and-white show one of the New York dealers, supposedly in the know, told him, 'Good show, Jackson, but could you do it in color?' A few weeks later another dealer said – to me this time: 'It's all right, we've accepted it.' The arrogance, the blindness was killing. And, as you see, not only from the outside world, but the art world itself.

[Lee Krasner in an interview with B. H. Friedman, in *Jackson Pollock: Black and White*, 1969]

Pollock and his Neighbours at the Springs, Long Island

Now my brother had a farm hand working for him. Charlie, an old man who didn't know much but who could drive horses and mow. Sometimes in the summer he moved the leaves along the side of the road for the Town. He was in here one day, the team was out in front. Pollock drove by here – he had acquired his beat up old model A Ford by then – and Charlie liked Jackson. He liked him, worked for him some, mowing around the yard. 'That old Pollock' he said, 'lazy son-of-a-bitch, aint he, Dan?' And I said, 'Charlie, what do you mean he's lazy?' 'Why I never see him do a day's work, did you?' he said. That was pretty much the local reaction; not bitter, not evil or vicious, but it was just the way he would talk about anybody else around here. See, at that time Jackson wasn't considered wild-hide or anything.

[D. T. Miller (local store-owner), in *Provincetown Review*, no. 7, Fall 1968]

Pollock 'a Great Painter'

He came in this day and he was speaking of a few things and was a bit mad and discouraged – discouraged isn't the word. He talked a bit about it and as he was going he stopped in the doorway and said to me 'Dan, I want to tell you something – I am a great artist. I don't give a damn what anybody said, I'm a great artist and I know it.' And do you know I believed him. I believed that he was.

[D. T. Miller, in *Provincetown Review*, 1968]

Pollock and Franz Kline (1910–62) in the Cedar Bar, New York

We all got a little of it. But Franz was the real one who gave it back, and then some. One time Franz and Nancy were sitting at the bar, talking, and unaware Jackson was behind them, staring at Franz. Jackson grabbed Franz by the hair and threw him backwards off the barstool onto the floor. Franz got up, straightened himself, glanced at Jackson, and said,

'Okay Jackson, cut it out.'

Jackson had backed away, slightly stooped, head thrust forward, eyes bright. He was so happy he glittered. After Franz had sat down Jackson did it again.

'Jackson!' Nancy cried.

But when Franz got up the third time, he wheeled, grabbed Jackson, slammed him up against the wall and let Jackson have it in the gut with a hard left right combination. Jackson was much taller, and so

[451]

surprised, and happy – he laughed in his pain and bent over, as Franz told me, whispered, 'Not so hard.'

[F. Dawson, *An Emotional Memoir of Franz Kline*, 1967]

Franz Kline on Pollock

When Pollock talked about painting he didn't usurp anything that wasn't himself. He didn't want to change anything, he wasn't using any outworn attitudes about it, he was always himself. He just wanted to be in it because he loved it.

[F. O'Hara, 'Franz Kline Talking', *Evergreen Review*, II/6 Autumn 1958]

Joseph Beuys (1921–86): His Air-crash in the Crimea

The event that was to have the most lasting effect on Joseph Beuys was his crash in the Crimea during the winter of 1943. After an attack on a Russian antiaircraft position, Beuys's Stuka was hit as it pulled out of the dive. Beuys and his second crewman were just able to get the machine back behind German lines. Then the altimeter suddenly failed, a blizzard came down, and the plane went out of control and crashed. Beuys was hurled out of the cockpit on impact and pinned under the tail. He lost consciousness. The other man was killed.

It was a miracle that Beuys survived; and he owed his survival to a group of nomadic Tartars who discovered the wrecked Stuka and its badly injured pilot in deep snow. They took him into one of their tents, devotedly tended the mostly unconscious man for eight days, salved his massive injuries with animal fat, and wrapped him in felt to warm him and help him conserve body heat. They fed him milk, curds, and cheese.

Beuys had suffered a double fracture at the base of his skull; he had shrapnel all over, only a portion of which could later be removed. He had broken his ribs, legs, and arms. His hair was singed to the roots, his nose smashed. Without the care of the Tartars, Beuys would have died. All this touched him deeply. When his health was more or less restored, his rescuers asked him to stay with them. This idea, he remembered later, was not unattractive. That brief life with the Tartars evoked images that he never forgot, and they reappeared, metamorphosed, in many of his Actions. Felt and fat became his basic sculptural materials.

[H. Stackelhaus, *Joseph Beuys*, 1991]

Beuys and the Hare

And the hare? Pure Beuys. 'I am not a human being,' Beuys once said, only half jokingly, 'I am a hare.' Another time he went so far as to assert: 'I am a really horny hare!'

. . .

For a time Beuys even drove a Bentley with a hare as a hood ornament. He ascribed extraordinary qualities to this creature of the steppes. For him, the hare had a direct connection with birth and with the earth into which it burrows. It is the symbol of incarnation and is closely associated with woman, birth, menstruation, and all the chemical changes that take place in the blood. All this is exemplified in *Hare's Grave*, of 1962–67, which contains no hare but rather a collection of chemical substances: pigments, alkaline solutions, medicaments, acids, iodine, colored Easter eggs. With this sculpture Beuys may have been deliberately reducing *ad absurdum* the realistic or naturalistic image promised by the title, in order to find a way to break through general, ingrained habits of seeing and thinking.

[H. Stackelhaus, *Joseph Beuys*, 1991]

Beuys's Ritual 'Death'

Just how deep, how alarmingly deep ran the connections between Beuys and the dark, the magical, and the shamanic emerges in the following story told by his friend, the Danish artist and scientist Per Kirkeby:

My wife and I were on a summer vacation in Spain with Beuys and his wife. We were in the south of Spain, inland, a long way from any water, among vast expanses of vineyards, where the soil was dry and crumbling. It was a weird, dusty landscape, shimmering in the heat . . .

Beuys was in very bad shape, with a chest ailment; that was why we had come here. One day I was in the small town nearby and overheard a conversation between the local doctor, whom Beuys had consulted, and our two winegrowers, who were always together. The doctor told one of them that if his wife went on using that thing it could have very harmful consequences for the foreigner.

Far away from any habitation, way out in the dusty landscape, they had set up a large tent. The kind that Roman generals have in spectacular movies. There lay the dying Beuys. I guess they were afraid of contagion. Some distance away from the tent stood the winegrowers with their wives. One of the wives was crying, screaming so loud that the sound carried all the way to the little group at the end of the tent, Beuys with eyes nearly sightless; my wife, who sobbed all day long; and myself. Beuys lay in that houselike tent with his head more or less out in the open, because one wall panel had been removed. His whole body was draped with a sheet, and his head was partly covered by a paper bag with holes for the eyes. The whole lower part of his face was ravaged by illness, wasted away, so that only the teeth in his upper jaw protruded, with the skin tightly stretched above them. In what had once been his mouth there were five or six cigars. Because he loved cigars. With his eyes he signaled to his wife to come and he raised his head so she could lay her hand beneath it. That was his last act of love. To me he said in a strange voice, deep down in his throat, that his artistic career had been shorter than we thought, less than a year, and that he was departing in helpless anguish at his fate.

[H. Stackelhaus, *Joseph Beuys*, 1991]

Beuys and the Baby's Bathtub

One early forerunner of his multiples was the simple little wooden box that Beuys first brought out in 1968 for two dollars and subsequently sold by the thousands. Inside it he drew a line with a pencil, above which he wrote the word *Intuition* – that was all. Simple though it may seem, this work is a piece of Beuysian philosophy: a representation of the insight that intuition is a higher form of reason. The box is empty only for those to whom intuition has no value, for those who like to be supplied with a recipe. Beuys issues no recipes. Here, as elsewhere, he inimitably supplies an energetic impulse.

That impulse was experienced in 1973, in a rather different way, by certain ladies of the Altenrath section of Leverkusen. Requested by their husbands to find some chairs for a summer gathering of the Social Democratic party (SPD) at the city's museum, Schloss Morsbroich, they found in a storeroom an old baby bathtub swathed in gauze bandages and equipped with Band-Aids, a lump of fat, and Vaseline ointment. They at once decided that this was just the right receptacle for rinsing beer glasses. So they set to work and cleaned all the 'garbage' out of the tub. In their energetic efforts for the SPD party they had unwittingly destroyed a work of art by none other than the celebrated Düsseldorf professor of sculpture, Joseph Beuys.

In the early 1960s Beuys had determined that this tub was the one in which he had been bathed as a baby by his mother. And so he decided to present a section of autobiography, which he did in his radical way, by using gauze and bandages to refer to the cutting of the umbilical cord, and Vaseline to refer to the constant care required by the infant Joseph. The *Bathtub* came into the possession of the Munich art collector and publisher Lutz Schirmer, who lent it with other Beuys objects to the Von der Heydt Museum in Wuppertal for a touring exhibition in 1972. The last venue on that tour was Schloss Mors-broich, where after it closed, the show's valuable contents were stowed away in a secure place – at least until those festive ladies came along.

When Schirmer got his *Bathtub* back and saw what had happened, it reminded him of nothing so much as a shaved cactus. He lodged a complaint with the state court in Wuppertal, which resulted – after some shilly-shallying and the calling of expert witnesses, including Beuys's Düsseldorf dealer, Alfred Schmela – in the payment of £30,400 in damages to Schirmer.

[H. Stackelhaus, *Joseph Beuys*, 1991]

Beuys and John Dillinger

In Chicago he commemorated Dillinger, the 'gangster's gangster', in his own way. On January 14, 1974, he rode in a cab along Lincoln Avenue. He was wearing a felt hat and a long gray coat with a fur collar. He stopped the cab outside the Biograph Theater, jumped out, ran as if fleeing from a hail of bullets, slumped into a snowdrift in front of the theater, and lay motionless. After a while he stood up. The movie was in the can, or on the videotape, as the case happened to be: Staeck/Steidl Productions presents *Dillinger: He Was the Gangster's Gangster*, starring Joseph Beuys.

[H. Stackelhaus, *Joseph Beuys*, 1991]

Beuys and the Coyote

The coyote, the prairie wolf, *Canis latrans*, is a nocturnal predator native to the forests and prairies of North and Central America. It lives mainly on small creatures and carrion, and it presents no threat to man. But of course the coyote is more than that. To the Indians, the coyote was a sacred animal; they revered it as one of the mightiest of their gods. But, as Caroline Tisdall tells us in her interpretation of Beuys's piece:

Then came the White Man, and the transition in the coyote's status. He was reduced from being an admirably subversive power on a cosmic scale to what C. G. Jung in his preface to Pueblo Indian legends called 'the Archetype of the Trickster'. His ingenuity and adaptability were now interpreted as low and common cunning: he became the mean coyote. And, having classed him as an antisocial menace, white society could take its legalized revenge on him, and hound him like a Dillinger.

For Beuys, Tisdall says, the persecution of the coyote was an example of man's tendency to project his own sense of inferiority onto an object of hate or a minority. This hatred and this sense of inferiority will always drive man to destroy the object of his hatred, the scapegoat and the eternal victim in every society – as the Europe of pogroms and concentration camps well knows, or prefers to forget. America is rich in minorities, but the Indians, as the aboriginal inhabitants, are a special case in the history of persecution. ' "The manner of the meeting was important,"' said Beuys, as quoted by Tisdall. 'I wanted to concentrate only on the coyote. I wanted to isolate myself, insulate myself, see nothing of America other than the coyote.'

And that was exactly how it was. At Kennedy Airport in New York, Beuys was wrapped in felt, laid on a stretcher, and driven by ambulance to the gallery. There, one room was divided in two by a wire grille, behind which his coyote awaited him. Beuys arranged strips of felt in the space, and every day he stacked the latest issue of the *Wall Street Journal* in two piles of twenty-five copies each. He wore brown gloves, had a flashlight with him, and leaned on a walking stick. And so he set out, gradually, to get close to the coyote.

Beuys wrapped himself in felt, with only the stick protruding, and lay down on the floor. A sculpture. He stacked other pieces of felt into a pile from which the flashlight shone. He talked to the coyote and encouraged him to tug at the felt strips and tear them. Then the situation was reversed; the coyote curled up on the felt, and Beuys lay down on the coyote's straw. From time to time, Beuys made 'music' with a triangle, which he wore suspended around his neck. Then the taped sounds of turbines broke the silence. Three days and nights later, the two were used to each other. Beuys said goodbye to Little John, hugging him gently. He scattered the straw in the room in which he had lived with the animal. Once more Beuys was wrapped in felt, laid on a stretcher, and taken to JFK airport in an ambulance. And so he left New York, having seen nothing of the city beyond the room with the coyote.

[H. Stackelhaus, *Joseph Beuys*, 1991]

Andy Warhol (?1930–87) and the Can of Soup

By the end of the year Andy was back where he had started. He had just come out of a 'nervous breakdown' and feared he might be slipping towards another. After he attended Claes Oldenburg's excellent Lower East Side exhibition, The Store, in early December with its garishly painted soft sculptures of some of his favourite subjects – underwear, ice cream and pies – he was so annoyed because he hadn't had the idea that when Ted Carey invited him to dinner Andy said he was too depressed to go out. Oldenburg's success was particularly painful because while Andy was friends with Claes and particularly with his swinging wife, Patti, she recalled that Claes 'did not like Andy's early work so there was some confusion there'.

Later that evening Ted stopped by with an interior designer who was struggling unsuccessfully to support her own gallery, Muriel Latow. Andy usually enjoyed Muriel's overwhelming personality but on this evening she and Ted could see that he was in a funk. He was desperate, he told them. He had to *do* something. Ted Carey:

Andy said, 'It's too late for the cartoons. I've got to do something that will have a lot of impact, that will be different from Lichtenstein and Rosenquist, that will be very personal, that won't look like I'm doing exactly what they're doing. I don't know what to do! Muriel, you've got fabulous ideas. Can't you give me an idea?'

Yes, she could, Muriel replied, but it would cost Andy some money.
    'How much?' he asked.
    'Fifty dollars,' she answered.

Andy promptly wrote out a cheque and said, 'OK, go ahead. Give me a fabulous idea!'

'What do you like most in the whole world?' Muriel asked.

'I don't know. What do I like most in the whole world?'

'Money,' she replied. 'You should paint pictures of money.'

'Oh, gee,' Andy gasped, 'that really is a great idea.'

In the silence that followed, Muriel elaborated. 'You should paint something that everybody sees every day, that everybody recognizes . . . like a can of soup.'

For the first time that evening, Andy smiled.

[V. Bockris, *Warhol*, 1989]

Warhol's Paintings of Marilyn Monroe

The show[1] was a controversial smash. Many of those who saw it joked about how terrible it was, but it almost sold out. Typical was the reaction of William Seitz, who bought a Marilyn for the Museum of Modern Art for $250. When Seitz's colleague, Peter Selz, called him and said, 'Isn't it the most ghastly thing you've ever seen in your life?' Seitz replied, 'Yes, isn't it. I bought one.'

[V. Bockris, *Warhol*, 1989]

Andy Warhol in 1965

Andy loved nothing better than being asked for his autograph. From that year on it was often difficult to be with him in a public situation. Strangers in restaurants interrupted dinner to obtain his signature on a scrap of paper, apologetically explaining that they were doing so on behalf of a child who was not with them at the moment. If we were shopping in Bloomingdale's, I'd overhear individuals stage-whispering to their companions, 'Look, over there, it's Andy Warhol,' evoking the disdainful response, 'Oh, I see him everywhere!'

[David Bourdon, quoted in V. Bockris, *Warhol*, 1989]

Warhol and Henry Geldzahler in the 1960s

His path was not always as smooth as his Wow! Gee whiz! pop persona suggested. Henry Geldzahler remembered a frantic call at

1. At the Stable Gallery, New York, October 1962.

1.30 a.m., only an hour after they had parted, insisting Henry meet him at the Brasserie in half an hour. When Geldzahler protested that he was already in bed, Andy said it was very important: 'We have to talk, we have to talk.' Imagining that something of creative import was coming down, and wanting to be in on its every moment, the fat man rushed to the restaurant to find a pale and trembling Andy perched on a banquette.

'Well,' Henry said, hurtling into the booth breathlessly, 'what is it? What is so important that it can't wait until tomorrow?'

Staring at him with wide-awake blank eyes, Andy replied, 'We have to talk, Henry. Say something!'

[V. Bockris, *Warhol*, 1989]

Warhol on the Attempt Made on his Life by Valerie Solanas

Before I was shot, I always suspected I was watching TV instead of living life. Right when I was being shot I knew I was watching television. Since I was shot everything is such a dream to me. I don't know whether or not I'm really alive – whether I died. It's sad. Like I can't say hello or goodbye to people. Life is like a dream.

[Interview with Laeticia Kent, *Village Voice*, 12 September 1968]

Warhol Encounters Willem de Kooning (b. 1904) at a Party, 1969

Warhol saw de Kooning, made a pilgrimage to him, said 'Hi, Bill,' and offered his hand. De Kooning was drunk and he suddenly turned to Warhol and said, 'You're a killer of art, you're a killer of beauty, and you're even a killer of laughter. I can't bear your work!' It was a very dramatic, ugly moment, face to face, and became the talk of the party. Andy smiled, turned away and said to Morrissey, 'Oh, well, I always loved his work.'

[Tom Hedley, quoted in V. Bockris, *Warhol*, 1989]

Warhol's Assistant Gerard Malanga on the 'Disaster' Series, 1983

Each painting took about four minutes, and we worked as mechanically as we could, trying to get each image right, but we never got it right. By becoming machines we made the most imperfect works. Andy embraced his mistakes. We never rejected anything. Andy would say, 'It's part of the art.' He possessed an almost Zen-like sensibility, but to the critics Andy became an existentialist because the accidents were interpreted as being intentional statements.

[Quoted in V. Bockris, *Warhol*, 1989]

Warhol Paints a Canvas

Monday, December 31, 1973: After three years finally get to see AW really paint. The outline of the face is traced from blowup of photo negative onto tissue and then tissue is placed over carbon, which is over raw canvas, and retraced by pressing carbon outline onto canvas. Then A slaps paint (acrylic) on with a large brush, more like housepaint brush than artist's brush, rarely cleaning brush, as he switches from area to area and color to color. He also uses hands, especially fingers, to create texture, gesture, blend colors. He doesn't clean hands much either, so colors merge, appear here and there, disappear rather arbitrarily. After it dries the photo negative is silkscreened (by Alex Heinrici at his own studio) onto the painted canvas.

[Author's diary extract, in B. Colacello, *Holy Terror: Andy Warhol Close Up*, 1990]

What Andy Warhol Prayed for

Jed Johnson says he once asked Andy what he prayed for and Andy said, 'Money.' I think he prayed for health because he often said to me, 'If you don't have health, Bob, you don't have anything. I know.'

[B. Colacello, *Holy Terror: Andy Warhol Close Up*, 1990]

Andy Warhol's Philosophy

The interviewer should just tell me the words he wants me to say and I'll repeat them after him.

I still care about people but it would be so much easier not to care . . . it's too hard to care . . . don't like to touch things . . . that's why my work is so distant from myself.

[460]

Machines have less problems. I'd like to be a machine, wouldn't you?

I tried doing them by hand, but I find it easier to use a screen. This way, I don't have to work on my objects at all. One of my assistants or anyone else, for that matter, can reproduce the designs as well as I could.

I like boring things.

I love Los Angeles. I love Hollywood. They're beautiful. Everybody's plastic, but I love plastic. I want to be plastic.

If you want to know all about Andy Warhol, just look at the surface of my paintings and films and me, and there I am. There's nothing behind it.

[Interview in the catalogue of the first Warhol retrospective exhibition, Moderna Museet, Stockholm, 1968]

Andy Warhol on Death

At the end of my time, when I die, I don't want to leave any leftovers. And I don't want to be a leftover. I was watching TV this week and I saw a lady go into a ray machine and disappear. That was wonderful, because matter is energy and she just disappeared. That could be a really American invention, the best American invention – to be able to disappear. I mean, that way they couldn't say you died, they couldn't say you were murdered, they couldn't say you committed suicide over somebody.

The worst thing that could happen to you after the end of your time would be to be embalmed and laid up in a pyramid . . .

[A. Warhol, *The Philosophy of Andy Warhol: From A to Z and Back Again*, 1975]

XXIII
CLASSICAL CHINESE PAINTING

ﻬ

The only culture, in addition to Western civilization, which seems to have established a tradition of collecting anecdotes about art, and in particular about artists as individual personalities, is the classical civilization of China. The Chinese sources remain very little known in the West – all but one of the anecdotes printed here come from a single publication, Osvald Sirén's massive multi-volume history of Chinese painting, which translates a number of stories, and paraphrases others.

Anyone who has read the other sections of this book will notice certain fundamental differences. The Chinese artist concerns himself with nature rather than man; he usually depicts landscape, not the human figure. He dislikes the idea of 'professionalism' in art – that is, of painting as an activity undertaken for money. The painter is a gentleman amateur – a scholarly official, or else a monk, or someone who has deliberately renounced worldly ambition, often after a distinguished official career. All of this is very different from the typical career pattern followed by a western artist.

There are, however, certain significant points in common. In one story, an artist who 'raised his brush and drew the halo in a single sweep with the force of a whirlwind' offers a striking parallel to the legend of Giotto's O. In another, where an artist advises a colleague to seek inspiration from the rough surface of a ruined wall, there is a resemblance to a procedure recommended by Leonardo da Vinci.

More significant still, perhaps, is the constant emphasis by Chinese writers on the notion that the artist is a special kind of person, someone fundamentally different from the rest of mankind. In fact this approach to art and its makers probably received greater emphasis in classical Chinese sources than it does in western ones. These special creative beings are, however, always painters not sculptors. There is no Chinese equivalent to Michelangelo; Chinese sculptors remained artisans.

[463]

My final story is for once linked to an event, not a personality. It comes from a Western source, and describes the casual brutality with which European troops destroyed a large part of the heritage of Chinese painting – the section of the great Imperial Collection which was housed in the Summer Palace.

Yen Li-pên (fl. c. AD 618–656) Paints a Bird

On a spring day, when [the Emperor] T'ai-tsung was strolling with some courtiers in the palace garden, he saw a strange bird bob up and down on the waves of a lake, which caused him great pleasure. He told the courtiers to compose poems about it, and asked them 'to get hold of Li-pên quickly for him to make a picture of the bird'. All the ministers began shouting for the 'painting-master', though Li-pên was already at the time a high official. He came running and perspiring and crouched down by the lake in order to paint. But the onlookers were all seated, and he felt greatly humiliated. When he came back home from this visit to the court, he said to his son: 'In my youth I liked to read and compose poetry, but now the emperor considers me simply as a painter and makes me do the work of a servant. What a humiliation! I warn you, do not practise this art!' But, as he was an artist by nature, he could never give up painting.

[Chinese source quoted in O. Sirén, *Chinese Painting: Leading Masters and Principles*, 1956]

Wu Tao-tzue (fl. 8th century AD) and the Perfect Halo

At the beginning of the Yüan-ho era (806–821), when I went up for examination (to the capital), I stayed in Lung-hsing ssŭ. There was then a man more than eighty years old (called Yin) who told me that when Wu painted the halo of a god inside the middle gate in Hsing-shan ssŭ all the people from the streets and market places of Ch'ang-an, old and young, learned men and common people, came in crowds to watch him until they formed something like a wall around him. He raised his brush and drew the halo in a single sweep with the force of a whirl-wind. And the people said: 'He must be aided by a god!'

[Chu Ching-hsuan, quoted in O. Sirén, *Chinese Painting: Leading Masters and Principles*, 1956]

The Strange Method of Wang Hsia, commonly called Wang Mo (Ink Wang; d. AD 803/3)

'He painted pine-trees, stones and landscapes, though not of a very noble and superior kind; yet much appreciated by the common people'. They were apparently too rough for the T'ang critic, who adds: 'I do not think that Mo's pictures are wonderful'.

The description of how Wang Mo executed these pictures sounds also more fantastic than convincing. It is said that when he got drunk he used to soak his long hair in a pail of ink and then fling or flop the ink on the silk, forming landscapes and figures that seemed to emerge out of clouds and mist.

[O. Sirén, *Chinese Painting: Leading Masters and Principles*, 1956]

Stories of Kao Chung-shu (mid tenth century AD)

From this time onward he led a wandering life, roaming about in the region between Ch'i, Yung, Loyang and the capital. Through his constant drinking he became increasingly reckless. Whenever he met some people, noble or mean, he simply shouted at them. But when he came to a place of beautiful scenery, he would linger there for ten or twelve days quite unable to go away. Sometimes he would not eat for more than a month; his body would not perspire even when exposed to the heat of summer days, and in the winter he hacked a hole in the ice on the river and took a bath. The people were much astonished at his endurance.

. . .

The emperor felt much sympathy for him, because of his talents, and showed leniency even when he behaved recklessly and neglected rules of propriety. But he became more and more addicted to wine and slanderous talking; at last he secretly sold documents from his office and kept the money. He was then sentenced to capital punishment, but by imperial favour this was reduced to flogging with bamboo twigs and banishment to Têng-chou (in Shantung) in the year 977. 'When he had reached Lin-i, in Ch'i-chou, he said to the official who escorted him: "I shall soon be gone". Then he made a hole in the ground, large enough to contain his face, and as he stooped down and looked into it, he passed away.

'He was buried at the side of the road in a mat. Several months later some old friends of his came to fetch the corpse in order to give it a proper burial. They found that his body was as light and empty as the shell of a cicada.'

[O. Sirén, *Chinese Painting: Leading Masters and Principles*, 1956]

Advice Given by Sung Ti (eleventh century AD) to a Colleague

'You should select a ruined wall and spread a piece of white silk over it. Then lean over the wall and look at it carefully morning and evening until you can see through the silk the protuberances and the flat parts with their curving forms, which all make up the picture of a landscape. Retain these in your mind and fix them in your eye. The raised parts are mountains, the low parts are waters, the hollows are valleys, the furrows are streams; the clear parts are the nearest, the obscure ones more distant. As the spirit grasps them and the thoughts give them form, it will seem to you as if there were human beings, birds, plants and trees flying and moving, coming and going. When they all are clear in your eye, you can play with the brush quite freely, uniting in silence with the spirit, and the scenery will be as made by Heaven and not like a thing made by man. That is called a living picture. From this time Yung-chih made great progress in painting.'
[Shen Kua in *Ming-ch'i pi-t'an*, quoted by O. Sirén, *Chinese Painting: Leading Masters and Principles*, 1956]

Stories of Ni Tsan (b. 1301, active until 1374)

While still a man of means and social standing, he was very active as a collector of antiquities and specimens of painting and calligraphy, which were kept in a special pavilion called *Chi'ing-pi ko*, where a circle of scholars often united to enjoy poetry and wine. The most distinguishing feature of this place and of its host seems to have been an extraordinary cleanliness. We are told that if a dirty man had entered the pavilion, the place where he had been seated was at once washed, and the host used to keep a basin of clean water at his side, so that he could wash his face and hands whenever he was going to paint. And 'this cleanliness was also evident in his conduct' – that is, in his purity of mind and heart.

. . .

From other records, we learn that when he had passed middle age (shortly before the fall of the Yüan dynasty), he distributed all his wealth among his relatives and started travelling in a house-boat along the rivers and lakes in Wu. He no longer found any pleasure in the company of the nobles and the rich, but put up at small country temples where he was satisfied with a wooden bench and a bamboo lamp. His pictures he gave away freely to the common people just as Wu Chên did, but if collectors offered him money, he refused to accede.

[O. Sirén, *Chinese Painting: Leading Masters and Principles*, 1956]

The Later Life of Weng Heng Shen, also called Cheng Ming (1470–1559)

After some time he resigned from all his official engagements and went back to his home town.

'There he simply amused himself with brush and ink. Crowds of visitors came to his door asking for paintings, but he only gave them away to scholars. When sons of old friends or relations in distress asked for his paintings he worked whole days for them untiringly. Other people such as provincial governors, prime ministers, members of the imperial family and rich merchants came to his door with gifts, but they did not even obtain entrance to his house. He was most particular not to establish any connexion with the imperial princes and the eunuchs and said that such was the law of the country. The reason for this (aversion) was his experience with Prince Ning, who once in the Chêng-tê period had tried to win him over with large sums of money (which he did not accept). As the prince was shortly afterwards completely routed by the government (forces), everybody praised Wên Chêng-ming.

'When at leisure he went out for strolls in the beautiful country around the city, and wherever he went, people were anxious to receive him. When he was staying at home many friends came to see him; they sat together burning incense and sipping tea, while they discussed paintings and calligraphy or examined antiquities and strangely-shaped stones. Many of the old stories about the men of Wu were then told, which made the guests forget the time. Such was the kind of life he enjoyed during the last thirty years of his life. When he died (1559) he was ninety (eighty) years old. At the moment he was still writing an inscription on a tablet; his brush stopped suddenly, and he passed away as happily as a butterfly. The people said that he did not die, but became an immortal.'

[Sixteenth-century Chinese source, quoted in O. Sirén, *Chinese Painting: Leading Masters and Principles*, 1956]

Shên-Chou (1427–1509) Withdraws from the World

When he had passed middle age and began to grow old, he withdrew from the world (suppressed his sound and hid his shadow), his only fear being that he could not do it completely. The governor Wang Shu from San-yüan did his utmost to attract Shên Chou to his office in order to obtain some advice from him in political matters, but Shên Chou simply refused to come. The next governor, P'eng Li, read his poem on the Hand-mill and found it deep and significant. He again invited Shên Chou at various times but the artist did not accept the invitations. When the governor finally by his command obliged Shên Chou to come to the office, they sat together talking for the whole day to the great satisfaction of the governor; but when he wanted to keep the artist there permanently, Shên Chou bowed deeply and said: 'I am a worthless fellow, not good enough to be your servant (ox or horse). In addition to this you should know that my old mother is so weak that she cannot move without the assistance of her son; therefore I hope that you will feel pity and let me go, so that I may return home, and the lives of my mother and her son may be saved. It would be the greatest kindness you could show me.' The governor sighed and consented.

[Chiang Shao-tsu in *Wu-sheng shih-shih*, quoted in O. Sirén, *Chinese Painting: Leading Masters and Principles*, 1956]

Pa-ta shan-jên (b. 1626, d. after 1692) Resists Collectors

If highly placed persons offered him a cask of wine worth many pieces of gold, they obtained nothing; if they brought silk for painting, he made no bones about accepting it, but said: 'I shall make myself stockings from this!' For this reason highly placed persons who wanted pictures by Pa-ta shan-jên turned to poor scholars, mountain monks, butchers and inn-keepers – *i.e.* to the kind of people who obtained pictures from him, because they had no ulterior motive, only the wish to make him feel free and happy. When these people invited him 'he would go at once, and at once get drunk, too!'

[O. Sirén, *Chinese Painting: Leading Masters and Principles*, 1956] Pa-ta shan-jên was a scion of the Ming imperial house who became a monk. He is the most famous of a group of 'eccentric' painters of the early Ch'ing Dynasty.

The Boxer Rebellion and the Burning of the Imperial Summer Palace

Aug. 14 [1900]. Holmes is writing about Chinese painting. He was told this anecdote of Sir Redvers Buller,[1] by Sidney Colvin. The show of Chinese Kakemonos had just been opened at the British, some years ago. 'Ah!' said Sir Redvers. 'How well I remember the sound of thousands of these roll paintings all fizzling together when we burned the Summer Palace; they were not thought worth taking away.'

[C. Ricketts, *Self-portrait, taken from the Letters and Journals*, 1939] The Chinese Imperial Summer Palace was destroyed as a punitive measure by an Anglo-French army in 1860.

1. Sir Redvers Buller (1839–1908), British general best remembered for his defeat at Colenso during the Boer War.

BIBLIOGRAPHY

Allingham, William, *A Diary*. Ed. H. Allingham and D. Radford. London, 1907

Amaury-Duval, P., *L'atelier d'Ingres*. Paris, 1878

The Arcimboldo Effect. Thames & Hudson, London, 1987

[d'Argonne, Bonaventure], *Mélanges d'histoire de littérature receuilles par M. Vigneul-Marville*. Paris, 1699–1700

D'Azara, Joseph Nicholas, *The Work of Anthony Raphael Mengs*. London, 1796

Baldinucci, Filippo, *Notizie de' professori del disegno da Cimabue in qua*. Florence, 1845–7 (first published 1681–6)

Barbier, Auguste, *Souvenirs personnels*. Paris, 1863

Bellori, Giovanni Pietro, *Vite de' pittori, scultori e architetti moderni*. Pisa, 1821 (first published Rome, 1672)

Bernard, Emile, *Sur Paul Cézanne*. Paris, 1922

Blanc, Charles, *Les Artistes de mon temps*. Paris, 1876

Blanche, Jacques-Emile, *Propos de Peintre: De David à Degas*. Paris, 1919

– *Manet*. Rieder, Paris, 1924

– *Propos de Peintre: De Gauguin à la Revue Négre*. Paris, 1928

– *Portraits of a Lifetime*. Trans. and ed. Walter Clement. J. M. Dent & Sons, London, 1937

– *More Portraits of a Lifetime*. Trans. and ed. Walter Clement. J. M. Dent & Sons, London, 1939

Bockris, Victor, *Warhol*. Frederick Muller, London, 1989

Boyer d'Agen [A. J. Boyé], *Ingres, d'après une correspondance inédite*. Paris, 1909

Burgess, James, *The Lives of the Most Eminent Modern Painters, who have lived since or were omitted by Mons. de Piles*. London, 1809

Caine, Hall, *Recollections of Rossetti*. London, 1928

Carr, J. Comyns, *Some Eminent Victorians*. London, 1908

Castagnary, Jules, *Fragments d'un livre sur Courbet*. Gazette des Beaux-Arts, Paris, 1911

Castiglione, Baldassare, *The Book of the Courtier*. Trans. Leonard Eckstein Opdyke. New York, 1905

Caylus, Conte de, *Vies d'artistes du XVIIIe siècle*. Paris, 1910

Cellini, Benvenuto, *The Life, written by himself*. Trans. Anne Macdowell. London, 1905 (first published 1730)

Champion, Pierre, *Watteau*. Paris, 1921 (reprints all the immediately posthumous lives of the artist)

Chantelou, Paul Fréart de, *Journal du voyage du Cav. Bernini en France*. Ed. Lalanne. Paris, 1885

Charteris, K. C., Evan, *John Sargent*. London, 1927

Claudet, Max, *Souvenirs, Gustave Courbet*. Paris, 1878

Clément, Charles, *Géricault*. Paris, 1868

Cochin, Charles Nicolas, *Essai sur la vie de M. Chardin*, 1780. In Charles Beaurepaire, *Précis analytique des travaux de l'Académie des Science, Belles Lettres et Beaux-Arts de Rouen*, vol. LXXVIII, 1875–6

Cocteau, Jean, *Picasso*. Paris, 1923

Colacello, Bob, *Holy Terror: Andy Warhol Close Up*. Harper Collins, New York, 1990

Colvin, Sir Sidney, *Memories and Notes of Persons and Places*. London, 1921

Comanini, Gregorio, *Il Figino, overo del fine dalla Pittura*. Dialogo, Mantua, 1591

Condivi, Ascanio, *The Life of Michelangelo Buonarroti*. Trans. Herbert Horne. London, 1904 (first published 1553)

Conway, William Martin, *Literary Remains of Albrecht Dürer*. Cambridge, England, 1889

Corot, raconté par lui-même et ses amis. Vesenaz, Geneva, 1946

Cotton, M.A., William, *Sir Joshua Reynolds and His Works*. London, 1856

Courbet, raconté par lui-même et ses amis. Vesenaz, Geneva, 1948

Crespi, Luigi, *Felsina Pittrice: Vite dei Pittori Bolognesi, Tomo III, che serve di supplemento all'opera di Malvasia*. Rome, 1769

Cumberland, Richard, *Anecdotes of Eminent Painters in Spain*. London, 1787

Cunningham, Allan, *The Lives of the Most Eminent Painters, Sculptors and Architects*. London, 1829

Dawson, Fielding, *An Emotional Memoir of Franz Kline*. Pantheon Books, New York, 1967

Delacroix, Eugene, *Journal*. Paris, 1893–5

Délecluze, E. J., *Louis David: Son Ecole et ses temps*. Paris, 1855

Descamps, J. B., *La Vie des peintres flamands, allemands et hollandais*. Paris, 1754

Diderot, Denis, *Memoires, correspondance et ouvrages inédits*, vol. 3. Paris, 1831

Duret, Theodore, *Histoire de Edouard Manet et de son oeuvre*. Paris, 1906

Edwards, R.A., Edwin, *Lives of Painters who have resided or been born in England*. London, 1808

Farington, R.A., Joseph, *Memoirs of the Life of Joshua Reynolds*. London, 1819

Félibien, A., *Entretiens sur les vies et sur les ouvrages des plus excellens peintres, anciens et modernes*. Paris, 1666–8

Fels, Marthe de, *La vie de Claude Monet*. Paris, 1929

Fletcher, Ernest, ed., *Conversations of James Northcote, R.A., with James Ward on Art and Artists*. London, 1901

Friedman, B. H., *Jackson Pollock: Energy Made Visible*. Weidenfeld & Nicolson, London, 1973

Gauguin, Paul, *Intimate Journals*. Trans. Van Wyck Brooks. London, 1923

Gauzi, François, *Lautrec et son temps.* David Perret, Paris, 1954

Geffroy, Gustave, *La Vie artistique, 6e serie.* Paris, 1900

Gigoux, Jean, *Causeries sur les artistes de mon temps.* Paris, 1885

Gilbey, Sir Walter, *The Life of George Stubbs, R.A.* London, 1898

Gilchrist, Alexander, *The Life of William Blake.* London, 1863

Gilot, Francoise, with Carlton Lake, *Life with Picasso,* McGraw-Hill, New York, 1964

Goncourt, Edmond et Jules de, *L'art du XVIIIe siècle, 2e series.* Paris, 1882

Goodrich, Lloyd, *Thomas Eakins.* Harvard University Press, Cambridge, Mass., 1982

Gros-Kost, E. *Courbet: Souvenirs intimes.* Paris, 1880

Haydon, Benjamin Robert, *The Autobiography and Journals.* London, 1853

Hazlitt, William, *Conversations of James Northcote, Esq., R.A.* London, 1830

Hibbard, Howard, *Caravaggio.* Thames & Hudson, London, 1983

Hill, George Birckbeck, *Letters of Dante Gabriel Rossetti to William Allingham, 1854–1870.* London, 1897

Hoschédé, Jean-Pierre, *Claude Monet, ce mal connu.* Pierre Cailler editeur, Paris, 1960

Houbraken, Arnold, *De groote Schoubergh der Nederlantische Konstschilders en schilderessen.* Amsterdam, 1718–21

Hueffer, Ford M., *Ford Madox Brown: A Record of his Life and Work.* London, 1905

Hunt, W. Holman, *Pre-Raphaelites and the Pre-Raphaelite Brotherhood.* London, 1905

Kahnweiler, Daniel-Henry, with Francis Crémieux, *My Galleries and Painters.* Trans. Helen Weaver. Thames & Hudson, London, 1971 (original French edition published by Gallimard, Paris, 1961)

Leslie, R. A., C. R., *Memoirs of the Life of John Constable, Esq., R.A.* London, 1845

Malvasia, Carlo Cesare, *Felsina pittrice, vite de' pittori bolognesi.* Bologna, 1841 (first published 1678)

Mancini, Giuli, *Considerazioni sulla pittura.* Rome, 1956–7 (written c. 1614–21)

Mander, Carel van, *Het schilderboek . . .* Haarlem, 1603–4; revised second edition, 1618

Mannlich, Johann Christian von, *Mémoires du Chevalier du Mannlich.* Ed. Joseph Delage. Paris, 1948

Marcel Duchamp. Ed. Anne d'Harnoncourt and Kynaston McShine. Catalogue of the retrospective exhibition held at the Museum of Modern Art, New York, and the Philadelphia Museum of Art. MOMA, New York, 1973

Mariette, P. J., *Abécédario.* Paris, 1851–3 (written first half of eighteenth century)

Marques, Alice Goldfarb, *Marcel Duchamp: Eros, c'est la vie.* The Whiston Publishing Company, New York, 1981

McCully, Marilyn, ed., *A Picasso Anthology*. The Arts Council of Great Britain in association with Thames & Hudson, London, 1981

Memes, J. S., *Memoirs of Antonio Canova*. London, 1825

Michiels, Alfred, *Rubens et l'école d'Anvers*. Paris, 1854

Moore, George, *Ave*. London, 1911

– *Vale*. London, 1914

– *Conversations in Ebury Street*. London, 1924

Naifeh, Steven, and Gregory White Smith, *Jackson Pollock: An American Saga*. Woods & White Inc., New York, 1989

Northcote, R.A., James, *Memoirs of Sir Joshua Reynolds*. London, 1813–15

Olivier, Fernande, *Picasso and his Friends*. Trans. Jane Miller. Heinemann, London, 1964 (original French edition, 1933)

Olson, Stanley, *John Singer Sargent, his Portrait*. Macmillan, London 1986

Palmer, A. H., *The Life and Letters of Samuel Palmer*. London, 1892

Palomino de Castro y Velasco, Antonio, *El parnaso espanol pintoresco laureado*. Madrid, 1947 (first published 1724)

Parmelin, Helene, *Picasso Plain*. St Martin's Press, New York, 1963 (original French edition, 1952)

Pennell, E. R. and J., *The Life of James McNeill Whistler*. London, 1908

The Percy Anecdotes, by Sholto and Reuben Percy [Clinto Robinson and Thomas Byerley] London 1821–3 (the title and fictional names of the authors of this collection are taken from the Percy Coffee House in Rathbone Place, London, where Robinson and Byerley used to meet to discuss material)

Piles, Roger de, *Dissertation sur les ouvrages des plus fameux peintres*. Paris, 1681

– *Abrégé de la vie des peintres*. Paris, 1699

– *The Art of Painting, with the Lives and Characters of 300 of the most eminent painters*. London, 1750

Pissarro, Camille, *Letters to his Son Lucien*. Ed. John Rewald. Routledge & Kegan Paul, London, 1980 (original French edition, 1930)

Pliny, *Natural History*. Trans. Philemon Holland. Second edition, London, 1634 (first edition, 1601)

Raffaëlli, Jean-Francois, *Promenades au Musée du Louvre*. Paris, n.d.

Redon, Odilon, *Lettres d'Odilon Redon*. Paris, 1923

Rewald, John, *Cézanne*. Paris, 1939

Ricketts, R. A., Charles, *Self-Portrait, taken from the Letters and Journals collected and compiled by T. Sturge Moore*. Ed. Cecil Lewis. London, 1939

Ridolfi, Carlo, *Le maraviglie dell' arte, overo, le vite degli illustri pittori veneti e dello stato*. Venice, 1648

Rossetti, William Michael, *Dante Gabriel Rossetti: His Family Letters, with a Memoir*. London, 1895

Rothenstein, Sir William, *Men and Memories*. Chatto & Windus, London, 1978

Sandrart, Joachim von, *Teutsche Akademie*. Nuremberg, 1675–9

Scott, William Bell, *Autobiographical Notes*. London, 1892

Sert, Misia, *Two or Three Muses.* Trans. Moura Budberg. Museum Press Ltd, London, 1953

Sirén, Osvald, *Chinese Painting: Leading Masters and Principles.* Lund Humphries, London, and The Ronald Press, New York, 1956

Smith, C. T., *Nollekens and His Times.* London, 1828

Southey, the Rev. Charles Cuthbert, ed., *The Life and Correspondence of the Late Robert Southey.* London, 1850

Speroni, Charles, *Wit and Wisdom of the Italian Renaissance.* University of California Press, Berkeley and Los Angeles, 1964

Spike, John T., *Giuseppe Maria Crespi and the Emergence of Genre Painting in Italy.* Catalogue of an exhibition held at the Kimbell Museum of Art, Fort Worth, Texas, 1985

Stackelhaus, Heiner, *Joseph Beuys.* Abbeville Press Limited, New York, 1991

Stein, Gertrude, *Picasso.* Beacon Press, Boston, 1959 (original French edition, 1938)

Susinno, Francesco, *Le Vite de' pittori messinesi, 1724.* Ed. V. Martinelli. Florence, 1960

Thornbury, Walter, *The Life of J. M. W. Turner, R.A.* London, 1862

Timbs, F. S. A., John, *Anecdotes from the Lives of William Hogarth etc.* London, 1865

Tischbein, Heinrich Wilhelm, *Aus Meinem Leben.* Berlin, 1922

Triper Le Franc, J., *Histoire de la vie et de la mort de Baron Gros.* Paris, 1880

Urbani, G. M., *Tiepolo e sua famiglia.* Venice, 1879

Valkenier, Elizabeth Kridle, *Ilya Repin and the World of Russian Art.* Columbia University Press, New York, 1990

Vallentin, Antonina, *Picasso.* Cassell, London, 1963 (original French edition, 1957)

Valéry, Paul, *Degas, Danse, Dessin.* Gallimard, Paris, 1938

Vasari, Giorgio, *Lives of the Most Eminent Painters, Sculptors and Architects.* Trans. Gaston Du C. de Vere. London 1912–14 (first published in Italian 1553; revised and enlarged second edition, 1568)

Verhaeren, Emile, *James Ensor.* (?Brussels, 1909)

Vigée Le Brun, Elizabeth-Marie, *Souvenirs.* Paris, 1835–7.

Vollard, Ambroise, *Renoir, an intimate record.* Trans. Harold L. Van Doren and Randolph T. Weaver. New York, 1925

– *En Ecoutant Cézanne, Degas, Renoir.* Bernard Grasset, Paris, 1938

Walpole, Horace, *Anecdotes of Painting in England, with some account of the principal artists.* London, 1780

Warhol, Andy, *The Philosophy of Andy Warhol: From A to Z and Back Again.* Harcourt, Brace, Jovanovich Inc., New York, 1975

Watson, Forbes, *Mary Cassatt.* Whitney Museum of Art, New York, 1932

ACKNOWLEDGEMENTS

For permission to reprint copyright material the publishers gratefully acknowledge the following:

From Jacques-Emile Blanche, *Portraits of a Lifetime*, translated by Walter Clement, copyright J. M. Dent & Sons Ltd, 1937; *from* Victor Bockris, *Andy Warhol*, copyright Frederick Muller, 1989; *from* Bob Colacello, *Holy Terror: Andy Warhol Close Up*, © 1990 by Robert Colacello, reprinted by permission of HarperCollins Publishers; *from* Fielding Dawson, *An Emotional Memoir of Franz Kline*, by kind permission of Fielding Dawson; *from* B. H. Friedman, 'An Interview with Lee Krasner Pollock', © Marlborough Gallery Inc., New York; *from* Claude Frieux, *Maiakowski par lui-meme*, © Editions du Seuil, 1961; *from* Lloyd Goodrich, *Thomas Eakins*, Harvard University Press, Cambridge, Mass., © 1982 by the President and Fellows of Harvard College; *from* Daniel-Henry Kahnweiler, *My Galleries and Painters*, copyright Thames & Hudson Ltd, 1971; from Laeticia Kent, interview with Andy Warhol, reprinted by permission of the author and *Village Voice*; *from* Steven Naifeh and Gregory White Smith, *Jackson Pollock: An American Saga*, copyright © 1989 by Woodward/White Inc., reprinted by permission of Clarkson N. Potter Inc., a division of Crown Publishers, Inc.; *from* Fernande Olivier, *Picasso and His Friends*, copyright William Heinemann Ltd 1964; *from* Lionel Preijer, 'Picasso découpe le fer', copyright *L'Oeil revue d'art* (No. 82, Octobre 1961); *from* John Rewald (editor), *Camille Pissarro: Letters to his Son Lucien*, copyright Routledge 1980; *from* Misia Sert, *Two or Three Muses*, copyright 1953 by Pitman Publishing; *from* Heiner Stackelhaus, *Joseph Beuys*, English language edition copyright 1991 by Abbeville Press, New York; *from* Elizabeth Krindl Valkenier, *Ilya Repin*, © 1990 Columbia University Press, reprinted by permission of the author; *from* Antonina Valletin, *Picasso*, copyright by Editions Albin Michel, English translation copyright © 1963 by Cassell & Company, reprinted by permission of the Macmillan Publishing Company; *from* interview with Andy Warhol in the exhibition catalogue of the Moderna Museet, Stockholm, reprinted by permission of the Moderna Museet, Stockholm.

Faber and Faber Limited apologize for any errors or omissions in the above list and would be grateful to be notified of any corrections that should be incorporated in the next edition or reprint of this volume.

INDEX OF ARTISTS